NEW
MANAGERIAL
MINDSETS

THE STRATEGIC MANAGEMENT SERIES

STRATEGIC THINKING
Leadership and the Management of Change
Edited by
JOHN HENDRY AND GERRY JOHNSON
WITH JULIA NEWTON

COMPETENCE-BASED COMPETITION
Edited by
GARY HAMEL AND AIMÉ HEENE

BUILDING THE STRATEGICALLY-RESPONSIVE ORGANIZATION
Edited by
HOWARD THOMAS, DON O'NEAL, ROD WHITE AND DAVID HURST

STRATEGIC RENAISSANCE AND BUSINESS TRANSFORMATION
Edited by
HOWARD THOMAS, DON O'NEAL AND JAMES KELLY

COMPETENCE-BASED STRATEGIC MANAGEMENT
Edited by
AIMÉ HEENE AND RON SANCHEZ

STRATEGIC LEARNING AND KNOWLEDGE MANAGEMENT
Edited by
RON SANCHEZ AND AIMÉ HEENE

STRATEGY STRUCTURE AND STYLE
Edited by
HOWARD THOMAS, DON O'NEAL AND MICHEL GHERTMAN

STRATEGIC INTEGRATION
Edited by
HOWARD THOMAS AND DON O'NEAL

STRATEGIC DISCOVERY
Edited by
HOWARD THOMAS, DON O'NEAL AND RAUL ALVARADO

MANAGING STRATEGICALLY IN AN INTERCONNECTED WORLD
Edited by
MICHAEL A. HITT, JOAN E. RICART I COSTA AND ROBERT D. NIXON

NEW MANAGERIAL MINDSETS
Edited by
MICHAEL A. HITT, JOAN E. RICART I COSTA AND ROBERT D. NIXON

STRATEGIC FLEXIBILITY: MANAGING IN A TURBULENT
ENVIRONMENT
Edited by
GARY HAMEL, C.K. PRALAHAD, HOWARD THOMAS AND DON O'NEAL

THE STRATEGIC MANAGEMENT SERIES

NEW MANAGERIAL MINDSETS

Organizational Transformation and Strategy Implementation

Edited by

MICHAEL A. HITT, JOAN E. RICART I COSTA
AND ROBERT D. NIXON

JOHN WILEY & SONS

Chichester · New York · Weinheim · Brisbane · Singapore · Toronto

Other Wiley Editorial Offices

John Wiley & Sons, Inc., 605 Third Avenue,
New York, NY 10158-0012, USA

WILEY-VCH Verlag GmbH, Pappelallee 3,
D-69469 Weinheim, Germany

Jacaranda Wiley Ltd, 33 Park Road, Milton,
Queensland 4064, Australia

John Wiley & Sons (Asia) Pte Ltd, 2 Clementi Loop #02-01,
Jin Xing Distripark, Singapore 129809

John Wiley & Sons (Canada) Ltd, 22 Worcester Road,
Rexdale, Ontario M9W 1L1, Canada

British Library Cataloguing in Publication Data

A catalogue record for this book is available from the British Library

ISBN 0-471-98667-4

Typeset in 10/12pt Palatino by Dorwyn Ltd, Rowlands Castle, Hants.
Printed and bound in Great Britain by Bookcraft (Bath) Ltd, Midsomer Norton, Somerset.
This book is printed on acid-free paper responsibly manufactured from sustainable forestry,
in which at least two trees are planted for each one used in paper production.

Contents

Contributors

JULIA BALOGUN
School of Management, Cranfield University, Cranfield, Bedfordshire MK43 0AL, UK

KAREN BANTEL
School of Business Administration, University of Michigan, Ann Arbor, MI 48109-1234, USA

HARRY BARKEMA
Tilburg University, PO Box 90153, 5000 LE Tilburg, The Netherlands

BRIAN K. BOYD
College of Business Administration, Arizona State University, Tempe, AZ 85287–4006, USA

DANIEL BYRD
School of Business Administration, University of Michigan, Ann Arbor, MI 48109–1234, USA

THOMAS ERICSON
Department of Management and Economics, Linkoping University, S-581 83 Linkoping, Sweden

DENNIS K.K. FAN
Department of Finance, Faculty of Business Administration, The Chinese University of Hong Kong, Hong Kong

SYDNEY FINKELSTEIN
Amos Tuck School of Business, Dartmouth College, Hanover, NH 03755, USA

JAUME FRANQUESA
Department of Management, Haworth College of Business, Western Michigan University, Kalamazoo, MI 49008-3806, USA

CLARA-EUGENIA GARCIA
Departamento de Economia de la Empresas, Universidad Carlos III de Madrid, C/Madrid 126, 28903 Getafe, Madrid, Spain

LUIS GOMEZ-MEJIA
College of Business Administration, Arizona State University, Tempe, AZ 85287-4006, USA

ISABEL GUTIÉRREZ
Departamento de Economia de la Empresas, Universidad Carlos III de Madrid, C/Madrid 126, 28903 Getafe, Madrid, Spain

MICHAEL A. HITT
Lowry Mays College of Business Administration, Texas A&M University, College Station, TX 77843–4221, USA

KAZUO ICHIJO
Faculty of Social Sciences, Hitotsubashi University, Japan

GERRY JOHNSON
School of Management, Cranfield University, Cranfield, Bedfordshire MK43 0AL, UK

EONSOO KIM
Graduate School of Business Administration, Korea University, Korea

TATIANA KOSTOVA
College of Business Administration, University of South Carolina, Columbia, SC 29208, USA

PIA LINDELL
Department of Management and Economics, Linkoping University, S-581 83 Linkoping, Sweden

CONSTANTINOS MARKIDES
London Business School, Sussex Place, Regent's Park, London NW1 4SA, UK

ESTEBAN MASIFERN
ILSE, International Graduate School of Management, Universidad de Navarra, Avda. Pearson, 21, 08034 Barcelona, Spain

JOHN McGEE
Warwick Business School, University of Warwick, Coventry CV4 7AL, UK

JOHN C. McINTOSH
Department of Management, University of Nebraska-Lincoln, Lincoln, NE, USA

LEIF MELIN
Jonkoping International Business School, PO Box 1026, S-551 11 Jonkoping, Sweden

YASMIN MERALI
Warwick Business School, University of Warwick, Coventry CV4 7AL, UK

WILL MITCHELL
School of Business Administration, University of Michigan, Ann Arbor, MI 48109-1234, USA

ROBERT D. NIXON
A.B. Freeman School of Business, Tulane University, New Orleans, LA 70118–5669, USA

IKUJIRO NONAKA
Institute of Innovation Research, Hitotsubashi University, Japan

MANUEL NÚÑEZ-NICKEL
Universidad de Jaen, Spain

VASSILIS M. PAPADAKIS
London Business School, Sussex Place, Regent's Park, London NW1 4SA, UK

JOAN E. RICART I COSTA
IESE, International Graduate School of Management, Universidad de Navarra, Avda. Pearson, 21, 08034 Barcelona, Spain

BRIAN SUBIRANA
IESE, International Graduate School of Management, Universidad de Navarra, Avda. Pearson, 21, 08034 Barcelona, Spain

JOAQUIM VILÀ
IESE, International Graduate School of Management, Universidad de Navarra, Avda. Pearson, 21, 08034 Barcelona, Spain

CHUN-CHEONG WAN
Department of Management, Faculty of Business Administration, The Chinese University of Hong Kong, Hong Kong

Series Preface

The Strategic Management Society was created to bring together, on a worldwide basis, academics, business practitioners, and consultants interested in strategic management. The aim of the Society is the development and dissemination of information, achieved through its sponsorship of the annual international conference, special interest workshops, the *Strategic Management Journal*, and other publications.

The Society's annual conference is a truly international meeting, held in recent years in Stockholm, Barcelona, Toronto, London, Paris, Mexico City, Chicago, and Phoenix. Each conference deals with a broad, current theme, within which specific sub-themes are addressed through keynote speeches and discussion panels featuring leading experts from around the world.

The Strategic Management Series is a cooperative effort between the Strategic Management Society and John Wiley & Sons. The series focuses on cutting-edge concepts/topics in strategic management theory and practice. The books emphasize building and maintaining bridges between theory and practice in strategic management. The work published in these books generates and tests theories of strategic management; additionally, it demonstrates how to learn, understand, and apply these theories in practice. The books in the series represent the products of Strategic Management Society sponsored Mini-Conferences and best volumes from the annual International Strategic Management Society Conferences.

The contributions in this volume are based on papers from the 1997 Strategic Management Society Conference held in Barcelona, Spain. The contributors represent an excellent set of authors from many regions of the world, in particular Asia, Europe, and North America. The following paragraphs provide an overview of the contents of this important book.

The new frontier, composed of rapid and unpredictable change and substantial uncertainty, requires new managerial mindsets that emphasize global markets and strategic flexibility and embrace change. To do so requires the harnessing and effective use of information technology (IT). IT affects firm structure and strategy implementation. Implementation processes are critically important to the success of strategic change. The book addresses two major themes, managerial mindsets and the implementation of strategy and strategic change.

Mindsets represent a shared, interconnected mental framework throughout a firm's managerial ranks. It is based on sensemaking that represents an intangible structure in the firm. IT supports sensemaking through linkages in a managerial network and the information that flows through this network. Through the structure and the information that IT provides, it affects a firm's strategic flexibility. Managerial mindsets oriented toward change and flexible IT architecture facilitate organizational transformations.

Implementation processes are particularly important for successful strategic change. A key element in implementation of strategy and strategic change is the managerial reward system. Managerial compensation affects managerial actions (e.g. to promote resource sharing across business units) and the firm's ability to effect change. Similarly, managerial ownership in a firm is often used to align managers' interests with those of the shareholders.

Therefore, *New Managerial Mindsets: Organizational Transformation and Strategy Implementation* addresses critically important topics relevant to firm success in the changing global competitive landscape.

Michael A. Hitt
September 1998

1

New Managerial Mindsets and Strategic Change in the New Frontier

Robert D. Nixon, Michael A. Hitt, Joan E. Ricart i Costa

We are entering a new frontier (Hitt, Ricart & Nixon, 1998). This new frontier entails a competitive landscape with rapid and unpredictable environmental changes. As a result, many firms will experience strategic discontinuities (Hitt, Keats & DeMarie, 1998). The new frontier is driven by substantial and continuous technological changes and improvements (Bettis & Hitt, 1995) and increasing globalization of business (Murtha, Lenway & Bagozzi, 1998). As we enter a new business frontier, new forms of managerial thinking, along with new organizational structures, will be required. This new frontier requires new managerial mindsets that are global in orientation and allow strategic and structural flexibility. In addition, the new business frontier will demand innovative methods of implementing such structural changes and of creating new managerial mindsets. As such, organizations must have the capability to create and implement strategic and structural changes that entail continuous technological improvements, particularly in information technology. While the design of these changes is critical, their implementation is even more crucial.

New Managerial Mindsets: Organizational Transformation and Strategy Implementation.
Edited by M.A. Hitt, J.E. Ricart i Costa and R.D. Nixon.
© 1998 John Wiley & Sons Ltd.

The new frontier requires that firms build the capability for strategic and structural flexibility along with the ability to integrate the two (Hitt, Ricart & Nixon, 1998; Kay, 1993). In effect, firms must develop the capability to "float like a butterfly and sting competitors like a bee" (Sifonis & Goldberg, 1996). One means of building strategic flexibility is to form organizational networks. These organizational networks function like a flexible architecture (Kay, 1993). According to Kay (1993), architecture is a network of relational contracts with parties internal and/or external to the firm. Thus, firms may establish relationships with and among their employees, suppliers, customers, competitors or other organizations engaged in related activities. The value of such architecture is in the capacity it creates for organizations to build knowledge and to respond in a flexible way to important external events or actions (Kay, 1993).

A critical element of a network architecture involving internal and external relationships is to achieve effective and open exchanges of information. This often requires efficient and current information technology. In fact, such technology can create a virtual organization in these networks (Sifonis & Goldberg, 1996). However, its availability notwithstanding, many organizations find it difficult to harness the power of information technology. Importantly, information technology has the power to transform industries and markets (Luftman & Oldach, 1996). Information technology infrastructure can be one of the most unique and significant long-term sources of strategic advantage (Weill, Broadbent & St Clair, 1996).

According to Daniels & Daniels (1996), information technology may be a critical element for firms to become global. Information technology allows the sharing of information, the connection of processes, and the customization of products on a worldwide basis. To do these things and remain flexible requires a modular form of information technology infrastructure. In fact, these advanced forms of information technology and public communication infrastructures (e.g. the Internet) are redefining industry structures (Sampler, 1998). The information technology redefines the industry both geographically and in terms of competition. Consequently, we are seeing the emergence of new electronic markets, but at the same time, the same technology facilitates intra-firm coordination, allowing for new forms of vertical integration or quasi-integration. Therefore, we need to better understand how to manage information technology in order to derive the benefits and use it to create a strategic advantage. This is no simple task, however.

Because of the new frontier driven by substantial technological change and globalization in business, the need for strategic and structural flexibility and the use of information technology to implement this flexibility and the change necessary to adapt to a new competitive landscape, new managerial mindsets are required. For example, managers must develop a global mindset that emphasizes organizational change and informs relationships and interactions within and external to the firm (Murtha, Lenway & Bagozzi, 1998). There is a need for new strategic mindsets that emphasize continuous learning. Movement into global markets and continuous development of new technology facilitate needed organizational learning (Barkema & Vermeulen, 1998). Organizational architectures can facilitate learning such as through technological strategic alliances (Das, Sen & Sengupta, 1998). Organizational learning builds a firm's knowledge and capabilities, thereby creating greater strategic flexibility. Strategic and structural flexibility is necessary for successful organizational transformation. According to Davidson & Movizzo (1996), organizational transformation can produce substantial results but the process can be long and painful, even for agile organizations. Unfortunately, most organizational transformations have been precipitated by crises (e.g. poor performance, significant competitor actions, etc.). However, future organizational transformations must be precipitated by proactive managerial action for the purpose of achieving greater alignment with a firm's competitive landscape.

Herein, we briefly review the underlying basis for the various parts of this book and the framework that suggests the significant value that each of the different chapters provide. All of these works provide a distinct piece of the puzzle to help us appreciate the importance of the new managerial mindsets in global markets. We begin by discussing the new managerial mindsets required to operate in this interconnected world, along with new developments and application of information technology and how the new managerial mindsets in technology help lead toward organizational change. We conclude by examining issues associated with some of the new developments in the relationships among strategies, competencies, firm performance, and strategy implementation.

INTERCONNECTED THINKING: NEW MANAGERIAL MINDSETS, ORGANIZATIONAL CHANGE AND INFORMATION TECHNOLOGY

The new competitive landscape will require that many organizations develop new managerial mindsets (Hitt, Keats & DeMarie, 1998). A managerial mindset is similar to the concept of dominant logic suggested by Prahalad & Bettis (1986) and explained further by Bettis & Prahalad (1995); it produces a form of managerial sensemaking. This sensemaking is important in relationships with other firms such as in strategic alliances and other network architectures. For example, having common or at least complementary managerial mindsets among the alliance partners could facilitate cooperation and coordination (Barr *et al.*, 1997).

In the new frontier, flexibility is key. Therefore, the new managerial mindset must entail an orientation toward change. Executives' cultural values can affect their orientation toward change and thus commitment to the status

quo (Geletkanycz, 1997). Unfortunately, managers, in general, are not necessarily open to change. These mindsets may be one of the reasons why firms
experience substantial inertia (Ruef, 1997) even in a period of dynamic environmental change such as exists in the new competitive landscape.

A primary catalyst for change is poor performance (Boeker, 1997). Poor
performance frequently produces a change in the person holding the chief
executive officer position. Other changes within the organization are then
more likely. However, it is much better to make changes when a firm is
performing well, thereby preparing for future changes in the competitive
landscape, than to wait until performance turns negative. Therefore, strategic leaders must have the courage to make changes when a firm has high
performance (Hitt, Keats & DeMarie, 1998).

Most firms make changes in reaction to changes in their competitive landscape or other parts of their environment (Rajagopalan & Spreitzer, 1997).
While this may be necessary, the most effective changes are proactive in
nature, in anticipation of changes in the environment. In this way, firms may
help shape their future environment. However, firms waiting until their performance turns negative will require a turnaround (Barker & Duhaime, 1997).
Turnarounds are, perhaps, the most difficult strategic changes to make and
often entail cost reductions to create greater efficiency. However, such
changes often do not deal with the specific problems and thus many turnarounds are not successful. Therefore, in a dynamic environment such as the
new competitive landscape, firms must create a process of continual transformation. This requires a significant change in many managerial mindsets.

There are several chapters in this volume that examine strategic thinking
in organizations and changing managerial mindsets. *Masifern and Vilà* argue
that managers must go beyond the notion of strategic thinking as a concept
of strategy, and develop the concept as a process and as a given state of
mind. They suggest that the process involves moving from an ideal (intended) strategy to a possible, achievable strategy. The outcome of this
process is a new mindset that guides managers' daily actions through a
shared, interconnected mental framework. *Balogun and Johnson* explore how
middle managers, as change recipients, perceive interacting facilitating and
obstructing processes as affecting the development of top-down, planned
strategic change implementation. They employ a sensemaking perspective
to explain how and why some emergent elements develop, and why this
approach sometimes introduces unintentional changes (some helpful, others
undesirable) into the strategic change process. An interesting chapter by
Lindell, Ericson and Melin combines concepts from an interconnected thinking perspective with those of organizational change to examine intangible or
invisible structures and processes that could facilitate a better understanding of the strategic change process. They suggest that a collective level of
shared thinking or sensemaking may represent a distinguishable structure

that is influential in the strategic transformation process. In support of this argument, Papadakis, Lioukas & Chambers (1998) concluded from their research that a new model of strategic decision making should be developed that incorporates a broader spectrum of theoretical arguments in addition to external control, strategic choice, and corporate inertia perspectives.

The new frontier is one of continually transforming organizations for large and small firms alike. In such organizations, information technology may be critical to communicate to all parts of an organization. As such, horizontal information systems, in conjunction with horizontal structures, may be critical for implementing change, particularly on a global basis (Hitt, Ireland & Hoskisson, 1997; Hitt, Keats & DeMarie, 1998). Furthermore, Henderson, Venkatraman & Oldach (1996) argue that the information technology must be aligned with firm strategy. *McIntosh and Kim* address this issue as they examine the competitive uses of information technology by comparing how Swedish, American, and Korean manufacturing firms use such technology to implement mass customization and time-based strategies in a global context. Their study explores how these firms reduce time-to-market, increase innovation, and reduce the cost of coordinating activities with network partners.

In addition to horizontal information systems interconnecting various parts of a global organization, information technology plays an important role in interconnecting firms to their customers and suppliers (Kay, 1993). The trans formation of industries such as computers, telecommunications, document production, and multimedia into information industries has changed the "normal" course of business and revolutionized the opportunities to integrate the flow of materials or services through contiguous stages of value-chain activities. Information integration has increased the opportunities for manufacturers to become their own distributer, wholesaler, and retailer. Even purchases such as automobiles are no longer restricted to traditional distribution channels (Taylor, 1996). For example, the chapter by *Subirana* explores the pivotal position of the Internet in the value chain. It presents a model of how transactions are performed on the Web and analyzes how value is added through the alliances formed by participants (e.g. media content and media distribution) within the transaction process.

Change to managerial mindsets and implementation of strategic change require new visions, strategies, structures, and managerial reward systems. These are the focus of the next section.

INTERCONNECTED PROCESSES: STRATEGIC IMPLEMENTATION IN A GLOBAL MARKET

Hitt, Ireland & Hoskisson (1997) argue that strategy formulation and implementation processes should be integrated. As such, implementation processes and actions are important for firm success. Implementation is particularly critical for strategic change. Strategy implementation in a global context is the focus of this section.

One of the positive outcomes of a new managerial mindset may be a more effective statement of the firm's mission. An effective mission statement is the topic of the chapter by *Markides and Papadakis*. They argue that an organization's mission statement must maintain a balance between extreme positions on a number of parameters, including, for example, specificity, flexibility, realism, and measurability. Suggesting there has been little research on the requirements, these authors present a model identifying five determinants of effective mission statements.

After the establishment of an organization's mission statement, the planned dissemination of that vision from a global corporate headquarters to the individual business units throughout the world markets is simultaneously an important and complex endeavor. Ghoshal & Nohria, (1993) argued that the role of the headquarters in information management and the dissemination of competencies among business units is crucial. An important determinant of how successful this dissemination and transformation process (of moving from one mode of behavior to a notably different one) will be is the headquarters–business unit relationship. While each headquarters–business unit relationship may be distinctively focused on maintaining an optimal fit between the headquarter's need for control and the business unit's need to be responsive to its individual competitive and national context, the chapter by *Merali and McGee* suggests that there are four archetypical headquarter styles, each with its own characteristics, filters and perceptions. They argue that when market conditions require restructuring, and thus a migration from one style to another, the relationship between the headquarters and the business unit may also need to be restructured.

The scope of corporate operations was transformed in the late 1980s and early 1990s, oftentimes changing the relationship between the headquarters and business units of large corporations. As such, many firms have downscoped to become less diversified, allowing top executives to focus their energies on managing the primary core businesses (Hoskisson & Hitt, 1994). This restructuring represents major strategic change and transformation. Strategic management scholars have suggested the need to explore several areas important to such structurings, including knowledge sharing (Nonaka & Takeuchi, 1995), compensation (Fisher & Govindarajan, 1992; Gomez-Mejia, 1992, 1994; Hoskisson *et al.*, 1989) and ownership structure (Fox & Hamilton, 1994).

To facilitate the sharing of knowledge, new structures are being devised to help organizations better implement critical knowledge-sharing strategies so crucial to successful navigation in the new frontier. There are multiple types of new structures being devised, to include network architectures (Kay, 1993) within and across organizations and what some have referred to as a cellular structural form (Miles *et al.*, 1997). The network or cellular form of organization often entails a set of businesses, each of which focuses on different products/service lines but which also has common attributes. In the cellular (sometimes called modular) form, these separate businesses operate relatively autonomously but also coordinate with one another in order to develop a competitive advantage for the larger organization. Not all of the units may cooperate or coordinate at any given time but there may be several sets of networks existing within the organization. In effect, these smaller relatively autonomous units form partnerships within the organization to compete in a larger market. Thus, the cellular form of organization is similar to the informal networks of smaller organizations that have been developed in recent years. It is a form that creates and allows the strategic flexibility that is so critical in the new frontier.

Several of the chapters presented in this volume focus on and explain new structural forms required for adaptation and managing a cellular form of organization from the corporate center. For example, *Ichijo and Nonaka* describe how some large Japanese electronic firms implement a related diversified strategy to compete more effectively in a global environment. This strategy involves centralized knowledge creation through cross-divisional interconnections that enable the sharing of the created knowledge among the firm's SBUs. They use Toshiba to exemplify the focus strategy and the challenges of managing integrating mechanisms to realize economies of scope. *Kostova* also considers the competitive advantages of successfully implementing knowledge transfer from the parent organization to foreign organizational units. She argues that both structural relationships (formal characteristics of an organizational unit relative to other units) and attitudinal relationships (widely shared attitudes or common mindsets of employees in an organizational unit toward the whole organization or another organizational unit) are important determinants of successful knowledge transfer.

A topic of increasing importance in recent years relating to strategy implementation is managerial reward systems designed to encourage managers to develop the appropriate strategies and to implement those strategies throughout the organization (Gomez-Mejia & Wiseman, 1997). Some of the reward systems have focused on top executives in order to manage the agency problem (i.e. to encourage managers not to overdiversify), while other reward systems are designed to help firms better implement strategies to promote sharing of knowledge and resources across organizational units and businesses. However, these reward systems have been greatly complicated by the increasing globalization. First, reward systems must be designed to appeal to those from diverse cultures and nationalities (i.e. Chen,

1995). Second, with the geographic distribution across national borders, managers may need incentives to cooperate. However, the types of incentives necessary to encourage managers to cooperate and share resources and knowledge across widely dispersed national geographic boundaries may be quite complex and difficult to design. Alternatively, such reward structures (e.g. managerial compensation systems) can be critical to establishing inter-unit coordination and cooperation, and to take advantage of potential synergies for sharing resources and knowledge across a firm's business units. This may require a cooperative structure (Hill, Hitt & Hoskisson, 1992).

Several of the chapters in this volume address managerial compensation within the context of an environment emphasizing the new focus strategy and/or how more related diversification strategies are effectively implemented and managed. For example, *Boyd, Finkelstein, Barkema and Gomez-Mejia* suggest that the type of compensation a CEO receives (cash versus equity) affects the implementation of a firm's diversification strategy. They argue that an emphasis on cash compensation reduces CEO risk bearing, and reduced risk bearing enhances the successful implementation of a related product strategy. Conversely, they argue that equity-based compensation increases risk bearing, thereby increasing the CEO's reluctance to implement a more focused diversification strategy. Compensation at the division level and its relationship to strategy implementation is the topic of the chapter by *Franquesa*. Here the focus is on how the match between the division's intra-corporate resource sharing and the division manager's compensation affects the proper implementation of a related diversification strategy.

Ownership structure also has had an effect on implementing refocusing strategies (Fox & Hamilton, 1994), particularly the extent of management ownership concentration (Lloyd, Hand & Modani, 1987). Research on management ownership concentration suggests that in highly concentrated firms, the manager's ownership has reached such a level that the manager's self-interest is in line with that of the outside shareholders (Morck, Schleifer & Vishny, 1988). These results suggest that where managerial ownership is more highly concentrated, implementation of refocusing strategies beneficial to shareholders will be more prevalent (Hoskisson & Hitt, 1994). However, the relationship between managerial ownership and diversification (lower) may be more apparent among Western-based firms than Asian-based firms, as suggested by *Fan and Wan*. They argue that firms with high management ownership concentration in Asian cultures have more incentives to adopt diversity for the purpose of reducing the risk of their undiversified portfolios even though implementing such a strategy may lead to inferior performance. As more firms enter global markets, especially as they extend from developed countries into developing economies, understanding the motivations for structural reformation (or avoiding such restructuring) may be important to the success of international alliances.

An emphasis on organizational restructuring/refocusing also has occasioned an increase in the importance of identifying and exploiting intangible resources (Barney, 1991; Prahalad & Hamel, 1990) that can lead to competitive advantages. Although conceptual arguments tend to suggest that intangible resources have positive effects on performance, the complexity of both intangible resources and performance as multidimensional constructs (Amit & Schoemaker, 1993) suggests that such intangibles may introduce competitive constraints, as well as competitive opportunities (Leonard-Barton, 1992). These opportunities and/or constraints may be magnified when the complexities associated with the global market are added. *Bantel, Byrd and Mitchell* explore these issues in their chapter as they examine how different types of intangible resources account for differential firm performance in high technology industries.

The ability, or even desire, of an organization to restructure (or resist restructuring) in order to achieve a greater focus on important resources and core competencies may be influenced by an organization's founding parameters. Organizational ecology suggests that as established firms interact with newly organized firms, the manner in which these new firms are initially structured may influence how quickly well established firms adapt or transform themselves (Carroll, 1987) from their original structure. Neo-institutional approaches suggest that observed homogeneity among firms is explained by imperatives of legitimacy and social fitness that lead to isomorphic structures (Powell & DiMaggio, 1991). However, in the new dynamic frontier, a question may arise as to whether the old or the new has the greater influence on the other. As new sets of resources and competencies are required to successfully compete in the global market (Prahalad & Hamel, 1990), founding conditions may play an increasingly important role in meeting the base requirements. The chapter by *Gutiérrez, Garcia and Núñez-Nickel* explains how a firm's founding conditions and context are embodied in a set of core characteristics that are translated directly, or indirectly, into organizational resources, routines, and competencies. They argue that the possession of such resources and competencies is not merely a historical accident but rather the reflection of evolution and previous events.

In summary, the new frontier entails a dynamic and competitive environment with new strategies. To make sense of this new frontier, we need to develop new managerial mindsets by encouraging strategic thinking and collective sensemaking. We must develop new structures necessary to compete effectively and survive in the global environment of business organizations by intensive use of information technology and the proper management of knowledge and flexibility. For these new structures to work, we must do diverse things, like developing new missions, designing new compensation systems, revising our management style, and considering the role of ownership in corporations. Understanding these issues is a broad agenda, as the chapters in this book show. The ideas presented provide a challenging new frontier for managers and researchers alike to explore the problems associated with implementing strategic change in an interconnected global market.

REFERENCES

Amit, R. & Schoemaker, P. (1993). Strategic assets and organizational rent. *Strategic Management Journal*, **14**, 33–46.

Barkema, H.G. & Vermeulen, F. (1998). International expansion through start-up or acquisition: a learning perspective. *Academy of Management Journal*, **41**, 7–26.

Barker, V.L. III & Duhaime, I.M. (1997). Strategic change in the turnaround process: theory and empirical evidence. *Strategic Management Journal*, **18**, 13–38.

Barney, J. (1991). Firm resources and sustained competitive advantage. *Journal of Management*, **17**, 99–120.

Barr, P., Bogner, W. Golden-Biddle, K., Rao, H. & Thomas, H. (1997). Cognitive processes in alliance: Birth, maturity and (possible) death. In H.Thomas, D. O'Neal and M. Ghertman (eds) *Strategy, Structure and Style*. Chichester, John Wiley & Sons, pp. 137–157.

Bettis, R.A. & Hitt, M.A. (1995). The new competitive landscape. *Strategic Management Journal*, **16**, 7–20.

Bettis, R.A. & Prahalad, C.K. (1995). The dominant logic: retrospective and extension. *Strategic Management Journal*, **16**, 5–14.

Boeker, W. (1997). Strategic change: the influence of managerial characteristics and organizational growth. *Academy of Management Journal*, **40**, 152–170.

Carroll, G.R. (1987). *Publish and Perish: The Organizational Ecology of Newspaper Industries*. Greenwich, CT: JAI Press.

Chen, C.C. (1995). New trends in rewards allocation preferences: a Sino-US comparison. *Academy of Management Journal*, **38**, 408–428.

Daniels, J.L. & Daniels, N.C. (1996). Building global competence. In J.N. Luftman (ed.) *Competing in the Information Age*. New York: Oxford University Press, pp. 97–133.

Das, S., Sen, T.K. & Sengupta, S. (1998). Impact of strategic alliances on firm valuation. *Academy of Management Journal*, **41**, 27–41.

Davidson, W.H. & Movizzo, J.F. (1996). Managing the business transformation process. In J.N. Luftman (ed.) *Competing in the Information Age*. New York: Oxford University Press, 322–358.

Fisher, J. & Govindarajan, V. (1992). Profit center manager compensation: an examination of market, political and human factors. *Strategic Management Journal*, **13**, 205–217.

Fox, M. & Hamilton, R. (1994). Ownership and diversification: agency theory or stewardship theory. *Journal of Management Studies*, 69–81.

Geletkanycz, M.A. (1997). The salience of culture consequences: the effects of cultural values on top management commitment to the status quo. *Strategic Management Journal*, **18**, 615–634.

Ghoshal, S. & Nohria, N. (1993). Horses for courses: organizational forms for multinational corporations. *Strategic Management Journal*, **10**(4), 323–338.

Gomez-Mejia, L.R. (1992). Structure and process of diversification, compensation strategy, and firm performance. *Strategic Management Journal*, **13**, 381–397.

Gomez-Mejia, L.R. (1994). Executive compensation: a reassessment and future research agenda. *Research in Personnel and Human Resources Management*, **12**, 161–222.

Gomez-Mejia, L. & Wiseman, R.M. (1997). Reframing executive compensation: an assessment and outlook. *Journal of Management*, **23**, 291–374.

Henderson, J.C., Venkatraman, N. & Oldach, S. (1996). Aligning business and IT strategies. In J.N. Luftman (ed.) *Competing in the Information Age*. New York: Oxford University Press, pp. 21–42.

Hill, C.W.L., Hitt, M.A. & Hoskisson, R.E. (1992). Cooperative versus competitive structures in related and unrelated diversified firms. *Organization Science*, **3**, 501–521.

Hitt, M.A., Ireland, R.D. & Hoskisson, R.E. (1997). *Strategic Management: Competitiveness and Globalization*. St Paul, MN: West.

Hitt, M.A., Keats, B.W. & DeMarie, S.M. (1998). Navigating the new competitive landscape: building strategic flexibility and competitive advantage in the 21st century. *Academy of Management Executive*, in press.

Hitt, M.A., Ricart, J.E. & Nixon, R.D. (1998). The new frontier. In M.A. Hitt, J.E. Ricart & R.D. Nixon (eds) *Managing Strategically in an Interconnected World*. Chichester: John Wiley & Sons.

Hoskisson, R.E. & Hitt, M.A. (1994). *Downscoping: How to Tame the Diversified Firm*. New York: Oxford University Press.

Hoskisson, R.E., Hitt, M.A., Turk, T.A. & Tyler, B.B. (1989). Balancing corporate strategy and executive compensation: agency theory and corporate governance. *Research in Personnel and Human Resources Management*, **7**, 25–57.

Kay, J. (1993). *Foundations of Corporate Success*. Oxford: Oxford University Press.

Leonard Barton, D. (1992). Core capabilities and core rigidities: a paradox in managing new product development. *Strategic Management Journal*, **13**, 111–125.

Lloyd, W., Hand, J. & Modani, N. (1987). The effect of the degree of ownership control on firm diversification, market value and merger activity. *Journal of Business Research*, **15**, 303–312.

Luftman, J.N. & Oldach, S.H. (1996). Introduction. In J.N. Luftman (ed.) *Competing in the Information Age*. New York: Oxford University Press, pp. 3–18.

Miles, R.E., Snow, C.C., Mathews, J.A., Miles, G. & Coleman Jr, H.J. (1997). Organizing in the knowledge age: anticipation of the cellular form. *Academy of Management Executive*, **11**(4), 7–20.

Morck, R., Schleifer, A. & Vishny, R. (1988). Management ownership and market valuation: an empirical analysis. *Journal of Financial Economics*, **20**, 293–315.

Murtha, T.T., Lenway, S.A. & Bagozzi, R.P. (1998). Global mindsets and cognitive shifts in a complex multinational corporation. *Strategic Management Journal*, **19**, 97–114.

Nonaka, I & Takeuchi, H. (1995). *The Knowledge-Creating Company: How Japanese Companies Create the Dynamics of Innovation*. New York: Oxford University Press.

Papadakis, V.M., Lioukas, S. & Chambers, D. (1998). Strategic decision making processes: the role of management and context. *Strategic Management Journal*, **19**, 115–148.

Powell, W.W. & DiMaggio, P.J. (1991). *The New Institutionalism in Organizational Analysis*. Chicago, IL: University of Chicago Press.

Prahalad, C.K. & Bettis, R.A. (1986). The dominant logic: a new linkage between diversity and performance. *Strategic Management Journal*, **7**, 485–501.

Prahalad, C.K. & Hamel, G. (1990). The core competence of the corporation. *Harvard Business Review*, **68**, 79–91.

Rajagopalan. M. & Spreitzer, G.M. (1997). Toward a theory of strategic change: a multi-lens perspective and integrative framework. *Academy of Management Review*, **22**(1), 48–79.

Ruef, M. (1997). Assessing organizational fitness on a dynamic landscape: an empirical test of the relative inertia thesis. *Strategic Management Journal*, **18**, 837–853.

Sampler, J.L. (1998). Redefining industry structure for the information age. *Strategic Management Journal*, **19**, 343–356.

Sifonis, J.T. & Goldberg, B. (1996). *Corporation on a Tightrope*. New York: Oxford University Press.

Taylor III, A. (1996). How to buy a car on the Internet. *Fortune*, 4 March, 164–168.

Weill, P., Broadbent, M. & St. Clair, D.R. (1996). IT value and the role of IT infrastructure investments. In J.N. Luftman (ed.) *Competing in the Information Age*. New York: Oxford University Press, pp. 361–384

Section I

Interconnected Thinking: Managerial Mindsets, Information Technology and Organizational Change

2

Interconnected Mindsets: Strategic Thinking and the Strategy Concept

ESTEBAN MASIFERN, JOAQUIM VILÀ

INTRODUCTION

Whereas during the 1970s and 1980s many chief executives channeled their energies towards the development of a strategy for their companies and for individual businesses, the emphasis shifted during the early 1990s to the search for sources of sustainable competitive advantage and is now moving to the issue of how to translate strategy into action. Progress in the strategic management field keeps shedding new light on the triggers of company performance, yet it is hard to claim that this has had a significant impact on the tasks of the majority of practising managers.

A number of factors have been pointed out to explain why developments in strategic management are applied at such a slow pace. Some authors (e.g. Prahalad & Hamel, 1994) refer to the excessive emphasis on analysis, to the detriment of creativity and exploration. It is claimed that analysis inhibits creativity, and precludes the chance to create regenerated strategies. Others state that most models and tools, even when presented as a definitive way to think about strategy, find application only in very limited settings (Coyne & Subramaniam, 1996). Still others suggest that the sluggishness in the practical use of strategy may be due to the artificial separation of formulation

New Managerial Mindsets: Organizational Transformation and Strategy Implementation.
Edited by M.A. Hitt, J.E. Ricart i Costa and R.D. Nixon.
© 1998 John Wiley & Sons Ltd.

and implementation. A major drawback in incorporating strategy in management practice is related to ignoring organizational issues in strategy formulation, a concern which the defenders of the state of practice, for example the deductive approaches of Planning, Programming and Budgeting systems during the 1960s and 1970s, tried to overcome (yet, most failed due to political pressures to avoid the loss of status and influence within firms). In the same line, more recently, academics have looked inside the organization and structure in detail only at the time of strategy implementation. In short, the source of the problem may lie both in the way the notion of strategy is approached and in the widespread tendency among scholars to separate responsibility for thinking and action within organizational hierarchies.

Strategic planning has been the dominant approach to the development of strategy for more than two decades, yet the limitations of formal planning, as it was conceived during the late 1970s, have been amply documented in the literature (*Business Week*, 1984; Lenz, 1987; Wilson, 1994), and, in recent years, formal planning has been one of the most favored subjects of attack among leading thinkers in the strategy field (e.g. Mintzberg, 1994). In many cases strategic planning turned out to be driven by techniques, not courageous inquiry. Critics of formal planning as a means to reach strategy advocate the advance of strategic thinking. Consequently, planning has failed to fulfill management expectations in as much as it has not produced strategic thinking (Hansen, 1991). Indeed, a number of authors add that strategic thinking has even disappeared altogether from the traditional planning processes. More recently, the claim that strategic thinking will overcome the design and behavioral limitations of formal planning and provide a road map for creating effective strategies is becoming popular. There is an extended view, defended by several writers (e.g. Ansoff, DeClerk & Heyes, 1979) that strategic planning leads to strategic management, which then somehow leads to strategic thinking. However, not much progress has been made in the definition and development of strategic thinking, nor in identifying the benefits it may bring to managers (Liedtka, 1998).

This chapter tries to bring together the limited research on process and content approaches to strategic thinking. We believe that, given the nature of the phenomenon, progress in this area depends on effective integration of both, and the weaker of the two will determine the prospects of any piece of research. Here, we try to go beyond the notion of strategic thinking as merely a particular way of thinking about strategy, and see it instead as a "way of doing" which is characteristic of a specific style of management. We suggest a process to facilitate developing the specific state of mind that characterizes strategic thinking. The process is related to moving from an ideal strategy (akin to the way *vision* and *intended strategy* are used in the literature) to a possible strategy. A new state of mind is an outcome of the former process, a result which subsequently guides the daily actions of managers. It is argued that strategy then turns out to be a shared framework in the minds of managers. Later, self-induced reflection itself shapes each individual's response to new information and becomes over time the driver of a refined state of mind built around an agreed-upon scheme, until a reconsideration of the strategy in place is called for.

The dominant approaches to strategy currently used in the field (as ex-post pattern of decisions, as vision, as positioning or as revolution, to mention the most frequently cited) provide only partial responses to practitioners' requests to make strategy a useful tool for management. We believe that the core of the problem may be due to a failure to capture the interconnected nature of the strategy creation. Academics have placed a major emphasis either on inside or outside aspects of the firm in the search for strategy, but rarely have proposed a feasible way to integrate both. Planners have traditionally looked outside, underrating the organizational factors. Most managers have limited their search of implementation alternatives to the confined range of organizational solutions their companies have had experience on. The current demands on management also request interconnection of the principles that guide action at different levels within the organization. The need to interconnect, setting direction, creating flexibility, and providing meaning as outcomes of the strategy creation process, is now stronger than ever.

We believe that the notions of strategic thinking and strategy presented here may shed new light on how to link aspects such as aligning efforts with the firm, providing guidance in the tasks of managers at different organizational levels as unexpected threats and opportunities unfold, and facilitating some aspects of strategy implementation. If we succeed in integrating some of these aspects, the viewpoint embraced by this chapter and similar research efforts may contribute to progress in both the academic demand for deeper understanding of the phenomenon and the managerial concern for an issue of high relevance.

STRATEGIC THINKING COMING INTO SHAPE

While the notion of "strategic thinking" has been increasingly used in the literature over the past two decades, it has been applied mainly in generic terms. Two basic concepts have received ample acceptance in the field until very recently. One assimilated strategic thinking to thinking about strategy and the other to an approach to strategy distinguishable from strategic planning.

In the first view, what determined the nature of strategic thinking was the nature of the issue under consideration (i.e. strategy). For instance, Raimond

(1996) compares the Western and Japanese modes of thinking about strategy, the first being rigorous, analytical, and quantitative, and the latter creative, imaginative, and concerned with values, emotional commitment, and energy. Or, in similar terms, strategic thinking has been conceived as thinking strategically. Bates & Dilliard (1993) propose a method for finding individuals with the ability and disposition to think strategically and in possession of certain capabilities. Strategic thinking, to Suutari (1993), is the ability to generate ideas and make decisions based on an understanding of the precepts of strategy formulation in accordance with the strategic objectives and direction of the business. Ginsberg (1994) conceives strategic thinking as the process concerned with the resolution of critical strategic issues (from the generation of the creative options needed to deal with each issue to their evaluation).

Practitioners use the term in a similar vein. To Lawrence Bossidy (1988), Allied Signal's CEO, strategic thinking identifies and synthesizes the forces which affect one's business, while strategic management uses strategic thinking to set business objectives and to communicate this direction to the organization. Kenichi Ohmae (1982), in his book *The Mind of the Strategist,* refers to strategic thinking as the combination of analytical method (testing out, digesting, assigning priorities to ideas) and mental elasticity (giving free rein to imagination and entrepreneurial flair in order to come up with bold and innovative strategic ideas).

In a second, yet very similar, approach, some authors have used strategic thinking interchangeably with the concept of strategic management. For example, Wilson (1994) reports that "having survived its original design flaws, strategic planning has evolved into a viable system of strategic management or strategic thinking." Näsi (1991, p. 27) approaches it as an overall concept, "a doctrine, a system of propositions and ideas about strategy and strategic action."

As the limitations of formal planning have become more apparent, a third, different and more concrete, approach to strategic thinking has resulted in an attempt to identify clearly the role of managers involved in strategic planning. Over the years, the rigid processes used in strategic planning were blamed for creating a climate that impeded creative thinking. Therefore, strategic thinking has been proposed as a way to return the thinking about strategic issues to the core of planning discussions. For example, Morrison and Lee, McKinsey partners, in a *Financial Times* article (1979, p. 21), refer to strategic thinking as the management tasks of dealing with substantive issues in strategy, in an attempt to redirect the attention away from planning mechanics. In a 1987 article from the *Economist* Michael Porter uses the notion of strategic thinking as thinking about strategic issues. He suggests expanding the scope of planning to include all elements of competitive analysis and thus avoid falling into the trap of planning routines (*Economist*, 1987).

Finally, the fourth major approach to the concept of strategic thinking, based on the nature of the process, has become increasingly prevalent over the past decade. Further insights drawn from the practitioner literature pivot on different aspects of its relationship to strategic planning. Robert (1993) suggests that strategic thinking precedes strategic planning—it generates a unique picture of what the organization should look like in the future, based on qualitative rather than quantitative variables.

Suggestions, presented by Reimann (1988), pointed out by high-level executives who participated as speakers at the Conference Board's 1988 Strategic Planning Conference, include "moving beyond the traditional mechanical approach toward a more creative and valuable process of strategic thinking." One finds claims such as "strategic thinking lives through dialogue or dies through writer's cramp," or "strategic thinking should occur where insight and knowledge meet." These statements are very inspiring if one has a grasp of what strategic thinking is; otherwise, the concept becomes a key missing piece, as is the case with "the vision of the final picture in the development of a giant jigsaw puzzle," to use an analogy found in the same report.

In summary, up to the early 1990s, strategic thinking had been dealt with in very general terms and without a specific meaning. Only recently has management research come to identify more concrete approaches to the notion. Mintzberg's work (1994) is illustrative of a growing line of research efforts where the term is not merely a catch-all for all sorts of notions about strategic management. Rather, he approaches strategic thinking as a particular way of thinking, albeit with specific characteristics. He further claims that strategic planning is an analytical process whose aim is programming already identified strategies. The result is a plan. Strategic thinking, on the other hand, is a process of synthesis, based on intuition and creativity, whose outcome is "an integrated perspective of the enterprise." Traditional planning tends to eliminate strategic thinking from the process. A similar comparison is presented by Näsi (1991), who distinguishes between the "hard line" analytical approach, focused traditionally on competition, and the "soft line" approach, emphasizing values and culture.

Liedtka (1998) approaches the notion of strategic thinking as derived from managerial competences. She defines strategic thinking as a particular way of thinking which includes five specific elements: it incorporates a systems perspective, is intent-focused, involves thinking in time, is hypothesis-driven, and is intelligently opportunistic. Having these competences is what characterizes the individual strategic thinker.

To Nadler (1994), strategic thinking is a creative process of thinking about forming, acting on, and learning about strategy. A collaborative process of formulating strategy generates shared learning, a frame of reference which constitutes the context for small decisions made over time.

Some authors suggest focusing on the consequences of strategic thinking rather than on the characteristics of a strategic thinker. Takur & Calingo consider strategic thinking to be the conceptual glue that holds the organization together in its pursuit of value creation, and suggest an illustrative analogy: "Strategic thinking can be imagined as the strand of rope on a string of pearls. The strand holds all the beads without being visible itself. Should some of the beads be removed to measure the breadth of the chain, the beauty or essence of the necklace would be destroyed" (Takur & Calingo, 1992, p. 48).

De Geus (1988), based on his experiences at Shell, claims that the real purpose of effective planning is not to make plans but to change the mental models that decision makers carry in their heads. In his view, planning provides the context which facilitates team thinking, the latter related to revising the view of the world of each team member. Planning becomes a key management system to accelerate institutional learning. Hendry, Johnson & Newton (1993) consider strategic thinking to be the cognitive processes through which organizations and environments are understood and strategies developed.

Strategic thinking, as structure of meaning, is presented as both the medium of social cognitive action and its product. To Boland *et al.* (1990) "the dynamic engagement [in an ambiguous situation] is the medium of strategic thought, and a newly reconstructed or enacted schema is the product of strategic thought."

We tend to agree with Hansen who, based on the experiences he drew from following up on the developments of a company over a 15-year period, concludes, "I am inclined to suggest that strategic thinking is more a state of mind than just another planning process" (1991, p. 129). The sections that follow present a possible process which can lead to strategic thinking, focusing however on a view of the notion as a specific state of mind. This is used as the foundation to elaborate a new approach to strategy as a derivative of strategic thinking.

STRATEGIC THINKING AS A PROCESS AND STATE OF MIND

We conceive of strategic thinking as a set of ideas, principles, policies, concrete rules, and operational approaches which shape the way managers think about their role and which guide their daily actions. This set of ideas and rules is more malleable than corporate ideology or organizational identity, which have a more permanent character. Also, strategic thinking is different from operational plans, which represent more concrete commitments and specific actions at given points in time.

As Peter Senge (1992) warns us, new ideas and insights will never be implemented unless they become part of a manager's mental model. Strategic thinking can guide managerial action only if it is embedded as a frame of reference. So, in this sense, strategic thinking can be thought of as a state of mind.

Each level within the company sets the guidelines and constraints under which strategic thinking is to be developed in lower levels. If aggregated frameworks are clearly set, and if these have been internalized in the minds of interested managers, then they actively manage the way in which a shared understanding builds up. Tregoe & Zimmerman (1980, p. 79) argue that "individual managers who can carry their organization's strategy in their head are always 'with it'. Every plan that must be developed, every decision that must be made, can be tested against this mental picture. This is day-to-day implementation in its most basic and important sense."

Strategic thinking, as structure of meaning, is not only an end product but also a context of social cognitive action. The process of building the set of ideas and insights which constitute strategic thinking is to be formally managed as a deliberate endeavor. It cannot emerge spontaneously nor come as the result of mere sedimentation of management practices, experiences, and habits over time. Yet some of the insights will, of course, come from self-induced reflection and mental discovery. However, unless a formal approach to strategy is set up, ongoing decisions are likely to be based on taken-for-granted assumptions, beliefs and values, which are encapsulated within managerial experiences and organizational culture (Johnson, 1992).

Hansen (1991) suggests approaching strategy as an outcome of strategic thinking, derived from a shared vision and representing the direction for the organization. Tregoe & Zimmerman defined strategy as the framework which guides those choices that determine the nature and direction of an organization (1980, p. 17). In a way that somehow integrates both, we conceive strategy as the output of a process guided to create a shared framework in the minds of managers. Strategy is narrower and more specific than strategic thinking. Strategy yields a common guideline, at different levels, made of specific agreements and decisions, that company employees internalize in their minds and pursue accordingly. Yet strategy does not dictate specific details on how to turn such a guideline into a reality. This is left to the interested manager.

The process suggested here differs significantly from more classical approaches to strategy formulation based on analytical tools and techniques. It starts by creating a gap, envisioning an ideal (in similar terms as a vision or strategic intent) and gradually settles down to a feasible position (Masifern, 1984, 1997). The resulting conceptual framework constitutes a shell that enables managers to arrive at decisions made in real time which are, moreover, coordinated and integrated on the basis of the agreed-upon strategy.

Therefore, strategic thinking contains features of both a process and a state of mind. It begins with a deliberate search, advances towards building a shared framework in the managers' minds, continues on to implementation in daily activity and then moves to a review and update of its basic content as conditions change both outside and inside of the company.

The sections that follow attempt to address each of these issues by outlining what we believe to be the key building blocks of our approach to strategic thinking.

STRATEGIC THINKING AS THE OUTCOME OF DOWNSCALING THE IDEAL STRATEGY TO A POSSIBLE STRATEGY

After reviewing some of the most important works on strategy definition, Hax & Majluf (1991) propose an integrative and comprehensive concept of strategy. These authors view strategy as "a fundamental framework through which an organization can assert its vital continuity, while, at the same time, it forcefully facilitates its adaptation to a changing environment" (1991, p. 6). The multidimensional approach that they suggest certainly overcomes most of the limitations of former perspectives which focused strategy on determining a set of decisions and actions oriented to create competitive advantage.

However, today's environment, characterized by high degrees of dynamism and complexity, imposes increasing demands on managers. Currently all levels of management confront situations that were unthinkable only a short time ago. Fast front-line execution has to be consistent with the corporate sense of unity, direction, and purpose, central to most traditional definitions of strategy. The rule that front-line managers have to wait for a decision to come from above no longer applies. Top managers need to transform their company in order to develop an organization capable of changing quickly and repeatedly (Masifern, 1984, 1997). Organizations will progressively give managers greater autonomy, but at the same time demand greater responsibility from them, and expect justification for their performance. Management procedures should contribute to the training of people in an effort to adapt to new job descriptions structured in organizations undergoing continuous transformation.

Traditional plans exhibit a tremendously fast rate of depreciation. Part of the problem is due to the fact that we progress through analysis at a much slower speed than that at which changes take place in the environment. By the time plans are printed and bound they have already become obsolete. Therefore, a number of authors exhort us to bring creativity and imagination into the strategy-making process (James B. Quinn, Tom Peters and Henry Mintzberg, to mention just a few). Yet the field has advanced to provide only limited guidance on the factors involved in the process of moving from creative thinking to action.

Managers need to operate under aligned frames of reference. The state of mind identified here as strategic thinking is the outcome of a formal process. A possible systematic approach to the development of strategic thinking is to involve managers in formal deliberation on how to move from the ideal strategy to a possible strategy for their unit of interest. Ideal strategy is defined as the strategy that best responds to external impacts[1] (Masifern, 1984, 1997). The ideal strategy is a distant target, a mental image of a utopian future state of the unit of interest. It is not constrained by any aspect of the current internal situation (position, capabilities, organizational design, etc.). The notion of ideal strategy can originate at each level within the organization, by teams of concerned managers at the focal unit of interest, and does not stem from high-level executives (beyond the institutional and corporate levels of strategy). The ideal strategy conveys the image of the best position in the light of the new reality that one expects. In a sense, it represents what we would like to do, much along the same line as Andrews (1987) and other authors have described it in the past.

The possible strategy is the result of scaling down the ideal strategy to a feasible end point. From the largely utopian image, we descend the steps created by limitations of resources, organizational culture, the law, current market trends, etc. Internal analysis plays a major role in arriving at the possible, but not the ideal, strategy. From an initial position of what we envision, we progressively reduce our ambitions by introducing aspects of internal and external acceptance, the cost levels involved, the assumable risks, and the like. The outcome of this process reshapes the conceptual scheme of the people involved and creates a new state of mind, the content of strategic thinking.

Conceiving of the ideal strategy is mainly a creative process, driven by logical reasoning, imagination and the will to transform reality. From this deductive process, specific sets of goals, ideas, and insights are derived. One could argue that an inductive logic, drawing a general view from particular aspects of organizational life, is a valid approach. However, we believe that at present the deductive mode of progressing offers more immediate results and higher original solutions, to the extent that one has some experience in deductive methods. We tend to suggest that analytical tools and procedures play a critical role in the validation of conclusions and that they may shed light by posing enlightening questions from different angles.

There are a number of implications which stem from the process outlined here. We will just touch on a few conceptual ones, and leave the more practical for a later section.

---

[1] Although a number of concepts have been introduced in the literature to tackle the notion of an *ideal*, such as strategic intent by Hamel & Prahalad, vision by Collins & Porras, idealized design by Ackoff, or target analogue by Holyoak & Thagard, we believe that none captures the full meaning of ideal strategy as presented here.

1. The popular academic debate between the dominant direction of influence between strategy and structure is seen under a new light. Structure[2]
   is not only a means to implement the strategy; it is also a determinant of
   the possible strategy, though not of the ideal strategy.
2. It is the possible strategy that is implemented, not the ideal one. Yet
   implementation is used not only to command the organizational resources and arrangements by means of which the possible strategy is to
   be carried out, but also to reduce over time the gap between the ideal and
   possible strategies. This process of articulating strategic thinking may
   add new insights on the usefulness of gap analysis in management to the
   work of Andrews (1987), Hamel & Prahalad (1989), Liedtka & Rosenblum
   (1996) and others. Building an area of agreement on the ideal strategy will
   contribute to the creation of a common sense of purpose in the company.
   Progressing towards consensus in solving the tension between ideal and
   possible strategy builds shared understanding. The desire to close the
   gap between the two becomes a driver for organizational learning.
3. A manager will hardly delegate to a collaborator unless both of them
   share a common understanding of purposes and priorities. Strategic
   thinking may bridge the gap between strategy formulation and implementation, which have advanced in the academic field as separate areas
   of concern, even though practising managers will claim that they are
   acting while they formulate and thinking while they implement.
4. Finally, Masifern (1997) and Vilà (1997) describe how the failure to make
   the distinction between the ideal and the possible strategy may be an
   important factor in explaining strategy incrementalism. Managers often
   recognize that strategies for consecutive years normally look very similar,
   a fact which is surprising considering the tremendous degree of change
   which most companies undergo. This fact is remarkable given that a most
   important role of strategy is adaptation to changing conditions. We argue
   that the failure to see the need to introduce changes in strategy may be
   the result of a behavioral limitation, not of a rational one, in the way we
   use techniques such as the SWOT analysis.

STRATEGIC THINKING AS A SPECIFIC FRAME OF REFERENCE

Managers can approach information processing in two dominant ways
(Walsh, 1995). Either they follow an approach whereby their past

---

[2] We use the notion of structure in its broader sense here, to include management structure,
management systems, management style, and people and the design of their job position; a key
aspect of implementation that is progressively introduced in the field as "organization."

experiences guide present information processing or they can let the current information context guide the process. Walsh claims that, in the former case, it is the cognitive structures generated from experience that affect individuals' abilities to attend to, encode, and make inferences about new information. In the latter case, new information itself shapes individuals' responses to it, which also includes the development of amended knowledge structures to be used in the first fashion.

Empirical researchers tend to link strategic thinking with mental representations of strategic decision makers (see Huff, 1990). Frame of reference is a general term for the knowledge structure that an individual draws upon to guide interpretation, inference, and action in any particular situation. However, we argue that the existence of a mental scheme is not sufficient to characterize the actions actually taken by a manager or team as strategic.

Based on the content and drivers for modification of a manager's mindset and whether the state of mind is individual or shared, we can categorize the frame of reference into four types, as shown in FIGURE 2.1.

Quadrant 1 represents a state of mind which is being updated solely on the basis of the accumulation of personal experiences, along with the values, beliefs, and habits resulting from full immersion in a given organizational culture. These individual characteristics result from the sedimentation of practices; they have an enduring character. We refer to an individual mindset which is modified on the basis of experience, values, beliefs, and habits

Content and drivers for modification

	Habits, values	Insights, decisions
Individual	Drifted frame of reference 1	2 Reflected frame of reference
Collective	3 Enduring organizational mindset	4 Strategic thinking

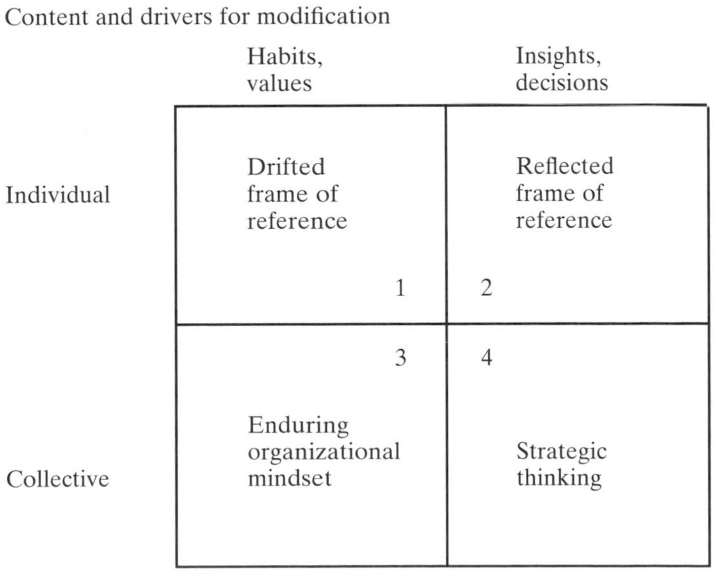

FIGURE 2.1 Types of frame of reference

as a drifted frame of reference. It is not modified through deep decisions and reconsideration by the focal person, but mainly through external stimuli (for example, new company values or new organizational rules) and ongoing personal incidents. The individual's innate gifts and personality features have a great deal of influence on the meanings and connections that constitute the actual content of the individual mindset.

Leaders who have held a position of power in the organization over a certain period may have little incentive to deviate from position 1, since it is likely that they have built a way of behaving in the organization that they find comfortable and that fits their own set of ideas. Finding a corporate leader settled in position 1 can explain, in part, why most organizations mechanically resist new truths and why it is so difficult to change the corporate mind. This is a topic of extensive coverage in the field. For instance, Chris Argyris (1985) has written about how individuals in companies engage in what he calls organizational defensive routines to preserve their status and abiding sense of security. The feeling of comfort is a major impediment to moving to quadrant 2.

Quadrant 2 represents a frame of reference that is updated on a continuous and deliberate basis. In light of new events that catch their attention, managers ponder the circumstances and adjust their mindset in the way that best fits the new reality. This mindset is driven by insights and formal decisions. Skills of reflection, as used by Peter Senge (1992), shape the mental model. The person in quadrant 2 is genuinely interested in finding flaws in his or her internal logic and correcting his or her view of the world accordingly. We can characterize this as a reflected frame of reference.

The boundary between drifted and reflected frames of reference is thin. It is reasonable to question whether a reflected mindset can be sustained if an individual tries to refine it just as an isolated effort. Quadrant 2 may easily regress into 1, since the significant activities are frequently shortchanged in most organizations as a result of resources, people, and management attention being directed to short-run demand. Cognitive limitations, such as our tendency to see mainly what we believe in, and organizational behavior realities, such as the difficulty of challenging the prevailing logic and the established order within most companies, all contribute to the conclusion that position 2 can hardly be thought of as a stable state of mind. We argue that a manager needs to be provided with a formal procedure in order to reach the idiosyncratic mode of reflective thinking. Even if there may be such a thing as an isolated strategic thinker, building the cognitive structure which characterizes strategic thinking will achieve the most desirable effect when it is conducted by teams of managers, formed by people who have to coordinate activities and integrate their efforts.

In quadrant 3 the characterization is of an enduring organizational mindset, an essentially inflexible collective mind that changes gradually. It is cultural in nature, in so far as it is the deeper level of basic assumptions, values, and beliefs shared by members of an organization that shape the individual's state of mind. Common patterns of behavior operate under the level of awareness and define the central "taken-for-granted" basis of the managers' role and their worldview. The realm of organizational culture (Schein, 1986) belongs to this cell. However, other characterizations also capture aspects of this sedimented collective mind. For example, Albert & Whetten's (1985) organizational identity defined as "managers'" beliefs about what is central, distinctive and enduring about their organization" may have some value here. Prahalad & Bettis (1986) introduce the notion of dominant logic as "mental maps developed through experience in core business." They suggest that managers conceptualize the business and make critical resource allocations based on representations that are likely to be of historical environments rather than of current circumstances.

It is certainly possible that organizational members act according to the leader's set of beliefs, or that of their immediate boss. Yet these people will not grasp the beliefs as their own. In the move from 1 to 3, the key ideas that shape mindsets belong to those who generated them, not to those who receive them. This situation differs from position 4, where all organizational members have to give up some personal preference in order to reach a common ground of shared understanding, consensus and commitment.

Quadrant 4 constitutes what we refer to as strategic thinking. As mentioned above, it represents a flexible frame of reference which is refined as a result of reflection, reconsideration, and new insights, and which places objectives and priorities as the common ground with other managers' frames with whom the focal manager has to interact. Some organizations facilitate the level of strategic thinking by putting in place a formal process aimed at producing a conceptual shell shared in the minds of managers. The drivers of the coupled frames of reference are new insights and formal decisions made through discussion, as a result of the managers' involvement in a deliberate reconsideration of the shared understanding which guides their actions.

Strategic thinking is put together and reshaped as a team formally develops consensus and commitment. The rules governing progress are not derived from hierarchy or command-and-control styles of management. There is no imposition of ideas by a leader or boss, but instead contributions for the best solution for the unit of interest are made by all. Every member of the team has to give up some personal preferences. The final outcome enhances the capacity for action of all people involved, yet it also curtails their freedom, to the extent that everybody is committed to the agreements reached. Commitments are made on the basis of purposes and priorities, not according to specific courses of action, as discussed below.

Strategic thinking represents a context where strategy and organization are to be developed taking into account aspects of both outside-in as well as inside-out approaches to strategy. Initially, external factors drive the willing-ness to transform reality. However, the realm of strategic thinking takes us into a dynamic setting where frequent organizational arrangements are in-troduced in a continuous attempt to move the company in the direction of the ideal strategy. New operating procedures are to shape habits and ways of working. Yet emergent values, beliefs, and personal experiences *per se* do not create strategic thinking. For the resulting frame of reference to con-stitute strategic thinking, it has to be the outcome of a deliberate process, with intentional and active participation of the focal manager. During the process, the major principles, basic assumptions, and key rules of organiza-tional action are validated and/or reconsidered. Subsequently, self-induced reflection will shape the individual's response to incoming information. These are the main reasons to assert that not just any state of mind amounts to strategic thinking. Besides, this is the rationale behind our claim that strategic thinking is the result of formal decisions that guide daily activity, and not just any mental frame that precedes action.

AN ALTERNATIVE APPROACH TO STRATEGY AS DERIVED FROM STRATEGIC THINKING

Tregoe & Zimmerman address a critical aspect of the link between formula-tion and implementation when they claim "Strategy as a framework must be carefully integrated into the thinking of managers, otherwise, strategy will simply not happen" (1980, p. 98). The notion of strategic thinking intro-duced here leads us to conceive strategy as a shared framework in the minds of managers. This represents an outcome crystallized as a conceptual shell which enables managers to arrive at decisions made in real time and which, more importantly, will coordinate and integrate individual efforts under one agreed-upon strategy. These authors add, "If key strategic choices are made in the absence of a [shared] framework, top management abdicates control and runs the risk of having a direction which is fragmented and in the hands of whoever is making these choices" (Tregoe & Zimmerman, 1980).

Strategy is at an intermediate level of specificity between strategic think-ing and plans (whether strategic or operational). Strategic thinking is far removed from clear-cut specifications. It will not actually be written down, so it leaves a lot of room for operational freedom. Plans are very specific; they represent concrete and well-spelled-out commitments. Codifying strat-egy, writing it down, is not a necessary goal, and we argue it should not be so. Strategy is about guiding action without close fastening or afflicting ties. Yet a team may wish to write out a few aspects of the strategy and make them clearly explicit in order to ensure that proper deliberation has taken place. Traditional approaches to strategy have suggested the need to articulate it, converting tacit knowledge into explicit. In today's environment, the critical task is internalization, using tacit and explicit knowledge to refine one's own mental framework and knowledge base.

The collaborative process of arriving at strategy generates shared learning, an agreed-upon reference which clarifies the context in which small decisions are to be made over time. The shared framework does not impose concrete courses of action on managers. This is very much in line with Robert (1993), who exhorted strategic thinking to provide a road map for creating an effective business strategy without dictating specific details. He added that this would create a common direction, a shared vision that all company employees could understand and follow. It would enhance communication and generate a set of filters through which day-to-day decision making could be rationalized.

During the 1970s, it was generally accepted to approach strategy in adaptive, contingent, and operating modes. Today it is imperative that strategy leave ample degrees of freedom, so that managers can accommodate their daily action to unforeseeable events. Attaining this would respond to Suutari's more recent concern for strategic thinking to provide the necessary bridge between the planned and the adaptive modes of strategy (Suutari, 1993).

In the past, planning significantly hindered the autonomy of the lower levels of management. Today, top managers have to avoid specifying the tasks of their collaborators. Middle-level managers exercise their intelligence when they decide how to attain the agreed-upon goals. Confronted with unexpected events, they assess if it is possible to act in the spirit of the shared framework. Eventually, significant challenges to the common logic will call for a collective revision and a new deliberate process of strategic thinking will start. But until this takes place, decisions in real time follow the dicta of a strategy in an ongoing process of adaptation. We believe this is a major advantage of the approach to strategy derived from strategic thinking when compared to the other ways of conceiving strategy making.

Mintzberg proposes viewing strategy as a perspective, its contents consisting of an ingrained way of perceiving the world (Mintzberg & Quinn, 1992, p. 16). In a former paper, Mintzberg (1985) suggests that managers consciously, but more often unconsciously, build an emergent strategy through their daily actions. In our opinion, to the extent that a shared framework is internalized in the minds of strategists, strategy turns out to be a guide for daily action, which nevertheless permits on-the-spot adjustment to circumstance. Once new developments unfold, a deliberate strategy fosters learning as alternative courses of action are compared. Some options stem from the previously formed strategy, others from a process of reflection which extends the shared mindset, yet others may require more profound reflection since they imply deviating from the agreed-upon framework. A reflected pattern of decisions guided by the deliberate strategy (a shared framework in the mind of strategists) will foster organizational learning before and after the new strategy is formulated, while a purely emergent strategy would preclude it.

IMPLICATIONS FOR MANAGERS

Even though most academics, business people, and consultants have widely recognized that the purpose of strategy formulation can no longer lie in generating strategic plans, critics of formal strategic planning have offered little guidance on how to overcome its limitations and address CEOs' concerns about turning a strategic vision into an operational reality.

The managerial approach outlined here is developed in a way that tries to respond to the concerns of top management on how to spread in their organizations the ability to manage by strategy in today's rapidly changing environment. Strategic thinking can contribute to this goal by aiding top management efforts in building a shared understanding of strategic issues and encouraging actions at the front line that are consistent with the strategy pursued by the firm. While more definitive conclusions require further empirical testing, it is nevertheless possible to single out a series of potential advantages associated with strategic thinking on the basis of the authors' experience of work completed for a few companies and the rationale advanced in this chapter:

- Daily actions are easily integrated, since they are born of the same framework. Managers make decisions in the light of a shared understanding of objectives and priorities, not of preconceived plans. Each manager can adapt strategy, from the time it was created as a shared framework, to accommodate external and internal changing conditions (to the extent that these are not radical changes and call for a re-evaluation of strategy). As a consequence, daily decisions are integrated under a shared understanding without having to wait until the next strategy meeting takes place.
- Decisions stemming from different departments display a higher level of coordination, since managers have a better understanding of the common purposes. Any manager follows at the same time the premises of both his or her basic discipline (e.g. finance, marketing, logistics, purchasing, and the like) as well as the guidelines of the strategy of the unit he or she serves in.
- Strategic thinking translates into speed, since it facilitates decision making. It also guarantees flexibility, since it allows change plans and the tailoring of actions to specific changing conditions. An organization which

has developed the ability of strategic thinking among its members can locate decision making close to where the action takes place. Freedom to decide enables fast responses.

- It may provide a common language that invites employees on all levels to engage in strategic conversations. Shared understanding depends on open communication, which both requires and contributes to aligned mental models and common language. Conversations articulate individuals' thinking, therefore they become a central vehicle to develop a coherent and evolving motion picture of strategy and organizational design.
- Strategic thinking makes delegation easier, since expectations are aligned and become more foreseeable both from the viewpoint of a manager as well as from that of his or her collaborators. Strategic thinking can also become a vehicle for self-control, since it facilitates self-evaluation of progress without having to resort to hierarchical means of supervision.
- Strategic thinking, to the extent that it is generated by a deductive approach process, breeds innovation. It facilitates the emergence of ambitious objectives, which is the essence of escaping from the inertia of current strategy and enabling drastic changes in the way the firm builds its future. Strategic thinking entails a process of creatively searching for alternative ways to close the gap between the ideal and possible strategy for the company as a whole and for its different units.

If strategic thinking contributes to a common language, shared understanding and organizational learning, it may become an important ingredient of the glue that will hold together the organizations of the future.

CONCLUSIONS

In line with the emerging stream of research in the strategy field that regards strategic thinking as a better way to approach the question of strategy than traditional strategic planning, we can argue that one of the most significant sources of competitive advantage for companies in the future lies in their ability to build a shared understanding. The approach outlined in this chapter sheds new light on the mainstream approach to strategy making. Strategic thinking, as described here, may provide the context required to align strategy formulation, some aspects of implementation (such as integration, coordination and delegation) and daily action. This notion of strategy leads to a fundamental issue in management: the fact that organizations are instruments to accomplish collectively what cannot be done alone.

When strategy is regarded as an internalized scheme, it may add to a series of concepts introduced in the management literature which attempt to identify the glue that holds an organization together. To mention only the work of a couple of seminal authors, Peter Drucker (1994) refers to "the theory of the business" as the set of fundamental assumptions that shape any organization's behavior, dictate its decisions and define what is considered meaningful results, and calls for treating this construct as a hypothesis subject to continuous test, or Philip Selznick's "character" of an organization (1957, p. 47), conceived as "distinct and integrated commitments to ways of acting and responding that are built right into it."

The way one approaches strategy has major implications for turning it into a reality. Implementation will not occur unless managers are involved in the strategy formation process and feel the resulting strategy as their own. This certainly is to be characterized as an intangible asset in academic terms. Yet we argue that strategic thinking feels almost tangible when one has it.

Successful business strategies result not from rigorous analysis, but from a particular state of mind (Ohmae, 1982, p. 4). The essence of strategy formation is not to create plans, but to build a shared framework in the minds of strategists. Given the persistence of change, it may be that in the near future, in strategically managed firms, good managers will not be those people who meet the plans, but those who are capable of changing plans according to strategy.

REFERENCES

Ackoff, R.L. (1981). *Creating the Corporate Future*. New York: John Wiley & Sons.
Albert, S. & Whetten, D. (1985). Organizational Identity. In L.L. Cummings & B.U. Staw (eds) *Research in Organizational Behavior*, vol. 7. Greenwich, CT: JAI Press, pp. 263–295.
Andrews, K. (1987). *The Concept of Corporate Strategy*. New York: Irwin.
Ansoff, H.I., DeClerk, R.P. & Heyes, R.L. (1979). *From Strategic Planning to Strategic Management*. New York: John Wiley & Sons.
Argyris, C. (1985). *Strategy, Change and Defensive Routines*. Marshfield, MA: Pitman.
Bates, D.L. & J.E. Dilliard (1993). Generating strategic thinking through multi-level teams, *Long Range Planning*, **26**(5), 103–110.
Boland, R.J., Greenberg, R.H., Park, S.H. & Han, I. (1990). Mapping the process of problem reformulation: Implications for understanding strategic thought. In A.S. Huff (ed.) *Mapping Strategic Thought*. New York: John Wiley & Sons.
Bossidy, L. (1988). Some thoughts on strategic thinking, *Executive Speeches*, January, 1–4.
Business Week (1984). The new breed of strategic planner, 17 September, 52–57.
Collins, J. & Porras, J. (1994). *Built to Last: Successful Habits of Visionary Companies*. New York: Harper Business.
Coyne, K.P. & Subramaniam, S. (1996). Bringing discipline to strategy, *The McKinsey Quarterly*, **4**, 14–25.
De Geus, A.P. (1988). Planning as learning, *Harvard Business Review*, March/April, 70–74.
Drucker, P. (1994). The Theory of Business, *Harvard Business Review*, September/October, 95–104.

Economist (1987). The state of strategic thinking, 23 May, 21–28.

Financial Times (1979). From planning to clearer strategic thinking. 27 July, 21.

Ginsberg, A. (1994). Minding the competition: From mapping to mastery. *Strategic Management Journal*, **15**, 153 174.

Hamel, G. & Prahalad, C.K. (1989). Strategic intent, *Harvard Business Review*, **67**, 63–76.

Hansen, S.O. (1991). Visions and strategic thinking. In J. Näsi (ed.) *Arenas of Strategic Thinking*. Helsinki: Foundation for Economic Education.

Hax, A.C. & Majluf, N.S. (1991) *The Strategy Concept and Process: A Pragmatic Approach*. Englewood Cliffs, NJ: Prentice Hall.

Hendry, J. & Johnson, G. with Newton, J. (eds) (1993), *Strategic Thinking: Leadership and Management Change*. Chichester: John Wiley & Sons.

Holyoak, K. & Thagard, P. (1995). *Mental Leaps: Analogy in Creative Thoughts*. Cambridge, MA: MIT Press.

Huff, A.S. (ed.) (1990). *Mapping Strategic Thought*. New York: John Wiley & Sons.

Johnson, G. (1992). Managing strategic change—strategy, culture and action. *Long Range Planning*, **25**(1), 28–36.

Lenz, R.T. (1987). Managing the evolution of the strategic planning process, *Business Horizons*, January/February, 34–39.

Liedtka, J.M. (1998). Strategic thinking: can it be taught? *Long Range Planning*, February, 120–129.

Liedtka, J.M. & Rosenblum, J.W. (1996). Shaping conversations: making strategy, managing change, *California Management Review*, **39**(1), 141–157.

Masifern, E. (1984). Dirección Estratégica, note SN-54, IESE Research Division, January.

Masifern, E. (1997). Strategy today, *Barcelona Management Review*, **6**, 95–108.

Mintzberg, H. (1985) Of strategies: deliberate and emergent. *Strategic Management Journal*, **6**, 257–272.

Mintzberg, H. (1994). *The Rise and Fall of Strategic Planning*. New York: Prentice Hall.

Mintzberg, H. & Quinn, J.B. (1992). *The Strategy Process: Concepts and Contexts*, New York: Prentice-Hall.

Nadler, D.A. (1994). Collaborative strategic thinking. *Planning Review*, **22**(5), 30–31.

Näsi, J. (1991). Strategic thinking as doctrine: development of focus areas and new insights. In J. Näsi (ed.) *Arenas of Strategic Thinking*. Helsinki: Foundation for Economic Education.

Ohmae, K. (1982). *The Mind of the Strategist: Business Planning for Competitive Advantage*. New York: McGraw-Hill.

Prahalad, C.K. & Bettis, R.A. (1986). The dominant logic: a new linkage between diversity and performance. *Strategic Management Journal*, **7**, 485–501.

Prahalad, C.K. & Hamel, G. (1994). *Competing for the Future*. Boston, MA: Harvard Business School Press.

Raimond, P. (1996). Two styles of foresight: are we predicting the future or inventing it? *Long Range Planning*, **29**(2), 208–214.

Reimann, B. (1988). Getting value from strategic planning. The Conference Board's 1988 Strategic Planning Conference. *Planning Review*, May/June, 42–48.

Robert, M. (1993). *Strategy Pure and Simple*. New York: McGraw Hill.

Schein, E.H. (1986). *Organizational Culture and Leadership*. San Francisco, CA: Jossey Bass.

Selznick, P. (1957). *Leadership in Administration: A Sociological Interpretation*. New York: Harper & Row.

Senge, P. M. (1992). Mental Models, *Planning Review*, **20**(2), 4–44.

Suutari, R. (1993). The case for strategic thinking. *CMA Magazine*, **67**(5), 17–21.
Takur, M. & Calingo, L.M. (1992). Strategic thinking is hip, but does it make a difference? *Business Horizons*, 48–54.
Tregoe, B.B. & Zimmerman, J.W. (1980). *Top Management Strategy: What it is and How to Make it Work*. New York: Simon & Schuster.
Vilà, J. (1997). Estrategia, planificación y actuación de directivos. In E. Masifern, J.E. Ricart & J. Vilà (eds) *Dirección Estratégica, Biblioteca IESE de Gestión de Empresas*, vol. 36, pp. 81–113.
Walsh, J.P. (1995). Managerial and organizational cognition: notes from a trip down memory lane. *Organizational Science*, **6**(3), 280–321.
Wilson, I. (1994). Strategic planning isn't dead—it changed. *Long Range Planning*, **27**(4), 12–24.

3

What Constitutes an Effective Mission Statement? An Empirical Investigation

CONSTANTINOS MARKIDES, VASSILIS M. PAPADAKIS

Does it matter what values you espouse? No one . . . has ever proved it does.
(Fortune, 1995)

There is general agreement in both the academic literature and managerial circles that every good company must have a clear sense of direction, preferably articulated in a mission or vision statement. A recent article in *Fortune* magazine (1997) argues that "top managers at the most admired companies [in the world] take their mission statements (MS) seriously and expect everyone else to do likewise." This belief, like motherhood and apple pie, is taken at face value: surely nobody can argue against it! As proclaimed by Newman (1992, p. 7)—with an obvious sense of irony—"Among the most highly prized possessions of a national or corporate leader, 'vision' is quickly moving up to the number one spot. Those without it are portrayed as stumbling in the dark from crisis to crisis. Those magnificent, charismatic leaders who have it, however, galvanize their constituents for a march to utopia, or at least a better quarterly profit".

While everybody seems to agree on the need for a good strategic objective, disagreements have arisen as to what constitutes a good or effective

---

New Managerial Mindsets: Organizational Transformation and Strategy Implementation.
Edited by M.A. Hitt, J.E. Ricart i Costa and R.D. Nixon.
© 1998 John Wiley & Sons Ltd.

objective. Some researchers have argued that most company objectives (as articulated in company mission and vision statements) tend to be useless primarily because they: (i) state the obvious, (ii) are too generic and thus fail to give guidance in making decisions and tradeoffs, (iii) are too fantastical or unrealistic, and/or (iv) are not shared by all the employees (Campbell & Yeung, 1991; Ireland & Hitt, 1992; Morris, 1996; Pearce & David, 1987).

Others have argued that developing an effective objective is a very difficult task because to be effective, the objective has to find the right balance on many parameters. Thus, for an objective to be effective it needs to be specific enough but not too constraining; it needs to be flexible and adaptable but should not be changed every year; it needs to be stretching and inspirational but not too unrealistic; it needs to be measurable but not constraining; it must be easy to understand but not simplistic; it must be based on real customer needs but mindful of the other stakeholders' needs as well; and it needs to set a time target but not compromise quality in the process (Collins & Porras, 1991, 1995; Grossman & King, 1993; Hamel & Prahalad, 1989; Ireland & Hitt, 1992; Mather, 1994; Trapp, 1995). Needless to say, achieving the right balance on all these parameters is extremely difficult.

While the literature on mission statements (MS) is full of prescriptions on how to develop a good one (Lipton, 1996; Piercy & Morgan, 1994), there is little empirical evidence (other than anecdotal case studies) to support the assertions made. Research in the area is still at an early stage (Larwood *et al.*, 1995). Clearly, more research on the assumed link between a clear sense of direction and superior performance is needed. For example David (1989) concluded that there is no difference between companies having and not having an MS on seven dimensions of financial performance, and Bart (1996) found rather weak direct links between MS and firm innovativeness.

Even the actual definition of mission "effectiveness" is disputed. Some researchers have suggested that whether a mission is effective or not should be measured by the degree to which the people in the organization have a clear sense of direction as to what their organization is trying to achieve (Graham & Havlick, 1995; Pearce, 1982). Others have argued that this is not enough—over and above setting direction, a mission statement must also inspire people and generate passion and commitment for the organization's way of doing business (Collins & Porras, 1991; Hamel & Prahalad, 1989). Yet others have pointed out that effectiveness should ultimately be reflected in the firm's performance, which should therefore be taken as the most accurate indicator of a mission's overall effectiveness (Bart, 1996; David, 1989).

In this chapter, we attempt to address this gap in the research by using questionnaire data suitable for multivariate analysis. Building on the work of Dutton & Ashford (1993) on "issue selling" we have developed a model that takes into consideration: (i) the actual content and characteristics of the MS, (ii) the process used to develop it, (iii) the process used to "sell" it to the rest of the organization, (iv) the credibility of the seller (i.e. top management), and (v) the commitment of the employee to the organization. We empirically test which of these factors influences the effectiveness of a company's MS.

Our chapter is one of the few *empirical* studies on this topic and so addresses an important gap in the literature. In addition, our study collects data from executives working in a variety of companies from several countries. Given the rapidly rising interconnectness of the world today, our study explores whether managerial problems and challenges are becoming common across countries and industries—and whether solutions to these problems are common across national boundaries. Finally, our study examines "effectiveness" in a variety of ways. This allows us to identify which variables consistently influence the effectiveness of mission statements. Thus, the managerial prescriptions we offer at the end of our chapter are grounded in actual empirical results.

THEORETICAL CONSIDERATIONS

An effective vision/mission has the potential to become the much needed "binding glue" and "guiding light" of the organization and contribute to more effective leadership, strategy implementation and change (Doz & Prahalad, 1987; Kotter, 1990). But an MS will be effective only if the majority in the organization believes in it, is committed to its accomplishment and behaves accordingly. For such a positive state of affairs to emerge, the employees must first be "convinced" of the value and usefulness of the organization's mission. In other words, the mission must be "sold" to them.

According to the literature on "issue-selling" (Dutton & Ashford, 1993; Dutton *et al.*, 1995; Thomas, Shankster & Mathieu, 1994), there are several factors which determine if an issue will be "sold" effectively or not. These factors include not only the inherent characteristics of the issue being sold but also the characteristics of the seller and the conditions under which the selling takes place. Based on this work, we propose the model shown in FIGURE 3.1 as a way of explaining whether an MS will be effective or not.

The model recognizes five major determinants of mission effectiveness. The first relates to the *inherent characteristics* of the MS itself (what we call mission-specific characteristics). Several authors have proposed that the content of the MS is important in determining effectiveness. For example, Pearce (1982) argues that a good MS must state clearly the basic product or service to be offered, as well as the primary market and the technology to be used in delivering the product. It must also state the organizational goals in a strategic sense and specify the organizational philosophy.

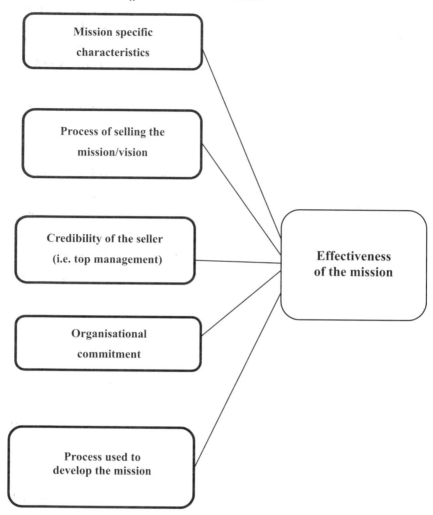

FIGURE 3.1   The determinants of mission-statement effectiveness

Similarly, Collins & Porras (1991) advise managers to develop missions that are clear and compelling, and are attainable only with effort (stretching targets). Managerial books by Jones & Kahaner (1995) and Graham & Havlick (1995) further propose that good MS must be short and clear, avoiding jargon or fancy language, so that everybody in the organization understands them.

The academic literature is littered with similar advice on how to make one's mission statement more effective. To name just a few of these prescriptions: the MS has to provide future focus for the organization (Wilson, 1992), energize as well as offer inspiration (Piercy & Morgan, 1994), use metaphors, vivid language and analogies (Conger, 1991; Collins & Porras, 1996), be specific and/or set measurable targets (Collins & Porras, 1996), be flexible and adaptable (Wilson, 1992), establish a critical goal and specify the key criterion for success (Wilson, 1992).

Influenced by the resource-based view of the firm, a number of authors have also proclaimed that the MS has to signal critical skills (Klemm, Sanderson & Luffman, 1991), reinforce corporate values (Conger, 1991; Klemm, Sanderson & Luffman, 1991; Piercy & Morgan, 1994), and define the structure, management systems and operating culture of the company (Wilson, 1992; Klemm, Sanderson & Luffman, 1991). According to Wilson (1992), one additional characteristic of a successful MS is its clarity in setting direction— a good MS should make it clear to employees how they can win the competitive battle in their industry. This again implies that the MS has to be grounded on reality (Lipton, 1996) and if possible guide decision making (Collins & Porras, 1996; Thornberry, 1997). These are some of the most frequently prescribed characteristics of effective MS according to both the academic and practitioner literature.

The actual *process used to "sell" the mission* to the employees is the second factor in our model. Three different literatures try to enrich our understanding of issue selling: the social problem theory, impression management and upward influence. The social problem theory explores how and why certain social problems emerge in a society (Schnieder, 1985). In the same vein, an issue becomes important if individuals successfully present these issues as such and others within the same organization are willing to buy into these claims. The impression management perspective presents issue selling as a social process which is trying to persuade individuals of the value of an issue by offering them tangible and/or intangible rewards (Schenkler, 1980). Finally, the upward influence perspective focuses on the characteristics of the seller, the target and the context to evaluate the relative effectiveness of the selling process (Schilit & Locke, 1982).

Dutton & Ashford (1993), in their study on issue selling, combined all three perspectives to identify several selling tactics—such as issue framing and packaging, the use of emotional language, the selling channel, the formality of the selling attempts, and many others—all of which influence whether the mission will be "bought" or not.

In the context of MS the issue of effectively selling the mission has also attracted some attention. Conger (1991) argues that leaders can craft commitment and confidence in the MS through their choice of words, values and beliefs. Several effective selling tactics have been proposed by Conger (1991), Grossman & King (1993) and Covin, Slevin & Schultz (1994). Such tactics include the demonstration of belief in the MS by top managers—often demonstrated through personal example, the effort to sustain enthusiasm in the MS, the willingness to celebrate actions that are compatible with the MS, and the willingness to challenge decisions if they are incompatible with the mission (Mather, 1994; Thornberry, 1997).

The third factor in our model is the *credibility of the seller*. According to Dutton & Ashford (1993), the characteristics of the issue seller (such as structural location and functional orientation) influence both the initiation of issue selling and the actual success of the selling process. Other factors might be the extent to which people believe that top managers are sincere in their overall behavior, or the extent to which top managers let middle managers feel a sense of equality when working together (Dwyer & Oh, 1987). Finally, personal competence should be one of the main factors adding to the credibility of the seller. In particular, we expect that top managers who are credible (for whatever reason) will be more successful in selling an organizational objective to the employees.

The fourth factor in our model measures the degree of *organizational commitment* of the individual employee. By commitment we mean the extent to which employees feel part of the team (as demonstrated by their willingness to go beyond the call of duty), or feel that there exist strong bonds between themselves and the organization (Mowday, Steers & Porter, 1979). By the same count, employees might demonstrate a negative commitment to the organization (as demonstrated, for example, by their willingness to leave the company for a more friendly environment, more status, personal freedom or a nominal payrise) (Dubinsky & Hartley, 1986). We assume that commitment to the organization could facilitate the acceptance of a demanding new goal.

The final factor proposed in our model of FIGURE 3.1 is the *process used to develop the MS*. For example, companies might want to develop their MS as part of their long-term planning effort, probably using a formal participative process, which involves several levels of management. Other companies might choose to restrict the development of their MS to just the top management ranks (e.g. only the board of directors and the top management team). Several authors have suggested that a group is more likely to accept an idea or goal if they are involved in the development of the goal and if they feel that their ideas and input were given serious consideration by top management (Oswald, Mossholder & Harris, 1994; Steward, 1996; Trapp, 1995). Similarly, Ireland & Hitt (1992) have proposed that the formality of the process used to develop the mission as well as the use of outside consultants could influence the ease with which employees accept the MS.

To summarize, we aim to test empirically whether the effectiveness of MS is determined by the five factors identified in FIGURE 3.1. Since each one of these factors encompasses a variety of dimensions, we also intend to test which of these dimensions are important and which are not. In the next section, we describe our methodological approach as well as how we operationalized all these variables.

METHODOLOGY

DATA COLLECTION AND SAMPLING ISSUES

The target population consisted of all the executives who attended an executive course at London Business School during the period 1989–1996. The course has been designed to meet the needs of high potential younger managers who, as future senior managers, will be responsible for the continued success of their organizations. Typically, participants are in their thirties with at least five years' managerial experience. They are employed in a wide range of organizations and in a variety of functions. The course is international, with participants bringing experience from around the world. We specifically targeted middle-level managers because we wanted to see *their* view on the value of mission statements. Most of the research on this topic focuses on the views of top-level managers, while ignoring the disposition of middle managers towards the mission. We believe that if middle managers do not embrace the MS, its likelihood of success is limited.

A ten-page questionnaire was sent to the target population of 519 middle managers. Following one repeat mailing, 245 managers returned completed questionnaires—a response rate of 47.2%, which is excellent for this type of research and the size of the questionnaire.

MEASUREMENT OF VARIABLES

1 Mission-specific Characteristics

Based on the rich normative literature we summarized above, we attempted to measure 17 different mission-specific characteristics. To measure these items we used agree–disagree format scales ranging from 1 to 7. These initial variables were factor analysed and five factors were derived (TABLE 3.1). It is worth noting that all five factors appearing in TABLE 3.1 reflect distinct, internally consistent patterns suggesting generic characterizations of MS. A specific name is assigned to each factor based on the variables' loading. The five factors are labelled as follows: inspiration, target setting, pragmatism, vividness and flexibility. These factors were used to build composite variables measuring these five characteristics. Details on the number of items on each composite variable and their reliability levels are presented in the Appendix.

2 Process of Selling the Mission (Selling Tactics)

Eight items were used to capture the characteristics of the selling process. These include, among others, demonstration on the part of top management of a deep belief in the MS, celebration of actions compatible with the MS,

TABLE 3.1 Factor analysis results of variables measuring mission-specific characteristics

	Factor loadings*				
	Factor 1: Inspiring	Factor 2: Sets targets	Factor 3: Pragmatic	Factor 4: Vivid	Factor 5: Flexible
1. Our mission statement (MS) has created a sense of urgency	0.85607				
2. Our MS has generated enthusiasm	0.83440				
3. Our MS provides a focus for the organization	0.79425	0.26298			
4. Our MS energizes the organization	0.72019			0.28471	
5. Our MS is inspirational	0.68351	0.27125		0.27616	
6. Our MS is nothing more than words on a piece of paper (R)	0.41543	0.30248	0.34158		
7. Our MS sets a measurable target		0.81039			
8. Our MS sets a reasonable time target		0.78430			
9. Our MS clearly tells us what we aim to achieve	0.36628	0.59590			
10. Our MS is specific	0.30485	0.52948			
11. Our MS does not signal the critical skills and capabilities of the organization (R)			0.72592		
12. Our MS is easy to understand			0.71060	0.33181	
13. Our MS reinforces our corporate values	0.26348		0.66282		
14. Our MS lets us know how we win in competition	0.28644	0.35787	0.57722		
15. Our MS uses metaphors and vivid language				0.89221	
16. Our MS is flexible and adaptable					0.90164
17. Our MS is based on real customer needs but does not neglect employees and the community		0.27356	0.36042		0.43638
Eigenvalue	6.34	1.39	1.33	1.13	1.02
Percentage of variance explained	37.3	8.2	7.8	6.7	6.0
Cumulative percentage	37.3	45.5	53.3	60.0	65.9

* Alpha factoring method was used, together with Varimax rotation and Kaiser normalization. Factor loadings less than 0.25 are not reported.

and linking of the mission with decision making (Bart, 1996; Collins & Porras, 1991; Wilson, 1992). Again, these items were factor analysed, resulting in two factors (TABLE 3.2). The first factor measures the extent to which top management demonstrates belief in the MS and the second measures the extent to which the MS is linked to actions and decisions. The reliability coefficients of the resulting composite variables are acceptable (see Appendix).

3 Credibility of the Seller (Top Management)

Following Dutton & Ashford (1993) and Dwyer & Oh (1987), our questionnaire tried to measure the credibility of top management using six items.

TABLE 3.2 Factor analysis results of variables measuring the characteristics of the process of selling the mission (selling tactics used by top management)

Selling tactics	Factor loadings*	
	Factor 1:	Factor 2:
	Top management demonstrates belief in the MS	MS is linked to decision making
1. Top managers believe in our MS (R)	0.822	
2. Top managers set personal example (R)	0.819	
3. Top managers sustain enthusiasm in our MS	0.729	0.418
4. Top managers reflect our values and objectives	0.658	0.351
5. Top managers mention our MS to externals	0.584	0.366
6. Top management celebrate actions compatible with our MS		0.824
7. We are encouraged to challenge decisions if they are incompatible with our mission		0.797
8. Top managers connect our mission-values with decisions	0.470	0.647
Eigenvalue	4.10	1.02
Percentage of variance explained	51.2	12.7
Cumulative percentage	51.2	63.9

* Alpha factoring method was used, together with Varimax rotation and Kaiser normalization. Factor loadings less than 0.25 are not reported.

Sample items include the extent to which people consider top managers sincere, whether they trust them, whether they consider them competent and so on (TABLE 3.3). These items resulted in one factor measuring the overall credibility of top management.

4 Organizational Commitment

Another broad category of factors influencing the effectiveness of MS is employee commitment. Based on Mowday, Steers & Porter (1979) as well as Dubinsky & Hartley (1986), ten items were used to capture the bonds between the employees and the organization. The items measure affective or attitudinal commitment. All items used are presented in TABLE 3.4. When factor analysed, the items resulted in two factors: employee commitment to the company and willingness to continue working for the company. The reliability coefficients for the resulting composite variables were 0.859 and 0.777, respectively.

5 Process Used to Develop the Mission

Our questionnaire tried to capture five elements of the development process, such as the extent to which the development of the MS was an important aspect of the company's long-term planning effort, the extent to which only a few individuals at the top were involved with its development, and the extent to which some kind of formal process was used (Klemm, Sanderson &

TABLE 3.3 Factor analysis results of variables measuring credibility of top management (the seller)

	Factor loadings*
	Factor 1: Top management credibility
1. People believe top managers provide inspiration	0.807
2. People consider top managers sincere	0.795
3. People trust top managers (R)	0.722
4. People are not suspicious of top managers (R)	0.707
5. Top and middle managers work as equals	0.706
6. People consider top managers as competent	0.695
Eigenvalue	3.29
Percentage of variance explained	54.8
Cumulative percentage	54.8

* Alpha factoring method was used, together with Varimax rotation and Kaiser normalization. Factor loadings less than 0.25 are not reported.

TABLE 3.4 Factor analysis results of variables measuring organizational commitment of the employee

	Factor loadings*	
	Factor 1:	Factor 2:
	Employee commitment to the company	Willingness to stay with the company
1. Employees feel part of the team	0.789	
2. There exist strong bonds between the employees and the organization	0.770	
3. Employees are fond of the organization	0.760	
4. Employees would make personal sacrifices	0.744	
5. Employees are proud to work for the company	0.726	
6. Employees go beyond the call of duty	0.715	
7. I would not leave the company for more friendly environment (R)		0.822
8. I would not leave the company for more status (R)		0.794
9. I would not leave the company for more personal freedom (r)		0.749
10. I would not leave the company for a 10% payrise (R)		0.669
Eigenvalue	4.20	1.74
Percentage of variance explained	42.0	17.4
Cumulative percentage	42.0	59.5

* Alpha factoring method was used, together with Varimax rotation and Kaiser normalization. Factor loadings less than 0.25 are not reported.

Luffman, 1991; Wilson, 1992). All five items were factor analysed, resulting in just one factor called participation in the development of the MS (TABLE 3.5). The reliability coefficient of the resulting composite variable is 0.714.

6 The Dependent Variable: Mission Effectiveness

As previously mentioned, our questionnaire consisted of three main categories of variables. The first group of variables attempted to measure the

TABLE 3.5   Factor analysis results of variables measuring the process used to develop the mission

	Factor loadings*
	Factor 1: Participation in the development of the mission
1. The development of a mission statement involves several levels of management including the board of directors and both senior and middle management	0.829
2. The development of our mission statement has been and is an important aspect of our long-term planning effort	0.695
3. The development of our mission statement is a top management function and involves few individuals within the organization (R)	0.690
4. We use a formal process to develop our mission statement	0.673
5. We do not have a mission as an inherent part of our strategic plan (R)	0.471
Eigenvalue	2.31
Percentage of variance explained	46.4
Cumulative percentage	46.4

* Alpha factoring method was used, together with Varimax rotation and Kaiser normalization.

characteristics of the MS, the process used to develop it and the tactics used to sell it to the rest of the organization. The second group of variables measured characteristics of the organization and its environment (e.g. environmental uncertainty, internal structure-systems, commitment of employees to the organization, corporate performance). The final group of variables consisted of scales attempting to measure the extent to which the respondents viewed their MS as effective or not. A number of different approaches were used to measure mission effectiveness. Two of them are reported here.

First, respondents were asked to comment on the overall value of the MS to their organization based on nine, seven-point, agree–disagree scales drawn from Klemm, Sanderson & Luffman (1991). These questions required managers to evaluate the extent to which they believe that their MS boosts managerial efficiency, leads to better leadership, links the company to its customers and suppliers, leads to improved staff efficiency, provides focus and direction, and so on. Finally, one other individual scale was used to measure MS effectiveness. It required respondents to provide an overall evaluation of how effective they believe the MS is. The reliability coefficients of the dependent variables are shown in the Appendix together with the number of items used in computing each of them.

EMPIRICAL RESULTS

TABLE 3.6 reports the intercorrelations among all the variables in the study. It is noteworthy that the correlation coefficients among the explanatory variables are not unduly high. Moreover, all correlation coefficients are in the expected direction. For example, the credibility of top management is, as expected, positively related to the perceived value of the MS. In the same vein, inspirational mission statements are considered as more effective and of higher value by employees.

TABLE 3.7 summarizes the results from the two regression models attempted. Both models are statistically significant at the 99% level and explain anything between 73% and 76% of the variation in the dependent variable.

TABLE 3.6   Intercorrelations among all variables

Variables	Mean	s.d.	1	2	3	4	5	6	7	8	9	10	11	12	13
1. Perceived value of the MS	4.30	1.13	1												
2. Mission effectiveness	4.67	1.41	80	1											
3. Inspiring	4.35	1.42	79	82	1										
4. Setting target	3.85	1.33	53	57	58	1									
5. Pragmatic	4.35	1.21	61	57	57	42	1								
6. Vivid language	2.67	1.61	17	15	23	14	10	1							
7. Flexible/adaptable	4.88	1.51	26	24	18	02	03	03	1						
8. Top management demonstrates belief in MS	5.02	1.16	64	69	63	31	46	08	21	1					
9. Top management links MS to decision making	4.14	1.38	61	60	62	38	41	12	16	61	1				
10. Credibility of top management	4.41	1.13	52	53	51	40	41	07	10	58	48	1			
11. Employee commitment to the organization	4.75	1.06	35	49	46	22	28	07	07	51	34	56	1		
12. Personal tendency *not* to leave the company	5.51	1.28	29	39	34	28	22	08	07	39	23	54	38	1	
13. Participation in the development of the MS	3.75	1.34	57	49	50	39	44	06	11	38	35	30	16	20	1

Decimals of correlation coefficients were omitted.
For coefficients greater than $r > 0.177$, $p < 0.01$.
For coefficients greater than $r > 0.12$, $p < 0.05$.
For coefficients greater than $r > 0.233$, $p < 0.001$.

TABLE 3.7   Summary table of regression analyses

Variables	Model 1: Perceived value of the MS (Vars of Question 11)	Model 2: Mission effectiveness (ONE SCALE) Q12
Mission-specific characteristics		
1. Inspiring	0.357***	0.402***
2. Setting target	0.057	0.164**
3. Pragmatic	0.236***	0.128*
4. Vivid language	0.023	−0.018
5. Flexible/adaptable	0.111**	0.091*
Selling tactics used		
1. Top management demonstrates belief in MS	0.119+	0.192***
2. Top management links MS to decision making	0.097+	0.065
Credibility of the seller		
1. Credibility of top management	0.104+	−0.065
Organizational commitment		
1. Employee commitment to the organization	−0.077	0.103*
2. Personal tendency *not* to leave the company	−0.043	0.069
Process used to develop the mission		
1. Participation in the development of the MS	0.152**	0.048
R^2	0.750	0.773
Adjusted R^2	0.731	0.756
F	40.3***	45.8***

+ $p<0.10$; * $p<0.05$; ** $p<0.01$; *** $p<0.001$.

Model 1 provides a very good fit. Here, we attempt to identify the key variables that explain whether employees perceive their company's MS as effective. The factors measuring mission-specific characteristics (with the exception of vivid language and target setting) appear to be significant. In particular, the factors "inspiring" and "pragmatic" are consistently significant in explaining the variation in our dependent variable. This highlights the difficulties in developing an effective MS: on the one hand, the MS has to be stretching and has to create a sense of urgency; on the other hand, it has to be grounded in reality and must be pragmatic. Obviously, there is a delicate balance that has to be struck between these two goals—if the MS is too stretching, employees will dismiss it as unrealistic; if it is too realistic, employees will dismiss it as boring and not motivational enough.

Perhaps the best way to resolve this dilemma is to develop a truly stretching and challenging objective but then spend a lot of effort and energy "selling it" to the employees. If top management does a good job in selling it to its people, then the objective might be perceived as challenging but achievable nevertheless (Collins & Porras, 1996). This suggestion is supported by the fact that the factor "selling tactics used" as well as the factor "credibility of the seller" comes out significant (at a 10% level of significance), and with the predicted signs.

It is interesting to note that the language used in the MS does not come out as a significant explanatory factor. This goes contrary to the prescriptive managerial literature, which encourages managers to use powerful and vivid language in their MS. This result is also contrary to current managerial practices where companies seem to compete as to who will come up with the most catchy slogan. Perhaps, it is the combination of vivid language with meaningful MS content that makes the difference.

Overall, four of the five factors identified in the theoretical section are significant in explaining the perceived value of the MS. The most surprising result is that organizational commitment is not significant in explaining the perceived value of the MS. Equally surprising is the finding that the credibility of the seller is also not significant in explaining mission effectiveness. These are results that need to be explored further.

The other factor that appears significant in explaining mission effectiveness is "employee commitment to the organization". We do not know how this organizational commitment is won but looking at TABLE 3.7, it seems that employee commitment increases when a team culture is developed in the organization. This would suggest that if all employees contribute—as a team—in the development of the mission, they will feel more committed to the organization and this, in turn, will translate into more commitment to the MS. This prediction is supported by the result that the factor "participation in the development of the MS" is a significant explanatory variable.

DISCUSSION, LIMITATIONS AND POSSIBLE EXTENSIONS

Our chapter is one of the few empirical studies on the topic of MS effectiveness. Our tests have allowed us to sift through the vast prescriptive literature on this topic and single out which of the many variables that are often suggested as predictors of MS effectiveness truly are. Thus, contrary to what other authors have suggested, we do not find any evidence that the language used in the MS has any effect on its effectiveness. Similarly, we do not find support for the proposition that organizational commitment contributes to MS effectiveness, while the credibility of the top management as an explanatory variable receives only partial support.

On the other hand, the variables "process used to develop the MS" and "selling tactics used" come out significant. When we examine the individual elements making up these two significant explanatory variables, further insights could be developed. For example, the elements making up the "selling tactics used" are presented in TABLE 3.2. These elements readily lead into managerially relevant prescriptions such as: to sell the MS, top managers must set the example, must demonstrate belief in the MS, must repeat the MS to outsiders, and so on. Similarly, the elements that make up the significant variable "process used to develop the MS" are presented in TABLE 3.5. These elements also readily lead to managerial prescriptions—such as "use a cross-functional team to develop the MS" or "use a formal process to develop the MS". Similar prescriptions can be developed for each one of the significant explanatory variables.

Our study also highlights the importance of not only developing a meaningful objective for the organization but also taking the time and making the effort to "sell" it to the people in the organization. In keeping with the prescriptions offered in the managerial literature (Markides, 1998), a mission statement—however grand and ambitious it may be—will be nothing more than empty words if it is not sold effectively to the rest of the organization.

It is interesting to point out that our basic findings do not change when we split our sample by the nationality of the respondents or the industry they come from. This result is in keeping with the theme of the SMS Conference: in an interconnected world, we would expect similarity in the challenges that businesses face across national boundaries as well as in the approaches adopted to face these challenges.

Even though our study fills an important gap in the literature of mission statements, it also suffers from a number of limitations which warrant discussion. First, its cross-sectional nature makes it impossible for us to safely argue for a specific direction of causality. For example, one might argue that the credibility of top management can be affected by the effectiveness of the mission statement as well. Second, despite the excellent response rate we have achieved, there might be some potential bias in the sample used. A small number of the respondents are likely to have been promoted to senior managers. Thus, some may be responding about their own credibility.

Finally, since the questionnaire was filled by one source within each organization, there is always the potential of common method bias. To minimize this problem we have used a number of precautions. First, the items used in the analysis were distributed throughout a lengthy questionnaire. Second, several different items were used, including anchored Likert scales, agree–disagree scales etc. Third, scale anchors were reversed in several places to reduce and compensate for the development of response patterns. These precautions enhance our belief in our data and make us believe that common method bias may not be a significant problem.

The present research effort has touched on only a few of the research questions in the area. Several extensions, both methodological and substantive, need to be made, and a number of points concerning overall research recommendations should be highlighted:

1. The research has found that MS effectiveness is dependent on a large number of variables. More work needs to be done to test the generalizability of the present results in other settings and sample designs. Another useful line of research would be to examine the same hypotheses in more narrowly defined samples, e.g. controlling for types of enterprises or different types of MS and for other context variables, so that consistent research findings can be accumulated and a more focused contingency theory on the effectiveness of MS developed.
2. Despite the fact that the regression models tested here appear to have a very good explanatory power, there still remains an unexplained percentage of variance. Further research can incorporate additional variables not considered in the course of this study (e.g. contextual elements such as reward systems, environmental attributes, organizational structure), and may adopt different and possibly more appropriate operationalizations of the constructs used here.
3. Theory is needed that more accurately reflects the effectiveness of an MS in its context and the relative weight of its determinants. Progress in this area could significantly improve both our understanding and eventually the quality of MS. A refinement of the formulation may be necessary before a more substantial explanation or prediction capability can be achieved.
4. The present work has established the multidimensional aspects of MS effectiveness and the multiple relationships with the main variables of the study. This enhances the need for producing a more integrated image of MS through the simultaneous study of a large number of qualities, and use of more sophisticated multivariate analysis. Simultaneous equation techniques would be useful to further examine determinants of the actual sets of relationships in practice as well as the direction of causality.
5. Future research efforts must also try to explore whether interactions between the five factors are significant in explaining MS effectiveness. For example, is the interaction between MS content and language used significant? Similarly, is the interaction between employee participation in developing the MS and employee commitment to the organization significant in explaining MS effectiveness? Future research efforts should also explore whether individual factors are important predictors even in the absence of the other factors. For example, is the factor "mission-specific characteristics" (and in particular the variable "inspiring") an important predictor in organizations where the MS was not "sold"

effectively to the employees? Could it be that it is the interaction between MS content and selling effort that explains effectiveness rather than one or the other?

Finally, it is important to note that, at least in this chapter, we have focused on the effectiveness and perceived value of MS as our dependent variables. No attempt was made to link this to actual organizational performance. Future research efforts must explore whether MS effectiveness is ultimately related to the organization's financial performance. Arguably, this is a difficult task to pursue and it may require a longitudinal research design. However, it is something that needs to be done because MS effectiveness is not a goal that should be pursued for its own sake—instead, it should be pursued only if it allows the organization to compete more effectively with its competitors.

APPENDIX

OPERATIONALIZATION AND RELIABILITY OF VARIABLES

Variables	Number of items in scale	Alpha reliability coefficient
Dependent variables		
1. Perceived value of the MS	9	0.854
2. Mission effectiveness	1	n/a
Mission-specific characteristics		
1. Inspiring	6	0.895
2. Setting target	4	0.734
3. Pragmatic	4	0.704
4. Vivid language	1	n/a
5. Flexible/adaptable	1	n/a
Selling tactics used		
1. Top management demonstrates belief in MS	5	0.834
2. Top management links MS to decision making	3	0.741
Credibility of the seller		
1. Credibility of top management	6	0.834
Organizational commitment		
1. Employee commitment to the organization	6	0.859
2. Personal tendency *not* to leave the company	4	0.777
Process used to develop the mission		
1. Participation in the development of the MS	5	0.714

REFERENCES

Bart, C.K. (1996). The impact of mission on firm innovativeness. *International Journal of Technology Management*, **11**(3), 479–493.

Campbell, A. & Yeung, S. (1991). Brief case mission, vision and strategic intent. *Long Range Planning*, **24**(4), 145–147.

Collins, J.C. & Porras, J.I. (1996). Building your company's vision. *Harvard Business Review*, September/October, 65–77.

Collins, J.C. & Porras, J.I. (1995). *Built to Last: Successful Habits of Visionary Companies*. London: Century, Random House.

Collins, J.C. & Porras, J.I. (1991). Organizational vision and visionary organizations. *California Management Review*, **34**(1), 30–52.

Conger, J.A. (1991). Inspiring others: the language of leadership. *Academy of Management Executive*, **5**(1), 31–45.

Covin, J.G., Slevin, D.P. & Schultz, R.L. (1994). Implementing strategic missions: effective strategic, structural, and tactical choices. *Journal of Management Studies*, **31**(4), 481–505.

David, F.R. (1989). How companies define their mission. *Long Range Planning*, **22**(1), 90–97.

Doz, Y.L. & Prahalad, C.K. (1987). A process model of strategic redirection in large complex firms: the case of multinational corporations. In A. Pettigrew (ed.) *The Management of Strategic Change*. Oxford: Basil Blackwell, pp. 63–83.

Dubinsky A.J. & Hartley, S.W. (1986). A path-analytic study of a model of salesperson performance. *Journal of the Academy of Marketing Science*, **14**(1), 36–46.

Dutton J.E., Ashford, S.J., Wierba, E.E., O'Neill, R. & Hayes, E. (1995). Reading the wind: how middle managers assess the context for selling issues to top managers. Working paper, University of Michigan, Ann Arbor.

Dutton, J.E. & Ashford, S.J. (1993). Selling issues to top management. *Academy of Management Review*, **18**(3), 397–428.

Dwyer R.F. & Oh, S. (1987). Output sector munificence effects on the internal political economy of marketing channels. *Journal of Marketing Research*, **24**(4), 347–358.

Fortune (1997). The world's most admired companies. 27 October, 40–56.

Fortune (1995). Brushing up your vision thing. 1 May, 87.

Graham J. & Havlick, W. (1995). *Mission Statements: A Guide to the Corporate and Nonprofit Sectors*. London: Garland Publishing.

Grossman, S.R. & King, J.M. (1993). Where vision statements go wrong. *Across the Board*, June, 56–57.

Hamel, G. & Prahalad, C.K. (1989). Strategic intent. *Harvard Business Review*, **67**(3), 63–76.

Ireland R.D. & Hitt, M.A. (1992). Mission statements: importance, challenge, and recommendations for development. *Business Horizons*, **35**(3), 35–42.

Jones P. & Kahaner, L. (1995). *Say it and Live it: The 50 Corporate Mission Statements that Hit the Mark*. London: Currency/Doubleday.

Klemm, M., Sanderson, S. & Luffman, G. (1991). Mission statements: selling corporate values to employees. *Long Range Planning*, **24**(3), 73–78.

Kotter, J.P. (1990). *A Force for Change: How Leadership Differs from Management*. New York: Free Press.

Larwood, L., Falbe, C.M., Kriger, M.P. & Miesing, P. (1995). Structure and meaning of organizational vision. *Academy of Management Journal*, **38**(3), 740–769.

Lipton, M. (1996). Demystifying the development of an organizational vision. *Sloan Management Review*, Summer, 83–92.

Markides, C.C. (1998). *Crafting Strategy: A Journey into the Mind of the Strategist.* Boston, MA: HBS Press.

Mather, R. (1994). Essential thinking for change: vision in an age of change. Andersen Consulting.

Morris, R.J. (1996). Developing a mission for a diversified company. *Long Range Planning*, **29**(1), 103–115.

Mowday, R.T., Steers, R.M. & Porter, L.W. (1979). The measurement of organizational commitment. *Journal of Vocational Behavior*, **14**, 224–247.

Newman, G. (1992). Worried about vision? see an optometrist. *Across the Board*, October, 7–8.

Oswald, S.L., Mossholder, K.W. & Harris, S.G. (1994). Vision salience and strategic involvement: implications for psychological attachment to organization and job. *Strategic Management Journal*, **15**, 177–489.

Pearce, J.A. II (1982). The company mission as a strategic tool. *Sloan Management Review*, **23**(3), 15–24.

Pearce, J.A. & David, F. (1987). Corporate mission statements: the bottom line. *Academy of Management Executive*, **1**(2), 109–116.

Piercy, N.F. & Morgan, N.A. (1994). Mission analysis: an operational approach. *Journal of General Management*, **19**(3), 1–19.

Schenkler, B.R. (1980). *Impression Management*, Monterey, CA: Brooks/Cole.

Schilit W.K. & Locke, E.A. (1982). A study of upward influence in organizations. *Administrative Science Quarterly*, **27**, 304–316.

Schnieder, J.W. (1985). Social problems theory: the constructionist view. *Annual Review of Sociology*, **11**, 209–229.

Steward, T.A. (1996). A refreshing change: vision statements that make sense. *Fortune*, 30 September, 107–108.

Thomas J.B., Shankster, L.J. & Mathieu, J.E. (1994). Antecedents to organizational issue interpretation. *Academy of Management Journal*, **37**(5), 1252–1284.

Thornberry, N. (1997). A view about vision. *European Management Journal*, **15**(1), 28–34.

Trapp, R. (1995). Sharing the corporate vision. *Update UK, News from Blessing/White*, Issue 5, Summer.

Wilson, I. (1992). Realizing the power of strategic vision. *Long Range Planning*, **25**(5), 18–28.

4

Bridging the Gap between Intended and Unintended Change: The Role of Managerial Sensemaking

JULIA BALOGUN, GERRY JOHNSON

INTRODUCTION

As organizations attempt to meet the challenges created by increasing globalization, more and more of them are undertaking change in their fight to remain competitive. However, it is acknowledged that planned change implementation is difficult and unpredictable (Kanter, Stein & Jick, 1992). It is also known that it is not possible to understand the incremental and emergent nature of strategic change within organizations without recognizing the impact of micro-organizational political and social processes (Johnson, 1987; Mintzberg, 1978; Pettigrew, 1985; Quinn, 1980). Yet few studies have explored in depth the implementation of a change initiative to examine how these micro-processes contribute to the way the implementation of strategy unfolds. The research presented here tackles this issue, by taking the importance attached to facilitating and obstructing processes during change (Huff, Huff & Thomas, 1992; Pettigrew, Ferlie & McKee, 1992),

New Managerial Mindsets: Organizational Transformation and Strategy Implementation.
Edited by M.A. Hitt, J.E. Ricart i Costa and R.D. Nixon.
© 1998 John Wiley & Sons Ltd.

and the relative neglect of the role of recipient interpretations in change (Bartunek *et al.*, 1996), as the starting point. It examines how facilitating and obstructing processes affect the way planned strategic change implementation develops, from the perspective of middle managers as change recipients.

The findings suggest that intentional and unintentional change cannot be viewed as two different types of change, but are inextricably linked, like the two sides of a coin. The intended elements of change, in the form of designed change interventions put in place by the instigators of change, achieve some of the planned change goals, but they also create other emergent effects for those involved in the changes, as the interventions interact with the context in which they are enacted. Some of these emergent effects are perceived by the change recipients to be helpful in moving change forward, but others are perceived to be undesirable and obstructive. Analysis reveals that it is these "positive developments" and "unintended consequences" (Giddens, 1976) that turn the implementation from a planned series of activities into an emergent incremental process.

Data for the study were obtained by tracking the progress of a planned strategic change implementation from the perspective of middle managers as change recipients, on a real-time basis via a diary mechanism. The research adopts a *sensemaking perspective* (Weick, 1995) to develop a framework for analysing the middle manager data. The analysis is used to propose a theory of mediation, which explains how positive developments and unintended consequences arise over time as a result of recipient interpretations of the planned change goals and interventions.

This research is able to provide fresh insights into how and why change implementation becomes an emergent process, by linking recipient sensemaking to both intended and unintended change outcomes. These findings have implications for change management practice and research. Viewed from the perspective presented here, managing implementation is as much about detecting and managing the unexpected consequences as it is about managing the planned elements. This challenges the traditional approach to change implementation, which equates success with the careful deployment and management of a series of planned interventions. The implication is that if implementation is carefully planned, and the right levers utilized, the plans will become a reality. The findings here, however, suggest that no matter how well the plans are prepared, interventions put in place will not only lead to intended outcomes, but also to other, unintended, outcomes.

After a brief presentation of the research agenda and methodology, the chapter illustrates, via case examples, the impact of unintended consequences and positive developments on change implementation, and also how they arise via recipient sensemaking. Finally, the implications of the findings are discussed, with particular regard to the practice of change management.

RESEARCH ON STRATEGIC CHANGE

There are a growing number of rich, qualitative, longitudinal, processual studies on change (Johnson, 1987; Pettigrew, 1985; Pettigrew and Whipp, 1991; Pettigrew, Ferlie & McKee, 1992). Most of this work looks at "extended strategic change" (Pettigrew, Ferlie & McKee, 1992, p. 150), encompassing patterns of change formulation and implementation in an organization over a period of several years. This research, in conjunction with other work on processes of strategy development (Bower, 1970; Mintzberg, 1978; Quinn, 1980), shows that strategic change is not a rationally planned series of events, but is better accounted for in terms of more micro-organizational political, cultural and cognitive processes. Yet although it is known that planned change implementation is difficult and unpredictable (Jick, 1993; Kanter, Stein & Jick, 1992; Pettigrew & Whipp, 1991), there are few studies concentrating specifically on the more micro-level patterns that occur during implementation to determine how they may account for this unpredictability. Within the research to date, there is also a relative neglect of the role of recipient interpretations during change, with a greater concern for the perspective of change instigators (Bartunek *et al.*, 1996). Research needs to consider the different understandings that may develop among different participants (Pettigrew, Ferlie & McKee, 1992), which requires an acknowledgment of change as a socially constructed process (Gioia & Chittipeddi, 1991).

It is clear from other strategic change research that importance is attached to facilitating and obstructing processes. Strategic change occurs when the forces for change become greater than and overcome the forces resisting change within an organization (Ginsberg, 1988; Huff, Huff & Thomas, 1992; Miller & Friesen, 1984). Therefore, interacting facilitating and obstructing processes may play an important role in the way a change implementation process develops. Yet only one study, by Pettigrew, Ferlie & McKee (1992), appears to examine explicitly the role of facilitating and obstructing processes at more micro-organizational levels during strategic change implementation.

This research builds on what is known about facilitating and obstructing processes, to investigate change implementation. The aim is to understand how and why the facilitating and obstructing processes perceived by change recipients during planned strategic change implementation arise through time, and how these interacting processes affect the way the implementation develops.

A CASE OF PLANNED CHANGE: THE RESEARCH SITE

The study examines the implementation of planned strategic change within the core business division of an organization, Anonco, launched in response to forthcoming changes in the organization's competitive environment.

Since a design team put together a blueprint for the changes, and then put an implementation programme in place, it was possible to demarcate the start of implementation and the intended "transition phase" (Beckhard & Harris, 1987), and to monitor the implementation through the transition.

The implementation followed a top-down, planned approach. A design team consisting of consultants and senior managers prepared the rationale and detail of the planned changes in terms of the proposed structure, outlines of job roles and responsibilities, and staffing levels. Some middle managers had been involved in the team to help design and document some of the more detailed workings of the new divisions. The individual divisions were to be responsible for their detailed implementation plans and the actual implementation of changes.

The restructuring involved splitting what was one division into three new divisions—a small Core Division and two support divisions, Maintenance and Services. The planned changes involved radical restructuring, downsizing, the introduction of many new working practices, and the start of a culture change to a less technical, more customer services oriented culture. By the end of the first year of change, Maintenance and Services were to start working on a contract basis with the new Core Division, and with each other, to create customer/supplier trading relationships between the three new divisions. The Core Division could eventually be allowed to seek outside providers of services should the support divisions not be able to offer services of equivalent quality and price.

The interventions put in place were primarily hard levers to do with structures, systems, and new job roles and responsibilities. The transition phase started with the appointment of three divisional directors and lasted for about a year until the contracts came into force between the divisions. The business was kept going during the transition by "business as usual": staff continued to do the work they used to do, while gradually taking up their new responsibilities, until the staff responsible for that old work in the new structure were able to pick it up. An extensive communications exercise was undertaken, with a launch video followed by workshops for all staff. The intent was to ensure that everyone understood the rationale for the changes and the new business vision. Change managers were appointed to each division to help the directors design and oversee all change-related activities.

METHODOLOGY

Other change research (Pettigrew, Ferlie & McKee, 1992) reveals facilitating and obstructing processes to be unpredictable. They emerge and recede through time, and are affected by unexpected events and the change context. It is for reasons such as these that Pettigrew (1990) argues that change research must be longitudinal and processual. Van de Ven (1992) supports this point of view. Therefore, a processual approach was adopted for this research.

The recipient group selected for the research were middle managers. They can play a key role in implementation, and are a group of people whose role in strategic change may have been underestimated and under-researched (Floyd & Wooldridge, 1992). However, the intent to focus on the perceptions of middle managers as change recipients alters the focus of the study from the change process, to how individuals experience the changes. As such, this makes the research an interpretive study to do with issues of sensemaking (Weick, 1995).

The tracking of implementation progress started in earnest four months into the transition phase, once middle managers had taken up their appointments in the new structure. Consistent with the interpretive orientation of the study, the technique selected for this was the use of diaries (Denzin, 1989). Diaries are an established means of collecting research data in sociological enquiries aimed at obtaining participants' perceptions and experiences. (See, for example, the work on teachers by Burgess (1984).) They enable researchers to gain an "intimate view" of organizational events from the perspective of those who actually experience them (Bogdan & Taylor, 1975).

There were 26 middle manager diarists spread across the three new divisions. Diarists were initially identified by the change managers from the new organization structure charts to ensure a good coverage of all different departments and interfaces. The change managers did not personally know all the diarists they asked to participate. Thus there was no preselection of diarists in terms of likely attitudes to change by the change managers. The three appointed divisional change managers also kept diaries.

The diaries contained five simple questions in the format of an unstructured questionnaire: What is going well and why? What is going badly and why? What problems do you foresee? What have been the significant events? and What rumours are circulating? They were at first maintained on a fortnightly basis, but this frequency was changed to monthly as the pace of change slackened. At the end of each recording period the diaries were forwarded to the researcher by the individuals themselves for addition to the research database (the actual diary entries were only ever seen by the diarist who wrote them and the researcher). The diary data were also used by the researcher to write reports for the three Divisional Directors on the progress of change in their divisions. These reports were written with the consent of the diarists, and were written in such a way that no one comment could be ascribed to any one diarist. The researcher made no recommendations as to what should be done differently in the reports. Divisional review meetings were also held with the diarists on a 6–8 weekly cycle, and more frequent contact with the diarists was maintained by regular telephone conversations. One-to-one in-depth, unstructured interviews took place with all diarists two months into the tracking, and again towards the end of the research. The interviews and telephone conversations enabled the researcher to probe queries prompted by the diary entries. The different types of data collected, along with documentation such as copies of briefing material and workshop documents, provided important data triangulation (Denzin, 1989).

An inductive data analysis approach was used which closely followed recommendations by Miles (1983) and Glaser & Strauss (1967). Classifications and categorizations of facilitating and obstructing processes were developed as the data were collected. Notes were kept of all facilitating and obstructing processes commented on by the diarists in the diaries, meetings and interviews. It became clear as the analysis progressed that at a descriptive level, although there was a very wide range of facilitating and obstructing processes in general, overall there were four main types of facilitating processes, and also four main types of obstructing processes. These are presented under the descriptive findings. Furthermore, it became clear that it was the emergent facilitating and obstructing processes that were contributing to the unpredictable nature of the change implementation.

However, explanation of the findings requires the development of a theoretical framework. This was done with the aid of a computer-based data analysis package, NUD.IST (non-numeric unstructured data indexing searching and theorizing: a computer package to aid users in handling non-numerical and unstructured data in qualitative data analysis. It does this by supporting processes of indexing (coding), searching and theorizing), and by employing the principles of qualitative data analysis and the constant comparative method (Miles, 1983; Glaser & Strauss, 1967). Grounded theory building was selected as the approach since this research was investigating a phenomena for which extant theory did not appear to be useful (Brown & Eisenhardt, 1997). All data were transcribed and then coded and analysed via the package. The findings are, therefore, on two levels. The first level is descriptive and to do with observations on the patterns of interaction between obstructing and facilitating processes perceived by the middle managers during implementation. The second level is theoretical, providing an explanation for the patterns observed.

FIRST-LEVEL FINDINGS: A DESCRIPTION OF THE ROLE OF FACILITATING AND OBSTRUCTING PROCESSES

At the first level, the research identified four different types of facilitating and obstructing processes encountered by recipients of change. Facilitating processes can be divided into *designed change goals*, the planned outcomes of the changes, such as new structure, roles and relationships; *designed change interventions*, the enablers put in place by the change instigators to help achieve the goals, such as communication, training and appointments; *positive developments*, outcomes perceived by the middle managers to be created by the change interventions and to be helpful in achieving the designed change goals, such as an understanding of the need for change; and *unplanned events*, such as *ad hoc* and supportive senior management behaviour.

Obstructing processes can be divided into *design issues*,[1] aspects of the designed interventions perceived to become problems and hinder the change process in some way, such as insufficient communication and inadequate transition management; *unintended consequences*, negative outcomes perceived by the middle managers to hinder the process of change and to arise from the interventions put in place, such as false expectations about the role of staff in the changes or interdepartmental rivalries; *inherent obstructing processes*, obstructions to the change process created by the existing way of operating and the organization's history, such as the old culture and old management style; and *unplanned events*, occurring internally and externally to the organization, such as uncertainty created by redundancies and pay reductions in other companies.

It is the interaction of the different facilitating and obstructing processes that caused the planned implementation to change from a planned series of activities into an *emergent incremental* process, in which intended and unintended changes are inextricably linked. As change progressed, the designed change interventions put in place through time helped to achieve some of the planned change goals, but also created other effects for those involved in the changes. Some of these effects were perceived by the diarists to be beneficial, helping to move change forward, but others were perceived to be undesirable and obstructive. These "positive developments" and "unintended consequences" (Giddens, 1976) were not only some of the most commonly occurring obstructing and facilitating processes, but they were also perceived by the diarists to be important in shaping the overall outcome of change interventions. They emerged through time as the change interventions put in place interacted with the context in which they were enacted.

Two illustrative examples follow. The first example shows how a series of unintended consequences developed from the restructuring interventions, and the second how a series of positive developments arose, leading to an emergent culture change in the Core Division. These examples are illustrated in FIGURES 4.1 and 4.2, via a type of causal network (Miles & Huberman, 1994). In the figures, the different types of obstructing and facilitating processes are represented by different symbols, and are cross-referenced alphabetically to the written explanations.

---

[1] These processes are called design issues rather than design problems, because although the middle managers participating in the research viewed them as problems, managers responsible for designing the change process did not necessarily agree. Further, the middle manager participants did not always agree about the nature of the problem.

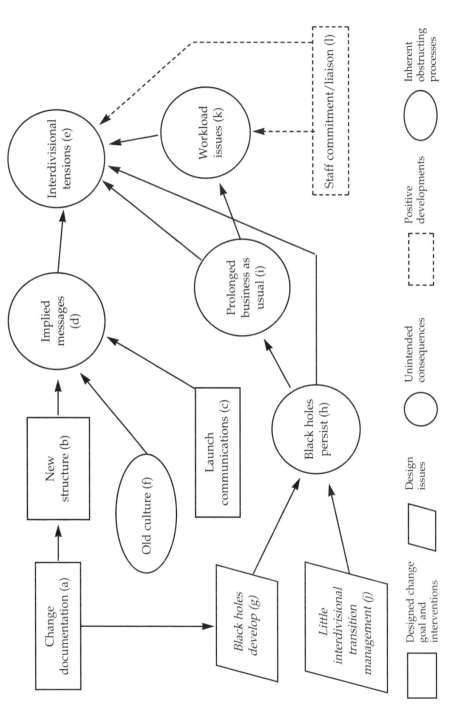

FIGURE 4.1 Process of development of inter-divisional tensions

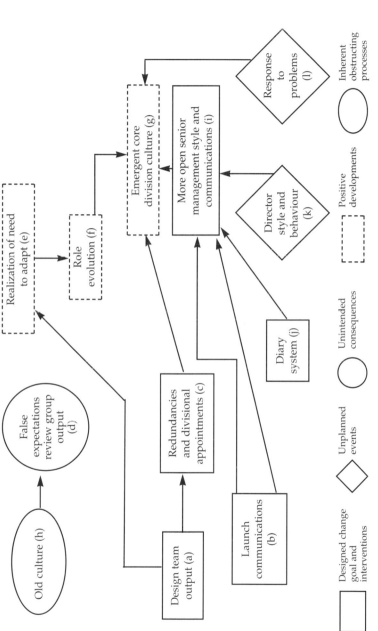

FIGURE 4.2 Process of emergent culture change

EXAMPLE 1: INTER-DIVISIONAL TENSIONS

The group responsible for planning the changes developed a *designed change goal* (a) of a *new structure* (b) with three divisions working together on a commercial basis. The aim was to create internal supplier customer relationships. Whereas the staff had worked closely together in the past, the new structure created an "artificial barrier", which was to help effect the change in relationships. Separate divisional identities had to develop to enable the divisions to perform effectively and efficiently what were different types of work and responsibilities.

However, despite the messages given to staff in the *launch communications* (c) of the intent for staff across the three divisions to work together to successfully establish cooperative working arrangements in the new structure, the form of the new structure *implied negative messages* (d) to some staff, particularly in Maintenance. "Maintenance staff have had a pride in the ownership of the company's assets but now are made to feel like contractors", and "Core Division all feel as if they will be all right, with no worries and the destiny of the others in their hands". Others felt the new structure created a perception of a core "elite", or that the new structure, because it "divided a united pack", would automatically have created tensions anyway. Thus, *interdivisional tensions* (e) developed. The new structure had "polarized opinions". There were now "feelings of competition" between the divisions, leading to "barriers". This was substantiated by examples of "protection of turf" and negative perceptions of the behaviour of other divisions. There were reported rumours such as, "Core Division are taking all the staff but little of the work and responsibility".

The messages read into the new structure by staff indicate how context affects the way interventions are received. There was a *long history* (f) of the staff in all three divisions working together as colleagues of equal status. Staff in Maintenance were used to viewing the assets of the company that they built and maintained as theirs, and they "had a pride" in this. Problems were sorted out between colleagues on the basis of "I owe you one". The new structure changed the traditional working relationships even though many staff were still doing the same work.

Meanwhile, *black holes* (g)—responsibilities not clearly specified by the design team—were developing. Managers could not always determine where responsibility for particular tasks lay, leading to disagreements as individuals tried to defend their own interests. "There is a great deal of uncertainty regarding the split of responsibility of who does what". Some of these black holes were resolved, but other *interdivisional issues persisted* (h), and led to an *extension of business as usual* (i) between some departments. The non-resolution of many of the "who does what" issues was blamed on a lack of *adequate interdivisional transition management* (j).

The *prolonged business as usual* (i) and *unresolved interdivisional problems* (h) also added to the *tensions* (e) between the divisions, particularly for Maintenance and Services. The ongoing need to continue to do their old duties as well as the new created a heavy *workload* (k) at a time when their staffing levels were being reduced. Maintenance and Service diarists felt that misunderstandings about business as usual, which "doesn't have any great degree of meaning" and was "used as an excuse", contributed to this.

Running alongside these problems, however, was a positive development. There was a recognition of the problems among staff and a desire to see the changes work. Despite the complaints, staff took *initiatives and liaised* (l) to keep the business going. On an individual basis, "we are liaising and working together as much as possible". Diarists felt staff commitment had been key. "The willingness of people to change" and "the cooperation and the commitment of the staff" were some of the aspects of change that had gone "really well". As a result, by the end of the first year, the new structure was in place with all staff in their new roles, and contract implementation under way as planned. Examples of business as usual did continue, as there were still some departments not ready to take up all their new duties as yet, particularly in the Core Division.

EXAMPLE 2: EMERGENT CULTURE CHANGE IN THE CORE DIVISION

One of the *stated intentions* (a) of the change process was to achieve a culture change, from a *technical, control culture* (h), to a more open, customer services culture. Although few specific actions aimed at achieving this were put in place, an emergent culture change did start to occur in the Core Division. A strong divisional identity was established, with more open communication and less of a control/blame management style.

Prior to the changes, staff fulfilled specific job roles, had little or no empowerment, and did not pass bad news upwards. A job was for life with the company. The *appointments* (c) to the Core Division rather than the organization as a whole, the *redundancies* (c), and the *launch communications* (b) talking about the new way of working all challenged the beliefs underpinning the old culture. A further challenge was the intention of the design team for middle managers to help finalize the boundaries of their departmental roles and responsibilities once appointed, rather than picking up a prespecified job role.

However, the influence of the *old culture* (h) led middle managers to develop *false expectations of the change design* (d). There was an expectation that the design team would "announce" at the start of the implementation "where all the boundaries lay", and that the structure would be "up and running" almost from day one. It became clear to the middle managers "from the minute people were put in place" that this was not the case. Details of departmental boundaries and job responsibilities were only given in outline in *change documentation* (a). As a result, although the middle managers initially experienced confusion, they started to *realize that they needed to adapt* (e) and from now on contribute to the design of their own job roles. This *evolution of staff roles* (f) contributed to the perception that a *new culture* (g) was developing in the division. Middle managers used to do a "routine job", whereas now they were expected to contribute to the "development of the section".

Other events also challenged old routines of behaviour. Senior managers were traditionally distant figures. Yet to launch the implementation, the *director and his senior managers* (b) ran and attended change workshops and departmental change plan events, and appeared to communicate openly, and to be interested in what staff had to say. The *director* (k) came across as "honest, open and totally committed to the success of the division and the business". Staff started to perceive a *different senior management style* with *more open communication* (i). The introduction of the *diary system* (j) also counteracted the old cultural norm of "bad news not passed upwards".

The perception that the senior management style was changing away from a control/blame culture to a new way of doing things was further reinforced by the *director's behaviour* (k). The director was "very approachable and open". He was also supportive of the diary system. He agreed to the creation of an *action report system* (l) whereby problems reported in the diaries were recorded and circulated to senior managers for comments and actions. *Action was taken as a result of the reported problems* (l) because the director insisted on it. Examples included the setting up of an office-move communications team in response to concerns about the planned relocation of the majority of the Core Division staff to one central office; contract briefings; and the issue of a special telephone directory in response to concerns about difficulties in identifying who was responsible for what.

However, not all changes were perceived positively—the removal of flexitime was highly unpopular, and the director received some criticism about his lack of visibility to more junior staff. The director therefore started to *attend team briefings* (l) so staff could talk to him. There was very positive feedback for this: "I would like to just voice appreciation really". Following the office move, organized by the move communications team, the director also set up a special *car parking scheme* (l) in response to complaints about a lack of parking at the new office. He set an example himself by parking in more remote parking areas, leaving those reserved for Core Division staff close to the office for those who needed them.

Finally, a *values and behaviours* programme was put in place at the start of the second year of change. However, the emergent culture change in the Core Division was already well under way by then, with social events such as a quiz night occurring to reinforce the new identity. "We have an identity and all staff do feel part of that".

CHANGE IMPLEMENTATION AS AN EMERGENT INCREMENTAL PROCESS

It has been shown that emergent processes, in the form of positive developments and unintended consequences, shaped the way change implementation developed at Anonco. Designed change interventions still played a positive role. Goals such as the restructuring and new ways of working were achieved, and many of the planned interventions did facilitate change. Yet it was these designed change interventions that led to the development of the unintended consequences and positive developments, since the emergent elements were created by the interaction between the change interventions and the context in which they were enacted by the change recipients.

As such, the findings support the increasing number of writers arguing that change implementation cannot be viewed as a rational, linear process (Johnson, 1987; Kanter, Stein & Jick, 1992; Pettigrew, 1985; Pettigrew, Ferlie & McKee, 1992). Change implementation becomes an *emergent incremental process* due to the impact of the unintended consequences and positive developments. Using Mintzberg's (1978) terminology, there were *intended* changes that became part of the *realized* changes, such as the new structure and job roles; *intended* changes that became *unrealized,* such as greater staff empowerment, which staff generally felt had not happened as yet; and *emergent* changes that also became part of the *realized* changes, such as the unintended consequence of interdivisional tensions, and the positive development of staff adaptation.

There is a pattern of individual deletions and additions to strategy (Huff, 1982). This pattern is incremental since it arises from "the apparent tendency of organizations to 'feel their way' through the uncertainty and complexity of their environment" (Johnson, 1987, p. 20). Here, formulation and implementation became mixed as original design decisions had to be altered, such as the delay of a departmental centralization in the Core Division. Additional interventions had to be put into place as some intended changes did not take place. For example, the values and behaviours programme was introduced to aid the intended cultural change. Other additional interventions were put in place to overcome some unintended consequences, such as the initiation of interdivisional senior manager meetings in response to the developing interdivisional friction. Yet this is only a *description* of what was observed, not an *explanation*. An explanation requires a theoretical framework which can provide understanding of why and how positive developments and unintended consequences arise.

SECOND-LEVEL ANALYSIS: AN EXPLANATION

In this research a more theoretical view was obtained by employing qualitative data analysis techniques and the constant comparative method (Glaser & Strauss, 1967; Miles, 1983) to allow the theory to emerge from the data. The analysis suggests that two concepts are important to an explanation of why unintended consequences and positive developments arise, and their impact on implementation: *mediating processes* and the *level of mediation*. To understand these concepts it is necessary to refer to what is already known about cognition and change.

Research into cognition has shown the importance of individual cognition and sensemaking. Organizations are socially constructed (Berger & Luckmann, 1966). Individuals' schemas and scripts affect the events they respond to and the way they respond (Barr, Stimpert & Huff, 1992). During times of stability, individuals typically act in a pre-programmed, unconscious manner as a result of these schemas (Fiske & Taylor, 1991; Gioia, 1986). The commonality between individuals' schema leads to an enacted reality (Weick, 1979) at group level in the form of routines, rituals, norms, systems, structures and assumptions and beliefs. The constant re-enactment of the group level reinforces and maintains the individual schemas.

In situations where individuals face change, when old schemas no longer apply, individuals encounter surprise (Louis, 1980), and start to act in a more conscious sensemaking mode (Weick, 1995). It is this more conscious sensemaking mode that is referred to as the *level of mediation*. The activity at the level of mediation is similar to Weick's (1979, p. 175) notion of selection, which answers the question "What's going on here?". One input to this activity is the enacted raw data, here represented by the changes perceived at the group level, and another the enacted interpretations that have worked in the past, here represented by individuals' schemas and scripts (see FIGURE 4.3).

Differences encountered at the group level which individuals cannot respond to via their existing schemas act as sensemaking triggers. Individuals move to a more conscious sensemaking mode to try to make sense of the differences within the context of their existing schemas and scripts,[2] and by sharing their experiences with others (Isabella, 1990). Therefore, the level of mediation is about the processes individuals within groups engage in when they encounter something different that cannot be explained by their existing schemas, to enable them to come to some sort of shared understanding

---

[2] Sensemaking does not occur in an acontextual fashion. Individuals have different perspectives depending on their previous experiences, positions within the organization, and self-interests (Dearborn & Simon, 1958). FIGURE 4.3 represents the components of the individual level in terms of scripts and schemas for simplicity, and channels all individual factors that may influence sensemaking through schemas and scripts.

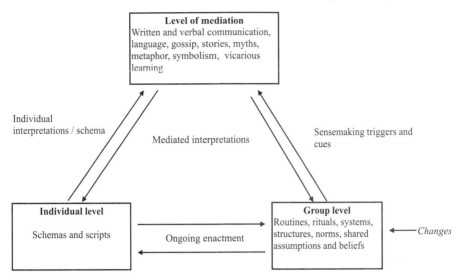

FIGURE 4.3   Level of mediation

about the implications of change for themselves. Individuals can only return to more automatic schema-determined responses and behaviours once some new shared understanding has developed.

The *mediating processes* are the sensemaking and sharing mechanisms used by individuals during times of change when operating in a more conscious sensemaking mode at the level of mediation, in an attempt to arrive at some understanding of the implications of the changes for themselves. The processes of mediation are an attempt to unpack the types of processes individuals engage in to help them answer the question "What's going on here?". They are about the interpretation of sensemaking cues, and the sharing of meaning inferred from these cues.

Therefore, processes of mediation to aid sensemaking are important during times of change, as other research also suggests (Gioia, 1986; Gioia & Chittipeddi, 1991; Isabella, 1990; Weick, 1995), and include communication and sharing mechanisms, both formal and informal (Isabella, 1990; Weick, 1995). However, what is key is not that mediating processes exist, or the form they take, but *how* they *mediate* between the enacted group level and the individual level, leading to unintended consequences and positive developments, and thereby an emergent and unpredictable implementation process. As an analytical device, the strength of the above framework is that it provides a perspective centred on the ongoing interpretation of events by change recipients throughout the change process. It also forces an explicit and detailed consideration of mediating processes and their role in change.

TABLE 4.1   Interdivisional tensions

	T1	T2	T3
Sensemaking triggers Designed change Goals & interventions	New structure Appointments Launch communications Change documentation	Contract training	Contracts issued Management procedures put in place Reducing business as usual
Unplanned events		Behaviour of others *but* also liaison	Liaison among staff to resolve contract problems
Mediating processes	Symbolism structure, etc. Rumours and stories Communicated messages	Symbolism of behaviour Rumours and stories Discussions re who does what, business as usual, contracts	Symbolism of behaviour and issue resolution Discussions to clarify outstanding problems
Existing schema/ scripts	Everyone works together for the company "I owe you one"	New structure = protect turf and competition	Structure = competition Contracts will make things worse Need to liaise
Change outcomes Unintended consequences and positive developments	New structure = protect turf and competition Interdivisional tensions	Interdivisional tensions Prolonged business as usual Fears contract impact Need to make it work Need for staff liaison	New structure can equal supplier/ customer cooperation Need for ongoing staff liaison

REVISITING UNINTENDED CONSEQUENCES AND POSITIVE DEVELOPMENTS

TABLES 4.1 and 4.2 rework the examples given earlier in terms of the model in FIGURE 4.3, to illustrate how the addition of the concepts of sensemaking triggers, mediating processes and schema enable an explanation to be developed for the patterns identified.

TABLE 4.2   Culture change, Core Division

	T1	T2	T3
Sensemaking triggers Designed change goals and interventions	Appointments Launch communications Director and his managers at communication events Diary system	Office move Office move communications team Action on problems Staff evolving own job roles	Car parking scheme Director attendance at team briefings
Unplanned events	Redundancies Director approachability	Support for diary system	Social events
Mediating processes	Symbolism appointments/ redundancies Director visibility Discussions re new environment	Stories re director Symbolism of response to staff problems, etc. Discussions re change significance for staff	Ongoing discussions re working environment in Core Division and significance for staff
Existing schema/ scripts	Job for life Tight job specifications Bad news not passed upwards Control culture	I work for Core Division Job if you perform Need to develop own job role Control culture	Less of a control/ blame culture Legitimate to pass bad news upwards Constant job evolution
Change outcomes Unintended consequences and positive developments	Job if you perform Need to contribute to design of own job role I work for Core Division	Legitimate to pass bad news upwards Less control/ blame Job roles not fixed—constant evolution	Core Division has own cultural identity Staff need to be flexible Less of a control/ blame culture

EXAMPLE 1: INTERDIVISIONAL TENSIONS

Time T1

In the early days of change the *sensemaking triggers* for the change recipients included the designed change goals and interventions, such as the implementation of the new three-divisional *structure*, the *appointments*, and the various launch *communication events* and *information*. These triggers led to a wide variety of *mediating processes*. First, *symbolism* as a *mediating process* played a role. The designed change goal of the new structure, with only a small number of *appointments* to the Core Division, was a symbolic act in itself, irrespective of what else was said or done (Johnson, 1990). The way the symbolic messages were then interpreted, leading to a *change outcome* of *interdivisional friction*, was affected by individuals' *schemas* since schemas provide "context specific dictionaries" (Berger & Luckman, 1966, p. 138) against which to compare and interpret current experiences. As described earlier, there was a long history of the staff in all three divisions working together as colleagues of equal power and status. Business used to be done on the basis of "I owe you one". The proposed contractual working *symbolically* challenged this. Contracts translated into only doing something if you got paid for it, supporting the *change outcome* of *look after your own patch*.

Other *mediating processes* at work were the *officially communicated messages* from the video and change workshops, namely the vision that staff were to work together to make the new structure work in the shorter-term, moving to a customer supplier relationship via contracts in the longer term. However, there were also *unofficially communicated messages,* such as the interdivisional attitudes staff were encountering and the *rumours* about this. These *mediating processes* therefore contributed to the *change outcome of interdivisional tensions*.

Time T2

As change progressed into the autumn, additional *sensemaking triggers* occurred. In some instances staff encountered *uncooperative behaviour* in other members of staff. This behaviour was underpinned by the interpretation of the new structure by these members of staff from time T1, now held in their *amended schema*. The uncooperative behaviour triggered *symbolic mediating processes* reinforcing earlier interpretations of *protection of own interests* and *change outcome* of *interdivisional tensions*. The behaviour also led to *mediating processes* of *rumours and stories* about tensions between divisions and examples of a lack of cooperation.

Mediating processes to do with a *lack of communication* and *information* were also at work. These processes were triggered by the *absence* of helpful sensemaking triggers. For example, when staff tried to resolve areas of responsibilities and black holes, they found they did not always have sufficient *information* in the *change documentation* to decide who was responsible for what. Since in situations of rapid change when there are high levels of uncertainty and equivocality (Daft & Weick, 1984), individuals will seek to clarify their situation to enable them to return to non-conscious responding (Weick, 1995), this led to much *discussion* and *debate*, and at times disagreements, among middle managers as they tried to resolve their responsibilities.

Meanwhile, there was a *growing concern* among Core Division staff in particular about the interdivisional tensions. "We want to work together . . . to succeed together". Thus as change progressed, the middle managers took the position that *liaison was needed to keep things going*, with some staff making efforts to liaise across interdivisional boundaries and others arranging meetings to try to resolve outstanding problems. "I am trying to see a number of my colleagues, so it's not a question of someone at the end of a phone, they've seen me." These *liaison attempts* added to the *sensemaking triggers* and created *symbolic mediating processes* that reinforced the growing belief in all three divisions of the need for liaison and the possibility of good working relationships.

As change progressed into the next year, the *sensemaking triggers* also included the *contract training* which was now under way. However, the training still did not provide contract details as the contracts were not ready yet. Therefore, the training triggered many *mediating processes* such as *discussions* about the contracts and *speculation* about their likely impact. Difficulties in implementing the contracts were anticipated, particularly in the Core Division. "We have got to run these contracts." As a result a *change outcome* of *fears about the impact of the contracts*, and the possibility that they may make the interdivisional tensions worse also developed.

Time T3

All of these issues persisted until the end of the first year of implementation, when the *contracts* were implemented and *contract management procedures* put in place. The *contracts* provided *information* enabling middle managers via *discussion* to resolve many of the black holes. As *discussions* led to resolution of outstanding problems, staff also started to realize that their earlier interpretations, that *contracts would make things worse*, were not being realized. The *increasing staff liaison*, the *positive outcomes of that liaison*, and the *non-appearance of anticipated problems* all acted as *sensemaking triggers* providing *symbolic* indications that the divisions could work together under the contracts.

EXAMPLE 2: CULTURE CHANGE

Time T1

At the start of the change process the *appointments* to the Core Division rather than Anonco as a whole, the *redundancies*, the effort put into the launch communications, and the attendance of the *director* and his *senior managers* at the communication events triggered *symbolic mediating processes* challenging assumptions of the old culture such as a job is for life, and beliefs about the senior management style. The introduction of the *diary system* was another *trigger* which *symbolically* challenged the routine of "bad news not passed upwards". These *mediating processes* were added to by *information* from the *launch communications,* and the need for middle managers to finalize their own job roles, triggering many *discussions* about the impact of the changes for staff.

Time T2

As implementation progressed from the autumn and into the next year, the perception of a control/blame culture started to change. More *actions* occurred, such as the office move, *triggering sensemaking* about the new versus the old. The existence of the diary system, the lack of comeback on the diarists for comments made, and the actions taken by the director in response to diary comments triggered many *symbolic mediating processes* which aided the *interpretation* that it was *legitimate to pass bad news upwards.* Other *mediating processes* occurring included *stories,* about such things as the director's management style, and ongoing *discussions* about the implications for staff of the new working environment. In particular, the need for staff to evolve their own job roles triggered many *discussions* about the flexibility now expected of staff.

Time T3

By the end of the first year of implementation, staff were starting to *talk openly* of a culture change in the division. There were many additional and supportive *sensemaking triggers,* such as the setting up of the car parking scheme at the new office, social events and the director's attendance at team briefings. These *triggers* led to additional *mediating processes* in the shape of ongoing *discussions* about the nature of the working environment in the Core Division. There were also other *discussions* and *stories* about differences between the Core Division and other divisions: "Whenever anyone else comes up with a good idea, we've already done it". This all supported the growing *interpretation* that the *Core Division* had its own *cultural identity.*

A THEORY OF MEDIATION

This chapter argues that change implementation can become an emergent and unpredictable process, because the ongoing mediating processes individuals engage in, in response to the planned initiatives and other message sending behaviours, shape the outcome of change interventions, leading to both positive developments and unintended consequences. The importance of such a theory of mediation lies not in the identification of the centrality of sensemaking processes during change, since we already know that sensemaking activity is important during times of uncertainty (Gioia, 1986; Gioia & Chittipeddi, 1991; Isabella, 1990), but in its explanatory power and the way it builds on existing theory. The theory of mediation proposed here links the change outcomes contributing to the emergent nature of implementation, in the form of unintended consequences and positive developments, to the mediating processes change recipients engage in as they try to understand the changes they are being asked to undertake. Therefore, it shows *how* sensemaking activity contributes to the emergent and unpredictable nature of change implementation.

The proposed theory of mediation has implications for change management, both theory and practice, although the focus of this chapter is the practitioner implications. Implementation becomes a series of mediated outcomes, rather than a series of planned outcomes, since it is underpinned by a cyclical process of recipient sensemaking. As such, intended and unintended change are not two different types of change, but inextricably linked like the two sides of a coin. This suggests that managing implementation is not so much about control, but more about trying to achieve an alignment of interpretations between the change instigators and the change recipients.

IMPLICATIONS FOR PRACTICE

The first implications for practice relate to the *nature* of change and implementation. The effect of designed change goals and interventions will be determined by the way they have been interpreted by the change recipients, which will not necessarily be the same as was intended. Change is therefore difficult to impose. Intended change will also create unintended change. Managers leading change should not reify change as something "done" to participants, since change recipients do not play a passive role. But if this is the case, how can change implementation be *managed*?

This research suggests, consistent with other research, that managing change is about the management of meaning (Isabella, 1990; Johnson, 1987; Pettigrew, 1985; Pfeffer 1981). Change will only occur if the individual interpretations underpinning old ways of behaving are changed to support new ways of behaving (Bartunek & Moch, 1987; Poole, Gioia & Gray, 1989). Yet this research also suggests that intended and unintended change are inextricably linked via processes of change recipient sensemaking, which raises questions about the use of the term *managing meaning* with its connotations of conscious meaning manipulation. Others similarly question the feasibility of consciously trying to put in place interventions designed to create certain interpretations for change recipients (Deal, 1985; Johnson, 1990; Moch & Huff, 1983). Naturally occurring rituals, artefacts and stories may have been found to aid change when they occur in a manner that can be interpreted as supportive of the desired change direction, but can they then be *deliberately* manipulated to achieve the same effect?

For example, the new divisional structure was imposed at the group level with certain intentions about the way it was to operate. Yet the way the structure actually operated was determined by the way the recipients interpreted its significance. One argument is that had the change leaders understood the role of mediating processes, and the power of symbolic as well as verbal messages, this could have been avoided. The change leaders did not manage meaning well enough. The alternative argument, and the one pursued here, is that if meanings cannot be managed, then managing change is more about *aligning interpretations*. Aligning interpretation is here seen as a two-way exercise. It involves not only giving meaning, but also understanding what meaning, both intended and unintended, has been inferred from the planned change activities, and other events and behaviours. Therefore, as other researchers suggest, it is necessary to attempt to facilitate developing interpretations by, for example, management of symbols, analogies and puzzles (Isabella, 1990), yet also to *monitor change progress* from the recipients' point of view. It is only possible to understand when and why change interventions are not having the desired effect, and what, if anything, can be done about it, if the interpretations the change recipients are arriving at are known. To return to the example of the new structure, it would not have been possible to put in place interventions to resolve the interdivisional tensions had the directors not known that they existed.

This research does not suggest that to facilitate the development of interpretations in line with that intended is impossible to achieve. The example of the emergent culture change in the Core Division shows how symbolic activity supportive of staff, stories and gossip about events and happenings, integration rituals (Trice & Beyer, 1984) such as social events, and verbal and written communication, all contributed to the development of interpretations about the new culture. The director's behaviour acted as a *catalyst* for new meanings, rather than being a direct manipulation of meaning. Therefore, this research, like other research, (Isabella, 1990; Johnson, 1990), suggests that what is important is a recognition by change leaders of the role of a variety of communication media, such as symbolic activity, stories, language and ritual, as well as verbal and written communication, during change, and the need for it to be mutually supportive and consistent. For this research also illustrates the impact in terms of unintended consequences, such as the interdivisional tensions, when espoused change is not supported by other non-verbal sensemaking triggers. The recipient interpretation process can be likened to a complex chemical reaction. Each intervention, action or event acts as only one catalyst for that reaction.

The nature of implementation also has a number of implications for the change *design*. First, changes to structures and systems are attempts to manipulate the enacted group level, but, as this research shows, the interpretations, and therefore the outcome, of such changes, are not predictable. Such changes may therefore have more chance of being successful if they are supported by other interventions aimed at facilitating supportive interpretation development. For example, the Maintenance division discovered a few months into the implementation that there was a misunderstanding among their managers of the way some aspects of the new structure were to operate. They organized a series of workshops, which provided managers with the opportunity to ask questions and share experiences and implementation problems they had encountered. The diarists subsequently rated these workshops as one of the most effective change interventions because they greatly helped their understanding. Planners of change need to design change interventions which focus on *both* systemic relationships such as roles, relationships and responsibilities (Beer, Eisenstat & Spector, 1990), *and* aiding individual understanding and interpretation development. Those interventions which, like the workshops, encourage individuals to air and share their interpretations, and stimulate experiential learning throughout implementation, are likely to be more effective than those that do not.

The second important design issue for change practitioners is to recognize the implications for transition management. Most of the management of change literature makes it clear that major change implementation is complex and difficult due to issues such as culture, politics and the need to manage the human aspects of change (Beckhard & Harris, 1987; Kanter, Stein & Jick, 1992; Kotter, 1995; Tichy, 1983). The tendency is to give lists of steps that will help if taken into account. As a result, the implication for the reader is often that change can be planned and managed according to design, as long as the necessary elements are given careful consideration. This in turn can encourage a reliance on careful and detailed planning. Furthermore, if the literature is referred to for advice on the *management* of *planned implementation*, in the main it advocates a traditional project management approach, with an emphasis on *control* (Buchanan & Boddy, 1992).

The theory of mediation suggests a different perspective on transition management. Since there is not necessarily a direct link between an intervention and its effect, managing change implementation is as much about the detection and management of the emergent elements of change as it is about the management of the planned elements. This changes the focus of attention for change agents. Change is about creating a feedback loop between the deliberate and emergent elements of change, which in turn involves working at the level of mediation. This was how the Core Division director facilitated culture change. He responded to staff concerns as they emerged, to address aspects of change that were not supportive of the type of culture he wanted in his division. In this way he used his behaviour as a bridge between the interpretations that were developing and the changes he wanted to achieve. This is not meant to imply that careful up-front planning and analysis is not worth doing. The issue is that transition management is also about keeping an unpredictable process on track, by creating linkages between intended and unintended outcomes of change.

Finally, the theory of mediation raises the issue of a bias for action in planning, the "tendency for action to dominate over legitimating and educational activities" (Pettigrew, 1985). The "process" or human agenda gets pushed to the background by project managers in favour of the content and control agendas (Buchanan & Boddy, 1992). This encourages the development of hard performance measures with a lower emphasis on softer measures such as staff morale and degree of understanding for change. This in turn enables managers to pay less attention to communicating with staff and helping them undertake change if they feel uncomfortable with this role. If, as the theory of mediation suggests, interventions aimed at aiding the processes of mediation are equally important (see above), planning and resourcing needs to allow for change management activities to do with a variety of communication mechanisms, as well as the hard interventions. This could be helped by expressing goals in terms of human issues as well as financial, pushing for the achievement of soft, less easy to measure targets as well as hard targets, and training to overcome the discomfort of dealing with human issues.

CONCLUSION

The purpose of this study was to examine how and why the facilitating and obstructing processes perceived by change recipients during planned strategic change implementation arise over time, and how these interacting processes affect the way the implementation develops. The main findings of the study are that planned change implementation becomes a series of mediated outcomes, rather than a series of planned outcomes, since the change process is underpinned by a cyclical process of recipient sensemaking. As a result intended and unintended change become inextricably linked. These findings advance existing research on change. It is known that change implementation can be an unpredictable process, with both an intentional and emergent character, and that sensemaking activity is important during times of change. The theory of mediation proposed here is able to show *how* such sensemaking activity contributes to the emergent and unpredictable nature of implementation.

One implication of this is that attempting to manage change as a series of stand-alone change initiatives may be inappropriate. Managing change is about facilitating an ongoing process of interpretation development, by recognizing the role of change recipient sensemaking during change. Coincidentally, this corresponds with the demands placed on organizations by their external environment. Many organizations now compete in a dynamic environment driven by the pressures of increasing globalization, which requires them to undergo continual change.

However, facilitating the alignment of interpretations requires a recognition of the centrality of the individual in the change process. Change cannot be reified as something "done" to change recipients. An organization's ability to drive change will depend on its ability to get its employees to align their behaviours and attitudes with the desired goals of change. An increasing danger is that as organizations become increasingly global in their sphere of operation, the centre may become more remote from the employees, at a time when achieving continual change requires them to put in place two-way organizational processes to maintain a better dialogue with their employees, and encourage a deeper understanding of what the organization is trying to achieve. Technological advances in communication, such as satellite broadcasting and electronic communication, which offer organizations an easy way of staying in touch with a globally dispersed workforce, may exacerbate the danger. This research shows that such means of communication are unlikely on their own to be effective when change requires a realignment of interpretations from employees.

Furthermore, the employees are the members of the organization most in touch with the markets and customers. Middle managers in particular play an important role in synthesizing information for top managers on internal and external events (Floyd & Wooldridge, 1992). Maintaining ongoing change to adapt to the dynamic environment in which an organization operates is about recognizing that change recipient experiences may lead them to interpretations that senior managers should know about and act on. Change may also involve senior managers in a realignment of their interpretations.

REFERENCES

Barr, P., Stimpert, J.L. & Huff, A. (1992). Cognitive change, strategic action, and organizational renewal. *Strategic Management Journal*, Summer Special Issue, 15–36.
Bartunek, J.M. & Moch, M.K. (1987). First-order, second-order, and third-order change and organization development interventions: a cognitive approach. *Journal of Applied Behavioural Science*, **23**, 483–500.

Bartunek, J.M., Davidson, B., Greenberg, D.N. & Humphries, M. (1996). Participation, complexity of understanding, and the assessment of organizational change, Academy of Management Meeting, Cincinnati.

Beckhard, R. & Harris, R.T. (1987). *Organizational Transitions*, 2nd edn. Reading, MA: Addison-Wesley.

Beer, M., Eisenstat, R.A. & Spector, B. (1990). *The Critical Path to Organizational Renewal*. Cambridge, MA: Harvard Business School Press.

Berger, P.L. & Luckmann, T. (1966). *The Social Construction of Reality*. New York: Anchor Books.

Bogdan, R. & Taylor, S.J. (1975). *Introduction to Qualitative Research Methods: A Phenomenological Approach to the Social Sciences*. Chichester: John Wiley & Sons.

Bower, J.L. (1970). *Managing the Resource Allocation Process: A Study of Corporate Planning and Investment*. Homewood, IL: Richard D. Irwin.

Brown, S.L. & Eisenhardt, K.M. (1997). The art of continuous change: linking complexity theory and time-paced evolution in relentlessly shifting organizations. *Administrative Science Quarterly*, **42**, 1–34.

Buchanan, D. & Boddy, D. (1992). *The Expertise of the Change Agent: Public Performance and Backstage Activity*. Englewood Cliffs, NJ: Prentice Hall.

Burgess, R.G. (1984). *In the Field: An Introduction to Field Research*. London: George Allen & Unwin.

Daft, R.L. & Weick, K. (1984). Toward a model of organizations as interpretations systems. *Academy of Management Review*, **9**, 284–295.

Deal, T. (1985). Cultural change: opportunity, silent killer or metamorphosis. In R.H. Kilman, M.J. Saxton, R. Serpa & Associates (eds) *Gaining Control of the Corporate Culture*, San Francisco, CA: Jossey-Bass.

Dearborn, D.C. & Simon, H.A. (1958). Selective perception: the identifications of executives. *Sociometry*, **21**, 140–144.

Denzin, N. (1989). *The Research Act: A Theoretical Introduction to Sociological Methods*. Englewood Cliffs, NJ: Prentice Hall.

Fiske, S.T. & Taylor, S.E. (1991). *Social Cognition*, 2nd edn. New York: McGraw-Hill.

Floyd, S. & Wooldridge, B. (1992). Dinosaurs or dynamos? Recognizing middle management's strategic role. *Strategic Management Journal*, **8**, 47–57.

Giddens, A. (1976). *New Rules of Sociological Method*. London: Hutchinson.

Ginsberg, A. (1988). Measuring and modelling changes in strategy: theoretical foundations and empirical directions. *Strategic Management Journal*, **9**, 559–575.

Gioia, D.A. (1986). Symbols, scripts, and sensemaking: creating meaning in the organizational experience. In H.P. Sims & D.A. Gioia (eds), *The Thinking Organization*. San Francisco, CA: Jossey-Bass.

Gioia, D.A. & Chittipeddi, K. (1991). Sensemaking and sensegiving in strategic change initiation. *Strategic Management Journal*, **12**, 433–448.

Glaser, B.G. & Strauss, A.L. (1967). *The Discovery of Grounded Theory: Strategies for Qualitative Research*. Chicago, IL: Aldine.

Huff, A.S. (1982). Industry influences on strategy reformulation. *Strategic Management Journal*, **3**, 119–131.

Huff, J.O., Huff, A.S. & Thomas, H. (1992). Strategic renewal and the interaction of cumulative stress and inertia. *Strategic Management Journal*, **13**, 55–75.

Isabella, L.A. (1990). Evolving interpretations as change unfolds: how managers construe key organizational events. *Academy of Management Journal*, **33**, 7–41.

Jick, T. (1993). *Managing Change: Cases and Concepts*. Homewood, IL: Richard D. Irwin.

Johnson, G. (1987). *Strategic Change and the Management Process.* Oxford: Basil Blackwell.

Johnson, G. (1990). Managing strategic change: The role of symbolic action. *British Journal of Management*, **1**, 183–200.

Kanter, R., Stein, M. & Jick, T. (1992). *The Challenge of Organizational Change.* New York: Free Press.

Kotter, J. (1995). Leading change: why transformation efforts fail. *Harvard Business Review*, March/April, 59–67.

Louis, M. (1980). Surprise and sensemaking: what newcomers experience in entering unfamiliar organizational settings. *Administrative Science Quarterly*, **25**, 226–251.

Miles, M.B. (1983). Qualitative data as an attractive nuisance: the problem of analysis. In Van Maanen, J. (ed.) *Qualitative Methodology.* Beverly Hills, CA: Sage.

Miles, M.B. & Huberman, A.M. (1994). *Qualitative Data Analysis: An Expanded Sourcebook.* Beverly Hills, CA: Sage.

Miller, D. & Friesen, P.H. (1984). *Organizations: A Quantum View.* Englewood Cliffs, NJ: Prentice Hall.

Mintzberg, H. (1978). Patterns in strategy formation. *Management Science*, **24**(9), 934–948.

Moch, M. & Huff, A.S. (1983). Power enactment through language and ritual. *Journal of Business Research*, **11**, 293–316.

Pettigrew, A.M. (1985). *The Awakening Giant: Continuity and Change in ICI.* Oxford: Basil Blackwell.

Pettigrew, A.M. (1990). Longitudinal field research on change theory and practice. *Organization Science*, **1**, 267–292.

Pettigrew, A.M. & Whipp, R. (1991). *Managing Change for Competitive Success.* Oxford: Blackwell.

Pettigrew, A.M., Ferlie, E. & McKee, L. (1992). *Shaping Strategic Change.* London: Sage.

Pfeffer, J. (1981). Management as symbolic action: the creation and maintenance of organizational paradigms. In L.L. Cummings & B. Staw (eds) *Research in Organizational Behaviour*, vol. 3, Greenwich, CT: JAI Press, pp 1–52.

Poole, P., Gioia, D.A. & Gray, B. (1989). Influence modes, schema change, and organizational transformation. *Journal of Applied Behavioural Science*, **25**, 271–289.

Quinn, J.B. (1980). *Strategies for Change: Logical Incrementalism.* Homewood, IL: Richard D. Irwin.

Tichy, N.M. (1983). *Managing Strategic Change: Technical, Political and Cultural Dynamics.* Chichester: John Wiley & Sons.

Trice, H.M. & Beyer, J. (1984). Studying organizational cultures through rites and ceremonies. *Academy of Management Review*, **9**, 653–669.

Van de Ven, A. H. (1992). Suggestions for studying strategy process: a research note. *Strategic Management Journal*, **13**, 169–188.

Weick, K.E. (1979). *The Social Psychology of Organizing*, 2nd edn., Reading, MA: Addison-Wesley.

Weick, K.E. (1995). *Sensemaking in Organizations.* Thousand Oaks, CA; Sage.

5

Collective Thinking in Strategic Change Processes

PIA LINDELL, THOMAS ERICSON, LEIF MELIN

INTRODUCTION

During the past decade, the process of strategic change has received increasing interest from management researchers. A number of studies focusing on the dynamics of strategy making have been carried out to improve our understanding of the phenomenon. However, in most cases strategic change is described as a rather uniform and homogeneous process—either evolutionary or revolutionary, proactive or reactive, rational or political. Such a view does not fully capture the complexity and dialectics of the process. Instead, strategic change should be understood as a combination of different types of processes shaped by the interplay between external forces and internal cognitive, cultural and political processes (Hellgren, Lindell & Melin, 1993; Melin & Hellgren, 1994). This view is based on the assumption of a socially constructed reality in which strategic thinking and acting are created through the interaction between different actors taking part in the process. Hence, the process is shaped by their experiences, interpretations and sensemaking of different events, and their preceding and succeeding actions. This view of strategic change as "chains" of strategic thinking and strategic actions is the point of departure for the study reported here.

New Managerial Mindsets: Organizational Transformation and Strategy Implementation.
Edited by M.A. Hitt, J.E. Ricart i Costa and R.D. Nixon.
© 1998 John Wiley & Sons Ltd.

STRATEGIC CHANGE AND COLLECTIVE THINKING

The cognitive dimension of strategic change has, more explicitly, been recognized since the mid-1980s (Prahalad & Bettis, 1986; Stubbart, 1989). When rational economic approaches have failed cognition has been identified as the missing link in understanding the diversification process (Duhaime & Schwenk, 1985; Jemison & Sitkin, 1986; Prahalad & Bettis, 1986; Kazanjian & Drazin, 1987; Ginsberg, 1990). There are also studies in which managerial cognition and strategic change are more generally discussed (Johnson, 1987; Schwenk, 1989; Gioia & Chittipeddi, 1991; Lyles & Schwenk, 1992; Gioia *et al.*, 1994). A dominating focus in these studies is on how a shared way of thinking emerges among strategic actors in the initiation of strategic change. Gioia & Chittipeddi (1991) use the concepts "sensemaking" and "sensegiving" to characterize this process, which is "simultaneously symbolic and substantive, involving reciprocal processes of cognition and action, and entails cycles of understanding and influence" (p. 447). It can also be influenced by political and organizational factors (Schwenk, 1989). An implicit assumption found in the literature is that a shared way of thinking is necessary for collective action to induce a change. At the same time, shared cognitions are regarded to be difficult to change (Lyles & Schwenk, 1992), which stresses the paradoxical character of the phenomenon. In our own studies of strategic change, we have also found that key actors in organizations think and act in accordance with certain patterns of shared thinking (Melin, 1991; Hellgren & Melin, 1993; Lindell, 1993; Ericson & Melin, 1997).

The phenomenon of shared thinking, which in the following we label *collective thinking*, has also been studied in other organizational studies, although not explicitly related to strategic change (Bougon, Weick & Binkhorst, 1977; Weick, 1979a; Hedberg, 1981; Smircich, 1983; Weick & Roberts, 1993). A number of concepts with different meanings have evolved from different contexts. This indicates that the phenomenon itself is not trivial, is complex, and that there is a need for further study and a more thorough discussion (Schneider & Angelmar, 1993; Weick & Roberts, 1993). As collective thinking may very well play an important role in strategy processes, analysis in a strategic context is important in contributing to our understanding.

RESEARCH QUESTIONS

The literature on collective thinking and strategic change, as well as our own empirical studies, raises several important questions that will be analysed and discussed here. First, what is collective thinking (including our definition of "collective")? What is the relation between the thinking of the individual and collective thinking? Second, if there is something such as collective thinking, how does collective thinking evolve and how does it change? Third, how is collective thinking related to strategic actions, i.e. what is its role in strategic change processes? To summarize, the purpose of this chapter is to identify the meaning and role of collective thinking in strategy processes. Through this focus, the overall aim is to enrich the general understanding of the cognitive dimension of strategic change.

In the following section we describe how the concept of collective thinking is defined and used in the literature and how it can be related to strategic change.

COLLECTIVE THINKING: A MULTIFARIOUS PHENOMENON

As the literature on collective thinking in strategic change is limited, we find it important to start answering our questions from a broader theoretical perspective. This means that we will first give a general presentation of the concept of collective thinking and then relate this knowledge to the process of strategic change.

WHAT IS COLLECTIVE THINKING?

On the individual level "thinking" could be characterized as a process in which we organize and interpret information, thereby creating meaning and making the world understandable (Gioia & Sims, 1986). It is mental structures in which we store knowledge that help us to do this. Usually these structures are considered to be free from emotions and affections. However, the need to take these aspects into consideration is stressed by Sims & Lorenzi (1992). It is argued that they are important in social life. Furthermore, mental structures could be seen as guiding action (Isenberg, 1986) as well as being created or changed by action (Weick, 1983).

If this characterizes thinking on the individual level, what is meant by collective thinking? In order to understand this phenomenon, several concepts have been developed: for example, cognitive consensuality (Gioia & Sims, 1986), organizational schemata (Bartunek & Moch, 1987), paradigm (Johnson, 1987), belief systems (Langfield-Smith, 1992), cause maps (Bougon, Weick & Binkhorst, 1977), shared meanings (Smircich, 1983) and interpretative systems (Daft & Weick, 1984). Most of these concepts are directly transferred from the individual level. This means that collective thinking could be characterized as a mental structure that is shared by individuals forming the collective that helps them to interpret and give meaning to information in the same way. However, even if individuals share some measure of understanding within a collective, research has, at the same time, shown the heterogeneity in individual thinking between actors. This collective thinking can be described as the lowest common denominator of individuals' thinking. From this it is gathered that groups and organizations can develop pluralistic and heterogeneous meanings at the same time that collective thinking can take place. As a consequence, we claim that several identities, cultures and cognitive spheres exist simultaneously within groups and organizations (Alvesson, 1993; Salzer, 1994). Further, collective thinking may not even be limited to a group or an organization (Alvesson & Berg, 1992). Certain beliefs and values can be shared by actors in several organizations, operating in the same industry (Porac, Thomas & Baden-Fuller, 1989; Spender, 1989; Melander, 1997). This means that our discussion on collective thinking refers to any group of actors, with the restriction that the actor is an individual. Hence, if nothing else is stated, the concept "collective" will be synonymous with group and organization.

In the view described here, collective thinking is derived from the thinking of individuals. However, it can also be seen as independent of individuals in as much as collectives might store sets of knowledge in procedures, norms, forms etc. (Duncan & Weiss, 1979; Hedberg, 1981; March, 1991). This makes collective thinking a supra-individual phenomenon. As Hedberg (1981, p. 3) claims, "Organizations do not have brains, but they have cognitive systems and memories". This idea is also found in McDougall's (1920) conceptualization of "group mind". Here the individual subordinates himself to the collective meaning of the group, which is a product of the thinking of the most dominant members. Each individual within the group has to share the group's idea and be emotionally dedicated to it. However, the creation of a strong group mind is, according to McDougall, independent of the homogeneity of the way of thinking and feeling of the individuals comprising the group. Instead, it depends on different factors, which can be summarized in the continuity of the group, its organization and its culture. These factors contribute to making the group and the group mind remain unchanged for a long period of time, despite shifts in group members. From this, it is gathered that it is possible for the individual to be a member of different groups with different minds as long as no rivalry and conflict between them exists. The role of culture as a carrier of collective thinking, preserving it independently of the individuals, is also found in Walsh & Ungson's (1991) concept "organizational memory", which refers to stored information from an organization's history that influences present decisions. Shared interpretations, which facilitate coherent problem solving and decision making, are embedded in systems and artefacts. Hence, time, organization and culture seem to be able to act as carriers of collective thinking, making it independent of the individuals, creating a supra-individual and a rather persistent collective thinking.

As shown earlier, the role of thinking is closely related to that of action. A dominating theme regarding collective thinking and action is that if behavior is to be considered as organized, there has to be some kind of coordination, or overlap, between the sensemaking of several individuals. As Smircich (1983, p. 64) states, "Organizations exist as systems of meanings which are shared to varying degrees. A sense of commonality, or taken for grantedness is necessary for continuing organized activity". Following this line of thought, there has to be some degree of shared meaning among individuals in an organization, since concerted action depends on a certain degree of shared values and understanding of how things are done (Gioia & Sims, 1986). Hence, intersubjective mental maps affect the behavior of the organization as a collective entity. This could be exemplified by McDougall's (1920) idea that an organized group that has developed a shared collective thinking is able to act in a more rational way and hence produce a successful outcome for the group.

However, this view is not the only one that deals with the action–thinking relationship. Other research shows that a group can take collective action even if there is no shared thinking within the group. Building on Weick (1979a), it is argued that a group makes sense in retrospect of the actions made by the group. Instead of sharing meanings, the group can share communication mechanisms that lead to collective action even if group members do not share a common goal underlying the action (Weick, 1979a; Donnellon, Gray & Bougon, 1986). However, following Gray, Bougon & Donnellon (1985) and Langfield-Smith (1992), we must look upon thinking and acting as two processes occurring simultaneously. Langfield-Smith (1992) argues that the development of collective thinking is highly dependent on collective action. Over time, collective action tends to generate collective thinking. This is due to the fact that the action generated by a group functions as a common point of departure for the sensemaking of the individuals within the group. This leads to our next questions: How does collective thinking evolve and how does it change?

How Does Collective Thinking Evolve and How Does it Change?

As indicated in the previous section, collective thinking is often seen as the outcome of interaction between different individuals. As Gray, Bougon & Donnellon (1985, p. 88) state, shared meaning coincides "when, through the course of regular social interaction, members begin to favor one subjective interpretation over others". As development and a change in thinking have to do with the development of (new) knowledge and (new) understanding, the process could also be seen as a learning process (Duncan & Weiss, 1979; Fiol, 1994). On the collective level, this process may result in something more than the cumulative learning of the individuals. This is based on the assumption that, over time, knowledge can be stored in procedures, norms, rules, forms and even myths (Hedberg, 1981; March, 1991). The supra-individual collective thinking thus created is something the individual can both contribute to and become socialized to. This mutual learning may eventually lead to a convergence between the individual's thinking and the thinking of the collective.

In the interaction process, studies have shown that striving for consensus seems to dominate, at least when the collective is relatively small (Nemeth, 1982, 1986). Regarding the relation between the individual's thinking and the collective's thinking, the adaptation of the former is brought about through active participation; that is, through both cognitive learning and cognitive rehearsal (Myers & Lamm, 1976; Myers, 1982). The assumption here is that "a thought is not a thought unless it is one's own" (Myers & Lamm, 1976, p. 617). In this process, a vision may act as a unifying force and sensegiving tool (Westley & Mintzberg, 1989; Collin & Porras, 1991; Gioia & Chittipeddi, 1991). Usually the process of adaptation means that the individual's thinking is adapted to the majority's (Nemeth, 1986). The adaptation is influenced by the individual's wish to conform with the positive expectations of others (Deutsch & Gerard, 1955) and to present himself favourably (Myers & Lamm, 1976). Another influencing factor is that individuals tend to accept information from others as evidence of reality (Deutsch & Gerard, 1955), where information tends to favour the initially preferred alternative (Myers & Lamm, 1976; Myers, 1982). An observed result of social interaction in small groups is that the exchange of arguments in a discussion even tends to enhance the dominating initial view in the group. If, on the other hand, the minority view comes to dominate, it will rather depend on the behavioural style of that group, e.g. the consistency of position over time and the confidence with which it is held (Nemeth, 1986). The forces and processes mentioned here have similarities with the political processes that play an important role in organizational life (Schwenk, 1989; Pfeffer, 1992) and which are considered an influence on collective thinking (Schwenk, 1989).

This discussion on the relation between the individual and the collective in the interaction process could also be compared with group learning, which may take place in a group characterized by frequent interaction and where knowledge and experience is continuously shared (such as a group of specialized physicians in a hospital). The group develops a shared cognitive frame, with shared understandings and tacitly coordinated behaviour (Miner & Mezias, 1996), and with a memory which differentiates this group from other groups. An interpretation here is that the outcome of the interaction process, the collective thinking, is genuinely shared by the individuals comprising the group. This is similar to the idea that the action generated by a group functions as a common point of departure for the sensemaking of the individuals within the group (Langfield-Smith, 1992).

However, the adaptation of an individual's attitudes to the group's is dependent on the individual's more deeply rooted values regarding the issue discussed and his relation to the group (Zaleska, 1982). If the individual continues to interact with the group it may lead to a "genuine change" in attitude. This is similar to what we have found in our studies on strategists' way-of-thinking (Hellgren & Melin, 1993; Lindell *et al.*, 1998). Our studies show that stable beliefs held by an individual act as a frame within which (the "core") changes are possible. On the other hand, Lyles & Schwenk (1992) divide the knowledge held by management into a relatively stable core and a more changeable peripheral set. Related to strategic change, this implies that the process is facilitated by the loose coupling between the core and the peripheral set. Our findings suggest that the scope of change is limited by the frame.

Thus, even if consensus is reached within a group, which could be described as collective thinking, it does not necessarily mean that the individual incorporates the thinking as his own. Therefore, distinguishing between consensus and the relative strength of a belief in a taken position is necessary (Stasser & Davis, 1981). The strength also relates to the changeability of the thinking in that a weaker belief, as in the core in our conceptualization, should be easier to change. However, the changeability might be influenced by emotions, as such forces may enhance commitment to beliefs (Sims & Lorenzi, 1992). This indicates that strategic change is difficult due to management's engagement in and emotional commitment to the present strategy, especially if the strategy is genuinely shared by the management; that is, based on their more deeply rooted values and attitudes.

The outcome of the interaction process, the collective thinking, can also be discussed in terms of quality and change regarding the collective as an entity. In Janis' (1972, p. 9) conceptualization of "groupthink", defined as "a mode of thinking that people engage in when they are deeply involved in a cohesive in-group", the wish to reach a complete agreement even results in poor performance of the group as different viewpoints are suppressed in the process, usually in favour of the ideas of the group leader. A similar reasoning is found in the convergent mode of thinking, which is "an activity of comparing and evaluating ideas" (Scheidel, 1986, p. 118). In convergent thinking the proposed ideas are taken into consideration, which may lead to "an unreflective acceptance of the majority position" (Nemeth, 1986, p. 23). In divergent thinking different viewpoints are considered and even encouraged. This will, according to Nemeth (1986), result in greater thought about the issue and hence better decision makers.

The idea that the outcome of the interaction process differs according to whether or not new aspects and alternatives are taken into consideration is similar to March's (1991) two modes of learning, labelled "exploration" and "exploitation". Exploration implies experimentation with new alternatives and ignorance of precedent rules and expectations. Exploitation, which is more common, is the refinement and extension of existing competencies. Most organizations have difficulties in finding the most fruitful tradeoff between these two learning modes, which means that there are often tendencies to increase exploitation and reduce exploration. Such a learning pattern makes "adaptive processes potentially self-destructive" (March, 1991, p. 73). Levitt & March (1988) talk about "competency traps" where an organization acquires short-term gains from continuing to develop current competencies, but runs the risk of being unable to move to a new, required competency (Miner & Mezias, 1996). Once again, this stresses the difficulties in changing collective thinking. The importance of openness towards different viewpoints in order to create change is also discussed by Fiol (1994), who argues that to promote the development of new knowledge and understanding (collective learning), "managers must actively encourage the development of different and conflicting views of what is thought to be true, while striving for a shared framing of the issues that is broad enough to encompass those differences" (1994, p. 418).

Following this line of thought, change in collective thinking, in terms of new knowledge and understanding, is both crucial and difficult to produce, and it is a process that seems to need thoughtful management. However, a collective may use two other types of knowledge acquisition, the vicarious type of learning, where one organization (collectives) borrows from or imitates others and the grafting type, where organizations (collectives) increase their store of knowledge by acquiring new members or a whole organization (collective) that possess different knowledge (Huber, 1991). This could be compared with an organization that copies a successful strategy or shifts management in order to create strategic change, or with two companies that merge. However, due to the interaction process and the role of the individuals' more deep-rooted values and beliefs in this process, this way of changing collective thinking may be rather difficult. One can expect that the imported collective thinking, including memory, is specific for that collective as well as for the importing organization. Therefore, one may assume that the interaction process must imply that these collective-specific memories create the basis for the joint development of a new shared storage of collective interpretations. This implies that there is need for experimentation and openness towards different viewpoints.

HOW IS COLLECTIVE THINKING RELATED TO STRATEGIC CHANGE?

In the previous sections, the relation between collective thinking and strategic change has been indicated mainly in terms of the difficulties in creating strategic change due to different characteristics of collective thinking and collective action. However, as shown, collective thinking can be characterized as a rather elusive phenomenon. It is complex and multifarious and it appears not only in the shape of genuine consensus, necessary for creating concerted action. Furthermore, the very need for collective thinking in order to create collective action or learning might be questioned. In short, it seems as if collective thinking can be either supra-individual or dependent on individuals, stable over time or temporary, general or issue-specific, genuinely shared or adopted, created through action or an action creator. This indicates that different types of collective thinking may be identified—types which may improve our understanding of collective thinking and its role in the process of strategic change.

Based on the discussion in the previous sections, other basic characteristics can be identified. Regarding our first question—What is collective thinking?—a basic definition, that can, at least implicitly, be found in the literature, is illustrated by the following: a shared manner within which a collective interprets and gives meaning to a certain event or issue or set of events and issues at a certain point in time. However, the extent to which the individuals genuinely share the thinking of the collective may vary. In a genuinely shared collective thinking there is homogeneity concerning deep-rooted values and beliefs within the collective. However, collective thinking might have the character of a manual adopted by the individuals and used to handle the actual events or issues in a collective manner. The reasons for the individuals might be political, or simply that they are commanded to. This gives an illusion of consensus and heterogeneity in the individuals' genuine thinking regarding the event or issue. It also means that, in some sense, collective thinking exists independently of individuals; that is, it is supra-individual. It is something that the individual adopts or subordinates to but not necessarily contributes to or shares.

The character of the collective thinking is also related to how it has evolved and thus to how it changes. What is identified at a certain point in time as collective thinking can over time be influenced by discussions, exchange of information and other actions; that is, the process of social interaction or learning. In the same way, collective thinking may emerge from the process if there is no shared thinking at the start. The process may result in different outcomes, which do not necessarily correspond to the thinking of the individuals and that of the collective. For each, the thinking may remain unchanged, be strengthened or change. If there is no genuine consensus at the start, it takes time to develop as it depends on the individuals' more deeply rooted values and their relations to the issue and to the collective. In the same way, a genuine change is difficult to produce. It is facilitated if there is an openness to different viewpoints in the process. However, political and organizational forces might influence the process and create an illusion of genuine consensus. As it is not genuinely shared, this type of collective thinking should be easier to change, but it may also become genuine through the interaction process. Another important aspect is the role of actions that express the collective thinking and preserve it in structures, systems, norms and traditions. Through this, the collective thinking and its supra-individual character is strengthened. However, collective thinking can also be of a more temporary and issue-specific nature.

The more basic characteristics of collective thinking presented above are based on the theoretical state of the art, but what is possible to find in practice, and more specifically in the process of strategic change? In order to further develop our understanding, we will use three longitudinal and in-depth case studies as a base for interpretation and enrichment of the phenomenon of collective thinking and its relation to strategic change. Through the integration of the findings from the literature review and from our case studies we will generate our conclusions. Relevant data from the case studies will be presented below as empirical illustrations of collective thinking in strategic processes in practice.

A TYPOLOGY OF COLLECTIVE THINKING

A NOTE ON METHODOLOGY

This study uses an interpretative approach for generating theory, where the output of the analysis is highly dependent on the researcher's ability to develop relevant theoretical statements in an iterative process with empirical insights. The bases for the empirical illustrations used in this chapter are longitudinal, in-depth case studies of strategic change in three different, large organizations—a university hospital, a department store chain and a multinational diversified company. The period studied in each case covers between 6 and 20 years of strategic change. The studies are in part historical reconstructions and in part real-time studies, where events in strategic processes were observed as they happened. We had very good access to the organizations studied, where we used both direct observation and in-depth interviews, supplemented with different documents from both external and internal sources. With this approach, we have been able to capture change processes both from the formation phase, where strategic ideas emerged, and from the implementation phase, where ideas of strategic change were to be realized within the organizations studied. Furthermore, this means that we have been able to capture not only strategic actions but also the thinking of individuals (e.g. CEOs and different managers) and of different groups (e.g. management teams). In the following section we present three illustrations from what could be interpreted as collective thinking.

COLLECTIVE THINKING: EMPIRICAL ILLUSTRATIONS

Swedish Match, a Multinational Diversified Company

Swedish Match, a multinational diversified company, has its main activities in consumer goods. In the mid-1970s the company found itself in a severe crisis as a result of an almost uncontrolled expansion in one of its businesses and the recession that succeeded the oil crisis. A new CEO and a new top management team were appointed. After some "emergency" actions, a new strategy including structural changes emerged after a thorough examination of each division. In this process, the top management team worked very closely with the management of the divisions. One might say that they acted as one team. During the following years, collaboration continued. The divestment of approximately half of the activities with a simultaneous corresponding expansion in the areas given priority occurred. During this process, the strategy had to be adjusted due to environmental changes and other conditions that turned out to be different to what was expected. After nearly ten years of hard work, a shared view on how the company should be managed had evolved including a number of critical factors for success. This was considered to facilitate strategic actions within the company. The CEO commented on this in the following terms: "We have a shared view on how to create profitability in mature markets. We seldom disagree when we face strategic problems. We also have a shared view on management and leadership".

In this illustration, the shared view can be interpreted as a genuine consensus on how the company should be managed as the strategic actors thought and acted in a similar way regarding strategic issues. Shared thinking had evolved through a continuous process of simultaneous thinking and acting. Hence, it could be characterized as the outcome of a learning process in which new knowledge was created. It is interesting to note that there was no shared thinking at the start of the strategic change process and the actors had no deeply-rooted individual beliefs concerning the strategic issues and no past prestigious commitments to the organization.

The University Hospital

In July 1992, it was decided that a new organizational structure was to be implemented at Linköping University Hospital. Until then, the hospital was made up of more than 40 relatively autonomous and specialized clinical departments, all reporting directly to the top manager of the hospital. In this change process, the purpose was to create an organizational structure that was made up of a number of so-called centres. A number of highly specialized clinical departments were to be gathered and integrated in larger organizational units, i.e. centres. In order to manage the further development of the centres, a manager was selected for each centre. All new centre managers were physicians within the hospital. Simultaneously, centre management teams were selected for each centre. These teams consisted of representatives from each of the clinical departments within the centre, from the administrators, from the staff, and the manager of the centre. We focused on the change process in one of the centres in the hospital organization.

In the change process, the aim of the centre manager was to create a management team where a genuine consensus prevailed prior to any decisions being made. However, due to different meanings, it was difficult to reach an agreement on the issues on the agenda. As a result, no decisions were made. The irresoluteness of the management team led to a stretched financial situation for the centre, and consequently a more pronounced pressure to change. The hospital manager insisted that the centre management team had to show results. In order to force the change process, external consultants were hired. However, the irresoluteness of the management team remained. Since the members of the centre management team refused to accept the changes, the hospital manager intervened. The hospital manager emphasized that the new organizational structure should be implemented even if there was strong resistance; that is, the decision was commanded and hence a result of a hierarchical process.

This case illustrates a situation in which there was no shared thinking regarding the issue at the start, and no genuinely shared thinking was produced through the interaction process, at least not within the time frame allowed by the top management of the hospital. As it was a crucial issue, meaning something quite new, it affected the deeply-rooted values of the individuals within the collective, which in addition was newly formed with members with different backgrounds. This supports what is found in the literature on the difficulty of changing the thinking and that genuine change takes time—time, which at least in this case, was not acceptable. Further, as the new organizational structure is now being implemented, it could be characterized as a manual used by the actors making them act, though not genuinely think, in a collective way. Only time will show whether it is to be genuinely shared through the interaction process. Hence, collective action in this illustration can be interpreted as being produced through the hierarchical structure and as being only an illusion of collective thinking.

Åhléns, a Department Store Chain

Åhléns is the only remaining department store chain in Sweden. This sector was most successful in the 1960s. At the beginning of the 1980s the company found itself in the midst of a crisis and there was a need for change. A new

CEO, who had no previous professional experience of consumer goods and retailing, was appointed with the mission to restructure Åhléns. The company had had profitability problems since the end of the 1960s, when a recession caused severe problems for the sector. At the same time, successful new retailing concepts were introduced, e.g. the externally located hypermarket and the centrally managed retail chain. These concepts started to outcompete department store chains during the 1970s. However, in Åhléns the old concept for success, which had evolved since the 1930s, remained unchanged. In short, it could be described in terms of centrally located department stores, decentralization, a broad assortment (general merchandising and food), low price and volume. The concept had become genuinely shared by managers at all levels and most of them had been socialized in it from the beginning of their professional careers. Over the years, the concept had been strengthened and manifested through strategic actions. At the end of the 1970s, the company had more than 100 stores located in Swedish town centres.

At the beginning of the 1980s, this concept met the way-of-thinking of the newly appointed CEO, which was inspired by the success recipes of the industry (Lindell, 1993). It involved stressing an upgraded and a centrally managed retail chain-like concept, contradictory to the established idea shared within the organization and to its expression in the structures, the systems and the culture. At that time, most of the managers had been with the company for at least twenty years and their average age was relatively high. Despite this mismatch between the "old concept" and the new, strategic actions were taken by the organization, changing the assortment, the structures and the systems in accordance with the new ideas. The number of stores was reduced from 120 to 80. The focus of the change was on general merchandising (50% of the turnover), especially clothing. But an upgraded concept was also introduced for the food division. The change also involved the structure of the organization, which meant that the managers of the department stores lost their power. To support the change process management training programmes were introduced. However, the strategy was never fully accepted, which affected the execution of the actions, and the expected profitability failed to appear. The old idea overshadowed the strategic change process and made it run less smoothly. Finally, this contributed to a new change of direction in 1988, which in short meant "back to basics". The new direction was introduced by a new CEO who had started his professional career in Åhléns 30 years earlier.

This illustration, describing the "old concept", could be interpreted as a genuine consensus on how to manage the company. However, it encompassed not only values and beliefs but structures and systems as well. It was a product of history and difficult to change, despite different kinds of external forces. Over the years the thinking and the actions had reinforced each other in one direction. The collective thinking that evolved from this process could be characterized as supra-individual.

Another observation in the Åhléns' illustration is that even if there is a genuine consensus, this can be subordinated to a new way of thinking commanded through the hierarchical structure. Hence, this is another example in which genuine consensus does not seem to be necessary for collective action. However, as indicated in the case, the quality of the actions might be questioned, as the actors might not understand or commit themselves to the new ideas—especially in a case like Åhléns, in which the new concept was contradictory to the old.

THREE BASIC TYPES OF COLLECTIVE THINKING

Based on the literature and the empirical illustrations, in this section we will identify three different types of collective thinking—the genuine consensus, the organizational heritage and the hierarchical type—which contribute to our understanding of the role of collective thinking in the strategic change process.

Genuine Consensus

In the empirical illustrations we have identified different types of what might be characterized as collective thinking following what is found in the literature. In the first and last illustrations (Swedish Match and Åhléns) there seems to have been a consensus on how the companies should be managed strategically—that is, a shared thinking between the strategic actors on how to interpret and give meaning to issues and events relating to strategy, and how to act on these. Further, it could be characterized as a genuine consensus because the actors had a very strong belief in it. A genuine consensus is the implicit characteristic of collective thinking in most of the literature. It takes time to evolve if it is not present, and once established it is difficult to change because it is anchored in the deeply-rooted beliefs and values of the individuals that form the collective. Hence, genuine consensus might be present more by coincidence within a collective when it faces a certain issue or it can be the outcome of a learning process in which chains of thinking and acting have interacted. One might expect that the former will be the case when the actors have a similar background, i.e. education or profession—that is, when each individual has been socialized in a similar way of thinking outside that of the collective in focus. As the genuine consensus is derived from the thinking of the individuals, it might also be dependent on how controversial the issue or event is and if it is simple or more complex; that is, how difficult it is to understand. A less controversial and/or simpler issue might be easier to have a shared view on. This corresponds to the idea that the thinking of the individual consists of more stable beliefs as well as more changeable ones (e.g. Lyles & Schwenk, 1992; Hellgren & Melin, 1993; Lindell *et al.*, 1998). Relating to our own studies, these show that the more stable beliefs held by an individual act as a frame within which changes in other beliefs are possible (Hellgren & Melin, 1993; Lindell *et al.*, 1998). It can be argued that if the issue or event concerns the more changeable part of each individual's way of thinking, it might be easier to reach a genuine consensus within the collective. If a genuine consensus is the outcome of a learning process this might have created values and beliefs that are part of each individual's frame of thinking and hence more difficult to, at least, change radically.

In both illustrations showing genuine consensus, it was the outcome of several years of interaction between the individuals forming the collective. In the Swedish Match illustration there was no shared thinking present at the start of the change process, at least not in terms of shared thinking anchored in the frames of the individual's way of thinking. Hence, it would have been easier to create. The long time scale can be explained by the difficulty of the issue—the overall strategy of the company. In the Åhléns illustration we can identify a genuine consensus regarding the strategic issue that evolved over decades and was based on the frames of thinking of the strategic actors. Hence, as shown in the illustration, the genuine consensus was difficult to change.

Based on the literature, focusing on the phenomenon of collective thinking and the support concluded by our findings in the empirical illustrations, we claim that there is a type of collective thinking that can be labelled *genuine consensus*. The genuine consensus is derived from the thinking of the individuals forming the collective and implies homogeneity in values and beliefs. It might be present more by coincidence within a collective when faced with a certain issue or it can be the outcome of a learning process. It depends on the background of the individuals and on how controversial and complex the issue or event is. The more complex and/or controversial the issue is from the individuals' point of view, the more difficult it is to create a genuine consensus if it is not present when the issue is faced. If a shared view exists on these premises, the more difficult it is to change. On the other hand, a genuine consensus might be easier to create and/or change if the issue is simple and/or less controversial. This also makes the character of the genuine consensus more temporary.

Organizational Heritage

In the Åhléns illustration we identify another type of collective thinking. In this case, collective thinking had become something more than a consensus based on the thinking of the individuals. One might say that it had gained a supra-individual character. The idea that collective thinking can be carried by the culture, in a broad sense, is found in conceptualizations such as "group mind" (McDougall, 1920) and "organizational memory" (Walsh & Ungson, 1991). This is also similar to the idea that an organization can learn in terms of storing knowledge in procedures, norms etc. (Duncan & Weiss, 1979; Hedberg, 1981; March, 1991). Hence, this type of collective thinking might be released from the individuals' way of thinking. Collective action in this case is not created through genuine consensus but through established structures, norms and procedures, which are the product of a former collective thinking (cf. Donnellon, Gray & Bougon, 1986; Weick, 1979b). That is, individuals might subordinate themselves to a collective thinking they do not genuinely share or contribute to. This gives an illusion of consensus. However, it might be genuinely shared by the individuals as in the Åhléns illustration. Together, these characteristics make it difficult to change as it is based on both the thinking of the individuals and on the structures, norms and procedures of the organization. If it is not shared, it might be due to the learning process, even if it is, as shown, both difficult and time-consuming. This process may also result in a new collective thinking, leaving new imprints in the organization. Following the literature and the findings in the Åhléns illustration, we will argue that it is meaningful to see this as a type of collective thinking, which we, due to its characteristics, label *the organizational heritage* type.

Illusionary Consensus: The Hierarchical Type

In the second illustration (the University Hospital) there was no genuine consensus on the issue faced by the collective. In this case, the collective was newly formed and the members had different backgrounds. Regarding the issue, there was no shared thinking present when it surfaced. It even challenged the individuals' ways of thinking in terms of their deep-rooted values and beliefs regarding the issue. Despite frequent discussions within the collective, no consensus emerged. This once again shows how difficult it is to create a genuine consensus, especially when the issue is complex and controversial from the individuals' point of view and under a limited amount of time. Due to the difficulties and to force action, the top management of the University Hospital commanded the collective to accept a certain view regarding the issue. The individuals subordinated themselves to this imposed view that forced them to act in a collective way. However, their deep-rooted values and beliefs were, at least not to begin with, changed accordingly. Thus, the thinking that was established could be characterized as supra-individual. This is in correspondence with the ideas presented in the previous section on organizational heritage. Even if the thinking is not genuinely shared within the collective, it functions as collective thinking. The individuals use it as a manual to interpret and give meaning to events and issues, and it serves as a base for collective action. In other words, it gives an illusion of genuine consensus in the collective. Thus, with support from the literature, we will label this form of collective thinking *the hierarchical* type. This is a collective thinking that is imposed on the collective through the organizational structure. This collective thinking represents an illusionary consensus. It should be stressed that this type might also be changed due to the process of learning resulting in a changed and/or genuinely shared collective thinking.

DISCUSSION

Based on the literature and our empirical illustrations, we have been able to identify three types of collective thinking with different characteristics. As opposed to the dominant view in the literature, collective thinking is not always derived from the thinking of the individuals that form a collective. Thus, collective thinking can be supra-individual. By showing the multifarious character of collective thinking, we argue that the three types contribute to our understanding of the phenomenon and its relation to collective action. However, we do not claim that this typology is complete. There may very well be other characteristics and/or types, but the ones presented here help us to shed light upon some important issues regarding collective thinking and strategic action. First, consensus is not a uniform concept, as it might be either genuine or illusionary. A genuine consensus is based in the participating individuals' shared and deep-rooted values and beliefs. An illusionary consensus represents rather the thinking a group of individuals have subordinated themselves to or adopted for different reasons. However, in both cases it serves as a basis for collective action. It could be questioned whether the illusionary consensus can be characterized as collective thinking, but as it functions as a collective thinking mechanism and there is support in the literature, we argue that it is both possible and relevant, and improves the understanding of the role of collective thinking in the strategic context.

Second, the type of consensus—genuine or illusionary—might affect the quality of the collective actions taken, which is illustrated in the description of Åhléns. One might assume that genuine consensus will result in better executed actions as they are based on the individuals' deep-rooted values and beliefs. This also relates to the behavioural learning view, where the degree to which the organization adapts to external events is a measure of the quality of the learning (Dodgson, 1993). This view is questioned by others, who argue that learning means changes in cognitive structures (e.g. Fiol, 1994). Thus, this would be an interesting issue for further research.

Finally, whether the consensus is genuine or illusionary has basically to do with the individuals' relationship both to the strategic issue and to the collective group, in terms of cognitive, bureaucratic and political processes. Thus, the typology of collective thinking can be improved by a further understanding of these processes.

COLLECTIVE THINKING AND STRATEGIC CHANGE

As cognitive processes are an important dimension of strategic change, we argue that our findings regarding the relationship between collective thinking and strategic action increase both our understanding of these processes, and the possibilities to manage them. To date, most of the literature on strategic change has focused on how consensus is reached in the beginning of a change process under the influence of different factors. This is described in the processes of sensemaking and sensegiving (Gioia & Chittipeddi, 1991). Implicated in this view is the assumption that consensus is a necessary condition for successful strategic change. Another implicit assumption is that strategic change is a step-wise process, and once consensus is established regarding the new strategy, the succeeding process is facilitated. However, the typology on collective thinking emphasizes the differences in consensus and indicates its consequences for collective strategic action. Hence, we find a more nuanced view on the conditions for successful implementation. In commenting on strategic change, one of the CEOs in our cases stated that "People do change over night if they are told to". According to our typology, this might be true, but as the consensus is most probably illusionary, the quality of the actions taken might be questioned. Furthermore, the typology also shows that if a genuine consensus is not present within the collective, such as a management team, when a certain strategic issue is faced, it takes time and resources to develop. On the other hand, if collective consensus of this genuine type is present it takes time to change it. This stresses the paradoxical nature of management's striving for both genuine consensus and for change, and the need for a balance between these efforts. This corresponds to what in the learning literature is discussed as the problem of the balance between the use of old competencies (exploitation) and the search for new (exploration) (March, 1991).

The findings presented here show that, independent of whether the consensus is genuine or not, the individuals' ability to change their ways of thinking is crucial in situations of strategic change. Furthermore, this ability seems to be dependent on the interaction within the collective group (in our cases mainly the management team). Thus, our understanding of collective thinking and strategic action can be further improved with better knowledge on how we learn in groups and especially how we learn to learn, that is, the processes of exploration (March, 1991) and deutero-learning (Argyris & Schön, 1978).

REFERENCES

Alvesson, M. (1993). *Cultural Perspectives on Organizations.* Cambridge: Cambridge University Press.

Alvesson, M. & Berg, P.O. (1992). *Corporate Culture and Organizational Symbolism.* Berlin: Walter de Gruyter.

Argyris, C. & Schön, D.A. (1978). *Organizational Learning: A Theory of Action Perspective.* Reading, MA: Addison Wesley.

Bartunek, J.M. & Moch, M.K. (1987). First-order, second-order, and third-order change and organizational development interventions: a cognitive approach. *Journal of Applied Behavioral Science*, **23**(4), 483–500.

Bougon, M.G., Weick, K.E. & Binkhorst D. (1977). Cognitions in organizations: an analysis of the Utrecht Jazz Orchestra. *Administrative Science Quarterly*, **22**(4), 606–639.

Collin, J.C. & Porras, J.I. (1991). Organizational vision and visionary organizations. *California Management Review*, **34**(1), 30–52.

Daft, R.L. & Weick, K.E. (1984). Toward a model of organizations as interpretation systems. *Academy of Management Review*, **9**(2), 284–295.

Deutsch, M. & Gerard, H.G. (1955). A study of normative and informational social influence upon individual judgement. *Journal of Abnormal and Social Psychology*, **51**, 629–636.

Dodgson, M. (1993). Organizational learning: a review of some literatures. *Organization Studies*, **14**(3), 375–394.

Donnellon, A., Gray, B. & Bougon, M.G. (1986). Communication, meaning, and organized action. *Administrative Science Quarterly*, **31**(1), 43–55.

Duhaime, I.M. & Schwenk, C.R. (1985). Conjectures on cognitive simplification in acquisition and divestment decision making. *Academy of Management Review*, **10**, 287–295.

Duncan, R. & Weiss, A. (1979). Organizational learning—implications for organizational design. In B. Staw (ed.), *Research in Organizational Behavior*, Vol. 1. Greenwich, CT: JAI Press.

Ericson, T. & Melin, L. (1997). Processes of divisionalization and actors' way-of-thinking—strategic change in hospital organizations, paper presented at the Advances in Management conference, Toronto, July.

Fiol, C.M. (1994). Consensus, diversity, and learning in organizations. *Organization Science*, **5**(3), 403–420.

Ginsberg, A. (1990). Connecting diversification to performance: a sociocognitive approach. *Academy of Management Review*, **15**(3), 514–535.

Gioia, D.A. & Chittipeddi, K. (1991). Sensemaking and sensegiving in strategic change initiation. *Strategic Management Journal*, **12**(6), 433–448.

Gioia, D.A. & Sims, H.P., Jr (1986). Introduction: Social cognition in organizations. In H.P. Sims & D.A. Gioia (eds) *The Thinking Organization: Dynamics of Organizational Social Cognition.* San Francisco, CA: Jossey Bass.

Gioia, D.A., Thomas, J.B., Clark, S.M. & Chittipeddi, K. (1994). Symbolism and strategic change in academia: the dynamics of sensemaking and influence. *Organization Science*, **5**(3), 363–383.

Gray, B., Bougon, M.G. & Donnellon, A. (1985). Organizations as constructions and destructions of meaning. *Journal of Management*, **11**(2), 83–98.

Hedberg, B.L. (1981). How organizations learn and unlearn. In P.C. Nyström & W.H. Starbuck (eds) *Handbook of Organizational Design.* London: Oxford University Press.

Hellgren, B. & Melin, L. (1993). The role of strategists' way-of-thinking in strategic change processes. In G. Johnson, J. Hendry & J. Newton (eds) *Strategic Thinking: Leadership and the Management of Change*. Chichester: John Wiley & Sons.

Hellgren, B., Lindell, P. & Melin, L. (1993). Strategic change as a prism of different perspectives—integrating multiple theoretical perspectives, paper presented at the *13th Annual Strategic Management Society Conference*, Chicago, September.

Huber, G.P. (1991). Organizational learning—the contributing processes and the literatures. *Organization Science*, **2**, 88–115.

Isenberg, D.J. (1986). The structure and process of understanding: implications for managerial action. In H.P. Sims & D.A. Gioia (eds) *The Thinking Organization: Dynamics of Organizational Social Cognition*. San Francisco, CA: Jossey Bass.

Janis, I. (1972). *Victims of Groupthink: A Psychological Study of Foreign-Policy Decisions and Fiascoes*. Boston, MA: Houghton Mifflin.

Jemison, D.B. & Sitkin, S.B. (1986). Corporate acquisitions: a process perspective. *Academy of Management Review*, **11**, 145–163.

Johnson, G. (1987). *Strategic Change and the Management Process*. New York: Basil Blackwell.

Kazanjian, R.K. & Drazin, R. (1987). Implementing internal diversification: contingency factors for organization design choices. *Academy of Management Review*, **12**, 342–354.

Langfield-Smith, K. (1992). Exploring the need for a shared cognitive map. *Journal of Management Studies*, **29**(3), 349–368.

Levitt, B. & March, J.G. (1988). Organizational learning, *Annual Review Sociology*, **14**, 319–340.

Lindell, P. (1993). Thinking, Acting, and Transformation—The case of Åhléns, Üa Swedish department store chain, paper presented at the *British Academy of Management Annual Conference*, Milton Keynes, September.

Lindell, P., Melin, L., Gamberg, J., Hellqvist, A. & Melander, A. (1998). Stability and change in a strategist's thinking. In E. Collin & J.C. Spender (eds) *Managerial and Organizational Cognition*. London: Sage.

Lyles, M.A. & Schwenk, C.R. (1992). Top management, strategy and organizational knowledge structures. *Journal of Management Studies*, **29**(2), 155–174.

March, J. (1991). Exploration and exploitation in organizational learning. *Organization Science*, **2**(1), 71–87.

McDougall, W., (1920). *The Group Mind*. Cambridge: Cambridge University Press.

Melander, A. (1997). Industrial wisdom and strategic change—the Swedish pulp and paper industry 1940–1990, Doctoral dissertation, Jönköping International Business School, Department of Management and Business Administration.

Melin, L. (1991). Ledares tänkesätt. In G. Arvidsson & R. Lind (eds) *Ledning av företag och förvaltningar—Förutsättningar, former, förnyelse*. Stockholm: SNS (in Swedish).

Melin, L. & Hellgren, B. (1994). Patterns of strategic processes: two change typologies. In H. Thomas, D. O'Neal, R. White & D. Hurst (eds) *Building the Strategically-Responsive Organization*. Chichester: John Wiley & Sons.

Miner, A.S. & Mezias, S.J. (1996). Ugly duckling no more: pasts and futures of organizational learning research. *Organization Science*, **7**(1), 88–99.

Myers, D.G. (1982). Polarizing effects of social interaction. In H. Brandstätter, J.D. Davis & G. Stocker-Kreichgauer (eds) *Group Decision Making*. London: Academic Press.

Myers, D.G. & Lamm, H. (1976). The group polarization phenomenon. *Psychological Bulletin*, **83**(4), 602–627.

Nemeth, C.J. (1982). Stability of faction position and influence. In H. Brandstätter, J.D. Davis & G. Stocker-Kreichgauer (eds) *Group Decision Making*. London: Academic Press.

Nemeth, C.J. (1986). Differential contributions of majority and minority influence. *Psychological Review*, **93**(1), 23–32.

Pfeffer, J. (1992). Understanding power in organizations. *California Management Review*, **34**(2), 29–50.

Prahalad, C.K. & Bettis, R.A. (1986). The dominant logic: a new link between diversity and performance. *Strategic Management Journal*, **7**(4), 485–501.

Porac, J.F., Thomas, H. & Baden-Fuller, C. (1989). Competitive groups as cognitive communities: the case of Scottish knitwear manufacturers. *Journal of Management Studies*, **26**(4), 297–416.

Salzer, M. (1994). *Identity across borders—a study in the IKEA-world*, Doctoral dissertation, Linköping University, Department of Management and Economics.

Scheidel, T.M. (1986). Divergent and convergent thinking in group decision-making. In R.Y. Hirokawa & M. Scott Poole (eds) *Communication and Group Decision-Making*. Beverly Hills, CA: Sage.

Schneider, S.C. & Angelmar, R. (1993). Cognition in organizational analysis: who's minding the store? *Organization Studies*, **14**(3), 347–374.

Schwenk, C.R. (1989). Linking cognitive, organizational and political factors in explaining strategic change. *Journal of Management Studies*, **26**(2), 177–187.

Sims, H.P. & Lorenzi, P. (1992). *The New Leadership Paradigm*. Newbury Park, CA: Sage.

Smircich, L. (1983). Organizations as shared meanings. In L.R. Pondy, P.J. Frost, G. Morgan & Th. C. Dandridge (eds) *Organizational Symbolism*. Greenwich, CT: JAI Press.

Spender, J.C. (1989). *Industry Recipes: The Nature and Sources of Managerial Judgement*. Oxford: Basil Blackwell.

Stasser, G. & Davis, J.H. (1981). Group decision making and social influence: a social interaction sequence model. *Psychological Review*, **88**(6), 523–551.

Stubbart, C.I. (1989). Managerial cognition: a missing link in strategic management research. *Journal of Management Studies*, **24**(4), 325–347.

Walsh, J.P. & Ungson, G.R. (1991). Organizational memory. *Academy of Management Review*, **16**(1), 57–91.

Weick, K.E. (1979a). *The Social Psychology of Organizing*. Reading, MA: Addison-Wesley.

Weick, K.E. (1979b). Cognitive processes in organizations. *Research in Organizational Behavior*, **1**, 41–74.

Weick, K.E. (1983). Managerial thought in the context of action. In S. Srivastva (ed.) *The Executive Mind*. San Francisco, CA: Jossey-Bass.

Weick, K.E. & Roberts, K.H. (1993). Collective mind in organizations: heedful interrelating on flight decks. *Administrative Science Quarterly*, **38**(3), 357–381.

Westley, F. & Mintzberg, H. (1989). Visionary leadership and strategic management. *Strategic Management Journal*, **10**, 17–32.

Zaleska, M. (1982). The stability of extreme and moderate responses in different situations. In H. Brandstätter, J.D. Davis & G. Stocker-Kreichgauer (eds) *Group Decision Making*. London: Academic Press.

6

Competitive Uses of Information Technology in the Global Environment: A Comparative Study of American, Swedish and Korean Manufacturing Firms

JOHN C. MCINTOSH, EONSOO KIM

INTRODUCTION

Competitive pressures in today's global economy increasingly demand that firms quickly create technologically advanced, customized products at relatively low cost. These objectives often require execution of complex, contradictory tasks such as simultaneously achieving global scale and scope economies while developing differentiated, world-class products. Firms have satisfied these objectives by managing a flexible network of global-

New Managerial Mindsets: Organizational Transformation and Strategy Implementation.
Edited by M.A. Hitt, J.E. Ricart i Costa and R.D. Nixon.

scale value chains composed of geographically far-flung subsidiaries, suppliers, and venture partners. Smooth operation of these chains poses significant managerial challenges. Sophisticated information processing capabilities are necessary for handling large volumes of business transactions and exchanging huge quantities of information across national boundaries. Additionally, significant activity-coordinating capabilities are required to orchestrate the efforts of many culturally diverse actors in the firm's far-flung, highly interconnected web of partners. For example, producing some global products entails surveying customers in diverse geographic contexts to identify the most desirable product features; disseminating this information to, and coordinating the efforts of, often far-flung product design teams; orchestrating the activities of suppliers to ensure that products are created in a timely fashion and at reasonable cost; and providing integrated logistics, inventory management, and order fulfilment to customers worldwide. These extensive and often contradictory requirements can be facilitated by standardizing managerial practices and hardware and software requirements worldwide. Indeed, we are currently witnessing a trend of global convergence in information technology. Nevertheless, differences in national regulations, cultures, and business practices pressure firms to adapt to local conditions.

In this chapter we examine how American, Korean, and Swedish global manufacturing firms use information technology to manage their interconnected webs of subsidiaries, suppliers, and venture partners in pursuit of mass customization and time-based strategies. We undertook this study for three reasons. First, American researchers contend that close coordination between the firm and a network of collaborators is required to successfully execute the preceding strategies (McFarlan, 1984; Cash & Konsynski, 1985; Clemons & McFarlan, 1986; Keen, 1988). The ubiquity of these strategies across firms, regardless of national origin, provides an opportunity to test the universality of this belief. Second, a significant body of research has accumulated over the past decade on how information technology (IT) can provide competitive advantage either by creating new business opportunities or by increasing the efficiency of existing business processes. Much of this work, however, is case-based, disjointed, and shows a conspicuous need for more empirical studies (Powell & Dent-Micallef, 1997). Third, very little research has been conducted on European firms, and virtually none on Asian organizations.

The current state of research on strategic uses of IT—equivocal findings, little work outside the US, and very few comparative studies—motivated us to address the question: Do American, Asian, and European manufacturing firms use information technology in the same way to leverage activities that enable pursuit of time-based and mass customization strategies?

We undertook this exploratory research because there has been so little comparative work. We surveyed a sample of American, Swedish, and

Korean global manufacturing firms to study country-specific choices of IT technologies and patterns of IT use. This chapter uses a small portion of that data to answer the preceding research question. We discovered that there are statistically significant differences in the way firms from different countries use IT to support time-based competition and mass customization. American firms tended to make the most extensive use of IT. Korean firms were close followers, while Swedish firms lagged behind. Business practices, cultural norms, and country-specific forms of organizing affected how firms used IT. American firms, for example, accustomed to efficient markets and high rates of change, used IT to identify appropriate external partners and were less concerned with using it to attenuate opportunism. Swedish firms, on the other hand, supported the established practice of doing business with a number of suppliers worldwide by using IT to reduce coordination costs and mitigate transaction risks. Relatively little emphasis was placed on searching for appropriate partners. Korean firms used IT to support their imitation strategy in the face of rapid technological change and organizational and cultural limitations. High levels of vertical integration characteristic of the Chaebol form and strong social norms which required conducting business with Chaebol mates inhibited rapid development of new capabilities. Korean firms used IT to access new product technologies from externals while maintaining the integrity of the Chaebol.

This chapter is organized as follows. We first identify two sets of factors (strategic enablers and meta-enablers) that support time-based and mass customization strategies. Strategic enablers are critical value chain activities, leverageable by IT, that allow firms to pursue particular strategies. Meta-enablers, on the other hand, are institutional arrangements between the firm and external parties, for example supply relationships and joint ventures, which facilitate performance of value-chain activities. Next, we discuss variable operationalization, instrument design, and respondent selection for a questionnaire which was sent to a sample of American, Korean, and Swedish global manufacturers. We then empirically validate our measures of how IT leverages strategic enablers and meta-enablers, and compare patterns of IT use across countries. We conclude by presenting implications, limitations of the study and future directions.

THEORETICAL FOUNDATIONS OF ENABLERS AND META-ENABLERS

In this exploratory research we drew on the strategic management, manufacturing strategy, and information science literatures to identify strategic enablers that allow firms to pursue time-based and mass customization strategies. Reducing product design time and prototype development time were identified as key enablers of time-based strategies. Market knowledge (information regarding customer tastes and preferences, which can be used to enhance product functionality and performance) and technology knowledge (information concerning technologies, which can be used to translate market needs into actual products) were identified as enablers of mass customization. Information intensive activities associated with finding appropriate partners, coordinating interfirm activities, and mitigating opportunism were identified as meta-enablers common to both time-based and mass customization strategies.

STRATEGIC ENABLERS OF TIME-BASED COMPETITION

Reducing time to market confers three competitive benefits to the firm. Time-sensitive consumers tend to be price-insensitive and are often willing to pay premium prices for first-to-market products. Firms with short product development cycles can incorporate more up-to-date features and technologies in their product offerings, respond faster to shifts in consumer preferences, and capture transient market opportunities (Stalk & Hout, 1990; Pine, 1993). Accelerating the product development process helps to avoid the rising opportunity costs of being late to market (Dumaine, 1989).

FIGURE 6.1 depicts IT's role in leveraging the strategic enablers *product development time* and *manufacturing time* to facilitate time-based competition. By reducing the time to perform these key inputs into the product creation process, the firm is able to reduce its time to market. IT can reduce cycle times for these two activities by allowing work which was formerly performed sequentially to be performed in parallel (Spencer, 1990). Scholars of concurrent engineering note that superior inter- and intra-functional integration, arising from IT, can truncate both product development and

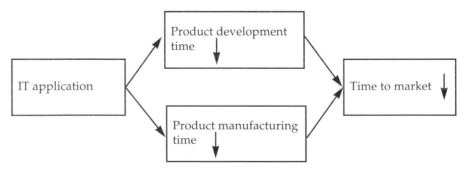

FIGURE 6.1   Use of information technology to leverage strategic enablers and reduce time to market

product manufacturing times (Pennell *et al.*, 1989). Firms may also reduce the length of the development phase by using IT to closely integrate activities between their functional areas and those of external partners who develop components or subsystems (Turino, 1990; DeCastro & Hoogerhuis, 1991; Markowitz, 1991; Sprague, Singh & Wood, 1991). Activity integration also streamlines processes and reduces cycle times by facilitating information flows among actors responsible for product development, design, and manufacture (Hitt, Hoskisson & Nixon, 1993). Finally, IT applications, in the form of computer aided manufacturing (CAM) and computer integrated manufacturing (CIM), can dramatically shorten manufacturing times (Goldhar & Jelinek, 1983; Gomory, 1989; Fawcett, Calantone & Smith, 1994).

STRATEGIC ENABLERS OF MASS CUSTOMIZATION

Mass customization can be enabled in two fundamental ways. First, in the context of existing products, the range of product options (the set of product features and possible levels of product performance) may be expanded to accommodate a larger number of customer tastes and preferences. For example, adding a magneto-optical drive to a personal computer expands its bundle of features and accommodates customers who want to utilize compact disks. In addition, creating product variants based on different performance levels of a key component can also facilitate mass customization. The firm may, for example, use 233, 133, and 90 megahertz microprocessors to create high, medium, and low performance versions of a personal computer. Second, entirely new products may be developed to satisfy actual and latent customer needs.

Strategic enablers of mass customization are market knowledge (information concerning customer tastes and preferences, which may be used to improve existing products or create entirely new ones) and technology knowledge (information concerning technological capabilities, which may be used to translate market knowledge into actual products). This division of inputs to mass customization arises from our conceptualization of the firm as an entity positioned at the boundary between markets and technologies. The firm is believed to scan its environment to gather market knowledge concerning actual and latent customer needs, and technology knowledge concerning existing and emerging capabilities that can be used to create products. The overlap between these two knowledge domains represents the firm's product opportunity set and the products it may create in pursuit of mass customization (McIntosh, 1995).

FIGURE 6.2 depicts how IT can be used to expand the firm's stock of market knowledge and technology knowledge and thereby enlarge its product opportunity set. Area A depicts the firm's product opportunity set prior to using IT. If IT is used to gather better information about tastes and

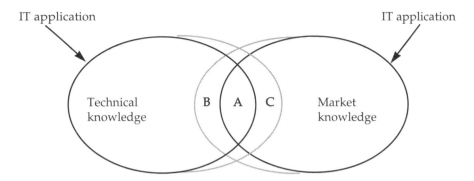

FIGURE 6.2   Use of information technology to increase the firm's knowledge of markets and technologies, and expand its product opportunity set

preferences of existing and potential customers, the firm's stock of market knowledge expands by B. This superior information may be used to create new product features, different levels of product performance, or entirely new products that satisfy a broader set of customer desires (Day, 1990; Glazer, 1991; Blaich & Blaich, 1993; Pine, 1993). When combined with the firm's existing technology knowledge, the product opportunity set enlarges to A+B. If IT is used to gather additional information about technological capabilities, the firm's stock of technology knowledge expands by C. This enhanced knowledge of product and process technologies may be combined with existing market knowledge to create new product features and different levels of product performance (Dixon & Duffey, 1990; Gerwin, 1994). The firm's product opportunity set now expands to A+C. If the firm applies IT to expand its knowledge stocks of both markets and technologies, its product opportunity set expands to A+B+C.

META-ENABLERS

Meta-enablers are institutional arrangements, used to access resources and capabilities of external parties, to facilitate performance of value-chain activities. Unlike strategic enablers, meta-enablers do not directly relate to the value chain activities that support a particular strategy. They are instead concerned with interfirm arrangements that integrate externals in the firm's web of value-chain activities.

Meta-enablers are important because rapidly shrinking process technology life cycles and increasingly transient market opportunities often make technologies obsolete before investment costs are recovered. Firms deal with this contingency by using institutional arrangements, increasingly augmented by IT, to realize the benefits of vertical integration without the risks of internalization (Porter & Millar, 1985; Johnston & Lawrence, 1988; Konsynski & McFarlan, 1990). Closer coordination with externals through IT linkages offers advantages of tightly coupled, stable relationships among firms (Clemons & Row, 1992), vertical quasi-integration (Cash & Konsynski, 1985), economies of scale (Porter & Millar, 1985; Rockart & Short, 1989), and economies of scope (McFarlan, 1984; Keen, 1988).

Although interorganizational coordination offers large strategic benefits, firms face transaction-specific risks (Clemons & Row, 1992). Assets specific to the relationship and specialized human resources may have no economically viable alternate use, and a partner's opportunistic behavior may result in losses. Information technology can, however, mitigate these transaction-specific risks. IT may be used to identify and evaluate potential suppliers and venture partners to ensure that they possess necessary resources and capabilities (Johnston & Vitale, 1988; Rockart & Short, 1989; Benjamin & Wigand, 1995). IT can reduce asset specificity in interfirm interactions (Malone, Yates & Benjamin, 1987; Clemons, Reddi & Row, 1993). Risks arising from close coordination, such as lock in, information asymmetries, and loss of resource control, may also be reduced (Bakos, 1991; Clemons & Row, 1992).

METHODS

In this section we use the preceding enablers and meta-enablers to discuss development of variables and questionnaire items to assess IT's effect on time-based competition and mass customization. We then detail how the survey was developed and how respondents were identified.

VARIABLE DEVELOPMENT

For strategic enablers of time-based competition, we created items that measure how IT leverages inputs into the process of reducing the cycle times of key value-chain activities. For strategic enablers of mass customization, we developed items that measure how IT leverages inputs into the process of expanding the firm's knowledge of markets and technologies. Because meta-enablers focus on facilitating institutional arrangements between the firm and externals, we do not measure inputs into value-chain activities arising from superior coordination with externals. Instead, we measure the information system's influence on interfirm coordination. In particular, we measure IT's impact on costs of finding externals, managing joint activities, and attenuating risk. The reader should note that the variable scores representing strategic enablers and meta-enablers were developed by averaging the response scores of questionnaire items associated with each.

Time-based Competition

We represented the strategic enablers of time-based competition with the variables: *product development time* (DEVTIME) and *manufacturing time* (MFGTIME). TABLE 6.1 presents these two strategic enablers and their associated questionnaire items. DEVTIME, which relates to product design activities, is measured by survey items which assess the role of the firm's information system in reducing time for prototype development and product introduction (Keen, 1988; Clark & Fujimoto, 1991; Pine, 1993). MFGTIME, a variable concerned with the speed of product manufacture, is measured by survey items which assess the information system's role in reducing time for machining, fabrication, and assembly (Gerwin & Tarondeau, 1989; Chang, 1993; Gerwin, 1993).

MASS CUSTOMIZATION

Our concept of the firm as an entity positioned at the boundary of markets and technologies led to the identification of market knowledge and technology knowledge as two key strategic enablers of mass customization. TABLE 6.2 presents each strategic enabler and its associated questionnaire items. We assessed market knowledge with two variables: *customer knowledge* (CUSTKNOW) and *market expeditioning* (EXPEDIT). CUSTKNOW relates to IT's impact on the firm's ability to gather information regarding tastes and preferences of *existing* customers (Wiseman, 1985). Firms engaged in mass customization may use this information to create product options that are finely targeted at customer needs. The variable CUSTKNOW is measured by items which assess the information system's ability to identify desires among existing customers for additional product features and higher levels of product performance.

TABLE 6.1   Strategic enablers of time-based competition and associated questionnaire items

Strategic enabler	Questionnaire items
Product development time (DEVTIME)	Extent to which IT reduces prototype development time
Product manufacturing time (MFGTIME)	Extent to which IT reduces new product introduction time Extent to which IT reduces time to manufacture a new product Extent to which IT reduces new product machining time Extent to which IT reduces new product assembly time

TABLE 6.2 Strategic enablers of mass customization and associated questionnaire items

Strategic enabler	Questionnaire items
Market knowledge (CUSTKNOW)	IT's ability to identify customer desires for additional product features
	IT's ability to identify customer desires for higher product performance
Market knowledge (EXPEDIT)	IT's impact on firm's ability to discover new product categories
	IT's impact on firm's ability to discover emerging markets
	IT's impact on firm's ability to identify new customers
	IT's impact on firm's ability to discover opportunities to customize existing products to appeal to potential customers
	IT's impact on firm's ability to identify new product applications
Technology knowledge (TSURVIN)	IT's impact on firm's ability to recognize (within the industry) technological developments to expand product features
	IT's impact on firm's ability to recognize (within the industry) technological developments to enhance product performance
Technology knowledge (TSURVOUT)	IT's impact on firm's ability to recognize (outside the industry) technological developments to expand product features
	IT's impact on firm's ability to recognize (outside the industry) technological developments to enhance product performance

In contrast, EXPEDIT refers to IT's impact on the firm's ability to gather information from *potential* customers. This is important because many firms face pressures to increase market share under conditions of increasingly fickle customer tastes and declining brand loyalty. Mass customizers often actively prospect for new customers, new markets, and new product applications. The survey measures EXPEDIT with items that assess the information system's ability to discover new product categories, and new product applications (Parsons, 1983; McFarlan, 1984); to discover opportunities to customize existing products to attract potential customers (Bakos & Treacy, 1986; Bakos, 1987); and to find new customers and emerging markets.

We assessed technology knowledge with two variables: *technological surveillance inside* the firm's industry (TSURVIN) and *technological surveillance outside* its industry (TSURVOUT). This distinction was made because firms increasingly face threats of technological obsolescence from rapid technological change, and the possibility that competitors from outside the industry may enter with an unanticipated, superior technology. Organizations pursuing mass customization often respond to this threat by looking both inside and outside their industry for technological developments that may be incorporated into products (Pine, 1993). The survey measures TSURVIN with items that assess the information system's ability to recognize, from within the industry, technological developments that can be used to expand product features and enhance product performance. TSURVOUT was measured with items which assess the same factors from sources outside the industry.

Variables Measuring Meta-enablers

Unlike strategic enablers, which are direct inputs into value-chain activities, meta-enablers are concerned with leveraging interfirm arrangements that integrate externals into the firm's value chain. We draw on a transaction costs lens to measure IT's effect on activities required to facilitate interfirm activities. We divide the process of enlisting cooperation of an external into three categories consistent with IT's characteristics: search costs, coordination costs, and risk mitigation. Table 6.3 presents each of these meta-enablers and their associated questionnaire items.

Table 6.3   The cooperation meta-enabler and associated questionnaire items

Strategic enabler	Questionnaire items
Search costs (FNDSUPL)	IT's impact on the firm's ability to locate suppliers of technologies that can be used to expand the bundle of features in existing products
	IT's impact on the firm's ability to locate suppliers of technologies that can be used to expand the performance of existing products
Search costs (FNDVENT)	IT's impact on the firm's ability to identify potential venture partners who can develop technologies to expand the bundle of features in existing products
	IT's impact on the firm's ability to identify potential venture partners who can develop technologies to expand the performance of existing products
Coordination costs (COCOST)	IT's impact on cost of coordinating activities with suppliers
	IT's impact on cost of coordinating activities with venture partners
Risk mitigation (RISKMIT)	IT's impact on the firm's ability to evaluate and choose the most appropriate suppliers
	IT's impact on the firm's ability to evaluate and choose the most appropriate venture partner(s)
	IT's impact on the cost the firm will incur if it changes suppliers

Search costs refer to costs the firm incurs to discover potential suppliers and venture partners who possess technological capabilities that may be used to expand product functionalities and enhance product performance (Rockart & Short, 1989; Benjamin & Wigand, 1995). *Search costs* are represented by two variables: *find suppliers* (FNDSUPL) and *find venture partners* (FNDVENT). FNDSUPL is measured by items which ascertain the firm's use of IT to locate suppliers of technologies (Bakos & Treacy, 1986) who can either expand the current bundle of product features, enhance product performance, or both. FNDVENT is measured by items which ascertain the firm's use of IT to identify potential venture partners (Porter, 1980; Porter & Millar, 1985) who can develop technologies that may be used to create the preceding product improvements.

Coordination costs are those associated with coordinating value-chain activities between the firm and an external (Cash & Konsynski, 1985; Johnston & Vitale, 1988; Rockart & Short, 1989). Examples include investing in development of data standards common to both organizations and purchasing dedicated networking capabilities (Johnston & Lawrence, 1988), the cost of exchanging product design information, and the cost of implementing design changes (Clemons, Reddi & Row, 1993). COCOST, the variable measuring coordination costs, is composed of items which assess the information system's impact on the firm's cost of coordinating activities with suppliers and venture partners.

Risk mitigation refers to costs of activities designed to reduce potential losses from a partner's opportunistic behavior. This incurs two fundamental costs: first, screening costs associated with identifying and evaluating a pool of prospective suppliers or venture partners and selecting the most appropriate one, and second, the costs of unraveling a connection with an unsatisfactory partner (Bakos, 1991; Clemons & Row, 1992). *Risk mitigation* is measured by the variable RISKMIT. This variable is composed of items which assess the information system's impact on costs the firm incurs to evaluate a pool of prospects and choose the most appropriate one and the system's impact on the cost the firm bears if it switches partners (Rackoff, Wiseman & Ullrich, 1985).

SURVEY DEVELOPMENT

A survey was used to gather data for this multinational study of how manufacturing firms use IT to leverage activities that enable pursuit of mass customization and time-based strategies. Using a seven-point Likert scale, an extensive questionnaire was developed to assess characteristics of the firm's information system, patterns of resource use, and resulting competitive effects. This preliminary questionnaire was administered to a panel of four North American academics whose research focuses on information technology. Refinements were made and the instrument was then piloted in a random sample of North American information systems executives working for manufacturing firms. Subjects were drawn from a commercial database published by Hugo Dunhill Mail Lists. After using their feedback to make additional refinements, the questionnaire was distributed to research collaborators in Korea and Sweden. The instrument was then translated into their respective language, back-translated by a panel of bilinguals in each country, and then compared to the English original for consistency. All inconsistencies were resolved and an interim survey was prepared for distribution.

The interim survey was piloted in samples of information system executives working in manufacturing firms in each country. Korean subjects were information systems executives enrolled in an upper-level executive workshop. Swedish subjects were information systems executives randomly selected from assorted directories of manufacturing firms. Feedback from these two pilot populations was used to refine further each instrument. The final products were back-translated into English, forward-translated into each collaborator's language, checked for consistency, and then back-translated into English. The final English back-translation was made so that researchers could evaluate the instrument in a language common to all team members. Researchers then met to decide on a final version of the questionnaire. Redundant items and those which reflected colloquial differences and idiosyncratic business practices were discarded.

Employing a modified version of Dillman's (1978) total design method, the questionnaire was then sent to one information system executive in a sample of global manufacturing firms in each country. Next, a first follow-up consisting of a reminder letter was sent one week after the initial mailing. A second follow-up consisting of a more urgently worded reminder letter and a duplicate survey was sent two weeks after the first follow-up. A third follow-up, made within two weeks of the second follow-up, consisted of a telephone request for participation and a re-mailing of the survey.

The American sample consisted of 325 information systems executives who appeared in the Hugo Dunhill Mail List database. Seventy-four complete questionnaires were returned for a response rate of 22.8%. The Swedish sample consisted of 149 information systems executives in manufacturing firms compiled from the client databases of two Swedish consulting firms and Dun & Bradstreet's *Directory of Principal International Businesses*. Fifty-two complete questionnaires were received for a response rate of 34.8%. The Korean sample consisted of 289 information systems executives in manufacturing firms selected from Dun & Bradstreet's *Directory* and assorted Korean directories of manufacturing firms. Eighty-one usable questionnaires were returned, giving a response rate of 28.0%.

RESULTS

We used ANOVA to compare firm size (number of employees) to determine if there were statistically significant differences across countries. Financial measures such as sales and net assets were not used because large differences in accounting conventions across nations were thought to yield numbers which are not comparable. Sample statistics were as follows: for 52 Swedish firms, mean employees = 7194.5 (S.D. = 13 047); for 74 American firms, mean employees = 6850 (S.D. = 7734.9); for 81 Korean firms, mean employees = 9180.3 (S.D. = 16 156). The ANOVA F-value of 0.7264 indicated no statistically significant difference across firms from all three countries.

Much preceding research on strategic uses of IT focused on categorizing strategic applications and developing conceptual frameworks. Relatively few studies identified dependent variables affected by IT and, in those cases, little work was done to validate them empirically. We tested the variables developed in this study for the following reasons. First, while adequately grounded in information science, manufacturing strategy, and strategic management theory, these variables suffer the limitation of not being previously empirically validated. Second, variables originally developed in the context of North American culture and business practices were used to compare IT use across three different nations. It is possible these measures were not appropriate because of cultural differences and variations in business practices in Asia and Europe. In the sections that follow, we first describe results from a reliability test, univariate analysis of variance (ANOVA) and multivariate analysis of variance (MANOVA). Next, we compare how firms from each country used IT to support time-based and mass customization strategies.

ASSESSMENT OF VARIABLES

Reliability

Coefficient alphas were calculated to estimate reliability of the variables. This statistic estimates the internal consistency of a scale based on the number of items and the average intercorrelation among items (Murphy & Davidshofer, 1991). We employed Robinson, Shaver & Wrightsman's (1991) criteria for estimates: alpha values of 0.80 or better are exemplary, and values of 0.70 to 0.79 are extensive. Alpha values varied from 0.70 for the variable RISKMIT to 0.91 for the variable MFGTIME. These values indicate that the measures could be considered reliable.

Multivariate Analysis of Variance (MANOVA)

MANOVA results for the two strategic enablers and meta-enabler appear in TABLE 6.4. Three MANOVAs were conducted to determine whether companies from each country differed on variables associated with those factors. Wilk's Λ statistic was used to determine if combinations of dependent variables were significantly different from each other. MANOVA results showed that Swedish, American, and Korean firms were significantly different from each other on the two strategic enablers and meta-enabler.

We chose MANOVA instead of running several ANVOAs for two reasons. First, this study used theory to group ten variables which represent strategic enablers and meta-enablers: two strategic enablers of time-based competition, four strategic enablers of mass customization and four meta-enablers. Grouping variables based on theoretical guidance was preferable to lumping them together (Stevens, 1992). As a result, using multiple ANOVAs would inflate the overall type I error. Ten univariate tests, each with a 0.05 type I error, would have 0.40 probability of false rejection (Stevens, 1992). Second, univariate tests ignore the interrelationships among variables.

Univariate Analysis of Variance (ANOVA)

Ten ANOVAs were run on each variable to determine if significant differences existed among firms from the three countries. Although ANOVA shows whether three or more groups differ significantly on a variable, there is a danger of an inflated type I error. We compensated for this by using the Bonferroni adjustment (0.05/10=0.005) to establish an appropriate alpha

TABLE 6.4   MANOVA results for strategic enablers

Strategic enabler	Test name	Value	Approximate F	Variable DF	Error DF	Significance of F
Time-based competition, MFGTIME, DEVTIME	Wilks	0.78504	13.05660	4.00	406.00	0.000
Mass customization, CUSTKNOW, EXPEDIT, TSURVIN, TSURVOUT	Wilks	0.90553	2.55603	8.00	402.00	0.010
Cooperation meta-enabler, FNDSUPL, FNDVENT, COCOST, RISKMIT	Wilks	0.53913	18.18650	8.00	402.00	0.000

level. Using this new significance level, we surmised that companies from the three countries differed significantly on all but two variables: CUSTKNOW (0.081) and TSURVIN (0.007). ANOVA results appear in TABLE 6.5.

INTERPRETATION OF RESULTS

In this section, we first interpret MANOVA results to determine if there are statistically significant differences in IT use across countries. We then use ANOVA results to rank-order variables across countries and interpret national patterns of IT use. We conclude by examining how firms from different countries use IT to support time-based competition and mass customization.

TABLE 6.4 presents MANOVA results from firm scores, by country, on variables representing IT's effects. Results show statistically significant differences in scores for Korean, American, and Swedish firms. This lends support to our belief that although there is worldwide convergence in IT technologies adopted by firms, country-specific differences lead to different patterns of IT use.

TABLE 6.5 presents ANOVA results for the ten strategic enablers and meta-enablers by country. Numbers in parentheses next to mean scores represent that country's rank relative to other countries on a particular variable. For example, in comparing scores for MFGTIME across countries, Americans ranked first, Swedes second, and Koreans third. We use TABLE 6.5 to compare patterns of IT use by firms from the three countries.

ANOVA-Fs show statistical significance for all variables except CUSTKNOW, consequently, this variable is not included in the ensuing

TABLE 6.5   ANOVA results for variables by country

Variable	Sweden ($N = 52$)		USA ($N = 74$)		Korea ($N = 81$)		ANOVA
	Mean	S.D.	Mean	S.D.	Mean	S.D.	F
MFGTIME	4.75(2)	0.99	5.55(1)	0.93	4.56(3)	0.97	22.19***
DEVTIME	5.00(2)	0.98	5.58(1)	0.89	4.57(3)	0.97	22.26***
EXPEDIT	3.85(3)	1.05	4.47(1)	0.72	4.38(2)	0.89	8.37***
TSURVIN	3.80(3)	1.42	4.26(2)	0.84	4.38(1)	0.95	5.10**
TSURVOUT	3.68(3)	1.34	4.28(1)	0.81	4.27(2)	0.99	6.32**
FNDSUPL	3.45(3)	1.13	4.60(1)	0.91	4.52(2)	1.10	22.11***
FNDVENT	3.44(3)	1.11	4.61(1)	0.72	4.27(2)	1.24	19.51***
COCOST	3.90(1)	0.93	2.66(3)	0.84	3.72(2)	0.87	40.73***
RISKMIT	4.03(1)	0.58	3.16(3)	0.70	3.85(2)	0.84	26.87***

*$p<0.05$; **$p< 0.01$; ***$p<0.001$.

discussion. This result is not surprising because sample firms are global players facing diverse customer tastes and preferences. They therefore need to keep abreast of changes in customer desires to ensure that product offerings are current.

Relative to Swedish and Korean firms, American firms appear overall to place greater emphasis on using IT to support enablers and meta-enablers of mass customization and time-based competition. Comparing country rankings on each variable revealed that American firms ranked first on six of the ten variables: MFGTIME and DEVTIME (time-based variables), EXPEDIT and TSURVOUT (mass customization variables), and FNDSUPL and FNDVENT (meta-enablers). Americans ranked second on TSURVIN (mass customization variable) and third on COCOST and RISKMIT (meta-enablers). The low rank for COCOST and RISKMIT appears to reflect America's change-oriented, market-driven economy. Under those conditions, firms are less likely to consider coordination costs and risk mitigation very important because an alternate partner can be found quickly if an existing partner proves unworkable. In a rapidly changing environment, quickly locating appropriate partners becomes a more important task. This interpretation is supported by the higher mean scores for search variables FNDSUPL (4.60) and FNDVENT (4.61) as compared to COCOST (2.66) and RISKMIT (3.16).

Overall, Korean firms ranked second in terms of IT use to support time-based and mass customization strategies. They ranked first on TSURVIN (mass customization variable), second on EXPEDIT and TSURVOUT (mass customization variables) and FNDSUPL, FNDVENT, COCOST and RISKMIT (meta-enablers). They also ranked third on MFGTIME and DEVTIME (time-based variables). The top rank on TSURVIN suggests that Koreans use IT to support their practice of imitating commercially successful products and competing on price. This interpretation is supported by two findings. First, the low rank on time-based variables, MFGTIME and DEVTIME, supports the belief that firms pursuing an imitation strategy need not emphasize rapid prototyping and short cycle manufacturing capabilities. Second, the rankings for search variables (FNDSUPL and FNDVENT), the coordination variable (COCOST), and the risk mitigation variable (RISKMIT) are consistent with the growing Korean practice of utilizing IT to connect with external entities with desirable resources and capabilities. This is necessary to compensate for the strategic inflexibility arising from the very high levels of vertical integration characteristic of the Chaebol form. Indeed, excessive vertical integration has led to "competitive sclerosis," a commonly cited factor in the pending bankruptcies of seven of Korea's 20 Chaebols (the *Economist*, 1997).

Overall, Swedish firms ranked last in terms of IT use to support time-based and mass customization strategies. These firms ranked first on CO-COST and RISKMIT (meta-enablers), second on MFGTIME and DEVTIME

(time-based variables), and third on EXPEDIT and TSURVOUT (mass customization variables) and the meta-enablers FNDSUPL and FNDVENT. Relative to American and Korean firms, Swedish firms place greater emphasis on IT to leverage coordination and risk mitigation. Although they surpass Koreans on IT uses to leverage time-based competition, they, however, lag behind both Americans and Koreans in regard to mass customization and interorganizational coordination.

The second overall rank for time-based variables indicates that Swedish firms are responding to global pressures to reduce cycle times and speed products to market. Swedish firms, nevertheless, tend to adapt rather slowly and still follow the practice of doing business with a small number of geographically far-flung suppliers. Large geographic distances between the firm and its suppliers require superior coordination capabilities, while large cultural differences increase the likelihood that differences in behaviors and values can lead to greater opportunism. The number one ranking of CO-COST and RISKMIT strongly suggests that IT is used to manage the complex coordination tasks necessary for smooth operation and to attenuate opportunism.

TABLE 6.6 ranks, in descending order, mean scores of strategic enablers and meta-enablers by country. We first interpret the pattern of IT use in each country to enable time-based competition and compare differences across national contexts. We then do the same for IT use to enable mass customization. The variables CUSTKNOW (0.081) and TSURVIN (0.007) were not included because they were not statistically significant at the 0.005 level.

Comparison of IT to Support Time-based Competition

For time-based competition, variables associated with the strategic enablers DEVTIME and MFGTIME ranked first and second, respectively, across all firms. This finding is consistent with the strategy literature, which notes that

TABLE 6.6   Rank ordering of mean variable scores by country

Sweden		USA		Korea	
Variable	Score	Variable	Score	Variable	Score
DEVTIME	5.00	DEVTIME	5.58	DEVTIME	4.57
MFGTIME	4.75	MFGTIME	5.55	MFGTIME	4.56
COCOST	4.01	FNDVENT	4.61	FNDSUPL	4.52
RISKMIT	3.87	FNDSUPL	4.60	EXPEDIT	4.38
EXPEDIT	3.85	EXPEDIT	4.47	FNDVENT	4.27
TSURVOUT	3.68	TSURVOUT	4.28	TSURVOUT	4.27
FNDSUPL	3.45	COCOST	3.02	RISKMIT	3.81
FNDVENT	3.44	RISKMIT	2.97	COCOST	3.80

businesses are increasingly using time as a competitive weapon. It is interesting to note that all firms ranked DEVTIME ahead of MFGTIME. This pattern is consistent with the product development literature, which notes that the product development phase is more time consuming than the manufacturing phase. Sample firms, regardless of national origin, appear to place greater emphasis on IT to reduce product development times.

Firms may facilitate time-based competition by delegating responsibility for component development to external parties such as suppliers and venture partners. IT may aid coordination by facilitating the process of evaluating and selecting appropriate externals. This practice is captured by the search variables FNDSUPL and FNDVENT. Because close coordination carries opportunism risks, RISKMIT may be leveraged by IT to reduce losses. Swedish firms ranked FNDSUPL seventh and FNDVENT eighth, while RISKMIT ranked fourth. Swedish firms appear to place stronger emphasis on IT to reduce opportunism risks rather than searching for appropriate partners. This pattern is consistent with the European practice of conducting business with a number of geographically dispersed partners.

American firms, in contrast, ranked FNDSUPL and FNDVENT fourth and third respectively. This ranking reflects the strong market orientation and high incidence of change in the US business environment. Korean firms ranked the same variables in third and fifth place, respectively. It is likely that Korean firms do not place very high emphasis on coordination with externals because their dominant organizational form, the Chaebol structure, tends to be highly vertically integrated. Additionally, business practices rooted in the Chaebol form discourage partnering with non-Chaebol externals. Therefore, using IT to facilitate coordination is not a priority. Similarly, the practice of doing business predominantly with Chaebol mates as well as strong social norms against opportunistic behaviors may explain why risk mitigation (RISKMIT) ranked seventh among Korean firms.

The tendency of American firms to rank COCOST and RISKMIT lower may be an outcome of the recent trend towards adopting a network or virtual form. Firms in industries such as electronics and automobiles are reducing the number of suppliers with whom they conduct business and are relying more and more on a small number of trusted suppliers. This approach may explain American firms' smaller emphasis on IT to mitigate risks. This interpretation is further supported by the fact that firms tended to rank search variables (FNDVENT and FNDSUPL) higher than coordination cost variables (COCOST and RISKMIT). Higher rankings of (FNDVENT) and (FNDSUPL) suggest that American firms emphasize using IT to locate appropriate externals rather than to mitigate risk. By using IT to find qualified suppliers and venture partners, firms may reduce the risk of adverse selection and may, therefore, not need to place a large emphasis on reducing effects of opportunism.

Comparison of IT to Enable Mass Customization

Both Swedish and American firms ranked the market expeditioning variable (EXPEDIT) fifth, while Korean firms ranked it fourth. These low rankings relative to time-based enablers (DEVTIME and MFGTIME) suggest that mass customization is of secondary importance. The higher ranking of EX-PEDIT by Korean firms suggests they may be attempting to leverage their competence in imitating successful products developed by creating product variants for new niches.

All firms ranked the technology knowledge variable TSURVOUT sixth. This outcome was rather surprising because it suggests that all firms place the same relative emphasis on importing technologies from outside their industry. At first glance, this seemed to fly in the face of conventional wisdom, which states that American firms tend to be very innovative, Swedish firms tend to lag on this dimension, and Korean firms tend to emulate successful products developed by competitors. We believe that this outcome may be due to the fact that we surveyed global manufacturing firms. The global reach of these firms implies that they face the same competitive pressures, including hypercompetition, which relies on technological advances to create temporary disruptions in the status quo. TSURVOUT's uniformly low ranking across all firms suggests that IT is used to scan the environment for potential technological threats.

The variables FNDSUPL and FNDVENT focus on IT's impact on locating suppliers who possess technologies and venture partners who can develop technologies to improve product functionalities and performance. Swedish firms ranked FNDSUPL in seventh place and FNDVENT in eighth place. This low ranking suggests they do not place great emphasis on using IT to enable the pursuit of mass customization. American firms, on the other hand, ranked FNDVENT in third place and FNDSUPL in fourth place. This result reinforces the conjecture that American firms are moving towards a virtual form and that IT is a key factor in leveraging the capabilities of network partners. The Korean ranking of FNDSUPL in third place and FNDVENT in fifth place is thought to arise from conflict between an imitation strategy, which calls for imitation of new product technologies, and the strategic inflexibility of the Chaebol form. These firms, faced with pressures to respond quickly and flexibly to fickle customer tastes and rapid technological change, are hampered by the rigidity of their organizational structure. Some Korean producers of consumer electronics cope with this contradiction by maintaining internal manufacturing competencies while seeking external partners who provide knowledge of new product technologies. By so doing, the firm maintains the integrity of the Chaebol while incorporating new technologies in its product lines.

Conclusion

This exploratory research empirically validated eight of ten variables thought to measure IT's effect on strategic enablers and meta-enablers of time-based and mass customization strategies. In addition, we discovered that although there is global convergence of information technologies adopted by firms, organizational, cultural, and country-specific differences shape patterns of IT use among firms. We believe that survival in today's increasingly volatile markets requires that firms develop the capability to quickly and seamlessly connect with external entities who possess resources and capabilities necessary to capture market opportunities. Our study shows that American firms come closest to this competitive ideal.

Although we are optimistic that the business environment is evolving towards a global network of friction-free electronic markets and virtual value chains, we believe that firms, including American companies, need to radically rethink the way businesses are organized. The Korean firms in our sample demonstrated that cultural norms and business traditions can limit how IT is used. While the slice of data used in this chapter did not highlight the following, we noted that all firms tended to create IT architectures to support existing functional silos. If our vision of a future business environment as a network of friction free electronic markets and virtual value chains is correct, the benefits of vertical integration will diminish greatly. Transaction costs economics posits that internalization takes place when coordination costs and transaction risks exceed the cost of conducting activities within the boundaries of the firm. IT innovations in the hospital supply industry and automated banking have demonstrated that not only coordination costs, but also transaction risks, can be attenuated through IT. If this trend continues, we anticipate that goods and services will be produced by constellations of separate companies, each conducting a small number of value-chain activities. We are concerned that cultural norms in the case of Koreans, long-standing business traditions in the case of Swedes, and administrative heritage in the case of Americans will perpetuate the practice of using IT to improve the efficiency of organizational forms which evolved in the industrial age and are increasingly inappropriate for the information age.

This study suffers from two limitations. First, because we selected one upper-level information system executive from each firm, it is likely that his/her perspective did not comprehensively portray IT use in that organization. Second, the sample size is too small to be completely representative of the underlying populations. We do not, however, consider this a significant weakness given the exploratory nature of this research.

In regard to future directions, we were intrigued by differences in the way firms used IT to partner with externals. Swedish firms placed greater emphasis on the coordination cost (COCOST) and risk mitigation (RISKMIT) variables as compared to search variables (FNDSUPL and FNDVENT). The American pattern, in contrast, was virtually reversed. This suggests that cultural norms may play a role in the way IT is used in partnering. A derivative of this research will link Hofstede's work on dimensions of culture to IT choices to unravel the effect of cultural values on IT deployment.

REFERENCES

Bakos, Y.J. (1987). Dependent variables for the study of firm and industry-level impact of information technology. *Proceedings of the Eighth Conference on Systems*, pp. 10–23.

Bakos, Y.J. (1991). Information links and electronic marketplaces. *Journal of Management Information Systems*, **8**(2), 31–52.

Bakos, Y.J. & Treacy, M.E. (1986). Information technology and corporate strategy: a research perspective. *MIS Quarterly*, **10**(2), 107–119.

Benjamin, R. & Wigand, R. (1995). Electronic markets and virtual value chains on the information superhighway. *Sloan Management Review*, Winter, 62–73.

Blaich, R. & Blaich, J. (1993). *Product Design and Corporate Strategy: Managing the Connection for Competitive Advantage*. New York: McGraw-Hill.

Cash, J.I. & Konsynski, B.R. (1985). IS redraws competitive boundaries. *Harvard Business Review*, **63**(2), 134–142.

Chang, M. (1993). Flexible manufacturing, uncertain consumer tastes, and strategic entry deterrence. *Journal of Industrial Economics*, **41**(1), 77–90.

Clark, K.B. & Fujimoto, T. (1991). *Product Development Performance*. Cambridge, MA: Harvard University Press.

Clemons, E.K. & McFarlan, F.W. (1986). Telecom: hook up or lose out. *Harvard Business Review*, July/August, 91–97.

Clemons, E.K. & Row, M.C. (1992). Information technology and industrial cooperation: the changing economics of coordination and ownership. *Journal of Management Information Systems*, **9**(2), 9–28.

Clemons, E.K., Reddi, S.P. & Row, M.C. (1993). The impact of information technology on the organization of economic activity: the move to the middle hypothesis. *Journal of Management Information Systems*, **10**(2), 9–35.

Day, G.S. (1990). *Market Driven Strategy—Process for Creating Value*. New York: The Free Press.

DeCastro, J. & Hoogerhuis, P. (1991). Concurrent engineering meets design automation. *Electronic Design*, 10 January, 79–88.

Dillman, D.A. (1978). *Mail and Telephone Surveys*. New York: John Wiley & Sons.

Dixon, J.R. & Duffey, M.R. (1990). The neglect of engineering design. *California Management Review*, **32**, 9–23.

Dumaine, B. (1989). How managers can succeed through speed. *Fortune*, **13**, 54–59.

The *Economist* (1997). South Korean manufacturing: the giants stumble. 18 October, 67–68.

Fawcett, S.E., Calantone, R. & Smith, S.R. (1994). An investigation of the impact of flexibility on global reach and firm performance, paper presented at the Academy of Management Annual Meeting, Dallas, TX.

Gerwin, D. (1993). Manufacturing flexibility: a strategic perspective. *Management Science*, **39**, 395–410.

Gerwin, D. (1994). Managing advanced manufacturing technology. In R.C. Dorf & A. Kusiak (eds) *Handbook of Design, Manufacturing, and Automation*. New York: John Wiley & Sons.

Gerwin, D. & Tarondeau, J.C. (1989). International comparisons of manufacturing flexibility. In K. Ferdows (ed.) *Managing International Manufacturing*. Amsterdam: Elsevier.

Glazer, R. (1991). Marketing in an information intensive environment: strategic implications of knowledge as an asset. *Journal of Marketing*, **55**, 1–19.

Goldhar, J. & Jelinek, M. (1983). Plan for economies of scope. *Harvard Business Review*, **61**, 141–148.

Gomory, R. (1989). From the "ladder of science" to the product development cycle. *Harvard Business Review*, **67**(6), 99–105.

Hitt, M.A., Hoskisson, R.E. & Nixon, R.D. (1993). A mid-range theory of interfunctional integration, its antecedents and outcomes. *Journal of Engineering and Technology Management*, **10**, 161–185.

Johnston, H.R. & Lawrence, P.R. (1988). Beyond vertical integration, the rise of the value-adding partnership. *Harvard Business Review*, July/August, 94–101.

Johnston, H.R. & Vitale, M.R. (1988). Creating advantage with interorganizational information systems. *MIS Quarterly*, **12**(2), 153–166.

Keen, P.G.W. (1988). *Competing in Time: Using Telecommunications for Competitive Advantage*. Cambridge, MA: Ballinger.

Konsynski, B.R. & McFarlan, F.W. (1990). Information partnerships—shared data, shared scale. *Harvard Business Review*, **90**(5), 114–120.

Malone, T.W., Yates, J. & Benjamin, I. (1987). Electronic markets and electronic hierarchies. *Communications of the ACM*, **30**(6), 484–497.

Markowitz, M.C. (1991). Concurrent engineering journey starts with the first step. *EDN*, **36**, 110–114.

McFarlan, F. (1984). Information technology changes the way you compete. *Harvard Business Review*, **63**(3), 98–103.

McIntosh, J.C. (1995). *A theory of product based competition*, doctoral dissertation. University of Illinois, Urbana-Champaign.

Murphy, K.R. & Davidshofer, C.O. (1991). *Psychological Testing: Principles and Applications*, 2nd edn. Englewood Cliffs, NJ: Prentice Hall.

Parsons, G.L. (1983). Information technology: a new competitive weapon. *Sloan Management Review*, **25**(1), 3–14.

Pennell, J.P., Winner, R.I., Bertrand, H.E. & Slusarczuk, M.G.M. (1989). Concurrent engineering: an overview for autotestcon, presented at the 1989 Autotestcon Conference, September 25–28, Philadelphia, PA, pp. 88–99.

Pine, B.J. (1993). *Mass Customization—The New Frontier in Business Competition*. Boston, MA: Harvard Business School Press.

Porter, M.E. (1980). *Competitive Strategy*. New York: Free Press.

Porter, M.E. & Millar, V.E. (1985). How information gives you competitive advantage. *Harvard Business Review*, **65**(3), 149–160.

Powell, T.C. & Dent-Micallef, A. (1997). Information technology as competitive advantage: the role of human, business, and technology resources. *Strategic Management Journal*, **18**(5), 375–405.

Rackoff, N., Wiseman, C. & Ullrich, W.A. (1985). Information systems for competitive advantage: implementation of a planning process. *MIS Quarterly*, December, 285–294.

Robinson, J.P., Shaver, P.R. & Wrightsman, L.S. (1991). Criteria for scale selection and evaluation. In J.P. Robinson, P.R. Shaver & L.S. Wrightsman (eds) *Measures of Personality and Social Psychological Attitudes*. San Diego, CA: Academic Press.

Rockart, J.F. & Short, J.E. (1989). IT in the 1990s: managing organizational interdependence. *Sloan Management Review*, Winter, 7–17.

Spencer, W.J. (1990). Research to product: a major U.S. challenge. *California Management Review*, **32**(2), 45–53.

Sprague, R.A., Singh, K.J. & Wood, R.T. (1991). Concurrent engineering in product development. *IEEE Design and Test of Computers*, **8**(1), 6–13.

Stalk, G. Jr & Hout, T.M. (1990). *Competing against Time—How Time-Based Competition is Reshaping Global Markets*. New York: Free Press.

Stevens, J. (1992). *Applied Multivariate Statistics for the Social Sciences*, 2nd edn. Hillsdale, NJ: Lawrence Erlbaum.

Turino, J. (1990). From design for test to concurrent engineering. In the proceedings of the Autotestcon 90, IEEE Systems Readiness Technology Conference, 19-21 September, 345–349.

Wiseman, C. (1985). *Strategy and Computers: Information Systems as Competitive Weapons*. Homewood, IL: Dow Jones-Irwin.

7

Transaction Streams and Value Added: Sustainable Business Models on the Internet

BRIAN SUBIRANA

INTRODUCTION

The market value appreciation of Internet services IPOs in the period 1980–1997 is $4773 million (Meeker, 1997). In only five years, the Internet may reach 150 million users. The Internet is used in practically all industries, in ever more global and sophisticated manners. The convergence of industries such as telecommunications, office equipment, consumer electronics, computers, and media and publishing into emerging information industries is having profound effects on the everyday businesses we take for granted. It is no longer necessary to buy newspapers at the local news stand because they can be read over the Internet. Encyclopedias are not mammoth books collecting dust on a shelf; rather, they are small interactive CD-ROMS to be enjoyed with a computer. And airline tickets do not need to be reserved through a travel agent for a fee; they can now be ordered directly through a computer.

To develop these types of information products, a company needs to combine content, editing and navigation, and then distribute the final product to the end customer. Currently, there is no one company that leads in all

New Managerial Mindsets: Organizational Transformation and Strategy Implementation.
Edited by M.A. Hitt, J.E. Ricart i Costa and R.D. Nixon.
© 1998 John Wiley & Sons Ltd.

of the different multimedia value-adding stages. Encyclopaedia Britannica has excellent text content, but to create its CD-ROM it must search out editing expertise in video and animation. Microsoft is a leader in developing software, and setting up its own network. But it must search elsewhere for content that can entice users to use its network. Tower Records sells music software to be used in stand-alone CD players, but it does not know how to deliver its products through air or cable channels of distribution. In order to be able to create these new products for the multimedia age, companies from the converging industries are making alliances. Thus, organizations that compete in the information industries find themselves in a difficult and complex situation. On one hand, they are pressed to position themselves to compete in the information society. On the other hand, they are finding it difficult to frame successful business models on which to direct their re-sources. The investment is often significant, and profit is slim (even the successful companies over-invest) and future perspectives are unclear.

Indeed, the overall direct volume of Internet transactions appears low according to some estimates. Some objective indicators, such as the amount of goods sold on the Internet in 1996 and 1997, confirm this. While analysts do not necessarily agree on the exact numbers (not even the orders of mag-nitude), most acknowledge that the growth potential for electronic com-merce is huge. Whether we measure transactions or the market for infrastructure, content, and services, most sources predict a two-order of magnitude increase in less than 5 years (300% to 600% annual compounded growth over this period).

In this chapter we analyse how transactions related to the exchange of goods and services are being performed on the Internet. The adoption of electronic markets in an industry has a disintermediation potential because it can create a direct link between the producer and the consumer (without the need for the intermediation role of distributors). Electronic markets lower the search cost, allowing customers to choose among more providers (which ultimately reduces both the costs for the customer and the profits for the producer). In this chapter we contend that electronic markets on the Internet have the opposite effect, resulting in an increase of intermediators. We introduce transaction streams which model how transactions are being conducted and help explain the types of new intermediators that are appear-ing. We also describe mechanisms by which companies are exploring ways of extending their transaction streams and introduce a model of how value is being crafted within transaction streams.

Understanding the current success stories on the Internet is an interesting endeavor for two reasons. First, it is an interactive environment with the full functionality of any other interactive environment (with some bandwidth limitations which restrict in some instances the exchange of real-time informa-tion such as video). This means that by understanding market dynamics on the Internet, one should be able to extrapolate and apply market behaviour in other interactive environments. Second, it is based on open standards and is largely unregulated. Thus, it is in constant flux, adapting itself to the evolving characteristics of the demand. We could say that the Internet is a lead user network—similar to Von Hippel's lead users concept (Von Hippel, 1988).

The chapter is structured in the following way. In the next section (Internet Functional Properties) we outline the functional properties that characterize the Internet, concentrating on those which impact how transactions are being performed. In the third section (Electronic Markets) we review the existing literature on electronic markets. In the fourth section, Transaction Processes, we describe the five fundamental steps in performing a transaction. In the fifth section (Transaction Streams), we introduce the transaction stream model and provide diverse examples of real transaction streams. The sixth section (Transaction Streams and Value Added) provides a model of how value is being provided within transaction streams. The final section (Conclusion: The Transaction Landscape) discusses the implications of the findings presented.

INTERNET FUNCTIONAL PROPERTIES

The Internet is a special medium because it has six properties that facilitate economic activities. In this section we will review each of them. Its first such property is the capacity to be used at any time, practically from anywhere and by anybody. This is a very powerful paradigm. No matter where your customers are, you can reach them. This has enabled the Internet to create communities of people with specific interests and low geographic density. An example is HotHotHot, a store devoted to spicy food. HotHotHot features a very complete selection of hot sauces and books. It includes a search engine and multiple delivery options. Operating a store like HotHotHot in every city around the world would probably not be profitable—however, the Internet enables interaction between the centralized store owner and the scattered customers.

The Internet's second property facilitating economic activity is its capacity for enabling various forms of interactive communication between players. The medium is extremely powerful as a communication vehicle. Through email (asynchronous one-to-one communication), chat (synchronous many-to-many communication), newsgroups (asynchronous many-to-many communication), and even voice and video, it has demonstrated its potential for establishing close personal links.

Third, the Internet can be used to provide services combining and selecting the offers of various providers. In this sense, it can be used to select the players that one wishes to invite to a given economic activity. This is important because such selection can be done automatically by a program that helps you navigate through the Internet. For example, one can present the information related to a given sporting event by combining information from different sources such as the weather report, the stock market, the player information and the event results all on a single page.

Fourth, a software "robot" can navigate on its own, performing a sort of "personal butler" role (Negroponte 1995). This is crucial because robots can be constructed to perform a myriad of relevant tasks, such as selecting vendors for a given product. In other words, robots can lower the search costs to a simple time delay produced by the interval required by the robot to query the different stores.

Fifth, the Internet has developed tools such as Java that allow the customization of the offer so that Internet interaction can also be customized with a program running on the client machine. By customization we mean that the interaction between the company and the user is tailored to the user. For example, advertising networks are able to track how many times a user has seen a given advertising banner. This information is then used to customize subsequent banner placements.

Finally, and most importantly, it is very inexpensive for both the user and the service provider. The entry barriers from a technical standpoint are very low. To start an Internet site, one can make use of space on an Internet Service Provider's server for a very low price. In fact, there are some services, such as Tripod, that offer free web page hosting. Thus, everybody can afford a web site. Because it is based on open standards, there are many competitive products covering most of the possible demand needs. This means that some new business concepts can be tested on a small scale at low cost relative to traditional testing arenas.

ELECTRONIC MARKETS

A transaction is the establishment of a contract between a set of agents (such as people and firms) to perform a given action. By "contract" we mean an agreement between a set of agents to perform a course of actions (usually with detailed implicit and explicit conditions and alternative paths). Here, "contract" should be understood in its broad sense as any commitment between parties to perform a given action—for example, purchasing a cinema ticket, placing an advertisement in a newspaper, purchasing a book, etc.

Previous work has stressed the roles of markets and hierarchies as distinct mechanisms for coordinating the transactions related to flow of materials or services through adjacent steps in the value-added chain (Malone, Yates & Benjamin, 1987). Markets coordinate the flow through supply and demand forces using external transactions between different individuals and firms.

Hierarchies coordinate such flow by directing it at a higher level in the managerial hierarchy. By reducing the costs of coordination, Malone, Yates & Benjamin (1987) contend that the evolution of information technology is leading to a shift toward proportionately more use of markets compared to hierarchies to coordinate economic activity. They also argue that electronic markets are a more efficient form of coordination for certain classes of product transactions whose asset specificity is low and whose products are easy to describe. Malone, Yates & Benjamin (1987) also suggest a transition from electronic single-source sales channels and separate database markets within the firm to linked databases between firms and finally to shared databases between them.

According to their view, electronic markets will evolve from electronic single-source sales channels to biased markets where the market maker is one of the providers, using the market transaction mechanisms in its favor, to unbiased markets, and finally to personalized markets. Personalized markets are those in which the customers can use customized aids in making their choices. For example, some airline reservation systems allow the user to set preferences such as departure time, seating assignment and rates, which are then used in subsequent transactions. The airline market is therefore customized to the users—different users have different options depending on their preferences.

Transaction streams model multi-tier individualized forms of coordination whereby the coordination role of transactions is leveraged among various transaction engines through instantaneous database transfers across multiple firms. In other words, successful business markets on the Internet do not use a market operator. Instead, there is a company that packages different components of one (or more) transaction(s) and delivers them in the form of a web page. By using these streams, firms such as PeaPod, DoubleClick, Amadeus, Federal Express, HotHotHot, Cyberslice, AdSmart, Alta Vista, Yahoo! and Amazon are using the latest and most up-to-date information to configure and complete business transactions.

Bakos (1991) analyses the impact of electronic markets through the analysis of search costs. Buyers must, directly or indirectly, pay search costs to obtain information about prices and product offerings available in the market. Electronic markets have a vast impact on search costs because of the coordinating effect of information technology. Using economic theory, he shows that this reduction in search costs plays a major role in determining the implications of these systems for market efficiency and competitive behaviour. This reduction results in direct efficiency gains from reduced intermediation costs and in indirect but possibly larger gains in allocation efficiency from better-informed buyers. The benefits realized by market participants increase as more organizations join the system, leading to network externalities (Katz & Shapiro, 1985).

However, the logic of Bakos (1991) is based on five economic characteristics of electronic market systems that have been changed by recent market and technological developments around the Internet. The first two characteristics that he analyses have been enhanced: first, search costs, as stated above, are reduced (through browsing or robot shopping) and, second, the benefits realized increase as more organizations can join the WWW electronic markets. However, the last three have been drastically changed by open standards such as TCP/IP, HTML, and Java and the vast market adoption of the Internet as a platform for economic activities. Indeed, Bakos' (1991) third argument was that "Electronic marketplaces can impose significant switching costs on their participants". However, in most Internet-enabled marketplaces, the switching costs are often nil. This is because the Internet provides an open standard for the information transmission (i.e. a dedicated line is no longer an entry barrier) and Java can be used to create an interface that can reduce the switching costs by translating among alternative interface options (i.e. the interface software is no longer a switching barrier). The entry costs (point four of Bakos argument) defined as large system development and maintenance costs, have also been substantially reduced. Many open solutions exist that can be adopted and integrated into a solution with a fraction of the development cost that has historically been necessary. When American Crown Food Co. was working on its attempt to introduce a link-up connection with its customers, it incurred very large organizational and technical costs. Pre-WWW network technology was expensive and proprietary. This explains why early success stories such as airline reservation and hospital supply were produced in markets with a high demand for immediate and distributed coordination.

Benjamin & Wigand (1995) evaluate how the emergence of a national infrastructure such as the Internet can change the different segments of an industry value chain. The analysis is centred around the National Information Infrastructure (NII) initiative and acknowledges that it is becoming increasingly difficult to delineate accurately the borders of today's organizations. In fact, we contend that such borders have become especially fuzzy in the past two years. The developments have made reality of what was once a vision of an Office of Technology Assessment report: "The network will, in many instances, serve as the market. When this occurs, market structure will depend as much on network characteristics and the economies of networks as it does on relationships among firms" (OTA, 1994).

The recent literature on the Internet is abundant. Both the academic and business sectors have covered this subject extensively. For example, a search on the Amazon book catalogue yields more than 250 titles matching "Internet and Business" for the period 1995–1997. Indeed, many believe that the paradigm shift that is necessary to live in the new information society is drastic and that we need to devote significant resources to reassessing our assumptions about economic interactions. Demand and supply of conceptual ideas is burgeoning.

McKinsey's work has resulted in numerous publications (Rheingold, 1993), among others, the best seller *Net Gain—Expanding Markets through Virtual Communities* (Hagel & Armstrong, 1997). They focus their analysis on virtual communities and argue in favour of "reverse markets"; that is, markets in which the balance of power between the provider and the customer will shift towards the latter. For example, electronic markets have benefited the airline industry by allowing disintermediation and the renegotiation of holdup situations. It is estimated that SABRE alone saved over a billion dollars through its Internet reservation system. A virtual community independent of the goods providers (unlike SABRE, which was initiated by American Airlines) with a significant share of the travel market could negotiate deals to transfer industry profit to the customer. Furthermore, it could retain and subsequently exploit customer behaviour information. This customer information would be of significant value to the provider. For example, customers belonging to a community of food lovers could allow the community to sell their yogurt consumption behaviour information. This information could then be sold to yogurt manufacturers for a given fee. The community members could receive financial rewards as a share of the price paid for the information and as discounted prices on future yogurt purchases.

TRANSACTION PROCESSES

Before we explain how transaction streams operate we must analyse in more detail how transactions are performed. In this section we will provide a definition of what constitutes a "transaction" and present a novel five-stage model of the process which precedes actualization of the transaction. Defining this process will support understanding of the different types of transaction streams to be presented in the following section. By "transaction" we understand the establishment (or cancellation) of some form of contract which includes a given economic activity (Haanes & Lowendahl, 1997). For example, when a customer purchases a flight reservation a contract is established between the customer and the airline. The economic activity that is involved in such a contract is the air transportation of the passenger. Electronic markets such as airline reservation systems have been developed to facilitate such transactions. In general, the agents involved in a given transaction are fairly similar. Often, an intermediary operates the market— in the case of air travel it is a computer reservation system (CRS) such as SABRE or Amadeus.

Before a transaction is completed five processes need to be enacted: player selection, contract condition setting, contract signature, contract storage and transaction action. We will refer to them as the transaction processes, and we now review each of them in turn. Player selection involves the selection of the economic agents that will be involved in the transaction. This is a critical component because it narrows the number of firms that will compete to get the contract to perform the action. CRS select the airlines that are connected to their systems and, in a given transaction, display only those that are relevant for preset travel itinerary conditions.

Contract condition setting refers to the process by which the involved parties negotiate the details of the action that is to be performed. For example, in the airline reservation system, SABRE provides the choices for given itinerary parameters. It has long been noticed that the amount of information that is necessary to determine the exact nature of a transaction contract is important to understand the market mechanisms involved. For example, if the product has a complex description and it is very specific the contract will most likely be set either inside a firm or through a hierarchy relation between providers (Malone, Yates & Benjamin, 1987). In other words, the process that details the clauses of the contract has implications for how the market for transactions operates. In the case of air tickets, the contract parameters and conditions are very standard and simple to expose and compare. If, in contrast, one is in the market to purchase a house, the complexity of the transaction contract has, so far, made it very difficult for electronic markets to participate in the process. Before a house purchasing transaction is completed procedures involving various tax forms, price negotiation, loan applications and registry verifications need to be performed. Before a final price is agreed upon, the seller and the buyer often engage in a cumbersome pricing discussion where pros, cons, trust and other factors are brought into the discussion. The buyer is often involved in a similar discussion with the bank to establish the loan conditions. In addition, even if the conditions were clear as in a repeat purchase, many of the above steps, as of yet, would have no legal enforcement if performed online. In other words, home purchasing transactions are, in general, too complex for current electronic market models.

The last three processes have to do with the contract and activity execution. Contract signature refers to the binding step in the process in which the transaction players agree on a course of action that clarifies how the transaction activities will be performed. This can be a short and standard agreement or a long, detailed and customized contract. Often a market intermediary sets some conditions to ensure the contract validity (identification, down payment, etc.). For example, a travel agent uses a CRS to close a travel contract by confirming the reservation in the system. Once this has been done, in the traditional CRS the contract (ticket) is issued as a paper document and stored in the airline database. Finally, the transaction action is the process by which the activity referred to in the contract is executed.

TRANSACTION STREAMS

In this section, we will introduce transaction streams. We will define them by first introducing an example related to the book distribution industry market; then we will present different schemes that people use to benefit from transaction streams. We will conclude this section with more examples of transaction streams.

There are hundreds if not thousands of bookstores on the Internet (Subirana & Zuidhof, 1996a). Their initial modus operandi appears fairly simple. An enterpreneur decides to make its database available on the Internet with the hope that customers will start surfing through the site and orders will land on his desk. This arrangement appears very similar to the sale of airline tickets through a traditional CRS, and is pretty much what Jeff Bezos (founder of Amazon) did when he left his job as a principal at D.E. Shaw in early 1994 to pursue retailing on the Internet. Music and books are some of the categories most suitable for Internet consumer retailing. There are more titles than any store can stock and a selection can be easily made by querying a title database. Books are also well-known commodities and easy to ship. In fact, in its first 30 days, Amazon shipped books to customers in all 50 US states and 45 countries around the world. The book market is also highly fragmented from the point of view of distribution, authoring and production. Some threat exists from large presence-based retailers such as Barnes & Nobel and Borders because they may leverage their brand recognition with their warehouse and book logistics experience.

The market is valuing Amazon more than other retailers. With comparable sales, the Internet Bookshop has only received marginal market appreciation. With 1996 sales of $17 million and $6 million in losses, Amazon had an IPO market value of $540 million. This figure can not be explained through an NPV analysis on book distribution based on a simple database and a warehouse. Indeed, there is more to book distribution on the Internet than most would have predicted just two years ago. For example, one of the novel and effective tools that Amazon.com is exploiting is the Amazon associate programme membership. Through the associates programme, Amazon provides the opportunity to link associate Internet sites to their own database. This means that the users of an associate site can purchase books preselected in the associate site. For example, in Netscape's developer area, there is a section with reviews about different books. The user can select a book and be redirected to the page that sells the book. Netscape has become an independent bookseller at practically no additional cost. The transaction profit is shared and Amazon gives a 5–15% share to the associates programme seller. So far it has over 8000 sign-up associates, including companies such as Netscape.

Observe that the associate programme changes two of the five processes involved in the book transactions above. First, the player selection is performed by the associate partner, Netscape in our example. Then, in the condition setting, Netscape is performing a prescreening of the 2.5 million books in the Amazon catalogue. By sharing part of the revenue, Amazon is benefiting from a very inexpensive and enthusiastic sales force. This is very attractive for organizations such as Netscape, which have access to a customer base interested in specific titles. Netscape can differentiate from its competitors by providing access to the appropriate books when its customers want it. In some ways, this can be considered a response by providers to reverse markets. To prevent the power shift to the customer, providers work together on a combined sales effort.

Transaction streams are electronic markets in which more than one organization controls the first four transaction processes. For example, in the Amazon associate programme, the referring Internet site controls the player selection while Amazon controls the rest of the transaction processes.

There are various types of emerging tools that companies use to stimulate transaction streaming. Here are five of the most common:

- Associate programmes: As described above with the Amazon example, this functionality allows companies to extend their reach by sharing audience and revenue with other Internet sites. For example, HotHotHot allows third-party sites to provide links to the HotHotHot home page. It offers 5% of the revenue generated by the customers coming through the link provided.
- Interest links: The special-interest mail-order world has received revamped impetus with the Internet. The player selection process used to be very ineffective as customers had to find and subscribe to a special-interest publication, order a catalogue, choose the merchandise and mail order it. The process took weeks, if not months. The Internet, however, allows transaction activity players to trigger the player selection process via links in specific Internet pages. Associate programmes can be seen as one special way of sharing the revenue of interest links where the associate programme managing company is the one performing the contract signature.
- Yellow pages: The All-Internet Shopping Directory provides extensive listings of Internet stores. Categories include Hobbies, Malls, Services and Business to Business. As with yellow pages, the directory provides various levels of services ranging from free hyperlinks to "focus" listings and banner advertisements. In its robust implementation, one could conceivably peruse a yellow page service for information up until the actual product description. This is what robots are best at.
- Robots: Robots are programs that can perform intelligent tasks such as finding the cheapest publicized price for a given product, or the most up-to-date zip code for a certain address. www.jango.com recently

introduced a beta version of Jango, an "intelligent shopping assistant", which accepts product descriptions and wanders the Internet to find them. In addition to finding product information, Jango is also able to fill in order forms to speed up the product ordering process. Shopping robots come in two varieties, as browsers running on client machines or as server software (Subirana, 1997b). Robots can be used to extend and automate the functionality of all transaction processes.

- Profile information: www.ffly.com claims to have a database of over one million users. Each user has a FireFly Passport that includes detailed user profile information (preferred movies, food bought, etc.) which is permanently updated as the user performs transactions. The Passport contains user information that can be carried to other sites to tailor server response. For example, FireFly has partnered with Filmfinder so that both use the same technology. This enables the two companies to benefit from collaborating in film query-related transactions. The Passport data can be linked with that from other member profiles to determine what films may be of interest based on the preferences demonstrated by other "similar" customers. This technology can be used to lower search costs and can ensure anonymity for certain transactions. This is very relevant as it can serve as the basis for the reverse markets discussed above (Hagel & Armstrong, 1997).

In fact, when Amazon buys advertising space in a search engine such as Alta Vista, the combined effect is often that of converting Alta Vista into a sort of up-front paid partner. Advertising banners can now be very targeted. For example, when a customer searches for the word "Netscape", an Amazon banner could display the number of Netscape-related books that are on its database. Furthermore, Amazon can create a banner with a search space so that the customer can choose to search either on the Alta Vista site or on the Amazon database. This case is interesting because the user is provided with alternative transaction paths while the involved firms are competing for his or her attention. The paper equivalent of directory searching does not enable the dynamic player selection and condition setting exhibited by successful Internet companies.

Alta Vista also has an associate programme to stimulate the usage of its database. Companies around the world are performing specialized queries on the database. The logic to support such a programme is that associate companies have better information from the user than Alta Vista. This means that they can use such information to design better queries while retaining the customer's attention. Observe that here, Alta Vista is only involved when the transaction action is performed. Since this programme can be combined with the associate programme of Amazon, the number of players involved in each transaction multiplies. In fact, in the second quarter of 1996, the top four engines (Yahoo!, Excite, Lycos and Infoseek) completed

IPOs. Yahoo! was the leader in 1997 with 40% market share of the pages delivered per day. Its stock market valuation in CQ2 was up $2.1 billion (to about $2.4 billion) since its IPO. The ability of a non-Internet brand to knock Yahoo! off its pedestal has not been demonstrated. Yet other search engines have worked arguably harder and smarter. In fact, some of the queries delivered by Yahoo! are managed directly through an associate programme by Alta Vista (owned by Digital).

An Internet advertiser is anyone who promotes their product/service via the Internet. This is normally accomplished by placing banners (small advertisements which link to the advertiser's home page) on sites throughout the Internet. Advertisers normally pay the publishers of the sites on which their banners appear. Individual advertisers, traditional ad agencies and cyber-ad agencies are all active advertisers on the Internet.

DoubleClick (founded March 1996) provides Internet advertising sales and management, and manages an Internet advertising network. DoubleClick's objective is to bring its network sites, Internet users and Internet advertisers together. In order to do so, it has created a comprehensive database of Internet user and organization profiles which is used for ad campaign targeting purposes. Additionally, DoubleClick categorizes every Internet page displaying DoubleClick ad banners in order to promote affinity targeting.

When an advertiser wants to place banners on the Internet, it must select among a host of available medium—in the tens of thousands in most cases. Such a selection is not as straightforward as selecting the airlines that are available to perform a given itinerary. Issues such as medium affinity, availability, etc. must be taken into account. Adsmart provides a service that is tailored to such a process. It contains a database of demographic and media data that can be used to select what are the most desired media. It also enables the creation of a full media plan which is then used to select the appropriate banner placement locations. In case of banner placement, the individual media (sometimes directly, sometimes through advertising networks) provides the availability of the different desired services.

The examples above are not isolated (Cronin, 1996; Granoff, 1997; Subirana 1996, 1997a, b, c, d; Subirana & Palavecino, 1997; Subirana & Zuidhof 1999; Subirana, Oghuledo & Santomá, 1996). Figure 7.1 shows a sample of companies that are involved in transaction streams. The companies are organized around two dimensions: transaction activity ownership and stream purpose. By high transaction activity ownership we mean that the company involved is the one that owns the transaction activity. The transaction stream purpose is divided into two categories depending on the objectives sought by the involved company: sell if the intention is to obtain more business and diversify/enhance if the company is seeking to improve its offer so as to attract more customers to its core product. Amadeus, a large CRS, has an associate programme, in contrast with SABRE, which has started an owned system called Travelocity. PeaPod, the online supermarket retailer, is targeting producers for selective advertising and supermarkets for pricing and delivery information. FedEx has developed software for direct package information querying, while Cyberslice partners with multiple pizzerias around the US to facilitate pizza home delivery and has an add banner programme through referral.

So far in this section we have described various examples of transaction streams. TABLE 7.1 shows three transaction examples of the five processes involved in transactions. The first is a CRS reservation system based on a traditional interface. In the second we have included a transaction stream with only one associate programme; we call it a single transaction stream. The third is a transaction stream for a banner placement transaction. We call this last example a "multiple transaction stream" because the number of involved players has grown. In this example, one can not simply consider the three most basic actors in an electronic market. Rather, the market operator, the customer and the provider roles are supplemented by a range of contributing associates.

One area in which transactions are becoming more streamed is in the insurance and endorsement of the contract signature and contract storage (Hodges, 1997; Markey, 1997). In the presence-based world, consumers rely on endorsements provided by third-party entities such as the American Automobile Association or the Michelin guides. On computer systems that span multiple administrative boundaries, and especially on the Internet,

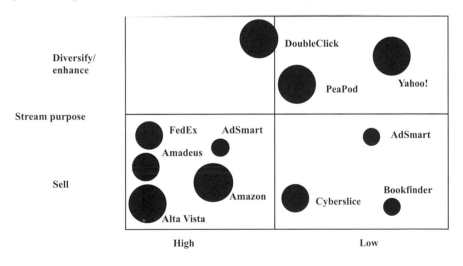

FIGURE 7.1   Stream purpose versus transaction action ownership

TABLE 7.1   Three transaction examples

Description	Electronic market: airline reservation	Single stream: airline reservation	Multiple stream: banner placement
Player selection	SABRE	Agency	AdSmart
Contract alternatives	SABRE	Amadeus	Advertising Agency or Pred. modelling Company
Contract signature	SABRE	Agency	DoubleClick
Contract repository	SABRE	Airline	Distributed
Transaction action	Airline	Airline	Alta Vista

such trust has proven difficult to establish. So far, global brands have been useful for providing assurance to customers. The lack of effective ways of managing the need for endorsement, security and insurance is a well-recognized barrier to the full acceptance of transactions on the Internet (Schwartz, 1997; Tapscott, 1996).

To respond to this transaction endorsement need, distributed approaches have been developed (Lai, Medvinsky & Clifford 1997). Before a transaction contract is signed, an assurance credential is granted to a server after meeting requirements imposed by the server issuing the credentials. The credential mechanism can be more tailored to the transaction needs than official licences. It can also be tailored to the user so that the transaction risk is managed dynamically by the user and not by the regulatory environment exclusively. Furthermore, proxies can be set in such a way that all the transactions realized by a given organization are endorsed and certified by an independent and trusted firm. Observe that the mechanism behind this process is similar to the FireFly Passport mentioned above but with a different purpose: instead of exchanging user demographic information to manage the transaction stream, the system exchanges endorsement and certification preferences.

This is an important issue; without the appropriate level of confidence the exchange of information among individuals and organizations will be limited. Lai, Medvinsky & Clifford (1997) propose a system based on a network of trust relationships that includes service providers, licensing agencies, insurance providers and endorsement agencies.

TRANSACTION STREAMS AND VALUE ADDED

The model represented in FIGURE 7.2 illustrates the different value-added components of information-intensive products. Three stages are presented. The first is content creation, for example, the writing of a case for a classroom discussion or the subsequent direction of a classroom discussion. The second component is packaging, which includes the editorial value of a case or a book publisher, and the process of selection or navigation performed by the classroom teacher. It also includes the value-added component of developing the MBA programme. Distribution includes the delivery means, such as a video conferencing link for distance learning or stand-alone distribution of paper cases; and the display device such as a TV, a computer for a CD-ROM case or paper for paper-based cases. Information industries share a remarkable similarity in this value-added proposition; indeed, content, packaging and distribution are ubiquitous in most of them.

Content includes such activities as entertainment, communication, learning, information and transactions. This list is not comprehensive but most applications can fit into one of these categories. Content providers participate in transaction streams because they often control the customer response in specific activities (i.e. the owner of HotHotHot knows when one of its customers may be interested in a book about spices and then can refer the customer to the Amazon Internet site).

Packaging has an editing component, which creates value by selecting what content should be included, and a navigation component, which adds value by providing mechanisms that help locate such content. Since the essence of transaction streaming is sharing the transaction process among different users, transaction streaming can be viewed as intrinsically related to packaging and navigation. The editing component is related to what transaction streams are being selected and the navigation is related to how the transaction streams are being accessed. Yahoo!, for example has its own content but is also a packager of content from many other companies charging on a per-transaction basis.

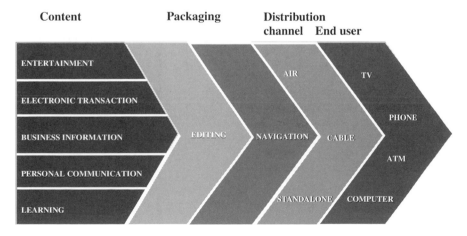

FIGURE 7.2   Value-added components of information products

Some companies are leveraging dominant positions in the distribution stage by crafting transaction streams through their services. For example, AOL has established lucrative deals with retailers to share their audience with them through interest links in their home page. The distribution stage of the multimedia value chain, as given in FIGURE 7.4, can be broken down into two parts: the distribution channel and the user environment. Through the distribution channel multimedia products and services are routed to the user environment. Within the user environment (either business or residential) multimedia services are further distributed to the actual user's geographic site, where services are consumed by the user.

Within the distribution channel (see FIGURE 7.3) we distinguish between the public or private telecommunications network and the gateway through which physical access is provided for the customer. The telecommunications network can either be publicly owned or owned by the enterprise, and operates at two different levels. At the level of telecom services several options are offered including wire or wireless services, and voice or data services. At the level of transmission media we distinguish among various alternatives for actual electronic transmission of multimedia services, such as transmission over cable or via satellite communications. The gateway provides the user with the physical connection to the telecommunications network, known in telephony networks as the "local loop". Currently, telephone companies and cable television companies are the main contenders in this segment of the distribution stage, but other players such as public utility companies (gas, electricity) have their own infrastructures and are potential entrants. Physical distribution takes place for stand-alone products like CD-ROMs and digital video discs. The logistics process for these multimedia products is equivalent to traditional distribution. Products are transported from the manufacturer over a physical network (e.g. road transportation) to the local store or kiosk. The customer buys the product and uses it within the user environment, e.g. on a personal computer. This example serves as an analogy for electronic distribution of multimedia services. Here, transportation of the product or service is performed over an electronic network, and

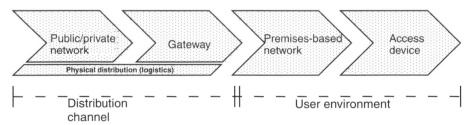

FIGURE 7.3 Distribution stage of multimedia value chain

the gateway serves as a shop window through which the customer can actually select and consume the preferred multimedia service from the user environment.

The user environment consists of two segments: the premises-based network and the access device. In the business environment premises-based networks are emerging in forms ranging from stand-alone desktops to integrated network solutions. Integration of voice and data networks, and the interconnectivity of local area networks (LANs, or networks connecting computers in a given location) are contemporary developments. Furthermore, virtual private networks (VPNs) are networks which connect computers in remote locations as if they were in the same physical location and provide business users with global operations with a transparent means of intra-company communication. The access device plays an important role, specifically in the residential environment, since its mode of operation influences the way multimedia services are and will be provided in the future. A primary access device has not yet emerged; the current contest between television and personal computers as main standards has only just begun.

CONCLUSION: THE TRANSACTION LANDSCAPE

This chapter describes a fundamental shift in industry structure for transaction-based economic activities. Such a shift is demonstrated by the fact that player selection, contract condition setting, contract signature, contract storage and transaction actions are being performed on the Internet by different players. This has a cascading effect. Each transaction process produces another transaction, which in turn results in more transactions. When a user purchases a product or a service, a transaction stream is triggered. We have argued that electronic markets are evolving from an intermediary-based model into a transaction stream model in which more than one agent controls the transaction contract process. Each transaction is generated through an individualized transaction stream. The number of players in a transaction stream is bound to increase.

The Internet provides tools to facilitate the streaming process. It enables different transaction participants to establish protocols to perform each of the five basic transaction components in a myriad of different ways. Associate programmes, interest links, yellow pages, robots and profile information, are just a sample of the tools being used. Different players add value through content, editing, navigation and distribution. As transaction streams evolve, new needs will appear. Currently, one of the greatest barriers to the full development of transaction streams is the lack of certification, security, licensing and endorsement authorities.

Based on the information presented here, it is possible that transaction streams will be present in many industries. Managers must then seek to benefit from such streams by integrating them into their current business models. The marketing arena is foreseen as one of the first to be affected. Traditionally exclusive distributor arrangements must be complemented with Internet presence through incorporation of some of the transaction streaming schemes presented above. The pricing policy through each of the transaction stream players deserves increasing attention. Existing practices tend to be fairly simple, but will become more complex as competition increases and experience is accumulated.

Companies participating in existing electronic markets must question whether benefit can be derived from operating the market within the Internet context. Internet compatibility would bring transaction stream opportunities that may increase the amount of transactions being performed. However, the broader reach may attract new players and bring profits down.

Transaction streams will become increasingly competitive. Companies must find ways to add value in their transaction streaming activities. Dell claims to sell over $4 million daily through in-company associate programmes which rely on their "business center solution". This service currently supports over 100 companies in management of their PC ordering needs. Furthermore, Dell is working to increase the value added to each customer by customizing current functionality offerings such as company reports, account team information, product information gathering and budget composition. These custom sites support the entire selling cycle, from pre-sales to post-sales.

Using this in-company associate programme, Dell is gradually transforming supply chains into seamless direct relationships between suppliers, manufacturers and their customers. Dell could provide the tools to foster third-party players to develop modules that enhance transaction streams involving Dell's products. Taken to an extreme, transaction streams can lead to the fragmentation of the various value-adding components in a transaction so that new organizational forms, such as the cellular form, become feasible (Miles *et al.*, 1997).

The future will belong to those companies that can successfully add value in the wave of transaction streams. A secure transaction ownership may only be possible when the ownership occurs at the transaction activity level. Transactions on the Internet will evolve into an ever increasingly complex environment where management will struggle to elucidate future profit arenas. The emerging electronic commerce landscape business is not cola-wars. It is a complex business that requires a manager to maintain many situational allies.

REFERENCES

Bakos, J.Y. (1991). A strategic analysis of electronic marketplaces. *MIS Quarterly*, 15 September, 295.

Benjamin, R. & Wigand, R. (1995). Electronic markets and virtual value chains on the information superhighway. *Sloan Management Review*, Winter, 62.

Cronin, M.J. (1996). *The Internet Strategy Handbook: Lessons from the New Frontiers of Business*. Boston, MA: Harvard Business School Press.

Granoff, P. (1997). Virtual vineyards. *MIT's Technology Review*, August/September.

Haanes, K. & Lowendahl, B.R. (1997). The unit of activity: towards an alternative to the theories of the firm. In H. Thomas, D. O'Neal & M. Ghertman (eds) *Strategy, Structure and Style*. Chichester: John Wiley & Sons, pp. 201–218.

Hagel, J. III & Armstrong, A.G. (1997). *Net Gain. Expanding Markets through Virtual Communities*. Boston MA: Harvard Business School Press.

Hodges, M. (1997). Building a bond of trust. *MIT's Technology Review,* August/September.

Katz, M.L. & Shapiro, C. (1985). Network externalities, competition and compatibility. *American Economic Reivew*, **75**, 70–83.

Lai, C., Medvinsky, G. & Clifford B. (1997). *Endorsements, Licensing and Insurance for Distributed Services.* Cambridge MA: MIT Press, p. 417.

Malone, T.W, Yates, J. & Benjamin, R.I. (1987). Electronic markets and electronic hierarchies. *Communications of the ACM*, **30**(6), 484.

Markey, E.J. (1997) A privacy safety net. *MIT's Techonogy Review*, August/September.

Meeker, M. (1997). *The Technology IPD Yearbook*. New York: Morgan Stanley Technology Group.

Miles, R.E., Snow, C.C., Mathews, J.A., Miles, G. & Coleman H.J. (1997). Organizing in the knowledge age: anticipating the cellular form. *Academy of Management Executive*, **11**(4), 7–24

Negroponte, N. (1995). *Being Digital*. New York: Vintage Books.

OTA (1994). *Electronic Enterprises: Looking to the Future*, OTA-TCT-600. Washington DC: US Government Printing Office.

Rheingold, H. (1993). *The Virtual Community*. New York: Harper Collins.

Schwartz, E.I. (1997) *Webonomics*, Broadway, New York.

Subirana, B. (1996). SI-88 Amalgamated Banks of South Africa Training TV Network (A): Multimedia learning and the transformation of the information industries, *Estudios Ediciones IESE*, University of Navarra, Spain.

Subirana, B. (1997a). SI-90 Amalgamated Banks of South Africa Training TV Network (B): Onto the Internet, *Estudios Ediciones IESE*, University of Navarra, Spain.

Subirana, B. (1997b) SI-91 J&J Internet Book Shopping Robot, *Estudios Ediciones IESE*, University of Navarra, Spain.

Subirana, B. (1997c). SI-101 Libresa (B), *Estudios Ediciones IESE*, University of Navarra, Spain.

Subirana, B. (1997d). SI-102 Libresa (C), *Estudios Ediciones IESE*, University of Navarra, Spain.

Subirana, B. & Palavecino, S. (1997). SI-104 Amadeus: Starting on the Internet and electric commerce, *Estudios Ediciones IESE*, University of Navarra, Spain.

Subirana, B. & Zuidhof, M. (1996a) SI-85 Libresa (A): CD-ROM encyclopaedias on a niche market, *Estudios Ediciones IESE*, University of Navarra, Spain.

Subirana, B. & Zuidhof, M. (1996b). SI-93 Readers Inn: Virtual distribution on the Internet on the transformation on the publishing industry, *Estudios Ediciones IESE*, University of Navarra, Spain (Available on CD-ROM).

Subirana, B., Oghuledo O. & Santomá, X. (1996). SI-95 OPI The Netscape Corporation, *Estudios Ediciones IESE*, University of Navarra, Spain.
Tapscott, D. (1996). *The Digital Economy*. London: McGraw-Hill.
Von Hippel, E. (1988). *The Sources of Innovation*. New York: Oxford University Press.

Section II

Interconnected Processes: Strategies, Competencies and Performance

8

Managing Cross-Divisional Interconnections to Create Knowledge-Based Competence in a Multidivisional Firm

KAZUO ICHIJO, IKUJIRO NONAKA

INTRODUCTION

The diversified form of business organization is a dominant form of modern business enterprise. Therefore, as Ramanujam & Varadarajan summarize (1989), diversification has emerged as a central topic of research in the strategic management literature. The recent structural change observed in a leading Japanese multidivisional electronics firm raises renewal interest in the structure and the management of multidivisional firms and the way they are affected by industrial characteristics. Facing drastic environmental changes characterized by such words as industry convergence, globalization, and time-based competition, Toshiba, one of the leading multidivisional electronics firms in Japan, created a cross-divisional unit. This cross-divisional unit, called the Advanced-I Group, was established to

New Managerial Mindsets: Organizational Transformation and Strategy Implementation.
Edited by M.A. Hitt, J.E. Ricart i Costa and R.D. Nixon.
© 1998 John Wiley & Sons Ltd.

cultivate new business frontiers using Toshiba's existing competitive strengths, i.e. technologies and expertise accumulated in Toshiba's various divisions.

The structural change observed at Toshiba provides empirical support to Chandler's (1994) argument that in industries in which new product development is a critical component of interfirm competition, where R&D expenditures are high, state-of-the-art facilities costly, and marketing requires specialized skills, the corporate office needs to concentrate on the entrepreneurial (value-creating) function. More importantly, however, this structural change also suggests the necessity for managing cross-divisional interconnections by establishing a cross-divisional unit to share, transfer, and create firm-specific organizational knowledge. It also suggests that the HQ unit should take the lead in this knowledge management at the corporate level.

This chapter describes the recent structural change at Toshiba and intends to develop new insights into the structure and the management of diversified multidivisional firms. Diversification alone will not produce superior performance (Chandler, 1962; Hill, 1994); the corporate management of a firm must adopt the appropriate internal organizational arrangements. We will analyze internal organizational arrangements at Toshiba from the knowledge creation perspective (Nonaka, 1991, 1994; Nonaka & Takeuchi, 1995). The objective of this chapter is to bring structure and knowledge management of multidivisional firms into focus in the study of multidivisional firms by elaborating why these structural changes were made. The importance of managing cross-divisional interconnections to develop knowledge-based competence of a related diversified firm will be emphasized in this chapter. For that purpose, the role of the HQ unit for managing cross-divisional interconnections and knowledge at the corporate level will be highlighted. Drawing on the knowledge creation perspective literature (Nonaka, 1991, 1994; Nonaka & Takeuchi, 1995), we will argue that a cross-divisional unit is established to develop new knowledge-based competence by integrating knowledge accumulated in different divisions. The cross-divisional unit will also facilitate the better use of the tacit knowledge of a firm, which is the most important source of innovation (Nonaka, 1991, 1994; Nonaka & Takeuchi, 1995) and the under-utilized resource residing in a firm (Teece, 1981). The chapter starts with a description of the characteristics of Japanese multidivisional electronics firms. It then summarizes environmental changes facing global electronics industries, paying attention to their impact on Japanese multidivisional electronics firms. Next, it elaborates the recent structural change observed at Toshiba. Finally, theoretical and management implications obtained from the study of Toshiba's strategy, structure, and management conclude the chapter.

CHARACTERISTICS OF JAPANESE MULTIDIVISIONAL ELECTRONICS FIRMS

GROWTH THROUGH RELATED DIVERSIFICATION

In the past 10 years, Japanese electronics firms achieved sustainable growth in the global electronics industry. According to Andersen Consulting analysis conducted in 1996/97 by faculty members of Stanford University, INSEAD and Hitotsubashi University, in 1985, eight Japanese firms were listed among the top fifteen electronics firms. In 1995, six of those eight Japanese firms were still on the list, with higher rank. In addition, one more Japanese firm joined the top fifteen. In contrast, among seven US and European firms which were on the list in 1985, only one firm was higher in rank in 1995.

This sustainability of Japanese electronics firms was partly due to their diversified strategies, i.e. diversification of their business based on their multidivisional structures. Here diversification is defined as the entry of a firm or business unit into new lines of activity, either by processes of internal business development or acquisition, which entails changes in its administrative structure, systems, and other management processes, following Ramanujam & Varadarajan (1989). One of the primary reasons for diversification is to maintain the long-term health of a firm in the competitive environment (Reed & Luffmann, 1986). The global electronics industry is characterized by rapid and drastic technological changes. Old technologies and products become obsolete very quickly: they are replaced by new technologies and new products. Rapid technological change sometimes makes it difficult for those firms whose business is narrowly focused to accomplish sustainable growth. They are liable to decline due to rapid technological change. According to the Andersen Consulting analysis, 88% of those companies that dropped out of the top 150 electronic system companies worldwide between 1885 and 1995 were specialists, i.e. non-diversified companies, such as Digital Equipment Corporation, which suffered from the decline of its business as mini-computers were being replaced by PCs and workstations.

On the other hand, diversification provided a security device to Japanese electronics firms against environmental changes. A case in point is Toshiba. Toshiba's early history has two strands. In 1875 Tanaka Seisho-sho (Tanaka Engineering Works), Japan's first manufacturer of telegraphic equipment, was established. Its founder, Hisashige Tanaka, was well known from his youth for inventions, which included mechanical dolls and a perpetual clock. Under the name Shibaura Seisaku-sho (Shibaura Engineering Works), his company became one of Japan's largest manufacturers of heavy electrical apparatus. On the other hand, in 1890, Hakunetsu-sha & Co., Ltd, was established as Japan's first plant for electric incandescent lamps. Subsequent related diversification saw the company evolve as a manufacturer of consumer products. In 1899, the company was renamed Tokyo Denki (Tokyo Electric Co.). In 1939, these two companies, leaders in their respective fields, merged to form an integrated electric equipment manufacturer, Tokyo Shibaura Denki (Tokyo Shibaura Electric Co., Ltd). The company was soon well known as "Toshiba," which became its official corporate name in 1978.

In 1983, Toshiba announced "E&E" as Toshiba's new corporate concept. E&E stands for Electronics and Energy. With this new corporate concept, Toshiba announced its related diversification strategy, which would consolidate its expertise and knowledge in virtually all areas of electronics and electrical products. Electronics creates the new systems and technology needed in today's highly advanced information society, while Energy— electricity—has been the firm foundation of Toshiba. Toshiba believed that the synergy created among E&E fields would be crucial for Toshiba to cultivate new business opportunities, as Toshiba would apply a wealth of expertise and knowledge in these areas to pioneer new products and technologies.

As a result of the related diversification in the fields of energy and electronics, Toshiba is currently a corporation manufacturing a wide range of products: information and communication systems (computer systems, telecommunication equipment, automation systems, medical electronics equipment, etc.), information media and consumer products (personal computers, word processors, copiers, storage devices, audio and video products, etc.), power systems and industrial equipment (industrial apparatus, power generating plants, transportation equipment, elevators and escalators, etc.), and electronic components and materials (semiconductors, electron tubes, optoelectronic devices, liquid crystal displays, batteries, printed circuit boards, etc.). This variety of products is developed and produced in four major business groups: the information and communication systems group, the electronic components and materials group, the information media and consumer products group, and the power systems and industrial equipment group.

Diversification enabled Toshiba to accomplish sustainable growth. For example, despite a steep drop in semiconductor memory prices and lower sales in power stations and equipment, Toshiba's consolidated net sales increased by 7% to 5453.4 billion yen in the fiscal year ending 31 March 1997. This decline of the semiconductor business and the power stations and equipment business was compensated by the growth of the personal computer and peripherals business. Thus diversification at Toshiba plays the role of a security device against rapid and drastic environmental changes.

ORGANIZATIONAL ARRANGEMENTS OF JAPANESE MULTIDIVISIONAL ELECTRONICS FIRMS

Since diversification alone will not produce superior performance, a firm must adopt appropriate internal organizational arrangements (Hill, Hitt & Hoskisson, 1992). In the following, we examine the organizational arrangements of Japanese multidivisional electronics firms, especially their centralization and integration arrangements to accomplish economies of scope (Hill, Hitt & Hoskisson, 1992; Hill, 1994) through related diversification.

According to the Andersen Consulting analysis, in Japanese multidivisional electronics firms, HQ units execute stronger controls over divisions. TABLE 8.1 shows that in Japanese multidivisional electronics firms HQ units have a stronger influence on crucial decision making issues than those in US multidivisional electronics firms. In addition, other key stakeholders such as an SBU general manager, SBU marketing manager, SBU engineering manager, and SBU manufacturing managers also have stronger influences on these decision making issues. Since each stakeholder has a "say" in each decision making issue, it took Japanese electronics corporations a long time to reach consensus. As a result, it may not be easy for Japanese multidivisional electronics firms to react to environmental changes quickly.

According to Chandler (1962), in M-form firms each division is autonomous with regard to day-to-day operations, and should be accountable

TABLE 8.1   Time-consuming decision making in Japanese multidivisional electronics firms

Decision making items	Corporate HQ	SBU general manager	SBU marketing	SBU engineering	SBU manufacturing
Marketing and pricing	[**]	[**]	[ ]	[**]	[**]
New market entry; market exit	[ ]	[**]	[ ]	[**]	[**]
New product development	[ ]	[**]		[ ]	[ ]
Selection of R&D project	[**]	[**]	[ ]	[ ]	[*]
Enlargement of production capacity	[ ]	[**]	[ ]	[*]	[*]
Purchasing of production facility	[*]	[**]	**	[*]	[ ]
Personnel	[**]	**	**	**	
Restructuring	[ ]	[**]	[*]	[*]	[**]

[**][ ][*] indicates that each decision maker has a stronger influence at Japanese companies than at US companies. * $p < 0.10$; ** $p < 0.05$.
Data source: Andersen Consulting Global Electronics Study.

for divisional profit and loss. The data about the decision making system of Japanese multidivisional electronics firms discussed above suggest that in Japanese multidivisional electronics firms, divisions lack complete autonomy, thus lacking M-form features. They can be categorized as multidivisional firms where top-management intervenes in the day-to-day operations of divisions, thereby violating one of the M-form principles, i.e. operating autonomy (Hill, 1994).

In related diversified firms, the corporate office retains some control over the functions common to the divisions to ensure interdependencies among divisions (Mintzberg, 1983). Centralization is a strong characteristic of Japanese multidivisional electronics firms. Other than the interference of a corporate HQ unit in the operating decisions of a division, they centralize those functions common to the divisions such as R&D. For example, Toshiba has structured its R&D organization around three major tiers. Corporate laboratories at the Research & Development Center carry out basic research with a 5–10-year horizon. The Center's activities are coordinated with those of seven Development Laboratories, each of which is attached to an individual business group and works on product-oriented technologies within a 3–5-year framework. Research at these laboratories leads to new products and models at the divisional engineering departments found in all Toshiba manufacturing facilities. In addition to the Research & Development Center, one other corporate laboratory, the Manufacturing Engineering Research Center, develops manufacturing technologies that are widely used within Toshiba.

The HQ unit also plays a crucial role in achieving lateral communication between divisions. Coordinating the activities of otherwise independent divisions becomes necessary so that skills can be transferred and resources shared (Porter, 1985; Hill, Hitt & Hoskisson, 1992). Coordination between divisions requires integrating mechanisms such as human resource transfer, task force, and permanent project teams (Hill, 1994). For example, in 1984, as a new initiative of E&E, Toshiba launched "Project I." Project I was a cross-divisional task force as a concentrated and ambitious strategic initiative to extend the company's knowledge into the information, integration, and intelligence of advanced information and communications systems (the "I" of "Project I" stands for Information, Integration, and Intelligence). By launching Project I, Toshiba wanted to develop its advanced information systems and products business by integrating Toshiba's intelligence, i.e. the knowledge existing in various divisions. Project I was established with Toshiba's knowledge intent to develop new knowledge in advanced information and communications systems. The highly successful product of Project I in its early phase was the development of T-1000, Toshiba's first notebook computer, and T-3100 released in the USA and Europe in 1986. Before then, Toshiba had not produced either mainframe computers or desktop PCs. In order to differentiate its business, Toshiba focused on the untapped note-book computer market. Since the desktop PC market was growing very quickly in the mid-1980s, very few companies were interested in the development of notebook PCs at that time. Therefore, Toshiba had to develop systems and devices (e.g. 3.5 inch floppy disk drive) for notebook PCs by itself. For that purpose, Toshiba's talented human resources, especially those who worked in the power systems and industrial equipment group, were requested to help people belonging to the information systems group to tackle this tough job. Since the power systems and industrial equipment group had been Toshiba's core business group, very talented engineers were working in this group. By means of this knowledge transfer, the development of the notebook PCs finally ended with enormous success.

Hill (1994) argues that there are two main avenues open to multidivisional firms for creating value: economies of scope and economies of allocation. The former requires that divisions share resources, transfer information, and act cooperatively, whereas the latter requires complete decentralization. Toshiba can be categorized as a multidivisional firm pursuing economies of scope, with the corporate HQ unit playing a strong leadership role in centralization and inter-divisional coordination to accomplish economies of scope. This entrepreneurial role (Chandler, 1994) of Toshiba's HQ unit can also be observed in other Japanese multidivisional electronics firms. A case in point is NEC. In 1977, NEC declared its famous C&C concept. C&C stands for computers and communication. This concept implied that NEC would grow its business in the computer and communication industry segments, and grow these two segments anticipating and intending their integration. Electronic devices such as semiconductors are an integral part of C&C, and are expected to act as the driving force behind technological innovations. R&D activities are centralized and their mission is to develop C&C technology that will form the foundation for all NEC businesses. Having introduced the concept of C&C, NEC has been developing its business by pursuing inter-divisional coordination in the fields of computers and communication.

TRANSFORMATION OF TOSHIBA

ENVIRONMENTAL CHANGES NECESSITATING STRATEGIC AND STRUCTURAL CHANGES

Just as the 1980s were for US industrial firms, the 1990s were for Japanese multidivisional firms a decade of reshaping corporate strategies and rebuilding organizational structures. Environmental changes necessitated the transformation of Japanese multidivisional electronics firms. The electronics industry has been becoming more and more unstable and uncertain, as a result of the convergence of various segments of the electronics industry, the velocity of technological changes, and globalization. Environmental changes necessitate organizational transformation since multidivisional firms create competitive advantages out of the very manner in which they adapt to international competition (Doz & Prahalad, 1994).

First, the word "convergence" characterizes the recent development of the entire electronics industry. It is expected and anticipated that the PC, the network, and the home electronics industry segments will converge. For example, PCs are closely related to networking and communications because of the rapid development of the Internet. On the other hand, in order to make current PCs more user-friendly, electronics corporations are trying to integrate PCs and home electronics. A case in point is the emerging digital TV, which is the integration of TV and PCs. The computer and consumer electronics industry segments are competing for future digital TV. A big-screen computer television such as Gateway 2000's Destination, designed for the family room and aimed at people who already own a home PC, was released to the market in 1996. On the other hand, in the same year, Japanese large electronics firms such as Sanyo and Sharp began to sell web TV boxes as consumer electronics products that allow consumers to browse the web on conventional televisions. These two distinct industries have already put a product on the market that tests the public appetite for interactive television. So far, however, neither has been a rousing success. Given this industry convergence, the necessity for cross-divisional coordination strongly arises so that knowledge, know-how, and skills about different electronics industry segments accumulated in otherwise independent divisions can be transferred and shared.

Second, the technological and industrial changes are becoming faster and faster. In order to survive in this rapidly changing environment, therefore, quick decision making and agile adaptation to environmental change are indispensable. However, Japanese multidivisional electronics firms are notorious for their slow decision making due to the complicated decision making system described above. This slow decision making prevents Japanese electronics corporations from adapting to the ever changing environment quickly.

FOCUS STRATEGY

Facing the environmental changes described above, Toshiba has begun to transform its strategies and structures. The ultimate goal of the transformation at Toshiba is to structure its diverse business activities so that each division is based on products that rank among the world's best. For that purpose, Toshiba has classified its various operating divisions as either high-growth, mainstream or emerging business. Toshiba publicly announced in its 1997 Annual Report that it would allocate a large share of resources to those classified as high-growth or emerging. A mid-term management plan to transform these goals into actions has been implemented. PCs, peripherals, semiconductors, LCDs and network computing products are classified as high-growth sectors. In these sectors Toshiba intends to foster growing businesses through direct investments as well as alliances with leading companies in Japan and overseas. The heavy electrical apparatus and consumer products segments fall into the mainstream category. Although these segments still have products that exhibit excellent growth potential, the growth rate and share of the mainstream business at Toshiba are becoming smaller.

The HQ unit of Toshiba examines the competitiveness and growth opportunities of each division and decides divisional profit performance targets based on this examination. Divisions warranting particular emphasis are those where Toshiba has a technological edge, as well as the rapidly growing market for information-oriented consumer products that incorporate digital technology. Strategically important businesses for Toshiba are the information infrastructure business, the information services and software business, and the advanced information and communication systems and equipment business. By taking selective approaches to each division, examining its strategic importance and competitiveness, Toshiba plans to restructure these mainstream categories and build a more solid operating base. Concentration and focus on the most competitive and promising divisions characterizes Toshiba's new organizational arrangements.

THE CROSS-DIVISIONAL UNIT AS AN INTEGRATING MECHANISM

The purpose of Toshiba's new focus strategy is to make Toshiba more competitive in the global high-tech industry segments (i.e. converging information, telecommunication, and so-called multimedia segments). In order to drive this strategy strongly and very quickly, in April 1994 Toshiba launched a new cross-divisional project, the Advanced-I Project. The name Advanced-I symbolically shows that this project is a successor of Project I. The Advanced-I Project's mission is to take the lead in Toshiba's strategic initiatives for becoming more competitive in the global markets of information infrastructure, information service and software, and advanced information and communication systems and equipment. In order to accomplish this mission, the activities of the Advanced-I Project are focused on: developing and promoting emerging multimedia businesses; implementing cross-divisional planning and coordination; leading cross-divisional projects for new product development; creating new businesses with alliance partners; and allocating special funds to accelerate business development in divisions. Toshiba has set the strategic priority on developing its technologies and products in the multimedia business. In order to be competitive in this business, Toshiba saw it as critically important to raise the speed at which it channels resources to this promising business. The Advanced-I Project has been established at the heart of this drive.

A new cross-divisional unit, the Advanced-I Group, was formed in July 1994 to structurally support the Advanced-I Project. The Advanced-I Group has four subdivisions (the Advanced-I marketing division, the Advanced-I planning division, the Advanced-I System LSI planning division, and the Multimedia division), and approximately 90 dedicated staff members belong to the Group. The Group is led by a senior executive vice president and three directors were appointed as its deputy executives. This involvement of directors (a total of four board members) into the Advanced-I Group suggests its strategic importance.

The Advanced-I Group holds a management committee meeting every two weeks. At this meeting, important decisions such as approvals for new business plans, investments, and alliances are quickly made. The characteristic of the Advanced-I Group as a cross-divisional strategic unit is well reflected in the membership of this management committee. Other than the four board members and the representatives of the Advanced-I Group dedicated members, chief technology executives of Toshiba's nine divisions are regular members of this committee. A chief technology executive is appointed in every division of Toshiba. The executive should have a wide range of knowledge about technologies and expertise accumulated in his or her division, human resources, and the strategic direction of his or her division. In the management committee meeting, they share business and technological updates for each division and also develop insights into the strategic direction of their own divisions based on these updates. Once the inter-divisional coordination is necessary, the chief technology executives are ready to name who in their divisions should be involved. In other words, the tacit as well as the explicit knowledge of each division embodied in each chief technology executive is accumulated and shared in the Advanced-I management committee. When the management committee agrees to form a cross-divisional project through this face-to-face cross-divisional knowledge sharing, the Advanced-I Group dedicated staff members play the coordination role in this project. The management committee also holds a "one-day meeting" every three months to conduct a progress check on the projects approved at the previous management committee meeting. In addition, every three months, the Advanced-I Group organizes a meeting inviting all of Toshiba's board members, including the chairman and CEO of Toshiba and representatives of all the divisions. About 120 delegates review the activities initiated by the Advanced-I Group and conduct intensive discussions about the future direction of the Advanced-I project.

The characteristics of the Advanced-I Group as a cross-divisional unit is also represented in its financial support from the divisions. The Advanced-I Group receives 0.5% of each division's sales, approximately 17–18 billion yen in total in 1996, to fund its activities. This financial support from each division group emphasizes the impression that the Advanced-I Group's mission is to lead the entire Toshiba company into new business opportunities by coordinating cross-divisional coordination. In return for this financial support from all the divisions of Toshiba, the Advanced-I Group is requested to take the lead in capturing new business opportunities integrating knowledge and expertise existing in Toshiba's different divisions.

The Advanced-I Group is currently describing its business domain by a matrix of nine areas, within which various new markets have already emerged, such as wireless communication infrastructure, or DVD, digital broadcasting, interactive TV and Internet appliances. Through the development of products, businesses and alliances, the Advanced-I Group is trying to position Toshiba to make wide-ranging contributions to the exciting future of multimedia.

SUMMARY

Toshiba created a cross-divisional unit, the Advanced-I Group, to seize business opportunities in advanced information and communication systems. The corporate HQ unit intends to establish leadership in all aspects of the development and application of digital technologies, including the emerging digital media networks that are converging information, communications, and visual media. Given the very rapid technological development and industry convergence in the information and telecommunication industry, it has become crucial for Toshiba to realize economies of scope. Economies of scope require the sharing of tacit and explicit knowledge, i.e. resources, skills, know-how and technologies, between two or more otherwise distinct divisions. In related diversified firms such as Toshiba, interdependent divisions need to be tightly coupled (Luke, Begun & Pointer, 1989) and integrating mechanisms for cross-divisional coordination such as taskforces are created (Galbraith, 1973). The complexity of the integrating mechanisms for cross-divisional coordination varies depending on the extent of interdependence (Hill, 1994), and a cross-divisional structure such as the Advanced-I Group has become necessary to facilitate knowledge transfer between divisions consistently and systematically. The Advanced-I Group is a horizontal, cross-divisional structure which provides a platform for cross-divisional coordination and collaboration as well as a platform for interfirm coordination and collaboration.

The advantage of the Advanced-I Group as the integrating mechanism is threefold. First, coordination between interdependent divisions becomes easier and faster. Knowledge accumulated in each division is shared through intensive face-to-face communication among chief technology executives who should be well aware of that knowledge, thus reducing uncertainties as to the true value of knowledge (Hill, 1994), which may impede collective activities. Second, the corporate HQ can reduce the performance ambiguity problem of cross-divisional activities (Govindarajan & Fisher, 1990; Gupta & Govindarajan, 1986) by being directly involved in the facilitation of these activities. Meetings are held every two weeks to review the progress of projects initiated by the leadership of the Advanced-I Group. Every three months, Toshiba's top management has intensive discussions with people involved in the Advanced-I Project to review the progress and develop insights into its future direction. Third, corporate initiatives for cultivating new business opportunities are facilitated by the Advanced-I Group, which receives strong support and commitment from Toshiba's board members, rather than by divisions and taskforces. The risk of these initiatives is not small since their success is highly uncertain, especially in the rapidly changing electronics industry. If these initiatives are handed over to divisions, the divisions may be reluctant to take risks and the initiatives may end up being pursued half-heartedly. In the Advanced-I project, the risk is taken by the corporate HQ unit. A cross-divisional taskforce can work well for a cross-divisional project. However, it is not appropriate if the project is accompanied by great uncertainty and risk. With these three advantages, the Advanced-I Group draws our attention as a cross-divisional coordination mechanism, especially in a rapidly changing and uncertain environment.

CONCLUSION: MANAGEMENT AND THEORETICAL IMPLICATIONS

KNOWLEDGE MANAGEMENT AND THE CROSS-DIVISIONAL UNIT

The most important implication of Toshiba's transformation described in this chapter is the necessity for managing divisional interconnections to develop knowledge-based competence in related diversified firms. Knowledge creation should be boundaryless, involving multiple disciplines, multiple functions, and organizational members with different experiences, as well as crossing organizational boundaries by extending to suppliers and customers, as well as competitors. Knowledge is socially created in context (Berger & Luckman, 1966). Therefore, creating a cross-divisional platform such as the Advanced-I Group is of fundamental importance for organizational knowledge creation because it provides a new context for knowledge creation across divisional boundaries. In order to develop knowledge-based competence in related diversified firms, it is critically important to generate a context in which people belonging to different divisions share both tacit and explicit knowledge. Tacit knowledge is the most important source of innovation (Nonaka, 1991, 1994; Nonaka & Takeuchi, 1995). However, it is under-utilized in a firm and is difficult to separate out for sale in markets (Teece, 1981). In order to make better use of tacit knowledge residing in a certain division for developing a firm's overall competence, a firm should generate a context in which tacit knowledge is shared at the corporate level so that it will be used in other divisions.

The importance of facilitating organizational knowledge creation consistently and intentionally by generating a new context for knowledge creation has been increasing in the face of industry convergence. The impact of environmental changes cannot be ignored as a key factor for leading Toshiba to establish the Advanced-I Group. Given the recent changes in the electronics industry, characterized as industrial convergence, the importance of converging various knowledge accumulated in divisions—that is, sharing, integrating, and transferring knowledge across divisional boundaries—has been greatly increased. Thus, industry convergence necessitates the establishment of integrating mechanisms between cross-divisional activities. If the environment is complex, the uncertainties as to cross-divisional activities are high, and the risk of the activities is not small; cross-divisional activities would not be facilitated without strong support from the HQ unit. Integrating mechanisms initiated and supported by the corporate HQ unit are more useful in this case.

KNOWLEDGE MANAGEMENT AND THE HQ UNIT

It is characteristic of a cross-divisional unit such as the Advanced-I Group that a corporate HQ unit plays the stronger role in coordinating cross-divisional activities. In addition, from the knowledge creation perspective, a cross-divisional unit strongly supported by a corporate HQ unit is more useful for knowledge management than a taskforce. Since a taskforce is established temporarily, the management of knowledge created from the taskforce may not be easy, especially after the activities of the taskforce are completed. On the other hand, a cross-divisional unit will take the responsibility for the sharing, transfer, and management of knowledge at the corporate level. As a result, knowledge creation and development will be conducted more systematically and consistently by a cross-divisional unit than by a taskforce (FIGURES 8.1 and 8.2).

Knowledge is partly tacit, individual as well as organizational (Nonaka & Takeuchi, 1995). It needs to be nurtured and stimulated, i.e. enabled, and it

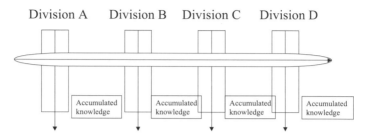

Objective: Sharing and synergizing division-specific
knowledge temporarily

FIGURE 8.1   The taskforce as a cross-divisional integrating mechanism. Required
management capabilities: boundaryless (internal)

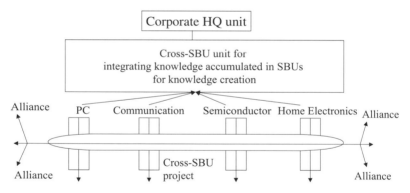

Objective: Sharing and synergizing division-specific knowledge
consistently and systematically

FIGURE 8.2   The cross-divisional unit in multidivisional electronic firms. Required
management capabilities: boundaryless (internal and external) and network

needs sensitive and aware managers to facilitate a social context in which it
can continue to grow. Therefore, in order to develop knowledge-based competence, corporations should pay attention to enabling conditions for knowledge development within them. There are important enabling conditions

for knowledge creation in corporations. These conditions exist in the vision, management, social relationships, boundary, and structure of corporations (Ichijo, Nonaka, & von Krogh, 1998). A cross-divisional unit such as the Advanced-I Group is a structural enabler for knowledge creation. As described in the introduction to this chapter, Chandler (1994) argues that in industries in which new product development is a critical component of interfirm competition, where R&D expenditure is high, state-of-the-art facilities costly, and marketing requires specialized skills, the corporate office needs to concentrate on the entrepreneurial (value-creating) function. Borrowing Chandler's argument, we argue that an HQ unit needs to concentrate on the knowledge management function to enable knowledge creation in a firm.

REFERENCES

Berger, P.L. & Luckman, T. (1966). *The Social Construction of Reality: A Treatise in the Sociology of Knowledge*. New York: Doubleday.

Chandler, A.D. Jr (1962). *Strategy and Structure: Chapters in the History of the Industrial Enterprise*, Cambridge, MA: MIT Press.

Chandler, A.D. Jr (1994). The function of HQ unit in the multibusiness firm. In R.P. Rumelt, D.E. Schendel & D.J. Teece (eds) *Fundamental Issues in Strategy: A Research Agenda*. Boston, MA: Harvard Business School Press, pp. 323–360.

Doz, Y.A. & Prahalad, C.K. (1994). Managing DMNCs: a search for a new paradigm. In R.P. Rumelt, D.E. Schendel & D.J. Teece (eds) *Fundamental Issues in Strategy: A Research Agenda*. Boston, MA: Harvard Business School Press, pp. 495–526.

Galbraith, J.R. (1973). *Designing Complex Organizations*. Reading, MA: Addison-Wesley.

Govindarajan, V. & Fisher, J (1990). Strategy, control system, and resource sharing: effects on business unit performance. *Academy of Management Journal*, **33**, 259–285.

Gupta, A.K. & Govindarajan, V. (1986). Resource sharing among SBUs: strategic antecedents and administrative implications. *Academy of Management Journal*, **29**, 695–714.

Hill, C.W.L. (1994). Diversification and economic performance: bringing structure and corporate management back into pictures. In R.P. Rumelt, D.E. Schendel & D.J. Teece (eds) *Fundamental Issues in Strategy: A Research Agenda*. Boston, MA: Harvard Business School Press, pp. 297–321.

Hill, C.W.L., Hitt, M.A. & Hoskisson, R.E. (1992). Cooperative versus competitive structures in related and unrelated diversified firms. *Organization Science*, **3**, 501–521.

Ichijo, K., Nonaka, I. & von Krogh, G. (1998). Knowledge enablers: developing and managing knowledge-based competence of a firm. In G. von Krogh, J. Roos and D. Klein (eds) *The Epistemological Challenge: Understanding, Managing and Measuring Organizational Knowledge*. New York: Sage.

Luke, R.D., Begun, J.W. & Pointer, D.D. (1989). Quasi firms: strategic interorganizational forms in the health care industry. *Academy of Management Review*, **14**, 9–19.

Mintzberg, H. (1983). *Structure in Fives: Designing Effective Organizations*. Englewood Cliffs, NJ: Prentice Hall.

Nonaka, I. (1991). The knowledge-creating company. *Harvard Business Review*, November/December, 96–104.

Nonaka, I. (1994). A dynamic theory of organizational knowledge creation. *Organization Science*, **5**, 14–37.

Nonaka, I. & Takeuchi, H. (1995). *The Knowledge-Creating Company: How Japanese Companies Create the Dynamics of Innovation*. New York: Oxford University Press.

Porter, M.E. (1985). *Competitive Advantage*. New York: Free Press.

Ramanujam, V. & Varadarajan, P. (1989). Research on corporate diversification: a synthesis. *Strategic Management Journal*, **10**, 523–551.

Reed, R. & Luffman, G.A. (1986). Diversification: the growing confusion. *Strategic Management Journal*, **7**, 29–35.

Teece, D.J. (1981). The market of know-how and the efficient transfer of technology. *Annals of the Academy of Political and Social Science*, 81–96.

9

Matching Diversification and Compensation Strategies

Brian K. Boyd, Sydney Finkelstein, Harry Barkema, Luis Gomez-Mejia

In 1985, Ed Brennan was appointed CEO and Chairman of Sears, Roebuck & Co. Brennan was a Sears insider, and this promotion was the reward for his plan to diversify the firm from retail to financial services. Acquisitions of Dean Whitter and Coldwell Banker, plus launching of the Discovery card, were argued to provide the basis for a spate of new offerings to Sears' customers. While socket wrenches and refrigerators appear to have little in common with negotiable securities or real estate, Brennan argued strongly for the synergies which could be derived from the combination of retail and financial services—in one proxy statement, for example, the company noted that the respective businesses were "more valuable to the shareholders when operating as segments of a single company than they would be if divested."

What were the outcomes of this diversification strategy? The focus on financial services led Sears to ignore its retail core, and the expected synergies never materialized. Ultimately, the plan—derided as the "stock and socks" model by much of Wall Street—led to disastrous results. Sears and Wal-Mart made a complete reversal in share of the discount retail market in the decade after Brennan assumed control. Additionally, there was a steady, downward trend in return on equity, return on assets, and profitability, with

New Managerial Mindsets: Organizational Transformation and Strategy Implementation.
Edited by M.A. Hitt, J.E. Ricart i Costa and R.D. Nixon.
© 1998 John Wiley & Sons Ltd.

major losses in 1992. Shareholders expressed their ire with a proxy resolution to strip Brennan of the board chair position—the first such resolution in a major US firm. In 1993, Brennan announced plans to divest the financial services segment and return the focus to the core retail business. Sears eliminated its long-running catalog operation, and closed 113 outlets. It also sold off Eye Care Centers of America, Coldwell Banker, Sears Mortgage, Pinstripes Petites, and spun off portions of Dean Whitter and Allstate. The workforce was also reduced by 50 000 people. For that year, the board of directors awarded Brennan a base salary of $1 million, another $2 million in bonus pay, and $700 000 in long-term compensation.

Currently, both diversification strategy and executive pay are high profile topics among shareholders, as demonstrated by a flurry of investor suits over ill-fated diversification strategies or "excessive" levels of CEO pay. It is surprising, then, that relatively little attention has been devoted to the intersection of these topics. In the Sears example, was Brennan overpaid, or was the level and mix of his income appropriate given the firm's diversification posture?

Historically, research on strategy implementation has highlighted how the interconnectedness—or lack thereof—of organizational subsystems can affect a number of outcomes, including firm performance. One prominent component of the normative implementation literature is the notion of "strategic" reward systems, or the matching of compensation practices to a firm's strategy. We explore the issue of strategic rewards in the context of corporate diversification. The dual choices of what type and degree of diversification to pursue are central to the strategic positions of most firms. While the 1980s were derided as an era of "merger mania," the dollar volume of M&A activity is considerably higher in the 1990s. Additionally, the research literature indicates that diversification strategies are often high-risk, with many firms accruing minimal or no benefits from such ventures.

Our chapter focuses on the role of executive pay in the effective execution of diversification strategies. We collected data on both diversification and pay strategies for a sample of 640 large US firms. Subsequently, we explored the following questions: How much, if at all, do firms "tailor" executive pay packages as a function of the firm's diversification strategy? and: Is this relationship different among high performing firms?

THEORY DEVELOPMENT AND HYPOTHESES

We begin with a summary of the separate research streams on corporate diversification and executive pay. Next, we discuss the prior literature which has examined these topics jointly. By integrating these papers, we identify a series of untested propositions.

CORPORATE DIVERSIFICATION

Driven by a wide set of forces, such as managerial preferences for personal risk (Jensen & Meckling, 1976), perceived opportunities to participate in new product markets (Porter, 1980), a desire for growth (Penrose, 1959), attempts to reduce unused productive and managerial capacity (Chandler, 1962), responses to antitrust enforcement (Fligstein, 1990), and many other reasons, diversification is a fundamental aspect of the strategic landscape of companies. The 1960s and 1970s were characterized by extensive "diversification" in the sense of firms expanding into many different businesses. Although much has been written about this era, perhaps the primary driver of the conglomerate strategy was the fundamental changes in antitrust regulation during this time. In 1950, Congress passed the Celler-Kefauver Act, which virtually outlawed both horizontal and vertical mergers because of their alleged anticompetitive characteristics. It was not until the Supreme Court rendered its first decision under Celler-Kefauver by voiding the proposed merger between Kinney Shoe and Brown Shoe Company in 1962, however, that vertical and horizontal mergers effectively became illegal. Thus, firms looking to grow via acquisition resorted to unrelated mergers that defined the conglomerate strategy.

With the changes in strategy came major organizational challenges. While many at the time argued that size and scale had inherent advantages, and "general managers" were capable of effectively running businesses in different industries, it became apparent that the conglomerate strategy was not without difficulties. Perhaps the most important challenge became that of generating reasonable rates of return as firms became bigger. In response, many companies turned toward portfolio planning techniques that sprang up in the 1970s as an attempt to address this problem of "profitless growth." The idea that a firm's full set of businesses needs to be evaluated in terms of growth potential and market position was an important insight, and helped many companies begin to make sense of their portfolios. Unfortunately, these portfolio planning methods also came with several flaws, including a disregard for potential synergies across businesses, the risks of writing-off so-called "dogs" when such businesses could still generate positive cash flow with little additional investment, the inherent cross-subsidization of businesses that covered up weaknesses in competitiveness, and other problems.

More recently, academic and practitioner emphasis has been toward building organizations which are more narrowly focused. Different versions of this logic have appeared over the past 20 years. For example, Rumelt's (1974) work highlighted the value of "related diversification" strategies, a key insight at the time in light of the strength of the conglomerate strategy during that era. Rumelt's work indicated that companies do best when they are focused around some set of core skills. As it turns out, however, most of the ensuing work has looked at relatedness more in terms of products and markets than in terms of core skills. Another version of the narrow focus theme emerged from Peters & Waterman's (1982) injunction to "stick to the knitting," which really hinged on the idea that firms do better when they do only one thing. Hence, this perspective was less about diversification than it was about no diversification. Finally, the most recent versions of the narrow focus theme have come from the work on core competence (Prahalad & Hamel, 1990; Quinn, 1992), which emphasizes the importance of expertise in a set of capabilities or competencies that can form the basis for a multi-business strategy. Here, relatedness is not defined in terms of products or markets, but in terms of competencies.

Given that the emphasis on focus can be dated back some 25 years, one would expect to find a strong research track record in support. As it turns out, there is probably no other question in strategy that has received comparable attention. Much of this work has concentrated on the relative efficacy of unrelated and related diversification. Related diversification strategies are expected to be beneficial because they allow firms to take advantage of (i) operational synergies in production, marketing, R&D, and administration achieved through economies of scale (e.g. Bain, 1959), vertical economies (e.g. Harrigan, 1984), and economies of scope (Seth, 1990), (ii) collusive synergies from market and purchasing power (Caves & Porter, 1977), (iii) managerial synergies from applying complementary competencies or replacing incompetent managers (Davis & Stout, 1992), and (iv) financial synergies from risk diversification and co-insurance (Lubatkin, 1983). Unrelated diversification strategies, in contrast, gain their primary benefit through the last of these synergies, those based on financial economies. As a result, there is a relatively strong *a priori* bias in favor of finding that related diversifiers do better than unrelated diversifiers.

The results that emerge from the empirical literature, unfortunately, are highly ambiguous. Although many will assert that the research record supports related acquisitions as a corporate strategy, numerous articles have concluded exactly the opposite (Ramanujam & Varadarajan, 1989). Indeed, many researchers continue to expect to find that related diversification is superior to unrelated diversification. Rather than rework this old hypothesis, it seems highly likely that the mixed results indicate that the simple relatedness idea is misspecified. That is, it is almost certainly the case that there are many contingencies that govern when a related diversification strategy is really the most appropriate one. For example, the performance consequences of diversification may be affected by the nature of the industries being consolidated (Hill & Hansen, 1991), the type of resources that can be transferred through diversification activities (Chatterjee & Wernerfelt, 1991), and a whole range of implementation issues that help determine whether relatedness translates into performance (Hoskisson & Hitt, 1990).

It is this last issue—effective implementation of diversification strategies—that holds great promise, we believe, for unraveling the puzzle of diversification strategy. Indeed, the challenge of implementing related diversification strategies may very well be an order of magnitude greater that that of implementing unrelated diversification strategies. After all, the effectiveness of a relatedness strategy depends on realizing synergies, while an unrelated strategy tends to have less synergistic potential, and, hence, provides a significantly less challenging implementation process. As Lubatkin & O'Neil (1987, p. 668) have argued, "administrative business risk" is greater when two related businesses are merged. Consider all that is needed for a related diversification strategy to be effectively implemented. Success here depends on realizing the strategic benefits of diversification by making synergies happen and positioning the new firm for growth. It requires effective interaction and coordination among business units to realize the strategic potential of this strategy at the same time that it necessitates special attention to human resource concerns. On the other hand, unrelated diversifiers do not require the same degree of cooperation, nor do they entail the same coordination costs, from the various businesses that make up the corporate parent. As a result, it is usually quite a bit less difficult to implement an unrelatedness strategy than one based on relatedness.

There are many aspects to the implementation question—such as cultural fit, management style similarities, and management reward systems—and it is here that there appears to be real promise in unraveling the performance consequences of diversification at the same time as there have been relatively fewer studies of this type. For example, several studies on mergers and acquisitions have highlighted the importance of cultural fit in post-deal integration (e.g. Chatterjee *et al.*, 1992). Differences in corporate cultures tend to create administrative conflicts and feelings of hostility after the acquisition is concluded (Sales & Mirvis, 1984). It is not hard to imagine that cultural problems in multi-business firms are even more severe when there are different business units operating with different goals, yet at the same time being impelled to "cooperate" to realize the synergies that are at the heart of the related diversification strategy.

Similar findings have been reported with respect to management style similarity, again with much of this work focusing on mergers and acquisitions. Management styles in different organizations can vary in terms of risk propensity, decision making approach, and even preferred control and communication patterns (Datta, 1991). Once again, it seems evident that similarity in management style can increase the likelihood that synergies will be realized because the interaction and coordination necessary for diversification success can proceed with less contentiousness than might otherwise occur (Larsson & Finkelstein, forthcoming). In all, this research on the implementation of diversification strategies holds great promise for unraveling the mixed results reported to date in the literature. In the following section, we explore in detail one particularly critical component of implementation: executive incentives and rewards.

EXECUTIVE COMPENSATION

An enormous amount of theoretical and empirical research has been done regarding what determines executive pay. This research has gone on for at least 70 years, and has accumulated towards a total of more than 309 studies (for reviews, see Gomez-Mejia, 1994; Gomez-Mejia & Wiseman, 1997). However, despite the enormous amount of research, there appears to be little convergence in this literature on what determines executive pay.

Firm Size

The most robust result in this literature is that CEO pay correlates with firm size. Most empirical studies measure a strong and highly (statistically) significant relationship. The higher pay of CEOs of larger firms can be justified by the larger complexity of their jobs (a human capital argument): they are on average responsible for more businesses, markets, products, and so on. However, a strong relationship between firm size and executive pay may also have adverse effects. The dominant paradigm in compensation research—agency theory—assumes that managers are inclined to serve their own interests, which do not necessarily coincide with those of the shareholders. From an agency perspective, offering a compensation scheme to managers is a way of "telling them what to do." Tying the managers' pay to firm size "tells" them to increase firm size, for which they are rewarded. Of course, growth is not always bad for shareholders. It is often a healthy strategy—if firms are small and relatively young, if the business is expanding rapidly, or if market share needs to be captured. In contrast, in older and more mature businesses, a strategy of consolidation and maintenance may serve the interests of the firms' owners better. However, a positive relationship between pay and firm size tells CEOs to increase firm size irrespective of what is optimal for shareholders, through start-ups or acquisitions, within the same industry or through diversification. Larger firms also imply more power, status, and perks for CEOs.

Diversification, especially unrelated diversification, allows CEOs to reduce their employment risk, even though such diversification may be bad for shareholders. Thus, a taste for growth—reinforced by a positive relationship between CEO pay and firm size—may imply strategic decisions that are undesirable for shareholders (Amihud & Lev, 1971; Gomez-Mejia, Tosi & Hinkin, 1987; Jensen, 1986; Morck, Shleifer & Vishny, 1990).

Firm Performance

Consequently—agency theorists argue—CEOs of large, open corporations should be controlled by a board of directors, which is responsible for the ratification of important strategic decisions, the hiring and firing of CEOs, and for setting their pay (Fama & Jensen, 1983). CEOs' pay should be structured in such a way that their interests are tied to those of the shareholders (Jensen & Meckling, 1976; Jensen & Murphy, 1990). Indeed, the relationship between CEO pay and firm performance is the most researched relationship in the compensation literature. Despite the enormous amount of evidence, there appears to be little convergence in this literature. Many studies have found a positive relationship between firm performance and CEO pay (see, for example, Gomez-Mejia, 1994), while others have found no relationship (e.g. Kerr & Bettis, 1987).

Perhaps the most comprehensive study to date on the relationship between CEO pay and firm performance was done by Jensen & Murphy (1990), who examined data on 1688 executives from 1049 corporations. CEOs often get large bonuses, of the same order of magnitude as their salaries. However, Jensen & Murphy's estimates imply that the *sensitivity* of bonuses for firm performance is low. Their estimates imply, for instance, that the average pay increase (salary and bonus) for CEOs who performed two standard deviations above normal (a gain of $400 million in shareholder wealth) was $5400. This was less than the average *weekly* income of the sample CEOs (approximately $9400). The estimated probability of dismissal in the case of bad firm performance was only a few percentage points higher than in the case of normal performance. Stronger pay–performance relationships were implied by the CEOs' options and stockholdings. The estimated total sensitivity of CEO pay for firm performance—which included the effects of pay, options, stockholdings, and dismissals—implied that, on average, CEO wealth changed $3.25 for every $1000 change in shareholder wealth. The authors suggested that the results in their study were inconsistent with agency theory, particularly since most managers held only trivial fractions of their firms' stock.

Explanations for Weak Pay–Performance Relationships

Various explanations have been forwarded for these weak results and low explained variances. First, agency theory formally does not say anything about the strength of the relationship between CEO pay and firm performance. A stronger relationship between CEO pay and firm performance implies stronger incentives but also more risk for managers, since firm performance is also influenced by external circumstances beyond the CEO's control, such as the growth of the economy, the actions of competitors, and so on. Thus a weak but statistically significant relationship between executive pay and firm performance is not necessarily inconsistent with agency theory.

Second, CEOs' pay may not only be tied to firm performance, but also to other informative measures of their performance, such as (changes in) the firm's market share, its success in developing new products, the firm's relative performance *vis-à-vis* competitors, whether or not the CEO has groomed a successor, and so on—variables which may correlate weakly with firm performance at the time of the evaluation. Third, there are many problems associated with estimating the pay–performance sensitivities implied by the stock options awarded to CEOs (see for example, Gomez-Mejia, 1994).

Fourth, firms often have weak boards of directors. This weakness may be caused by the size of the board (too large), by having too many inside directors on the board, and because outside directors do not own shares in the firm and may therefore lack the incentive to discipline the CEO (Jensen, 1993). These problems may transfer to the renumeration committee, responsible for setting CEO pay. Outside directors serving on these committees may be particularly sensitive to CEO pressure if they were nominated during the present CEO's tenure, or if they depend on the CEO for their business (e.g. in the case of banks, insurance companies, or consultancy firms). Indeed, Jensen & Murphy's (1990) results indicate that CEO pay elements such as salary and bonus, and also dismissals, for which the board is responsible, are relatively insensitive to firm performance. Recent evidence from the UK, where renumeration committees have become more common since the recommendations of the Cadbury report in 1992, shows that CEOs of firms with a renumeration committee received *higher* pay (salary and bonus) than CEOs of firms without such a committee. Apparently, these committees tend to increase CEO pay if it is below the "going rate" (the average pay for a CEO of a firm with similar size and performance)—often following the advice of consultants—but are less inclined to decrease CEO pay if it is above the going rate. Thus board characteristics, and in particular characteristics of the renumeration committee, may explain (at least part) of the weak pay–performance relationships found in earlier compensation studies.

Fifth, recent evidence suggests a more complex relationship between CEO pay and firm performance (see also Finkelstein & Boyd, 1998), because the relationship between the manager's pay and firm performance is moderated by other factors, such as diversification (Gomez-Mejia, 1992). This emerging literature suggests that the variance explained can be increased substantially if such contingencies are explicitly modelled.

LINKING DIVERSIFICATION AND EXECUTIVE PAY

As noted previously, many studies have examined the relationship between corporate diversification and performance. Not only are these results mixed at best, but very little is known about "how firms implement diversification strategies . . . and the performance consequences of different approaches to implementation" (Ramanujam & Varadarajan, 1989, p. 354). A key implementation factor that may influence the relative success or failure of a corporate diversification strategy is the nature of the executive compensation scheme. Prior studies have found that variations in the extent and process of diversification tend to be associated with particular reward system profiles. For instance, Berg (1969, 1973) found that pay in large diversified firms is characterized by high risk sharing, lower fixed pay, decentralization, rewards based on business unit performance, and heavy emphasis on quantitative performance measures. While Berg did not differentiate between related and unrelated diversification, his findings suggest that this compensation profile was consistent with organizational features typical of conglomerates: independent business units, minimal resource sharing, and large information asymmetries between corporate headquarters and business units.

Similarly, several studies (Lorsch & Allen, 1973; Balkin & Gomez-Mejia, 1990; Gomez-Mejia, 1992; Hoskisson, Hitt & Hill, 1993) found that the design of the reward system reflects corporate-division and inter-division relations. As firms diversify by acquiring business units that share little in common, the firm tends to adopt a compensation profile that avoids the need for corporate headquarters to judgmentally assess the tasks and relative contributions of employees in different parts of the corporation. For instance, Hoskisson, Hitt and Hill (1993) found that corporate executives of highly diversified firms faced an increased span of control and greater diversity among divisions, limiting their understanding of the internal affairs of these multiple and disparate divisions. As a result, these executives emphasize financial results to evaluate divisional managers, and decentralize operating authority to divisions. In a review of this literature, Gomez-Mejia & Balkin (1992) concluded that the most appropriate pay profile for these firms consists of greater variable pay and risk sharing, quantitative performance measures, closer linkage between performance of the operating unit (rather than the corporation as a whole) and pay for divisional managers, and decentralized compensation decisions.

A contingency framework guides most of this research, with the central argument that the effectiveness of corporate strategy implementation "depends significantly on the existence of a match between compensation strategies and diversification strategies. If different compensation strategies are needed for the effective implementation of diversification strategies, then it follows that systematic matching of compensation and diversification strategies will have a positive impact on firm performance" (Gomez-Mejia, 1992, p. 381).

Strangely enough, the empirical research cited above has been focused almost exclusively on overarching compensation strategies for the entire organization (Balkin & Gomez-Mejia, 1990; Gomez-Mejia, 1992; Kerr, 1985) or divisional managers (Berg, 1969, 1973; Napier & Smith, 1987). There is very little empirical or conceptual work on how the compensation of the CEO varies as a function of corporate diversification, and the interactive effect of these two variables on firm performance. This lack is surprising given that the CEO is the main strategist for the firm (Mintzberg, 1990).

One would expect that the design of the CEO compensation package may have a direct bearing on business decisions affecting the relative success or failure of any corporate diversification strategies. Some of these key decisions include the level of business risk adopted by a firm (e.g. Coffee, 1988); investments of the firm's capital (Morck, Shleifer & Vishny, 1988); growth strategies such as mergers and acquisitions (Kroll, Simmons & Wright, 1990); and industry segments within which a firm chooses to compete (Gomez-Mejia, 1994). For example, top managers may avoid entering product markets characterized by volatile stock prices (e.g. as in various segments of the electronics industry) if a substantial portion of their pay is linked to equity market performance measures (Boschen & Smith, 1995).

CEO compensation may be both a cause and an effect of the corporate diversification strategy chosen. Although there is virtually no empirical research that explores the direction of the relationship, it would be a cause if the pay package induces the CEO to pursue a particular diversification strategy. It would be an effect if the board of directors designs an appropriate incentive structure for the CEO to implement the diversification strategy chosen. In either case, all of the business decisions noted above that have been found to respond to the CEO's incentive structure are likely to have performance consequences as a function of the fit between CEO pay and corporate diversification strategies. For example, a related diversification strategy calls for CEO decisions that involve more risk taking (because of greater asset specificity), more internally generated growth, an evolutionary expansion strategy, and overlapping industry segments for the firm's products (Gomez-Mejia & Balkin, 1992). By extension, if the CEO compensation package is conducive to certain types of business decisions and those decisions have performance consequences that vary according to corporate diversification strategies, then how the CEO is paid is likely to interact with diversification strategy to affect firm performance. For example, Hoskisson, Hitt & Hill (1993) found that reliance on financial results caused the divisional managers of diversified firms to emphasize short-term financial outcomes, leading to lower R&D expenses! From a contingency perspective, this means that the dysfunctional effect of the CEO incentive structure on the observed performance of related or unrelated diversified firms partly depends on the appropriate match between the design of the properties of the CEO pay package and type of corporate diversification.

In the present study, we argue that the type of diversification pursued by a firm is associated with certain CEO pay factors, and deviations from the prototypical pay scheme unique to a particular diversification strategy tend to result in lower performance. Specifically, as argued below, related diversified firms are more likely to emphasize cash compensation than unrelated diversified firms. Those related diversified firms that adopt this CEO pay policy are more likely to be high performers. Conversely, unrelated diversified firms are more likely to compensate the executive in the form of equity based pay, and related diversified firms that adopt this pay policy are more likely to be poor performers. There are several reasons for these expectations, as noted below.

A received wisdom in much of the diversification strategy literature is that an unrelated diversification strategy represents an attempt on the part of the firm to spread business risks across various industry segments and thereby avoid the pitfalls of being dependent on the fortunes of a small set of product offerings (Ramanujan & Varadarajan, 1989). Therefore, a related diversification strategy demands greater risk taking on the part of the CEO because of greater dependence on fewer products and greater investments in assets and knowledge that are specific to the firm. An empirical study by Hoskisson & Hitt (1988) provides indirect evidence for this tendency. These authors found that the more unrelated the firm's diversification, the less risk is observed in the CEO's decisions. A follow-up study by Hoskisson & Johnson (1992) found that firms that become more related in their product offerings after experiencing a major reorganization tend to be associated with riskier business decisions. Conversely, firms that become more unrelated in their product offerings following a major reorganization exhibit a more conservative posture in decision making.

A successful related diversification strategy also requires more centralized control on the part of top executives because there is a greater degree of interdependence and resource sharing across divisions (Pitts, 1976). Because these firms are associated with a more intimate form of control by top management and demand a unitary corporate-wide perspective, the burden of business risk in decision making is shifted to top executives in corporate headquarters.

The remuneration package of the CEO should fit the desired CEO risk taking attributes of related product firms. In their classical study, Amihud & Lev (1971) found that top managers are more likely to move the firm into an aggressive program of mergers and acquisitions, even at the expense of profitability, because of their belief that greater diversification leads to lower risk to their pay and employment security. Much of the agency literature supports this basic proposition: the more risks executives are made to bear, the more likely they will be risk averse in decision making. Specifically, normative agency scholars have argued that risk bearing increases risk aversion by aggravating the overinvestment problem faced by managers since their financial well being and employment security are dependent on a single firm.

To the extent that related product firms reward the executive with cash compensation they reduce the risk bearing of the CEO since this form of pay is less subject to perceived losses. When a CEO compensation scheme emphasizes ex-ante contingent pay (variable pay that is contractually linked to risky firm performance targets, such as market returns), executives are tempted to pursue conservative firm strategies that smooth income streams and create growth at the expense of business synergies, both of which are inimical to the needs of related diversifiers.

Cash compensation is less risky to the executive than equity-based compensation, for three reasons (Tosi & Gomez-Mejia, 1989). First, cash compensation suffers less variability or fluctuation from year to year so that the executive's income stream is fairly stable and secure, while equity-based pay can be subject to large fluctuations depending on market forces and firm-specific factors. Second, cash compensation is less subject to downside risk, or the simultaneous potential for large gains or losses. The less likely it is that the executive's income will go down if performance indicators decline, the lower the risk exposure of the executive. This effect is clearly more pronounced for equity based pay, and hence involves more risk bearing for the executive. Third, the longer the time period under consideration, the more uncertainty faced by the firm and the greater the possibility of unforeseeable events developing that may have a negative impact on the executive's earnings. Unlike equity-based pay, which is tied to distant performance indicators, cash compensation has a much shorter time horizon. Fourth, compensation risk increases if the criteria used to reward the executive are based on market performance indicators (e.g. stock prices) because the executive has limited influence on those indicators.

Following the above logic, we argue that cash compensation for the CEO reduces risk bearing and this reduced risk bearing enhances the successful implementation of a related product strategy. While long-term incentives are presumably designed to help executives think and act more like owners, these incentives also concentrate much of their wealth in a single firm. In comparison, most stakeholders can spread their risk across multiple firms. Therefore, the emphasis on equity-based pay leads to higher risk sharing by CEOs, simply because of the difficulties in diversifying their risk portfolio. As noted by Wiseman & Gomez-Mejia (1998, p. 9) "stock options create risk bearing when executives anticipate the returns from exercising those options in the future. Loss averse managers respond to this risk by preferring actions that preserve this anticipated value over actions that enhance their value." The following hypothese derive from the above arguments:

Hypothesis 1: Emphasis on cash compensation will be higher among related versus unrelated diversifiers.

Hypothesis 2: Support for hypothesis 1 will be greater among high versus low performing firms.

Hypothesis 3: Emphasis on equity-based compensation will be higher among unrelated versus related diversifiers.

Hypothesis 4: Support for hypothesis 3 will be greater among high versus low performing firms.

METHOD

The sample was designed to provide a representative range of executive compensation practices in large US firms. The initial pool included all firms listed in the 1987 *Fortune 1000*. Privately held firms, mutual associations and cooperatives, and US subsidiaries of foreign firms were identified and excluded from the pool, since executive compensation data are generally not available from these firms. Our final sample of 640 firms were then randomly selected from the remaining list, and encompassed all of the SIC broad industrial classes. A total of 53 two-digit SICs and 190 four-digit SICs were included in the final sample. No four-digit industry group accounted for more than 7% of the total sample, and no two-digit industry accounted for more than 12% of the sample. Thus, the sample is sufficiently randomized to guard against potential industry effects, and to ensure that our results are generalizable. Given the extreme range of industries—nearly 200 industry groups being represented in our sample, with many of our sample firms competing in multiple segments concurrently—it was impractical to impose any sort of industry controls. Also, the sample size was based on a self-imposed goal to collect data on 60–70% of *Fortune* firms in the hopes of getting a broad distribution on both compensation and diversification practices.

MEASUREMENT OF PREDICTOR AND OUTCOME VARIABLES

Diversification

Diversification strategy is typically broken out into two dimensions: emphasis on related or unrelated (conglomerate) diversification. Palepu's (1985) entropy scores du and dr were calculated using the Compustat Business Segment database, supplemented by 10-K statements as needed. Then, using the respective midpoints of these two measures, we classified sample firms as "high" or "low" on the two dimensions. (Note: levels of dt and du varied widely across firms—i.e. while many companies had scores of zero on either, many others reported very high levels of diversification. Given the extreme non-normality of the distribution for these variables, we chose to rely on dichotomous measures instead.

CEO Compensation

There are two primary elements to CEO pay: total cash compensation and long-term or deferred income. The first component—*total cash compensation*—is measured as the sum of salary and bonus, and has been used in many studies of executive pay (e.g. Boyd, 1994; Finkelstein & Hambrick, 1989; Hill & Phan, 1991). More recent studies of executive pay, however, also employ measures of *long-term compensation* in their analyses (e.g. Seward & Walsh, 1996; Zajac & Westphal, 1995), a trend that may be driven by recent SEC requirements to disclose the dollar value of stock options in annual proxy statements. Two options are generally available for valuing long-term compensation. The first approach, which includes Black-Scholes and its variants, uses a sophisticated model to project the value of such compensation. A second approach (Lambert, Larcker & Weigelt, 1993) is to value stock options at 25% of their exercise price. In our sample, the correlation between Black-Scholes and discount valuation measures was extremely strong (0.98), and other work (Finkelstein & Boyd, 1998) has reported superior reliability with the discounted valuation versus Black-Scholes methodology. Therefore, long-term compensation was operationalized in this study as the number of shares multiplied by 25% of the exercise price. Separate analyses (not reported here) used the Black-Scholes model to operationalize long-term compensation, and found no difference in the support for hypotheses across valuation methodologies. Data for all compensation measures were collected from proxy statements for 1987.

Firm Performance and Size

Prior firm performance was operationalized as the composite of return on equity for the years 1985 and 1986. Financial data were taken from Compustat, and supplemented by annual reports as needed. *Subsequent performance* was operationalized as the composite of return on equity for the years 1987 through 1991. *Firm size* was measured with the logarithm of net sales for 1986.

RESULTS

DESCRIPTIVE ANALYSES

The "average" firm in our sample had revenues in excess of $1 billion annually—the mean for company sales in 1986 was $3.9 billion, and the median was $1.6 billion. Additionally, the mean return on equity for sample firms was 11% for 1986. CEO cash compensation ranged from a low of $101 000 to approximately $6.3 million; on average, the CEOs in our sample earned $707 591 in cash compensation. Using the discounted valuation method, the present value of the typical long-term compensation award was $166 311; this value ranged from a low of zero to a high of $9.5 million. In aggregate, the present value of the typical long-term incentive award represented 24% of base salary and bonus.

The next component of our descriptive analysis was to determine the breakout of firms by diversification strategic orientation. The largest single group were firms best described as core businesses—relatively low levels of related or unrelated diversification. These firms comprised 44% of our sample. Firms with high levels of unrelated or conglomerate diversification made up 20% of the sample, and related diversifiers—what we will call synergy seekers—were a smaller pool at 9% of the sample. The remaining 29% of our sample were hybrid diversifiers, with high levels of both related and unrelated diversification.

For comparison, we analyzed the mean profitability of each of these strategy categories. Strategies which emphasized related over unrelated diversification generally had higher returns. The pure forms of the two diversification options had markedly different rates of return: the synergy seekers reported a mean ROE of 16%, while the conglomerates reported a ROE of only 3%; these results are consistent with the normative arguments for focused diversification strategies mentioned earlier. Hybrid diversifiers reported a ROE of 13%, and single businesses reported 10% ROE.

The pursuit of diversification has historically been the province of larger firms. We tested this assumption by comparing the degree of correlation between each diversification posture and firm size, measured as the logarithm of net sales. Both related and unrelated diversification reported correlations with firm size ($r = 0.13$ and 0.08, respectively) that were statistically significant, but limited in magnitude.

TESTS OF HYPOTHESES

As an informal test of hypotheses, we compared the means of both compensation measures separately for both high and low performers on the two diversification dimensions. These results are shown in TABLE 9.1. t-tests reveal that high performing firms awarded higher levels of both cash and incentive pay for either strategy type. However, these simple analyses fail to include the effects of other predictors of pay, so we conducted ANOVA models using controls for firm size and prior performance. These models, shown in TABLE 9.2, report somewhat different findings. The results of hypothesis tests are as follows:

TABLE 9.1   Compensation levels by diversification strategy

Pay variable	Diversification	Low	High	t-statistic	Significance level
Cash	Related	13.27	13.40	2.70	0.007
	Unrelated	13.26	13.37	2.69	0.007
Long-term	Related	6.73	7.95	2.66	0.008
	Unrelated	6.78	7.52	1.73	0.08

TABLE 9.2   ANOVA models for compensation variables

Variable	Full sample	High performers	Low performers
Dependent variable: cash compensation (logarithm)			
du	2.90 (0.08)	2.44 (0.11)	0.92 (0.33)
dr	9.12 (0.002)	10.11 (0.002)	1.69 (0.19)
Size	185.93 (0.0001)	44.08 (0.0001)	143.83 (0.0001)
Prior performance	4.26 (0.04)	0.09 (0.76)	6.93 (0.009)
Model R^2	0.26	0.21	0.31
Dependent variable: long-term compensation (logarithm)			
du	1.93 (0.16)	0.89 (0.34)	1.02 (0.31)
dr	9.07 (0.002)	3.08 (0.08)	5.97 (0.01)
Size	18.48 (0.0001)	9.02 (0.003)	9.80 (0.002)
Prior performance	0.00 (0.98)	0.29 (0.59)	1.00 (0.32)
Model R^2	0.04	0.05	0.04

- Hypothesis 1 proposed that emphasis on cash compensation will be higher among related versus unrelated diversifiers. As shown in the table, this hypothesis was supported: after controlling for firm size and prior performance, related diversification reported a highly significant link with cash compensation ($p = 0.002$), while the link from unrelated diversification was marginally significant ($p = 0.08$).
- Hypothesis 2 proposed that support for hypothesis 1 will be greater among high versus low performing firms. Again, this hypothesis was supported: the effect of related diversification was highly significant among high performers ($p = 0.002$), and non-significant among the subsequent low performers ($p = 0.19$). Unrelated diversification was not linked to cash compensation in either subset.
- Hypothesis 3 proposed that emphasis on equity-based compensation will be higher among unrelated versus related diversifiers. This hypothesis was not supported—in fact, a contrary relationship was found. Related diversification had a significant, positive relationship with long-term

compensation ($p = 0.002$), while emphasis on unrelated diversification had no effect on this portion of compensation.

- Hypothesis 4 proposed that support for hypothesis 3 will be greater among high versus low performing firms. This hypothesis was not supported: related diversification had a positive effect on long-term compensation in both high and low performing subsets; however, unrelated diversification had no significant effect in either case.

DISCUSSION

Our analyses answer a number of questions about the successful design of executive pay systems, but raise several others. The most salient finding is that high and low performing firms use very different tactics in rewarding—and motivating—their top executives. As noted earlier, the successful management of a series of related businesses is a much riskier proposition than managing a conglomerate or single business. By corollary, the immediate measures of success—i.e. synergy building—are going to be more ambiguous and problematic to measure than for the single or conglomerate business. This reality is manifested in several ways. Not only do high performers award more cash compensation for related diversification, but they also place less emphasis on prior performance. These results, coupled with a weaker influence of firm size and overall small effect of size for high performers, suggest another key difference between high and low performers. Overall, the low performers seem much more algorithmic in setting pay. The high performers, in contrast, place more emphasis on other factors not mentioned here. One promising opportunity for future studies, then, is to better identify the factors used by high performers to set pay in the face of related diversification.

These results also extend on the agency rationale of why firms diversify. As noted previously, diversification can be seen as an outgrowth of CEO self-interest—risk spreading, empire building, and costly acquisitions as a basis to justify higher levels of pay. While CEOs do earn more in larger firms, the pursuit of unrelated diversification is completely unrelated to either aspect of pay. That this relationship holds for both high and low performers is especially interesting.

One limitation of this study is that we had to combine salary and bonuses because most firms do not disaggregate these items. It is possible that short-term incentives (i.e. bonuses) increase risk to the CEO, leading to more conservative strategic decisions. While the combined cash measure we use may be obscuring some of the results, prior studies support that bonuses are largely insensitive to performance (Jensen & Murphy, 1990), and that the amount received does not vary much from year to year.

Future research on corporate diversification and executive compensation can take several forms. Perhaps at the top of the list is the need for work that examines in a qualitative manner how incentives affect decisions to engage in diversification activity. While our findings in this study are suggestive, work of a more qualitative nature has the potential to examine such attributes of compensation systems as the degree of monitoring, the criteria used to reward individuals, and the reactions of executives and other stakeholders to compensation systems. For example, it would be interesting for future research to examine how shareholders react to changes in pay systems in related versus unrelated firms.

In addition, there are several important issues related to how diversified firms are managed that seem important to investigate. One of the most important challenges in diversified organizations is how to combine the desire for business unit autonomy with the quest for synergistic sharing and learning across business units. What types of pay systems are best able to accomplish these dual goals? What conditions make it more likely for such systems to be successful? When we consider what mechanisms are available to CEOs and boards of directors to simultaneously promote independence and sharing, incentive systems seem particularly important. Yet, the research literature in strategy does not offer very much theory, or practical guidance, on this question.

Compensation design is important, yet not the only factor that determines whether or not an executive will pursue unrelated diversification. Here we have argued that equity-based incentives lower the performance of unrelated diversified firms. It is still possible that executives with that type of compensation arrangement may pursue unrelated diversification to lower their employment risk.

REFERENCES

Amihud, Y. & Lev, B. (1971). Risk reduction as a mangerial motive for conglomerate mergers. *Bell Journal of Economics*, **12**, 605–617.

Bain, J.S. (1959). *Industrial Organization*. New York: John Wiley & Sons.

Balkin, D.B. & Gomez-Mejia, L.R. (1990). Matching compensation and organizational strategies. *Strategic Management Journal*, **11**, 153–169.

Berg, N.A. (1969). What's different about conglomerate management? *Harvard Business Review*, **47**(6), 112–120.

Berg, N.A. (1973). Corporate role in diversified companies. In B. Taylor & K. MacMillan (eds) *Business Policy Teaching and Research*. New York: Halstead Press.

Boschen, J.F. & Smith, K.J. (1995). You can pay me now and you can pay me later: the dynamic response of executive compensation to firm performance. *Journal of Business*, **68**(4), 577–608.

Boyd, B.K. (1994). Board control and CEO compensation. *Strategic Management Journal*, **15**(5), 335–344.

Caves, R.E. & Porter, M.E. (1977). Entry barriers to mobility barriers: Conjectural decisions and contrived deterrence to new competition. *Quarterly Journal of Economics*, **91**(2), 241–261.

Chandler, A.D. (1962). *Strategy and Structure*. Cambridge, MA: MIT Press.

Chatterjee, S. & Wernerfelt, B. (1991). The link between resources and type of diversification: theory and evidence. *Strategic Management Journal*, **12**, 33–48.

Chatterjee, S., Lubatkin, M.H., Schweiger, M. & Weber, Y. (1992). Cultural differences and shareholder value: linking equity and human capital. *Strategic Management Journal*, **13**, 319–334.

Coffee, J.C. (1988). Shareholder versus managers: the strain in the corporate web. In J.C. Coffee, L. Lowenstein & S. Rose-Acherman (eds) *Knights, Raiders, Targets*. New York: Oxford University Press, pp. 40–60.

Datta, D.K. (1991). Organizational fit and acquisition performance: effects of post-acquisition integration. *Strategic Management Journal*, **12**, 281–197.

Davis, G.F. & Stout, S.K. (1992). Organization theory and the market for corporate control: a dynamic analysis of the characteristics of large takeover targets, 1980–1990. *Administrative Science Quarterly*, **37**, 605–633.

Fama, E.F. & Jensen, M.C. (1983). Separation of ownership and control. *Journal of Law and Economics*, **26**, 301–325.

Finkelstein, S. & Boyd, B.K. (1998). How much does the CEO matter? The role of managerial discretion in setting CEO compensation. *Academy of Management Journal*, **41**, 179–199.

Finkelstein, S. & Hambrick, D.C. (1989). Chief executive compensation: a study of the intersection of markets and political processes. *Strategic Management Journal*, **10**(2), 121–134.

Fligstein, N. (1990). *The Transformation of Corporate Control*. Cambridge, MA: Harvard University Press.

Gomez-Mejia, L.R. (1992). Structure and process of diversification, compensation strategy, and firm performance. *Strategic Management Journal*, **13**, 381–397.

Gomez-Mejia, L.R. (1994). Executive compensation: a reassessment and a future research agenda. *Research in Personnel and Human Resource Management*, **12**, 161–222.

Gomez-Mejia, L.R. & Balkin, D.B. (1992). *Compensation, Organizational Strategy, and Firm Performance*. Cincinnati, OH: South-Western Publishing.

Gomez-Mejia, L.R. & Wiseman, R.M. (1997). Reframing executive compensation: an assessment and outlook. *Journal of Management*, **23**(3), 291–374.

Gomez-Mejia, L.R., Tosi, H. & Hinkin, T. (1987). Managerial control, performance, and executive compensation. *Academy of Management Journal*, **30**(1), 51–70.

Harrigan, K.R. (1984). Formulating vertical integration strategies. *Academy of Management Review*, **9**, 638–652.

Hill, C.W.L. & Hansen, G.S. (1991). A longitudinal study of the cause and consequences of changes in diversification in the U.S. pharmaceutical industry 1977–1986. *Strategic Management Journal*, **12**, 187–200.

Hill, C.W. & Phan, P. (1991). CEO tenure as a determinant of CEO pay. *Academy of Management Journal*, **34**(3), 707–717.

Hoskisson, R.E. & Hitt, M.A. (1988). Strategic control systems and relative R&D investment in large multiproduct firms. *Strategic Management Journal*, **9**, 605–621.

Hoskisson, R.E. & Hitt, M.A. (1990). Antecedents and performance outcomes of diversification: a review and critique of theoretical perspectives. *Journal of Management*, **16**, 461–509.

Hoskisson, R.E. & Johnson, J.A. (1992). Corporate restructuring and strategic change: the effect on diversification strategy and R&D intensity. *Strategic Management Journal*, **13**(8), 625–634.

Hoskisson, R.E., Hitt, M.A. & Hill, C.W.L. (1993). Managerial incentives and investment in R&D in large multi-product firms. *Organization Science*, **4**, 325–341.

Jensen, M.C. (1986). Agency costs of free cash flow, corporate finance, and takeovers. *American Economic Review*, **76**(2), 323–329.

Jensen, M.C. (1993). The modern industrial revolution, exit, and the failure of internal control systems. *Journal of Finance*, **48**(3), 831–880.

Jensen, M.C. & Meckling, W.H. (1976). Theory of the firm: managerial behavior, agency costs, and ownership structure. *Journal of Financial Economics*, **3**, 305–360.

Jensen, M.C. & Murphy, K.J. (1990). Performance pay and top-management incentives. *Journal of Political Economy*, **98**(2), 225–264.

Kerr, J.L. (1985). Diversification strategies and managerial rewards: an empirical study. *Academy of Management Journal*, **28**(1), 155–179.

Kerr, J. & Bettis, R.A. (1987). Boards of directors, top management compensation, and shareholder returns. *Academy of Management Journal*, **30**(4), 645–664.

Kroll, M., Simmons, S.A. & Wright, P. (1990). Determinants of chief executive officer compensation following major acquisitions. *Journal of Business Research*, **20**(4), 349–366.

Lambert, R.A, Larcker, D.F & Weigelt, K. (1993). The structure of organizational incentives. *Administrative Science Quarterly*, **38**(3), 438–461.

Larsson, R. & Finkelstein, S. (Forthcoming). Integrating strategic, organizational, and human resource perspectives on mergers and acquisitions: a case survey of synergy realization. *Organization Science*.

Lorsch, J.W. & Allen, S.A. (1973). *Managing Diversity and Interdependence*. Boston, MA: Harvard Business School Press.

Lubatkin, M. (1983). Mergers and the performance of the acquiring firm. *Academy of Management Review*, **8**, 218–225.

Lubatkin, M. and O'Neil, H. (1987). Merger strategies and capital market risk. *Academy of Management Journal*, **30**, 665–684.

Mintzberg, H. (1990). The manager's job: folklore and fact. *Harvard Business Review*, **68**(2), 163–176.

Morck, R., Shleifer, A. & Vishny, R.W. (1988). Management ownership and market evaluation. *Journal of Financial Economics*, **20**, 293–315.

Morck, R., Shleifer, A. & Vishny, R.W. (1990). Do managerial objectives drive bad acquisitions? *Journal of Finance*, **45**(1), 31–48.

Napier, N.K. & Smith, M. (1987). Product diversification, performance criteria and compensation at the corporate manager level. *Strategic Management Journal*, **8**(2), 195–201.

Palepu, K. (1985). Diversification strategy, profit performance, and the entropy measure. *Strategic Management Journal*, **6**, 239–255.

Penrose, E.T. (1959). *Theory of the Growth of the Firm*. Oxford: Blackwell.

Peters, T.J. and Waterman, R.H. (1982). *In Search of Excellence*. New York: Harper & Row.

Pitts, R.A. (1976). Diversification strategies and organizational policies of large diversified firms. *Journal of Economics and Business*, **8**, 181–188.

Porter, M.E. (1980). *Competitive Strategy*. New York: Free Press.

Prahalad, C.K. & Hamel, G. (1990). The core competence of the corporation. *Harvard Business Review*, May/June, 71–91.

Quinn, J.B. (1992). *Intelligent Enterprise*. New York: Free Press.

Ramanujam, V. & Varadarajan, P. (1989). Research on corporate diversification: a synthesis. *Strategic Management Journal*, **10**, 523–551.

Rumelt, R. P. (1974). *Strategy, Structure, and Economic Performance*. Cambridge, MA: Harvard University Press.

Sales, A.L. & Mirvis, P.H. (1984). When cultures collide: issues in acquisitions. In J. Kimberly and R. Quinn (eds) *The Challenge of Managing Corporate Transition*. Homewood, IL: Dow Jones and Irwin, pp. 107–133.

Seth, A. (1990). Value creation in acquisitions: a re-examination of performance issues. *Strategic Management Journal*, **11**, 99–115.

Seward, J.K. & Walsh, J.P. (1996). The governance and control of voluntary corporate spin-offs. *Strategic Management Journal*, **17**(1), 25–39.

Tosi, H.L. & Gomez-Mejia, L.R. (1989). The decoupling of CEO pay and performance: an agency theory perspective. *Administrative Science Quarterly*, **34**, 169–190.

Wiseman, R.M & Gomez-Mejia, L.R. (1998). A behavioral agency model of managerial risk taking. *Academy of Management Review*, **23**(1), 133–153.

Zajac, E.J. & Westphal, J.D. (1995). Accounting for the explanations of CEO compensation: substance and symbolism. *Administrative Science Quarterly*, **40**(2), 283–308.

10

Division Managers' Compensation: The Contingencies of Centralization and Directionality of Intra-Corporate Sharing

JAUME FRANQUESA

INTRODUCTION

It has been suggested elsewhere that the economic benefits from related diversification come from the exploitation of economies of scope, or synergistic economies (Berg, 1973; Galbraith & Kazanjian, 1986; Hill & Hoskisson, 1987; Hill, Hitt & Hoskisson, 1992; Teece, 1980, 1982). Economies of scope are the result of exploiting interrelationships between divisions, and require some degree of resource sharing and/or skill transfers across businesses (Porter, 1987). Despite its potential benefits, the pursuit of economies of scope across related businesses poses important implementation challenges. In particular, in the context of the decentralized M-form, exploitation of economies of scope complicates the problem of divisional control, as resource sharing introduces performance ambiguity and

New Managerial Mindsets: Organizational Transformation and Strategy Implementation.
Edited by M.A. Hitt, J.E. Ricart i Costa and R.D. Nixon.
© 1998 John Wiley & Sons Ltd.

lack of divisional accountability, as well as the need for division managers to behave in a cooperative fashion with each other (Galbraith & Nathanson, 1978; Hill, 1988; Hill & Hoskisson, 1987; Hoskisson, 1987). These premises have been the basis for explaining general differences in the coordination and control mechanisms employed in related versus unrelated diversified firms (Hill, Hitt & Hoskisson, 1992; Kerr, 1985; Pitts, 1974; Vancil, 1979).

Prior research suggests that the potential synergistic benefits from resource sharing vary across strategic business contexts, which implies that different divisions within the related diversified firm should engage in different amounts of resource sharing (Govindarajan & Fisher, 1990; Gupta & Govindarajan, 1986; Porter, 1985). Research suggests also that, for the intended benefits of sharing to be fully realized, control mechanisms should match the resource sharing context of individual units. As a result, different control mechanisms are required across divisions of the firm (Govindarajan & Fisher, 1990; Gupta & Govindarajan, 1986). Following the *differentiated fit* perspective (Ghoshal & Nohria, 1989; Govindarajan, 1988; Nohria & Ghoshal, 1994), the present study adopts the individual division as the unit of analysis, and takes a contingent approach based on its resource sharing activities.

The control mechanism under study is the compensation contract for division general managers. Consistent with prior research on executive pay for middle-level managers (Fisher & Govindarajan, 1992; Napier & Smith, 1987; Stroh *et al.*, 1996), the present study focuses on annual (or short-term) bonus compensation. In practice, division managers' incentive compensation is a complex phenomenon that may include cash bonuses related to the achievement of short-term or annual objectives, cash bonuses related to the achievement of long-term (three to five year) objectives, and different forms of equity compensation, such as shares of restricted stock, phantom stock, or stock options, mostly also associated with long-term plans. Nonetheless, previous studies have found short-term cash bonuses to be the most important component of incentive compensation for division general managers (Galbraith & Merrill, 1991; Hoskisson, Hitt & Hill, 1993).[1] Past analyses indicate also that only the short-term bonus plan tends to be used in a contingent manner across SBUs, while the use of equity-based awards does not seem to respond to motivational reasons (Galbraith & Merrill, 1991;

---

[1] Based on a sample of 79 SBUs, Galbraith & Merrill's study reported that while 91% of division general managers received some sort of incentive compensation, only 27% participated in some form of long-term performance plans. On average compensation from long-term performance plans represented only 3% of the executive's total incentive compensation. Based on a sample of 108 corporations, Hoskisson, Hitt & Hill (1993) found that 40% of the firms surveyed were placing an emphasis on short-term division financial incentives, while only 7% placed emphasis on long-term measures of divisional performance as a basis for awarding bonuses to division general managers. Data collected from the 101 division managers included in the present study suggest also that the annual cash bonus is the most important component of incentive compensation for division general managers.

Merchant, 1989). More importantly, the decision to focus on short-term bonus plans here is warranted because the main focus of the present study is on the contractual adjustments necessary to solve the problems of division managers' control that emerge as a result of resource sharing. When effective, the elements of long-term or equity-based compensation respond rather to an attempt to curb the control problems created by the shortened time horizon and risk exposure of managers when evaluating investment decisions (Lambert & Larcker, 1985; Lewellen, Loderer & Martin, 1987). Since I am not concerned with intertemporal aspects of the problem of control in this chapter, the long-term dimensions of executive compensation are de-emphasized.

There is a body of literature that has produced evidence that proper implementation of a related diversification strategy requires a match between the magnitude of a focal unit's intra-corporate resource sharing and several features of the bonus contract for its manager. Contractual variables that have been related to the magnitude of interdivisional sharing are (i) the relative use of subjective versus formulaic approaches to awarding bonuses (Pitts, 1974; Vancil, 1979; Kerr, 1985; Gupta & Govindarajan, 1986; Govindarajan & Fisher, 1990; Hill, Hitt & Hoskisson, 1992); and (ii) the relative importance of incentives based on the performance of an entire cluster of divisions (Pitts, 1974; Kerr, 1985; Gupta & Govindarajan, 1986; Hill, Hitt & Hoskisson, 1992). The conclusions that emerge from previous findings in this area are that the higher the magnitude of resource sharing by a focal division,[2] the more should its general manager's bonus depend on subjective awards and group-performance criteria. The motivation for the present study is that such conclusion may not be warranted in all cases, and that a more fine-grained analysis of the problem of control introduced by resource sharing may result in both significant contributions to current theory of corporate strategy implementation as well as more effective recommendations to corporate contract designers.

A number of theoretical contributions suggest that, in addition to measuring the volume and strategic value of activities shared by a focal division (Govindarajan & Fisher, 1990; Gupta & Govindarajan, 1986), the allocation of decision rights over the shared resources will also have important control implications (Jensen & Meckling, 1992; McCann & Ferry, 1979; Pfeffer & Salancik, 1978; Vancil, 1979). On the one hand, the problem of managerial control will tend to be more prevailing and costly to solve as decision rights over resources to be shared are decentralized to individual divisions, rather

---

[2] From a control stand-point, the magnitude of a division's sharing should be measured by taking into account both the volume and the criticality of the activities being shared (i.e. how important are the shared activities for the focal division to compete) (Gupta & Govindarajan, 1984, 1986; Pfeffer & Salancik, 1978).

than being centralized at the group or corporate level (Huber & McDaniel, 1986; Jensen & Meckling, 1992; Vancil, 1979). Research in the international management area provides supporting evidence of the different control implications of centralized versus decentralized forms of resource sharing (Bartlett & Ghoshal, 1989; Ghoshal & Nohria, 1989; Roth & O'Donell, 1996). Also, for those cases where authority resides at the division level, the nature of the problem of control will be fundamentally different depending on the focal manager being the holder of such decision rights or not, and thus becoming either the "provider" or the "recipient" of services from the shared resource (Gupta & Govindarajan, 1991; McCann & Ferry, 1979; Pfeffer & Salancik, 1978; Pitts, 1980; Vancil, 1979).

In other words, past studies may have characterized and measured resource sharing in too general terms. This may have hindered our ability to fully comprehend the nature of the problem of control for each individual division manager as a result of sharing, and to study appropriate incentive contract solutions in each case. Recently, Franquesa (1997) has developed a theoretical model which explores the different nature of the problem of division managers' control, given differences in the magnitude, centralization, and directionality of sharing by their units. The model builds upon an agency theoretic perspective proposed by previous authors (Baker, 1992; Merchant, 1989) and integrates a series of results from modern economic theory of contracts (Baker, Gibbons & Murphy, 1994; Holmström & Milgrom, 1991) . This chapter reports the results of a first empiral test of Franquesa's (1997) model, and is organized as follows: the first section reviews theoretical arguments and presents the main hypotheses. Hypotheses relate different types of resource sharing to the appropriate compensation mechanisms from the viewpoint of division effectiveness. The second section describes the research methods used to test the model, including the sample, and measures. In the third section empirical results are presented. Finally, the results are discussed and the chapter concludes with implications for research and practice.

THEORETICAL BACKGROUND

DIFFERENT FORMS OF RESOURCE SHARING

To study the implications of resource sharing for the problem of control of individual division managers, we need to develop a measure of sharing at the division level, which captures the nature and extent of the division's interdependencies with other units of the corporation. Prior authors have operationalized the construct of resource sharing at the division level as the "magnitude" or importance, for the division, of the activities being shared.

In previous studies, the level of resource sharing is defined as the volume of activity sharing, multiplied by the extent to which the activity is critical for the focal division to compete (Govindarajan & Fisher, 1990; Gupta & Govindarajan, 1986). While volume and criticality of sharing seem important dimensions, they may still not provide a complete account of the nature and extent of the division's intra-corporate dependencies. According to Pfeffer & Salancik's (1978) resource dependency theory, the interorganizational dependence of a focal organization is determined by three critical factors: (i) the importance for the focal unit of the resource being exchanged (which includes both the magnitude of the exchange and the criticality of the resource); (ii) the extent to which either the focal or another organization controls the use of the resource; and (iii) the extent to which there are alternative sources for the shared resource that the dependent organization might turn to. As it stands, the current model of implementation of related diversification strategy is built upon the first of these dimensions only (Govindarajan & Fisher, 1990; Gupta & Govindarajan, 1986). Nonetheless, it has been proposed that the authority (or lack of it) of a focal division over resources being shared will be a major determinant of the nature of the problem of control for its general manager (Pitts, 1976, 1980; Vancil, 1979). Thus, it seems that the second of Pfeffer & Salancik's dimensions in particular (i.e. the extent to which the focal division controls the use of resources being shared) may have important implications for the design of effective incentive mechanisms within related diversified firms. In this section, I propose a classification of different forms of resource sharing based on the internal distribution of decision-rights over resources being shared.

There are two aspects relative to the location of decision rights over shared resources that will largely determine the role played by individual divisions in the resource sharing process: (i) the allocation of decision rights over the shared resource either at corporate or division level, which I will refer to as *centralization* or *decentralization* of sharing (Pitts, 1976, 1980; Vancil, 1979); and (ii) in the case of decentralized sharing, the ownership or not of such decision rights by the focal unit, which has implications for the *directionality* of sharing (Gupta & Govindarajan, 1991; McCann & Ferry, 1979; Vancil, 1979). Corporate managers must first choose between *centralized* or *decentralized* coordination of the sharing process for each given resource. In the case of centralized (or vertical) coordination of sharing, decision rights over a shared resource are allocated to a corporate- or group-level functional manager who provides services to a cluster of divisions. In the case of decentralized (or lateral) coordination of sharing, authority and decision rights over the shared resource are assigned to a division manager, who must provide services for other divisions (Galbraith, 1994; Vancil, 1979). Second, in the context of decentralized forms of sharing, the role played by a focal division will be different depending on whether the shared resource is under its authority or not (Pitts, 1980; Vancil, 1979). In the case where the focal division "owns" the resource, its manager must act both as a general manager of his/her division and as a functional manager for other divisions. In the case where the focal division does not own the shared resource, its manager must try to influence the use of the resource in the best interests of his/her division (Vancil, 1979). An alternative way to character-ize these different divisional roles is through the *directionality* of the flow of inter-divisional exchanges, where one division becomes the "provider" while the rest are "receivers" of services from the shared resource (Gupta & Govindarajan, 1991; McCann & Ferry, 1979; Vancil, 1979). The different nature of the problem of control under centralized versus decentralized forms of sharing, and at the two ends of the flow of transactions, will be explored in the next section.

In sum, both the centralization of decision rights and the directionality of inter-divisional transactions from a focal division's point of view have im-plications for the role that is to be played by the division in the activity sharing process, and hence for the nature of the problem of control of its manager. Combining these two dimensions of sharing, I will distinguish three different forms of resource sharing from a division's point of view. FIGURE 10.1 illustrates the three different forms of sharing:

1. *Centralized resource sharing,* or the focal division's use of services from corporate- or group-level functional resources. This form of resource

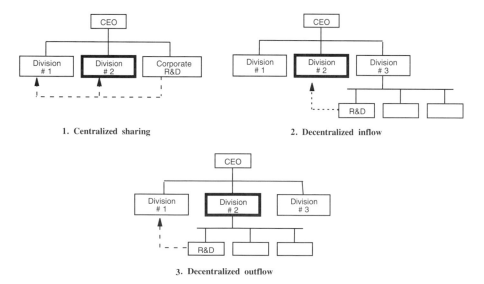

1. Centralized sharing   2. Decentralized inflow

3. Decentralized outflow

FIGURE 10.1   Three forms of resource sharing

sharing includes not only services from physical and human resources owned by the corporation, but also services that are subcontracted to outside providers by the corporate center to be used across several divisions.[3]

2. *Decentralized inflow sharing*, or focal division's use of services from functional resources under the control of another division.
3. *Decentralized outflow sharing*, or the use by other divisions of services from functional resources under the control of the focal division.

Vancil's (1979) work documented the existence of these three forms of sharing within diversified firms, although his observations with respect to decentralized forms of sharing were limited to the sharing of manufacturing resources. The work of several authors in the international management arena further suggests that the use of decentralized forms of resource sharing may be growing among multinational companies (Bartlett & Ghoshal, 1989; Ghoshal & Nohria, 1989; Roth & Morrison, 1992; Roth & O'Donnell, 1996). Nevertheless, at the beginning of this research, the relative incidence of centralized versus decentralized forms of resource sharing within modern related diversified firms was largely an empirical question. Data collected for the present study showed that these three different forms of sharing are indeed commonplace and a significant organizational phenomenon within related diversified firms.

The basic tenet of this chapter is that the relative involvement of a focal division in each of the three forms of sharing defines its role within the related diversification strategy of the firm, and dictates the nature of the problem of control for its general manager. The differentiated control problem for each division manager, in turn, determines the compensation devices that will be appropriate in each case. I now turn to a review of the theoretical model that accommodates the expected relationships between compensation features and divisional performance under different forms of resource sharing.

THE PROBLEM OF CONTROL WITHIN RELATED DIVERSIFIED FIRMS

Division-level managers can be considered agents of group-level or corporate executives (Baker, Jensen & Murphy, 1988; Hoskisson *et al.*, 1989). The agency relationship emerges because corporate managers are delegating

---

[3] Except the case where the division manager holds the right of not using the services from this subcontractor contracted by corporate, or the right to renegotiate the conditions of the service provided to better fit divisional needs.

operating decisions to division managers, so that they can concentrate on strategic decision making (Chandler, 1962). Control of division managers, then, consists of division managers making decisions and acting in what top management believes to be the best interest of the corporation.[4] The challenge for corporate managers (what I refer to as the *problem of control*), then, consists of instilling division managers' decisions that are consistent with and support the implementation of the intended corporate strategy of the firm, and to do that at a minimum cost for the firm. In other words, the problem of control is defined as the problem of designing the most efficient (i.e. least costly) incentive mechanism so that the interests of division general managers are aligned with the best interest of the corporation, as dictated by its intended corporate strategy.

As discussed above, the present work is based on the precept that the nature of the problem of control of division general managers is different under different forms of sharing. This section discusses how the problem of control is affected by considerations of centralization and directionality of sharing, and proposes appropriate administrative solutions in each case. The analysis starts with a key assumption. To guide the analysis, I assume that the core component of all efficient compensation packages for division general managers is a *base-line contract*, which consists of a linear combination of fixed salary and a cash bonus based on division profits (Baker, 1992; Merchant, 1989). In other words, for theory development purposes, we are choosing to focus on compensation contracts based on *financial* rather than *strategic* control of division managers (Hoskisson, Hitt & Hill, 1993). The attractiveness of this theoretical perspective is that it allows for an elegant formulation of the problem of control of division managers, and it is also well suited for the application of the rationale and results from modern economic theory of contract formulations. The problem of control originated by different forms of sharing will be best conceptualized against the backdrop of this assumed base-line contract.

Let us assume, first, that all division managers are compensated on the basis of the base-line contract. The base-line contract for each division manager is defined as the compensation scheme (i.e. combination of salary and bonus) that is optimal when his or her division is self-contained and does not engage in any resource sharing activities.[5] In other words, we define the base-line as the optimal contract at the point of zero resource sharing. As a

---

[4] An implicit assumption throughout the discussion is that corporate managers are properly motivated so that their interests are aligned to the interests of the corporation (i.e. its shareholders). Such an assumption is critical to the model developed here. In the absence of incentives for top management it is unlikely that efficient compensation contracts will be adopted for divisional managers (Baker, Jensen & Murphy, 1988; Gomez-Mejia, 1994).

[5] The model is abstracting from time horizon and risk exposure problems (i.e. dynamic or intertemporal aspects of the problem of control).

result of different levels of business risk and different levels of managerial risk aversion, the relative weights of salary and bonus in the base-line contract may be slightly different for each division and each manager. Nevertheless, what is important to us here is that, in all cases, managers' contingent compensation depends on division profits.

Let us now add sharing. As a focal division engages in different forms of sharing, the base-line contract for its general manager becomes less appropriate and its use generates *motivational distortions* in the new strategic context of the unit. There are two types of motivational distortions created by the base-line contract in a resource-sharing context: *performance ambiguity* and *performance incompleteness. Performance ambiguity* is at work when division profits constitute a poor signal of a division's contributions to its own financial performance[6] (Govindarajan & Fisher, 1990; Gupta & Govindarajan, 1986; Hill, 1988; Hill & Hoskisson, 1987; Lorsch & Allen, 1973; Merchant, 1989; Vancil, 1979). *Performance incompleteness* is at work when a division's financial performance reflects only part of its expected contributions to corporate value (Hirst, 1981), as the division is also contributing to the performance of other divisions.[7] The effect of performance ambiguity is that divisions can no longer be held accountable for their own earnings (Hill, 1988); the effect of performance incompleteness is that divisions should no longer be held accountable only for their own earnings.

Different forms of resource sharing introduce different motivational distortions, and/or the same distortions but to different extents. Franquesa (1997) argues that inflow sharing creates a problem of performance ambiguity, while outflow sharing creates both performance ambiguity and performance incompleteness problems. Further, although performance ambiguity is associated with all forms of sharing, its effects are stronger in the case of decentralized forms of sharing than in the case of centralized sharing. FIGURE 10.2 summarizes the motivational distortions that define the problem of control under each form of sharing. In this model, then, the differentiated

---

[6] *Performance ambiguity* emerges as a result of sharing because returns earned by a focal division may now be due to contributions (demerits) within that division, or to contributions (demerits) by another division or corporate department that are tightly coupled with it (Hill, Hitt & Hoskisson, 1992).

[7] In the literature, authors have rather referred to a *need to behave in a cooperative manner*, for divisions of the related diversified firm (Gupta & Govindarajan, 1986; Hill, Hitt & Hoskisson, 1992; Kerr, 1985; Pitts, 1974; Salter, 1973), which is another way to describe the same problem. I prefer to build on Hirst's (1981) concept of *incompleteness* of performance measures here, because it conveys that this aspect of the control problem is also related to a lack of adequacy of division profits as a measure of divisional contributions to corporate value. In other words, by choosing this characterization I am emphasizing that both dimensions of the problem of control that emerge as a result of sharing have to do with a loss of *outcome measurability* (Eisenhardt, 1985; Ouchi, 1979) of divisional profits as a signal of division managers' contributions. A conceptualization like that is more appropriate for the application of an agency-theoretical perspective later in this chapter.

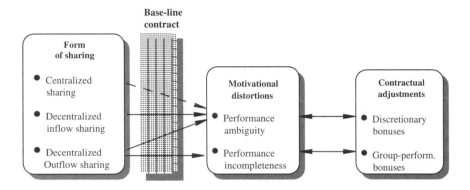

FIGURE 10.2   Control implications of directionality of sharing

problem of control of each individual manager is defined as the type and extent of motivational distortions caused by the base-line contract, given the magnitude, centralization, and directionality of sharing by his/her division.

Division general managers will behave in the best interest of the corporation only to the extent that motivational distortions are reduced. Thus, in this model, the search for solutions to the problem of control consists in finding appropriate *contractual adjustments*, or ways to patch the base-line contract (which was optimal in the absence of sharing), so that motivational distortions are reduced (Baker, Gibbons & Murphy, 1994; Merchant, 1989). FIGURE 10.2 also depicts the appropriate *contractual adjustments* to correct each motivational distortion. Concurring with prior research, we expect that the use of *discretionary bonuses* will lessen the problem of performance ambiguity (Govindarajan & Fisher, 1990; Gupta & Govindarajan, 1986; Hill, Hitt & Hoskisson, 1992; Merchant, 1989), while the introduction of *group-performance incentives* will be a useful way to correct the problem of performance incompleteness (Gupta & Govindarajan, 1986; Hill, Hitt & Hoskisson, 1992; Lorsch & Allen, 1973).

OPTIMAL USE OF DISCRETIONARY BONUSES: IMPLICATIONS OF CENTRALIZATION

Resource sharing can be conducted either in a centralized or decentralized fashion. In both cases sharing creates a problem of performance ambiguity, but this problem is more perverse under decentralized forms of sharing (Jensen & Meckling, 1992). As a result, given any magnitude of resource sharing by a focal division, the resulting levels of performance ambiguity will tend to be smaller if the sharing is effected in a centralized rather than a decentralized fashion (Franquesa, 1997).

In a recent paper, Baker, Gibbons & Murphy, (1994) have formally analyzed the determination of optimal compensation schemes that combine both explicit and implicit contracts.[8] Their results show that, as the objective performance measure (e.g. divisional profits) becomes more distortionary (i.e. with higher levels of performance ambiguity), the optimal compensation scheme is characterized by a larger implicit-contract bonus rate (i.e. larger proportion of discretionary compensation) and a lower explicit-contract bonus rate (i.e. a lower proportion of base-line incentives). This formal result, then, seems to confirm the intuition of prior management theorists, who have long argued for the use of discretionary bonuses as an appropriate administrative response to increasing levels of performance ambiguity (Gupta & Govindarajan, 1986; Hill, Hitt & Hoskisson, 1992; Ouchi, 1979; Salter, 1973). Baker, Gibbons & Murphy (1994) are further able to show that, due to the underlying problem of trust associated with subjective forms of compensation, discretionary bonuses should not be used under small levels of performance ambiguity. Their analysis concludes that implicit contracts will be part of optimal compensation packages only after the motivational distortions created by the explicit contract are large enough to offset the motivational distortions introduced by the use of implicit contracts themselves, in the form of mistrust by agents.[9] In sum, according to Baker, Gibbons & Murphy's (1994) results, the use of discretionary bonuses in association with low levels of performance ambiguity will be negatively associated with division effectiveness. In turn, at high levels of performance ambiguity, the use of discretionary bonuses in direct proportion to increases in the level of performance ambiguity will be positively associated with division effectiveness. Thus, given low levels of performance ambiguity from the base-line contract in the case of centralized sharing, and high levels of performance ambiguity in the case of decentralized forms of sharing, the following hypotheses can be formulated:

Hypothesis 1a: The interaction of *centralized* sharing and *discretionary* bonuses is negatively related to division effectiveness.

Hypothesis 1b: The interaction of *decentralized inflow* sharing and *discretionary* bonuses is positively related to division effectiveness.

Hypothesis 1c: The interaction of *decentralized outflow* sharing and *discretionary* bonuses is positively related to division effectiveness.

---

[8] They use a repeated-game model similar to Bull's (1987), which requires the implicit contract to be self-enforcing for the firm (i.e. the firm will be better off, in the long-term, by not reneging on the implicit contract) in order for the employee to trust subjective assessments of performance.

[9] In the terms of their self-enforcing model, for small distortion levels of the objective measure the principal will not have enough incentives to honor the implicit contract, and hence the agent will not trust the principal's subjective evaluation.

OPTIMAL USE OF GROUP-PERFORMANCE BONUSES: IMPLICATIONS OF DIRECTIONALITY

As a focal division engages in outflow sharing, its manager becomes both a general manager for the division as well as a functional manager for other divisions (Vancil, 1979). As a result, a problem of control emerges because, under the base-line contract, the division manager is rewarded based on the profits of his/her unit, but is not made accountable for the impact that his/her decisions have on the profits of other divisions. The *incompleteness* of the base-line contract (i.e. incompleteness of division profits as a measure of the total set of intended division manager's contributions to firm value) will prompt the focal manager to behave in a parochial manner (Lorsch & Allen, 1973), and potential economies of scope will not be fully realized.

Note that performance *incompleteness* emerges as a result of outflow sharing; but not as a result of inflow sharing. In the case of inflow sharing, division managers do not have control over the use of the shared resource, and thus cannot generate externalities on other divisions that also depend on services from this resource. More importantly, coordination requires that managers of inflow-sharing divisions try to influence decisions in the use of the shared resource that will work to the best advantage of their own divisions (Vancil, 1979). This is the way in which critical information relative to the best uses of the resource will reach the manager that holds decision rights over it. In other words, parochialism may actually be a healthy managerial behavior in the case of inflow-sharing units, as they cannot generate externalities for other divisons, and as they add value by procuring their own self-interest (Franquesa, 1997).

The best available strategy to amend the problem of performance incompleteness is to add an additional contract based on the performance of the group of dependent subsidiaries (Gupta & Govindarajan, 1986, 1991; Salter, 1973). The optimality of such a strategy is supported by a classical result in the moral hazard literature, proved independently by both Holmström (1979) and Shavell (1979). This result, known as the *sufficient statistic condition*, establishes that any available outcome measure will enter the optimal contract if and only if it contains some information about the agent's contributions that is not already captured by any other signal already used in the contract (Hart & Holmström, 1987). Thus, in the case of managers of outflow-sharing divisions, given that their intended contributions extend beyond increasing the value of their own divisions, it is expected that optimal contracts will combine the base-line with an additional contract based on a measure of their cross-business contributions. By contrast, in the case of inflow-sharing divisions, the profits of the division will be a sufficient statistic of expected divisional contributions, so that the addition of group-performance bonuses would represent a departure from optimal compensation. Accordingly, I expect:

Hypothesis 2a: The interaction of *centralized* sharing and *group-performance* bonuses is negatively related to division effectiveness.

Hypothesis 2b: The interaction of *decentralized inflow* sharing and *group-performance* bonuses is negatively related to division effectiveness.

Hypothesis 2c: The interaction of *decentralized outflow* sharing and *group-performance* bonuses is positively related to division effectiveness.

METHODS

SAMPLE

The population for this study was drawn from Standard and Poor's Compustat Business Segment data tapes for 1996, and consisted of highly related diversified manufacturing firms within the database. I first selected all firms that reported their main area of operations in the industrial manufacturing segment (SIC codes 2000–3999). Next, the related diversification component of the entropy index of diversification (Jacquemin & Berry, 1979; Palepu, 1985) was computed for these firms. A group of 166 firms that fell within the upper 25% of the related entropy distribution was identified as the target population. Thus, this study focuses on firms that show a relatively high index of relatedness across their businesses. Average sales for the target population were $5.95 billion in 1995; 128 of the selected firms were headquartered in the US, the rest based in other countries.

Next, information on US-based divisions of the population firms was searched and compiled into a mailing database. Names and addresses of division general managers were sought through *Standard & Poor's Register of Directors and Executives*, and the *Directory of Corporate Affiliations*. Annual reports of a number of these firms were also consulted to check and update the information published in the directories. Sufficient information on division managers' names and addresses was found for a group of 74 firms.[10] Data was gathered through a mail survey administered to division general managers within these firms. The survey was mailed during the summer of 1997. Of the 792 division general managers who received questionnaires, 127 (16%) responded, of which 101 (12.8%) were usable responses and 94 (11.9%) were both usable and complete. The sample of usable responses

[10] We found names and addresses of division general managers for 117 of the target firms, but given our interest in measuring cross-divisional sharings, as well as budgeting constraints for this project, we decided to survey only firms where we had identified at least six different SBUs. As a result, the sample was slightly biased toward larger firms. A number of firms were also dropped because of differences in the information provided by the two directories, which could not be reconciled with the help of annual reports either.

represents divisions of 46 different corporations, with sales for these companies ranging from $54 million to $62 billion, with the average firm sales being $9.5 billion in 1996 (s.d.= 14.2 billion). Division sales, in turn, ranged from $3 million to $6 billion, with the average sales level being $474 million in 1996 (s.d.= 822.7 million). The average number of division employees was 1657 in 1996.

MEASUREMENT

The questionnaire was developed through a review of past research and identification of validated instruments that would be appropriate for this study. Preliminary drafts of the questionnaire were discussed with scholars to assess content validity, and a final draft was pretested with a sample of four division managers, two corporate vice presidents and a director of compensation at large related diversified firms not included in the study. These executives were participants of training courses at a leading American university, and the researcher had the possibility to hold an interview with them, immediately after they had completed the questionnaire, to check on clarity and relevance issues. As a result of this effort a series of modifications and additions were adopted in the final version of the questionnaire. TABLE 10.1 contains summary statistics and TABLE 10.2 contains zero-order correlations for the variables employed in the present study.

Division Effectiveness

The dependent variable for this study is adapted from a validated measure of divisional effectiveness at strategy implementation (Gupta & Govindarajan, 1984). This measure is an index of the extent to which the division has reached goals established at corporate level, and hence the extent of compliance with the principal's objective. Such a construct is deemed appropriate for the present research, as a measure of the immediate outcome of better or worse governance of the agency relationship between corporate and division managers, and arguably also as an indicator of shareholder value created by individual divisions.[11] Respondents were asked to report their performance on the construct dimensions over the previous two years.

---

[11] It is likely that this construct will capture changes in shareholder value at the division level better than any externally imposed index of performance for all divisions. Nonetheless, since this chapter focuses on implementation of corporate strategies, I am not interested in ultimate effects on shareholder value, but rather in the intermediate effects on corporate managers' value and satisfaction.

TABLE 10.1   Descriptive statistics ($n = 101$ divisions)

Variable	Usable observations	Minimum	Maximum	Mean	SD
1. Effectiveness	101	1.653	4.595	3.320	0.668
2. Sharing					
a. Centralized inflow	101	0.000	0.610	0.179	0.139
b. Decentralized inflow	101	0.000	0.279	0.028	0.064
c. Decentralized outflow	101	0.000	16.250	1.560	2.685
3. Compensation					
a. Bonus size	99	1.000	10.500	5.586	2.260
b. Discretionary bonus	99	0.000	1000.000	112.491	185.961
c. Corporate bonus	98	0.000	1000.000	114.566	173.948
4. Controls					
a. Log company $m sales	101	3.999	11.036	8.226	1.503
b. Log division $Th sales	95	8.006	15.520	11.928	1.662
c. Log division employees	95	2.398	9.470	6.341	1.573
d. Unrelated diversification	101	−0.055	1.108	0.273	0.343
e. Competitive strategy	100	4.750	10.000	7.545	1.207
f. Industry dummies (not shown)					

Gupta & Govindarajan's (1984) instrument provides a complex measure of effectiveness which has been shown to have both content and convergent validity in different samples (Govindarajan, 1988; Govindarajan & Fisher, 1990; Roth & O'Donell, 1996).[12] The original measure is based on a weighted-average index of ten performance dimensions. After pretest I added some performance dimensions and deleted others. I also changed the wording of the questions slightly. As a result, the index employed in this study was based on 17 performance dimensions: sales, market share, cash flow from operations, operating profits, ROS, ROI, and EVA, as financial criteria; cost control, product quality ratings, new product development,

---

[12] Govindarajan's (1988) study found this measure to be positively correlated with superiors' assessments of overall subsidiary performance, as well as with the incentive awards received by the focal subsidiary manager compared to the average awards received by the manager's peers. With respect to the convergent validity of this measure, Govindarajan & Fisher (1990) and Roth & O'Donell (1996) found that the index of division effectiveness as reported by division managers was strongly correlated with the same index as reported by corporate or headquarters managers.

TABLE 10.2 Correlation coefficients ($n = 101$ divisions)

Variable	1	2a	2b	2c	3a	3b	3c	4a	4b	4c	4d
						Correlation coefficients					
1. Effectiveness											
2. Sharing											
a. Centralized inflow	-0.03										
b. Decentralized inflow	-0.09	0.22**									
c. Decentralized outflow	-0.19*	0.36***	0.15								
3. Compensation											
a. Discretionary bonus	-0.00	-0.20**	-0.14	-0.11							
b. Group performance bonus	0.04	0.32****	0.14	0.20**	-0.11						
c. Control form	0.03	0.01	0.07	-0.6	-0.08	-0.06					
4. Controls											
a. Log company $ sales	-0.13	0.19*	0.07	0.22**	-0.04	0.15	-0.02				
b. Log division $ sales	-0.00	0.25**	0.12	0.17*	-0.13	0.24**	0.12	0.59***			
c. Log division employees	-0.08	0.04	– 0.09	0.05	-0.11	0.15	0.07	0.49**	0.88****		
d. Unrelated diversification	0.08	-0.30***	-0.00	-0.09	-0.05	-0.14	0.03	0.26**	0.16	0.25**	
e. Competitive strategy	0.42***	0.02	-0.05	-0.16	0.12	0.07	-0.12	-0.11	-0.06	-0.01	-0.07
f. Industry dummies (not shown)											

* $p < 0.10$; ** $p < 0.05$; *** $p < 0.01$; **** $p < 0.001$.

market development, personnel development, development of unique divisional skills, and personal goals, as non-financial criteria; and finally product, market, and technical support to other divisions, as cross-sharing criteria. On each dimension respondents were asked to rate on a five-point Likert scale ranging from "not important" to "extremely important" the degree of importance superiors attached to the criteria when establishing goals or mandates for the division. In a different question, respondents were also asked to rate on a five-point scale ranging from "not at all satisfactory" to "outstanding" their division's performance relative to superiors' expectations, over the previous two years, and for each of the same 17 dimensions. This question was adapted from a previous questionnaire by Lorsch & Allen (1973). Finally, an overall index of division effectiveness over the past two years was constructed as a weighted-average performance on the 17 dimensions, using the responses on dimensional importance to determine weights. The final effectiveness measure then ranges from 1 to 5.

Inflow Sharing

As discussed in the literature review section, any measure of resource sharing needs to take into account both the amount and criticality of resources being shared (Gupta & Govindarajan, 1986; Pfeffer & Salancik, 1978). Accordingly, the inflow-sharing constructs were computed as weighted averages of the volume of services provided to a focal division from other parts of the corporation on an array of 12 different functional areas, with the importance of each area used as weights (Gupta & Govindarajan, 1984, 1986). On the one hand, respondents were asked to rate on a five-point Likert scale ranging from "not important" to "extremely important" the criticality of each of 12 functional activities for the division to succeed in its marketplace. These activities resulted from pretest and interviews with managers and were: science/basic research, product/process engineering, procurement, human resource management, manufacturing, distribution and sales, after sale service/support, marketing, finance, information systems, government liaison, and other administrative tasks. The wording for this question was adapted from Gupta & Govindarajan's (1984) and Lorsch & Allen's (1973) similar instruments. On a different question, for each of 12 functions, respondents were asked to consider all activity conducted for the benefit of their divisions' products and to break it down in terms of the percentages carried out by the division itself, or provided by a corporate- or group-level functional department, by an outside firm contracted by corporate, or by another business unit. The total reported percentage activity for each function was to add up to 100%. A similar measure was used by Vancil (1979) to capture the extent of transfer of goods among profit centers, as well as the extent of services provided by corporate level departments.[13] Two different measures were developed from this data, using the reported importance of the various functions to compute percentage weights. The percentage activity transferred from corporate- or group-level functional departments, as well as from corporate contractors, was used to compile a weighted-average index of the magnitude of *centralized sharing* by each division, while the percentage activity transferred from other divisions was employed to construct a weighted-average measure of the magnitude of *decentralized inflow sharing* by divisions. Both measures may, in theory, vary from 0 to 100%, and can be interpreted as the extent to which the success of the focal division in its marketplace depends on decisions and actions taken by others.

To assess construct validity for these measures, I computed their correlation with an Aston-group type measure of autonomy/centralization of the division (Inkson, Pugh & Hickson, 1970; Pugh *et al.*,1968, 1969). For 16 decision areas I asked respondents if they could make decisions independently, and if not who within the organization would have to actually approve the decision before legitimate action could be taken. The division's lack of autonomy was here captured by two different indices: an index of *vertical centralization*, which counts the number of decisions that are taken at a higher level of authority, and an index of *lateral centralization*, which counts the number of decisions that need to be approved by a peer division manager. As expected, the *vertical centralization* measure was found to be positively correlated with the index of *centralized sharing* ($r = 0.54$, $p < 0.001$), while the *lateral centralization* measure correlated with the *decentralized-inflow sharing* index ($r = 0.34$, $p < 0.001$).

Outflow Sharing

A weighted-average measure of sharing across the same 12 functional activities enumerated above was also sought for this construct. In this case, however, respondents were asked to consider all activity carried out by a corresponding department within their division, and to provide an estimate of the percentage activity that was performed on behalf of other divisions within the firm. Next, respondents were also asked to assess on a five-point Likert scale ranging from "not important" to "extremely important" the criticality of each of 12 functional activities for the "typical" division being

---

[13] The main difference with the Vancil (1979) measures is that those were rather capturing the level of costs allocated to the unit for services rendered from elsewhere in the organization, while the measures used in the present study capture the actual percentage activity that is being transferred. Our emphasis on percentage activity rather than cost is justified by the focus of the present study on effectiveness and value creation by the division, rather than on efficiency and value appropriation.

served. A weighted-average index of outflow sharing across the 12 functional activities was computed, using the importance of the activity for others as weights. Accordingly, the scale for this measure ranges from 0 to 60. To test for construct validity I computed an index of the importance that corporate superiors place on cross-divisional support, within the set of goals for each division. As expected, the importance of divisional support goals correlated positively with the index of *outflow sharing* ($r = 0.38$, $p < 0.001$).

Compensation Variables

Three different compensation variables were developed. The compensation questions asked about the current compensation plan, and then in a different question I asked if major changes had been made over the past three years on the compensation package and/or on the way in which short-term bonuses were computed. Division managers who reported a major shift in the way bonuses were determined over the previous three years were excluded from analysis. Thus, the compensation features for each division manager in the final sample were believed to have been in place and relatively unchanged for at least the three years prior to our survey.

To measure *discretionary bonuses* I used Gupta & Govindarajan's (1984) instrument and scaled it according to the size of the short-term bonus. Respondents were asked whether superiors relied on a strict formula, a completely subjective approach, or on a combination of both approaches when determining their short-term bonuses. In the last case, respondents were also asked to indicate the percentage of bonus that was decided in a discretionary manner. Percentage discretionarity took a value of zero for bonuses that were reported to be strictly formula-based, and a value of 100 for bonuses reported to be completely subjective. The reported percentage of bonus that is discretionary was multiplied by the size of the typical short-term bonuses (i.e. relative to salary) to create a final measure of the relative size of discretionary bonuses.

Group-performance bonuses were also defined as a percentage of salary, and were measured as the product of the relative influence of corporate performance on bonuses by bonus size. Respondents were asked to report the percentage influence that several performance aggregates had on the size of the short-term bonuses they typically received on their jobs. Reported percentages were to add to 100%. The reported percentage influence of overall corporate performance on bonuses was multiplied by bonus size (i.e. relative to salary) to determine the amount of pay associated with group-level performance.

A third compensation variable was developed which is an index of *financial versus strategic control* of division managers. This measure was included in the analysis to examine if the assumption of financial control of managers, which was made during theory development, was binding, so that the model would not be generalizable and apply only to contracts of such a form. An index was computed as the difference of the overall weight given to financial criteria minus the overall weight given to non-financial (i.e. strategic) indicators, when reporting the importance of each criteria as goals emphasized by corporate superiors.

Control Variables

Our dependent variable is in essence a multidimensional index of performance variables. I decided to control for any organization size, strategy, and industry effects on these performance measures. Both corporate and division size were included as control variables. Company size was defined as the logarithm of annual corporate sales. Division size was measured both as the logarithm of division sales and as the logarithm of division employees.

Controls for strategy were also included at the corporate as well as the division levels. The sample for this study was derived from a population of highly related diversified firms. Thus, it makes little sense to control for the extent of related diversification. Following the studies of Hill and colleagues, I did however control for the extent of unrelated diversification (Hill & Hoskisson, 1987; Hill, Hitt & Hoskisson, 1992). The unrelated component of the entropy measure (Jacquemin & Berry, 1979; Palepu, 1985) was used to measure the extent of corporate unrelated diversification. Division strategy was defined as a continuum from a low-cost to a differentiation positioning, and measured using Gupta & Govindarajan's (1984) instrument.

Finally, to control for industry effects, industry dummy variables were added to the model.

ANALYSIS

Hypotheses were tested by means of hierarchical OLS regression on division effectiveness, where control variables, main effects, and multiplicative interaction terms were included consecutively (and in this order) into the regression model. After fitting a base regression, which included control variables only, the analysis proceeded separately for each of the two compensation variables of interest (i.e. contractual adjustments). In both cases, the hierarchical procedure continued as follows. First, a main effects model was fitted that extended the control model to include effects for the compensation variable and the three forms of resource sharing. Next, an interaction term was added between the compensation variable and the index of financial versus strategic control. This additional term is included to check on the possibility that the use of the compensation features of interest have different effects on division effectiveness depending on the financial versus strategic emphasis of the base-line bonus contract. As such, this interaction term acts like a multiplicative control (i.e. a control on the association between the compensation variable and the dependent variable, before we introduce our moderating variables of interest). Finally, I ran the full model, which included controls, main effects, the interaction between the compensation variable and the index of control form, plus the interaction effects of the compensation variable with the three sharing constructs. The partial F-test of the full model, as well as the regression coefficients for the interaction terms and their significances were used to test the hypotheses.

RESULTS

The base regression, which includes only control variables, is reported in TABLE 10.3. The control model was strongly significant ($p < 0.001$) and explained 46% of the variance in division effectiveness. Several coefficients in

TABLE 10.3   Regression results: base regression ($n = 94$)

Independent variables	Effectiveness[a][b]
Company size	−0.197*
	(−1.67)
Division sales	0.480**
	(2.19)
Division employees	−0.349*
	(−1.711)
Unrelated diversification	0.112
	(1.06)
Competitive position	0.512***
	(5.12)
Industry dummies:	
SIC22	−0.099
SIC26	0.199*
SIC28	0.018
SIC30	0.232**
SIC32	0.058
SIC33	−0.202*
SIC34	0.039
SIC35	0.163
SIC36	0.178
SIC37	0.161
SIC38	0.067
F-statistic	3.881***
R^2	0.456

[a] Standardized regression coefficients (*t*-statistics in parentheses).
[b] * $p < 0.1$; ** $p < 0.05$; *** $p < 0.01$.

this regression deserve comment. First, corporate size was negatively associated with divisional effectiveness. In this sample of divisions of highly related diversified firms, this result may have to do with overdiversification in the case of related diversified firms that grow too large. Second, division sales was positively associated with effectiveness, while number of division employees was negatively associated with effectiveness. These results may have to do with higher productivity of labor (over and above industry effects) being associated with higher division effectiveness. Finally, there was no corporate strategy effect but there was a strong competitive strategy effect. The positive coefficient on Gupta & Govindarajan's (1984) competitive strategy variable suggests that divisions that hold a strong differentiation advantage are more effective than others.

Results from the hierarchical regression procedures are reported in TABLE 10.4, which includes standardized regression coefficients for main and interaction effects, as well as the increase in R^2 and partial F-test associated with each new group of variables incrementally added to the model. To maintain simplicity, the regression coefficients of the control variables for these models are not reported, as they are essentially the same as those reported in TABLE 10.3.

The main effects models (equations 1 and 4) showed a negative and significant effect of decentralized inflow sharing on division effectiveness. This was an unexpected and surprising finding, which seems to indicate that, for most firms, the administrative costs of this form of sharing offset any benefits in the form of economies of scope. The lack of other significant main effects for sharing variables suggests that, on average, the pursuit of larger extents of cross-divisional sharing in either a centralized or outflow-sharing fashion has no effect on division effectiveness. Thus, to the extent that support is found for the hypotheses developed in this chapter, results will suggest that no benefits accrue from intra-corporate sharing unless proper implementation is taken into account and appropriate administrative mechanisms are set in place. The main effects for the compensation variables were not significant either. The lack of significance for compensation variables is consistent with the theoretical model presented in this chapter, as well as prior *differentiated fit* type models, where a compensation feature is not expected to have positive or negative effects on divisional performance across all divisional contexts (Ghoshal & Nohria, 1989; Govindarajan, 1988; Govindarajan & Fisher, 1990; Gupta & Govindarajan, 1986; Nohria & Ghoshal, 1994).

The partial F-tests for equations 2 and 5 were not significant, indicating that the multiplicative control term is not contributing to the explanatory power of the model. Thus, before we include the interaction terms of interest in the model, there is no evidence to suggest that different benefits accrue from the use of discretionary and group performance bonuses in contexts

TABLE 10.4 Regression results: main and interaction effects on effectiveness (n = 94 divisions)

Results for:	Regression equation number	Standardized regression coefficients (t-statistics)								Partial F-tests		
		Com-pensation variable	Central-ized inflow	Decent-ralized inflow	Decent-ralized outflow	Compen-sation by control form	Compen-sation by central-ized inflow	Compen-sation by decent-ralized inflow	Compen-sation by decent-ralized outflow	R^2	Increase R^2	Partial-F (degrees of freedom)
Discretionary bonuses	1	−0.09 (−0.933)	0.006 (−0.053)	−0.216** (−2.016)	−0.170 (−1.653)					0.463	0.059	7.948*** (4.73)
	2	−0.186 (−1.614)	0.000 (0.002)	−0.218** (−2.053)	−0.166 (−1.629)	0.179 (1.486)				0.479	0.016	2.209 (1.72)
	3	−0.151 (−1.177)	0.078 (0.604)	−0.226* (−1.899)	−0.311** (−2.551)	0.287** (2.258)	−0.331* (−1.939)	0.047 (0.350)	0.337** (1.990)	0.518	0.039	5.590*** (3.69)
Group performance bonuses	4	−0.046 (−0.416)	0.026 (0.218)	−0.197* (−1.859)	−0.139 (−1.541)					0.458	0.054	7.183*** (4.73)
	5	−0.061 (−0.485)	0.019 (0.151)	−0.192* (−1.773)	−0.154 (−1.453)	0.044 (0.256)				0.458	0.000	0.066 (1.72)
	6	0.317 (1.523)	0.234 (1.336)	−0.243** (−1.848)	0.082 (0.408)	0.172 (0.974)	−0.510* (−1.718)	0.017 (0.132)	−0.295 (−1.257)	0.504	0.046	6.347*** (3.69)

* $p < 0.1$; ** $p < 0.05$; *** $p < 0.01$.

where control is strategic in nature, as compared to contexts where the emphasis is rather on the attainment of financial targets.

In equation 3, I introduced the interaction terms between discretionary bonuses and each of the three forms of sharing. The partial F-test for this regression was significant, indicating that at least one of the coefficients of interest was statistically different from zero. Jointly, these interaction terms explained an additional 4% of division effectiveness variance. Coefficient signs were all in the expected direction, and two out of three were significant. Thus, these results provide considerable support for Hypothesis 1. The negative and significant coefficient for the interaction between discretionary bonuses and centralized sharing provides support for Hypothesis 1a, and suggests that, in contrast to the recommendations of the extant models of strategy implementation (Govindarajan & Fisher, 1990; Gupta & Govindarajan, 1986; Hill, Hitt & Hoskisson, 1992), the use of discretionary bonuses in combination with the most common form of resource sharing is actually detrimental to division effectiveness. The positive, but non-significant, interaction effect between discretionary bonuses and decentralized inflow sharing provides only tentative support for Hypothesis 1b. There is no concluding evidence that suggests motivational benefits as a result of matching the size of discretionary bonuses to the level of decentralized inflow sharing. The positive and significant coefficient for the interaction with decentralized outflow sharing provides support for Hypothesis 1c, and indicates that the implementation of increasing levels of outflow-sharing should be supported with the use of larger discretionary bonuses. Overall, these results provide strong support for the basic tenet of this chapter, that effective implementation of resource sharing requires the use of different administrative solutions for different forms of sharing.

Also in this equation, I found evidence of a negative main effect of decentralized outflow sharing, as well as a positive effect from the interaction of discretionary bonuses with control form. Both effects deserve brief comment here. The negative main effect of decentralized outflow sharing suggests that divisions that are more involved in this form of resource sharing tend to be less effective at attaining corporate goals than other divisions. This is again a counterintuitive result, similar to the one discussed previously for decentralized inflow sharing. The difference, in this case, is that the main effect emerges after introducing the interactions of interest. In other words, this negative main effect appears after controlling for proper implementation of sharing. Thus, the change in this estimate from equation 2 to equation 3 suggests that some divisions in this sample are more effective as a result of outflow sharing, while others are less effective as a result of it, and that the ones that are more effective are precisely the ones that match the levels of outflow sharing with the size of discretionary bonuses. The immediate and important conclusion is that, unless decentralized outflow sharing is accompanied by the use of discretionary bonuses, it will be detrimental for the firm.

After accounting for the effects of different implementation practices, I found also evidence of a positive interaction effect between discretionary bonuses and the form of division managers' control. This result suggests that the use of discretionary bonuses is more beneficial the greater the emphasis on financial control of division managers. One possible explanation may be that resource sharing generates less performance ambiguity when division managers are evaluated on the basis of non-financial criteria. The conclusion here is that my model will apply somewhat differently if strategic control is in place, as implementation of decentralized forms of sharing will require comparatively smaller discretionary bonuses when these are awarded on the attainment of strategic goals.

To summarize, two of the three hypotheses about the effectiveness of discretionary bonuses under different forms of sharing were supported. Further, accounting for these effects resulted in negative main effects for the two decentralized forms of sharing, as well as evidence of a confounding effect of the form of control on the benefits of discretionary bonuses.

Equation 6 shows the results of fitting the full model using group performance bonuses as the compensation variable. The addition of the interaction effects of interest resulted in an increase of 4.6% in R^2, and a partial F-test significant at $p < 0.001$. Nevertheless, only the interaction effect with centralized sharing returned a significant regression coefficient. This effect was in the expected negative direction and provides support for Hypothesis 2a. It suggests that, as divisions engage in larger extents of centralized sharing, providing larger group-performance bonuses for their managers results in lesser divisional contributions to corporate value. This result is at odds with conclusions by prior authors (Gupta & Govindarajan, 1986; Hill, Hitt & Hoskisson, 1992) about the positive effects of using group performance bonuses in resource sharing contexts. Overall, the results from equation 6 provide weak support for my second set of hypotheses, and are equally at odds with my model too. Particularly disturbing is the fact that there is no indication of positive effects of using group performance bonuses in correspondence to larger levels of outflow sharing.

DISCUSSION

The empirical analysis grants ample support for the hypothesized implications of using discretionary bonuses under centralized versus decentralized forms of sharing. Results indicate that the use of discretionary bonuses is positively associated with division effectiveness, as divisions engage in greater levels of decentralized-outflow sharing, but negatively associated with effectiveness, when divisions engage in centralized sharing instead. This finding proves the value of distinguishing features of centralization and directionality of sharing when designing compensation contracts for division managers. It also provides tentative support for the conceptual arguments articulated in Franquesa (1997) about the lower levels of performance ambiguity resulting from centralized, as compared to decentralized, forms of sharing. The missing piece from the empirical results is the lack of support for Hypothesis 1b, as the interaction of discretionary bonuses with decentralized inflow sharing was found not to be significant. It is possible that the limited size of the study sample alone explains the lack of a statistically significant effect. An alternative possibility, of course, is that the theoretical model is incorrect, and that there is truly no motivational benefit resulting from the use of discretionary bonuses in association with decentralized inflow sharing.[14] If such were the case, a completely formulaic base-line contract would provide the same motivational benefits as a combination of formula-based and discretionary bonuses. In other words, these two administrative solutions would be motivationally *equifinal*. Further research is needed on the motivational effects of discretionary bonuses when used in combination with decentralized inflow sharing, as the present study is inconclusive in this respect.

The results were less supportive of the second set of hypotheses, which relate to the use of group performance bonuses in inflow versus outflow forms of sharing. The negative interaction effect of group performance bonuses with centralized sharing landed support for Hypothesis 2a, but no support was found for the other two hypothesized interaction effects. In particular, the lack of any positive motivational effects of group performance bonuses, in combination with any form of resource sharing, was in itself an empirical *anomaly*, given the results of past studies (Gupta & Govindarajan, 1986; Hill, Hitt & Hoskisson, 1992). One possible explanation for the lack of expected results is that the form of division managers' control (i.e. financial versus strategic) might be confounding the interaction effects of interest. In other words, given that financial control was a driving assumption for the purposes of theory development, some of the hypothesized relationships may not generalize to both financial and strategic

---

[14] One possible explanation may derive from the fact that a satisfactory solution to the agency problem in the case of decentralized inflow sharing divisions may depend critically on division managers exerting efforts to influence, in their favor, decisions relative to shared resources (Merchant, 1989; Vancil, 1979). If this is the case, then the use of discretionary bonuses (which in essence discounts externalities imposed on the focal division's profits) would have both a positive motivational effect (by reducing the performance ambiguity problem), as well as a negative motivational effect on managers of decentralized inflow divisions (by discouraging the pursuit of influence on decisions that have an impact on the value of the division). The two effects would tend to offset one another, and hence the lack of a significant net effect on division effectiveness.

control contexts. To explore this possibility, I decided to fit an additional model that included all of the variables in equation 6, plus two additional three-way interaction terms between group performance bonuses, form of control, and each of the two decentralized forms of sharing. For the computation of these three-way interaction terms, the index of control form was converted to a binary variable, by assigning a value of 1 to index scores above the median (i.e. observation with higher emphasis on financial control), and 0 to scores below the median (i.e. observations with higher emphasis on strategic control). This was done to distinguish the two fundamental forms of control, and to facilitate interpretability of findings. As a result, the three-way interaction terms were really two-way interaction effects, which were included in the model for division managers that operated under financial control, and not for those operating under strategic control.[15] Regression results for this model are reported in TABLE 10.5. The addition of the three-way interaction terms resulted in an increase of 4.2% in R^2, and a significant partial F-test. More importantly, the two effects were strongly significant and in the hypothesized direction, providing support for Hypotheses 2b and 2c. Thus, once I controlled for possible confounding effects of the form of control on the two lacking interaction effects, I found complete support for my model. These results suggest that the use of group performance bonuses is positively associated with division effectiveness for outflow sharing divisions, but negatively associated with effectiveness for divisions engaging in inflow forms of sharing. A caveat of these results, though, is that while the negative effect with centralized forms of sharing generalizes to both financial and strategic control contexts, the results with decentralized forms of sharing apply only to circumstances where the emphasis of the short-term bonus plan is on financial control. In other words, support for some of the hypothesized effects is found only for the class of contracts that was assumed in the theoretical model, and not for others.

Two other regression coefficients in TABLE 10.5 deserve comment. On the one hand, I found no evidence of a significant negative effect on decentralized inflow sharing, as was found in all prior regressions. The fact that this effect loses its significance, after we control for the effects of using group performance bonuses in association with this form of sharing, suggests that the previously observed negative main effect may have responded to inappropriate implementation practices on the part of surveyed firms.[16]

---

[15] I also ran a model with a continuous three-way interaction. Results were essentially the same, with even stronger significance levels for the effects of interest. Still, the binary three-way interaction was preferred for clarity of interpretation and parsimony reasons.

[16] Another possibility is that the result is due to additional multicolinearity introduced in the model by the three-way interaction effects. Nevertheless, variance inflation factors for all variables remained low throughout the analysis. The v.i.f. for decentralized inflow sharing in the last model was 2.48, up from 2.41 in equation 6.

Table 10.5 Regression results: confounding effect of control form on group performance bonuses ($n = 94$ divisions)

Results for:	Regression equation number	Standardized regression coefficients (t-statistics)								Partial F-tests		
		Com-pensation variable	Central-ized inflow	Decent-ralized inflow	Decent-ralized outflow	Compen-sation by control form	Compen-sation by central-ized inflow	Compen-sation by decent-ralized inflow	Compen-sation by decent-ralized outflow	Compen-sation by decent-ralized inflow by control form	Compen-sation by outflow by control form	Partial-F (degrees of freedom)
Group performance bonuses	6	0.317 (1.523)	0.234 (1.336)	−0.243* (−1.848)	0.082 (0.408)	0.172 (0.974)	−0.510* (−1.718)	0.017 (0.132)	−0.295 (−1.257)			
	7	0.405* (1.970)	0.250 (1.469)	−0.200 (−1.537)	−0.036 (−1.177)	0.077 (0.340)	−0.524* (−1.754)	0.026 (0.204)	−0.302 (−1.269)	−0.313** (−2.230)	0.377** (2.197)	6.187*** (2.67)

* $p < 0.1$; ** $p < 0.05$; *** $p < 0.01$.

Also, after effectively controlling for the interaction terms of interest, we found evidence of a positive and significant main effect of group performance bonuses on division effectiveness. This effect is independent of the amount of sharing, and irrespective of the financial versus strategic nature of control. Accordingly, it suggests that there may be other reasons for group performance bonuses being beneficial within related diversified firms, besides resource sharing considerations.

CONCLUSIONS

This study developed and tested a theory of division managers' control under resource sharing contexts, which takes into account not only the magnitude, but also the centralization and directionality of sharing (Gupta & Govindarajan, 1991; Vancil, 1979). A classification of three different forms of resource sharing was presented, to reflect distinctions of centralization and directionality from a focal division's point of view. These different forms of sharing represent alternative ways in which the corporation might choose to involve a division in the pursuit of intended economies of scope, and thus they largely define the role that is to be played by the division in the implementation of the corporate strategy of the firm. Accordingly, it was postulated that the nature of the problem of control of division general managers would be different under each form of sharing, and a theoretical model was developed that predicts the administrative mechanisms required to solve the problem of control in each case. The model adopted an agency theoretic perspective, and departed from an assumed base-line contractual relationship between corporate and division managers, based on division profits. Motivational inadequacies of the basic contract in the presence of sharing were analyzed, and a series of hypotheses was proposed about the compensation strategies that would prove more effective at amending distorted motivation, and governing the agency relationship, under each form of sharing. Hypotheses were tested with data from a sample of 101 division managers of 46 related diversified manufacturing corporations.

The findings can be summarized as follows: (i) the alignment of discretionary and group performance bonuses with the magnitude of resource sharing was found to have very different effects on division effectiveness depending on the centralization and directionality of such sharing; (ii) the use of discretionary bonuses was found to be positively related to division effectiveness when used in association with decentralized outflow sharing, but negatively related to effectiveness when used in association with centralized sharing; (iii) the use of group performance bonuses was found to be positively related to effectiveness when used in association with decentralized outflow sharing, but negatively related to effectiveness when used in association with either centralized or decentralized forms of inflow sharing; and (iv) these findings apply universally, except for the effects of combining group performance bonuses with decentralized forms of sharing, which apply only where the short-term bonus plan emphasizes financial performance. These results provide strong support for the theoretical model of differentiated control problems under sharing outlined in this chapter, with five out of six hypotheses being corroborated by the data. In conclusion, this study suggest that, in contrast to recommendations by previous authors (Govindarajan & Fisher, 1990; Gupta & Govindarajan, 1986; Hill, Hitt & Hoskisson, 1992), not all forms of resource sharing require the same type of administrative solution, and failure to consider differences in centralization and directionality of sharing will result in detrimental performance implications.

This work represents both an empirical and a theoretical contribution to prior research on implementation of corporate strategy. In the past, authors have built upon general conceptualizations of resource sharing that consider only the magnitude of a division's exchanges with other units of the diversified firm (Govindarajan & Fisher, 1990; Gupta & Govindarajan, 1986). By dividing this generic construct into three different elements, the present research has proven that centralization and directionality of sharing also have important implications for the differentiated nature of the problem of control of division managers, and has provided new insights into effective compensation contracts within related diversified firms. From a theoretical standpoint, this study extends prior attempts to apply agency theory to the analysis of effective motivational contracts for division general managers (Choudhury, 1985; Govindarajan, 1988; Govindarajan & Fisher, 1990; Hoskisson, Hitt & Hill, 1993; Hoskisson et al., 1989; Merchant, 1989; Roth & O'Donnell, 1996). By adopting the assumptions and rationale behind economic theory of contract formulation, the model presented in this chapter is capable of integrating results from modern developments in this area, and deriving testable hypotheses from them.

There are several implications for managers that derive from the evidence presented in this chapter. First, the use of appropriate compensation mechanisms in association with resource sharing seems to have important performance implications. This is particularly true in the case of decentralized forms of resource sharing, which seem to have tougher implementation requirements. The evidence suggests that when sharing is pursued through direct exchanges between divisions it tends to result in lower division effectiveness (and ultimately loss of corporate value), unless supported by appropriate compensation. Second, corporate managers should pay attention to differences in the magnitude, centralization, and directionality of sharing by focal divisions, when designing compensation contracts for their managers. Third, results suggest that for division managers who are more dependent on services transferred from centralized functional units (i.e. centralized sharing) corporate managers should set small group performance bonuses and avoid the use of discretionary bonuses altogether. The correlation coefficients reported in TABLE 10.2 indicate that corporations do tend to match higher levels of centralized sharing with lower discretionary bonuses ($r = -0.2$, $p < 0.05$), which would be in line with the recommendations of this study. However, TABLE 10.2 also shows that corporate managers tend to match higher levels of centralized sharing with higher group performance bonuses ($r = 0.32$, $p < 0.01$), which, as the evidence shows, tends to result in lower division effectiveness. Corporate managers would be well advised to discontinue this last practice. Fourth, for divisions that depend on services provided by other divisions, rather than corporate services (i.e. decentralized inflow sharing), corporate managers should also set comparatively small group performance bonuses. Finally, for divisions that control core resources and capabilities that are to be leveraged across the organization (i.e. outflow sharing), the level of expected cross-divisional contributions should be matched with larger portions of pay that depend on discretionary awards and on the performance of the corporation as a whole. In sum, corporations will benefit from assessing the role that each division is supposed to play within the intended network of intra-corporate sharing, and designing compensation plans accordingly.

There are several limitations of the present study. Obvious limitations are the use of self-reported and perceptual data, as well as its cross-sectional nature. Given the constructs of interest, the use of self-reported data was imperative. Care was taken to build upon previously validated measures, and to check on construct validity whenever the measures used departed from proven instruments. Budgetary, time, and access constraints prevented collection of longitudinal data, which would have contributed to the strength of the findings as arguments are based on causality. Again, efforts were made to moderate this limitation, by building the necessary time lags within the questionnaire itself. I asked respondents to report compensation variables in the current period, and then asked if there had been important changes in compensation for the previous three years. Respondents who reported important changes were selected out, so that the compensation variables in the final sample are believed to approximate compensation features that were present three years prior to data collection. Effectiveness in turn is measured as the average for the past two years, so the performance variable would be lagged by at least one and a half years. I selected this design because pretests indicated that it was clear, and that it was not imposing excessive demands on the memory of respondents.

The study also presents a methodological limitation deriving from the use of a bivariate approach to fit. Both administrative solutions and resource sharing are characterized in terms of their separate components rather than as an overall gestalt or configuration (Drazin & Van de Ven, 1985; Miller, 1981). Thus, the study analyzes the performance effects of sharing–compensation relationships one compensation variable at a time, and one form of sharing at a time. Thus, I need to assume that the analysis of fit between resource sharing and compensation can be decomposed into the sum of separate interaction effects for each pair of compensation variables. Future research needs to be conducted to identify patterns in which different forms of resource sharing are combined by divisions of related diversified firms, and to analyze the performance and control implications of these patterns of divisional sharing, including internal consistency effects of the various elements of pay. Further research is also needed to explore effective administrative mechanisms when control of division managers is strategic rather than financial in nature. The results from the present study show that, in particular as it relates to the implementation of decentralized forms of sharing, the model that was developed and tested here may not apply when division managers operate under strategic, rather than financial, control. Thus, future work needs to explore, both theoretically and empirically, the implications that enforcement of different forms of control may have on the desirability of other elements of compensation.

REFERENCES

Baker G.P. (1992). Incentive contracts and performance measurement. *Journal of Political Economy*, **100**(3), 598–614.

Baker, G.P., Jensen, M.C. & Murphy, K.J. (1988). Compensation and incentives: practice vs. theory. *Journal of Finance*, **43**(3), 593–616.

Baker, G.P., Gibbons, R. & Murphy, K.J. (1994). Subjective performance measures in optimal incentive contracts. *Quarterly Journal of Economics*, **59**, 1125–1156.

Bartlett, C.A. & Ghoshal, S. (1989). *Managing Across Borders: The Transnational Solution*. Boston, MA: Harvard Business School Press.

Berg, N. (1973). Corporate role in diversified companies. In B. Taylor & K. MacMillan (eds) *Business Policy: Teaching and Research*. New York: Wiley.

Bull, C. (1987). The existence of self-enforcing implicit contracts. *Quarterly Journal of Economics*, **102**, 147–159.

Chandler, A.D. (1962). *Strategy and Structure*. Cambridge, MA: MIT Press.

Choudhury, N. (1985). Incentives for the divisional manager. *Accounting and Business Research*, **16**, 11–21.

Drazin, R. & Van de Ven, A.H. (1985). Alternative forms of fit in contingency theory. *Administrative Science Quarterly*, **30**, 514–539.

Eisenhardt, K.M. (1985). Control: organizational and economic approaches. *Management Science*, **31**(2), 134–149.

Fisher, J. & Govindarajan, V. (1992). Profit center manager compensation: an examination of market, political and human factors. *Strategic Management Journal*, **13**, 205–217.

Franquesa, J. (1997). The differentiated problem of division managers' control, working paper, Purdue University.

Galbraith, J.R. (1994). *Competing with Flexible Lateral Organizations*. Reading, MA: Addison-Wesley.

Galbraith, J.R. & Kazanjian, R.K. (1986). *Strategy Implementation: Structure, Systems and Process*. St Paul, MN: West Publishing.

Galbraith, J.R. & Nathanson, D.A. (1978). *Strategy Implementation: The Role of Structure and Process*. St Paul, MN: West Publishing.

Galbraith, C.S. & Merrill, G.B. (1991). The effects of compensation program and structure on SBU competitive strategy: a study of technology-intensive firms. *Strategic Management Journal*, **12**, 353–370.

Ghoshal, S. & Nohria, N. (1989). Internal differentiation within multinational corporations. *Strategic Management Journal*, **10**, 323–337.

Gomez-Mejia, L.R. (1994). Executive compensation: a reassessment and future research agenda. *Research in Personnel and Human Resources Management*, **12**, 161–222.

Govindarajan, V. (1988). A contingency approach to strategy implementation at the business unit level: integrating administrative mechanisms with strategy. *Academy of Management Journal*, **31**, 828–853.

Govindarajan, V. & Fisher, J. (1990). Strategy, control systems, and resource sharing: effects on business-unit performance. *Academy of Management Journal*, **33**(2), 259–285.

Gupta, A.K. & Govindarajan, V. (1984). Business unit strategy, managerial characteristics, and business unit effectiveness at strategy implementation. *Academy of Management Journal*, **27**(1), 25–41.

Gupta, A.K. & Govindarajan, V. (1986). Resource sharing among SBUs: strategic antecedents and administrative implications. *Academy of Management Journal*, **29**, 695–714.

Gupta, A.K. & Govindarajan, V. (1991). Knowledge flows and the structure of control within multinational corporations. *Academy of Management Review*, **16**(4), 768–792.

Hart, O. & Holmström, B. (1987). The theory of contracts. In T.F. Bewley (ed.) *Advances in Economic Theory: Fifth World Congress*. Cambridge, MA: Cambridge University Press.

Hill, C.W.L. (1988). Internal capital market controls and financial performance in multidivisional firm. *Journal of Industrial Economics*, **37**, 67–83.

Hill, C.W.L. & Hoskisson, R.E. (1987). Strategy and structure in the multiproduct firm. *Academy of Management Review*, **12**, 331–341.

Hill, C.W.L., Hitt, M.A. & Hoskisson, R.E. (1992). Cooperative versus competitive structures in related and unrelated diversified firms. *Organization Science*, **3**(4), 501–521.

Hirst, M.K. (1981). Accounting information and the evaluation of subordinate performance: a situational approach. *Accounting Review*, **56**, 771–784.

Holmström, B. (1979). Moral hazard and observability. *Bell Journal of Economics*, **10**(1), 74–91.

Holmström, B. & Milgrom, P. (1991). Multi-task principal-agent analyses: incentive contracts, asset ownership, and job design. *Journal of Law, Economics, and Organization*, **7**, 24–52.

Hoskisson, R.E. (1987). Multidivisional structure and performance: the contingency of diversification strategy. *Academy of Management Journal*, **30**(4), 625–644.

Hoskisson, R.E., Hitt, M.A. & Hill, C.W.L. (1993). Managerial incentives and investment in R&D in large multiproduct firms. *Organization Science*, **4**(2), 325–341.

Hoskisson, R.E., Hitt. M.A., Turk, T.A. & Tyler, B.B. (1989). Balancing corporate strategy and executive compensation: agency theory and corporate governance. *Research in Personnel and Human Resources Management*, **7**, 25–57.

Huber, G.P. & McDaniel, R.R. (1986). The decision-making paradigm of organizational design. *Management Science*, **32**(5), 572–589.

Inkson, J.H.K., Pugh, D.S. & Hickson, D.J. (1970). Organization context and structure: an abbreviated replication. *Administrative Science Quarterly*, **15**, 318–329.

Jacquemin, A.P. & Berry, C.H. (1979). Entropy measure of diversification and corporate growth. *Journal of Industrial Economics*, **27**(4), 359–369.

Jensen, M.C. & Meckling, W.H. (1992). Specific and general knowledge, and organizational structure. In L. Werin & H. Wijkander (eds) *Contract Economics*. Oxford: Basil Blackwell, pp. 251–274.

Kerr, J. (1985). Diversification strategies and managerial rewards: an empirical study. *Academy of Management Journal*, **28**, 155–179.

Lambert, R.A. & Larcker, D.F. (1985). Executive compensation, corporate decision-making and shareholder wealth: a review of the evidence. *Midland Corporate Finance Journal*, **2**, 6–22.

Lewellen, W., Loderer, C. & Martin, K. (1987). Executive compensation and executive incentive problems: an empirical analysis. *Journal of Accounting and Economics*, **9**, 287–310.

Lorsch, J.W. & Allen III, S.A. (1973). *Managing Diversity and Interdependence: An Organizational Study of Multi-Divisional Firms*. Boston, MA: Division of Research, Graduate School of Business, Harvard University.

McCann, J.E. & Ferry, D.L. (1979). An approach for assessing and managing inter-unit interdependence. *Academy of Management Review*, **4**(1), 113–119.

Merchant, K.A. (1989). *Rewarding Results: Motivating Profit Center Managers*. Boston, MA: Harvard Business School Press.

Miller, D. (1981). Toward a new contingency approach: the search for organizational gestalts. *Journal of Management Studies*, **18**, 1–26.

Napier, N.K. & Smith, M. (1987). Product diversification, performance criteria and compensation at the corporate manager level. *Strategic Management Journal*, **8**, 195–201.

Nohria, N. & Ghoshal, S. (1994). Differentiated fit and shared values: alternatives for managing headquarters–subsidiary relations. *Strategic Management Journal*, **15**, 491–502.

Ouchi, W. (1979). A conceptual framework for the design of organization control mechanisms. *Management Science*, **25**, 833–848.

Palepu, K. (1985). Diversification strategy, profit performance and the entropy measure. *Strategic Management Journal*, **6**, 239–255.

Pfeffer, J. & Salancik, G.R. (1978). *The External Control of Organizations: A Resource Dependency Perspective*. New York: Harper & Row.

Pitts, R.A. (1974). Incentive compensation and organizational design. *Personnel Journal*, **53**, 338–344.

Pitts, R.A. (1976). Diversification strategies and organizational policies of large diversified firms. *Journal of Economics and Business*, **28**, 181–188.

Pitts, R.A. (1980). Toward a contingency theory of multibusiness organization design. *Academy of Management Review*, **5**(2), 302–210.

Porter, M.E. (1985). *Competitive Advantage*. New York: Free Press.

Porter, M.E. (1987). From competitive advantage to corporate strategy. *Harvard Business Review*, **65**(1), 43–59.

Pugh, D.S., Hickson, D.J., Hinings, C.R. & Turner, C. (1968). Dimensions of organization structure. *Administrative Science Quarterly*, **13**, 33–47.

Pugh, D.S., Hickson, D.J., Hinings, C.R. & Turner, C. (1969). The context of organizational structures. *Administrative Science Quarterly*, **14**, 94–114.

Roth, K. & Morrison, A.J. (1992). Implementing global strategy: characteristics of global subsidiary mandates. *Journal of International Business Studies*, **23**, 715–735.

Roth, K. & O'Donell, S. (1996). Foreign subsidiary compensation strategy: an agency theory perspective. *Academy of Management Journal*, **39**(3), 678–703.

Salter. M.S. (1973). Taylor incentive compensation to strategy. *Harvard Business Review*, **51**(2), 94–102.

Shavell, S. (1979). Risk sharing and incentives in the principal and agent relationship. *Bell Journal of Economics*, **10**(1), 55–73.

Stroh, L.K., Brett, J.M., Baumann, J.P. & Reilly, A.H. (1996). Agency theory and variable pay compensation strategies. *Academy of Management Journal*, **39**(3), 751–767.

Teece, D.J. (1980). Economies of scope and the scope of the enterprise. *Journal of Economic Behavior and Organization*, **1**(3), 223–247.

Teece, D.J. (1982). Towards an economic theory of the multiproduct firm. *Journal of Economic Behavior and Organization*, **3**, 39–63.

Vancil, R.F. (1979). *Decentralization: Managerial Ambiguity by Design*. New York: Financial Executives Research Foundation.

11

Management Ownership Concentration, Diversification Strategy and Firm Performance in an Emerging Economy: An Agency Perspective

DENNIS K.K. FAN, CHUN-CHEONG WAN

INTRODUCTION

As globalization is moving at a faster pace, an increasing number of firms are seeking to gain competitive advantage through expanding into emerging economies. As a result, joint ventures and strategic alliances have become the two most popular forms of international partnership. It has been reported that one of the crucial factors in the success of international ventures is partner selection (Hill, 1994). The selection criteria may vary among different countries; however, understanding firm behavior in major emerging economies will contribute greatly to the partner selection process. This is particularly so in today's highly interconnected world. As evidenced by the recent financial turmoil which broke out in the last quarter of 1997 in Asia, even economies with very strong foreign exchange reserves, such as

New Managerial Mindsets: Organizational Transformation and Strategy Implementation.
Edited by M.A. Hitt, J.E. Ricart i Costa and R.D. Nixon.
© 1998 John Wiley & Sons Ltd.

Singapore and Hong Kong, could not shield themselves from the crisis. The failures of a number of large local corporations in the region, as a result, have further demonstrated the importance of choosing the right partner in international ventures. We believe that the ownership structure of a potential partner is one of the most important factors that an international investor needs to focus on. This is because the ownership structure of a firm has important implications for the incentive structure of the managerial team and thus their performance. One recent development in the Pacific region is that the South Korean government has lifted the restrictions on the maximum stockholding foreign investors are allowed to hold in Korean corporations. This signifies the importance of ownership structure in corporate management. The move is also expected to have profound impacts on the economy of the nation.

In this chapter, we attempt to look into the impact of the ownership structure of some large corporations in an emerging economy on one major corporate strategy—diversification. Diversity as a corporate strategy has been under scrutiny. Prior research has amply documented a relationship between diversity and firm performance on the one hand, and on the other, a non-monotonic relationship between management ownership concentration and performance. These two streams of research have, however, appeared to be quite independent in the literature. One purpose of this chapter is to provide a synthesis of these two lines of research. Specifically, we propose to investigate the interrelationships among diversification, management ownership concentration, and firm performance within the framework of agency theory. We suggest that managers of high management ownership concentration firms have more incentives to adopt diversity for the purpose of reducing the risk of their undiversified portfolios even if such a strategy will lead to inferior performance.

Our empirical evidence is drawn from Hong Kong. As a typical emerging market in the Asian Pacific region, Hong Kong is under the strong influence of oriental culture. The prevailing form of high ownership concentration for Hong Kong firms is partly due to their entrepreneurial background as well as the emphasis of control by family stockholdings. It makes the blending of ownership and management a common characteristic of a large number of firms. This has appeared to be a major difference between the ownership structure of typical Asian firms and that of Western firms. The choice of strategies by the owner managers of Asian firms, if they follow traditional Asian practices, therefore, may not be anticipated by investors from Western cultural backgrounds. Such a cultural clash or interorganizational misunderstanding is often deemed to be a major cause of joint venture failures. Studying the implications of different ownership structures on performance, as well as the way strategic decisions are related in very different cultures, is of importance in its own right. Our results could also be useful references to international investors who are interested in engaging in joint-venture businesses in economies which have characteristics similar to those of Hong Kong. The chapter is organized as follows: the next section provides the theoretical considerations, and the methodology, including sample construction and measurement, is presented in the third section. Empirical results are reported in the fourth section, followed by a summary and discussions in the final section.

THEORETICAL CONSIDERATIONS

Several arguments have been put forward in the past few decades to justify diversification as a corporate strategy. One of the major arguments is that there exist general management skills applicable to different kinds of businesses (Drucker, 1954; Judelson, 1969; Katz, 1955; Koontz, 1961). It is believed that these skills when possessed by the top management of a diversified company can contribute to the efficient operation and sound performance of the company. Without question, this theory works well at times of sustained economic growth when most firms, diversified as well as non-diversified ones, are performing well. When, however, as in the late 1960s, many of the largest conglomerates in the US were outperformed by the market, scepticism arose concerning the validity of this argument. The study by Hitt & Ireland (1986) examines the ability of diversified firms to enhance their performance by applying distinctive competencies of the respective firms across business units. They reported that the ability may vary with the degree of the firm's diversification. Specifically, their empirical results show that general administration activities appear to be negatively related to performance for firms with unrelated businesses.

Since the early 1970s, diversification as a corporate strategy has been under scrutiny both in theory and in practice (Goold & Luchs, 1993). Scepticism about the rationale for diversification has been heightened against the backdrop of the tremendous wave of takeover activities since the 1980s. During this period, huge profits were often realized as an outcome of restructuring, divestitures and spin-offs (Bowman & Singh, 1993; Jarrell, Brickley & Netter, 1988; Jensen, 1986). The takeover activities have, in fact, forced many US companies to restructure their organizations and to refocus their businesses in order to maintain their competitiveness. In particular, firms that were overdiversified were forced to downscope to avoid being targeted for takeovers (Hoskisson & Hitt, 1994).

It has been alleged that the track record of diversification strategies of many large US conglomerates has been dismal (Porter, 1987). A number of studies have documented that corporate diversification is negatively related to firm performance (Bettis, 1981; Christensen & Montgomery, 1981;

Hamilton & Shergill, 1993; Rumelt, 1974, 1982), although a few studies have reported no significant relationship between the two variables (Lloyd & Jahera, 1994). In a more comprehensive study, Lang & Stulz (1994) showed that in their sample, throughout the 1980s, diversification was negatively related to firm performance, as measured by Tobin's q. Although the literature inclines to support a negative relationship between diversity and performance, Hoskisson & Hitt (1990) argue that this relationship is strongly affected by the means of the implementation of the strategy. Furthermore, the causality between the two variables has yet to be confirmed. It is argued that poor performance of a firm may prompt more diversification whereas high performance may lead to lower diversification, or they may be reciprocally interrelated.

If diversity has a negative impact on a firm's performance, it is of extreme interest to find out what drives a firm to diversify. It may be argued that lower performance is a tradeoff for lower shareholder risks. However, corporate diversity is generally recognized to be an inefficient means of reducing the risks of shareholders because, in a capital market where transaction costs are relatively low, risk reduction through diversification of a firm's operations adds no value to shareholders, as shareholders have a less expensive way of diversifying their investment by simply holding a portfolio of stocks of different industries.

Among the many justifications of diversification researchers have put forward, the synergy effect has received the most attention. Many researchers even view synergy as the only possible justification (Kanter, 1989; Porter, 1985; Trautwein, 1990). It has, however, been reported that in practice relatively few firms have been able to gain synergy benefits from diversity (Campbell & Luchs, 1992; Ramanujam & Varadarajan, 1989). Hoskisson & Hitt (1990) suggest an integrated model of antecedents and moderating variables associated with diversification strategy and performance outcomes. They argue that a number of factors, including the internal governance, resources of the firm, managerial motives, and incentives, as well as the external industry structure, may have an impact on the diversification strategy.

In this chapter, we attempt to look into the issue by focusing on the interrelationships among management ownership structure, diversification strategy and firm performance. We believe that viewing the issue in the perspective of agency in general and corporate governance in particular will provide insights into the motivation of firm managers adopting a diversification strategy. In the literature, the studies on the relationship between diversity and performance and those on the relationship between management ownership concentration and performance have appeared to be quite independent. Yet, we suggest that a synthesis can be reached within the framework of agency theory. This synthesis could also provide a rationale for diversification. We conjecture that a firm's corporate strategy decisions are closely related to its management ownership concentration.

The separation of ownership and control has given rise to problems associated with the agency relationship, in which there is divergence of interests between the management of a corporation and its shareholders (Barnea, Haugen & Senbet, 1985; Fama & Jensen, 1983; Jensen, 1986; Jensen & Meckling, 1976). Such agency problems are particularly acute for larger firms. Investigating corporate strategies from the perspective of agency theory is not new in the management literature. Recent studies include those of Baysinger & Hoskisson (1990), Hoskisson & Hitt (1990), Hoskisson *et al.* (1996), Hoskisson, Johnson & Moesel (1994), and Hoskisson & Turk (1990). The implications of management ownership structure for corporate strategies have not been extensively investigated, however. We argue that corporate diversity is closely related to the management ownership structure of a firm. Consider an owner manager of a firm in which high management ownership concentration is required to maintain control of the firm. The portfolio of this owner manager is, therefore, relatively less diversified than it would otherwise be. This is particularly so for larger firms because it requires a much larger investment to maintain control. In order to reduce the risk of their investments, owner managers will have the incentive to diversify the operations of the firm even if such a strategy will result in lower performance. In other words, operations diversity serves as an alternative to portfolio diversification for the purpose of risk reduction. It thus follows that firms with higher management ownership concentration are more inclined to adopt diversification strategies than those with lower management ownership concentration.

Management ownership concentration has been found to have an impact on the performance of a firm. Morck, Schleifer & Vishny (1988) reported empirical evidence of a non-monotonic relationship between management ownership concentration and performance. Specifically, high performance is associated with both low and high, but not medium, levels of management ownership concentration. To explain this phenomenon, it is argued that managers who have small stockholdings will be more subject to the discipline of the managerial labor market and thus will have the incentive to work toward value maximization. Conversely, for the medium ownership concentration firms, more agency problems can be expected as the managers have gained sufficient voting power to secure their managerial positions. For the high ownership concentration firms, the managers' ownership has reached such a level that their self-interest is in line with that of the outside shareholders. Therefore, the implication is that the managers of the medium ownership concentration firms are more inclined than the low and high ownership concentration ones to deviate from a value-maximization strategy in their pursuit of personal benefits. This argument is further supported by Finkelstein (1992) and Finkelstein & Hambrick (1996). They suggest that management ownership increases managerial power and gives managers more discretion.

A logical implication of the above arguments is that when the management ownership is small, there should be more involvement on the part of the board of directors in formulating corporate strategies for the purpose of guarding against severe deviation from firm value maximization. In fact, Johnson, Hoskisson & Hitt (1993) reported a negative relationship between the equity ownership of top management and the involvement of the board of directors. Furthermore, they also reported a positive relationship between ownership by outside directors and their board involvement in making strategic decisions.

Based on the discussions above, in the following section we will investigate empirically, using Hong Kong data, the interrelationships among management ownership structure, diversification strategy, and firm performance. In particular, we will test the hypothesis that the higher the management ownership concentration of a firm, the more it is inclined to adopt diversification strategies. Furthermore, we will examine the robustness of the non-monotonic relationship between ownership structure and firm performance, as well as the relationship between diversification strategy and firm performance.

METHODOLOGY

SAMPLE

The sample of this study was drawn from a set of the largest corporations in Hong Kong, an emerging economy which has maintained high economic growth since the 1950s. The initial sample consisted of the largest 120 firms listed on the Hong Kong Stock Exchange in terms of market capitalization as at the end of 1990. The annual reports, the Pacific-Basin Capital Markets (PACAP) databases and local trade magazines provided the necessary business and financial data for this study.

Utilities, banking, and finance companies were omitted from the sample since these firms are subject to heavy government regulations in their scope of business in Hong Kong. Firms for which sufficient information was not available and those delisted after 1990 were also discarded. Furthermore, to reduce noise, only those firms with consistent diversification strategies for the years 1990 and 1991 were retained in the sample. After applying the above criteria, 62 firms remained in the final sample.

MEASURES

Management Ownership Concentration

The ownership data for the fiscal year ending 1991 were used in the cross-sectional analysis in this study. Following Demsetz & Lehn (1985), the management ownership concentration (MOC) of a firm is measured by the percentage stockholding of the ten largest directors. In the examination of the relationship between MOC and firm performance, each firm's MOC is classified as low ($0\% \leq MOC < 5\%$), medium ($5\% \leq MOC < 50\%$), or high ($50\% \leq MOC$). The use of 5% and 50% for the classification is arbitrary. However, we believe that 5% is a reasonably low stock ownership while 50% or above means a controlling stockholding. In our final sample, 23 (37%) firms were classified as having low MOC, while 17 (27.5%) and 22 (35.5%) of them were classified as having medium and high MOC, respectively. The distribution of the sample firms by MOC for each industry is shown in TABLE 11.1.

Diversification Strategy

The industry profile reported in the annual report, supplemented by local trade magazines, was used for identifying the diversification strategy of a firm. A two-level categorization scheme based on Rumelt's (1974) study was adopted initially and then a three-level categorization scheme was used to test for the robustness of the results.

In the two-level scheme, a firm is classified as either dominant or diversified. A dominant firm must have 70% or more of its sales derived from one single industry. Otherwise, it is considered as a diversified firm. In our final sample, there were 33 (53.2%) dominant and 29 (46.8%) diversified firms. The distribution of the sample firms by industry and diversification strategy based on the two-level classification is shown in TABLE 11.2.

In the three-level scheme, the diversified firms are further divided into related and unrelated diversifiers. If sales from related industries (e.g. manufacturing and retailing of watches) summed up to 70% or more of the total sales, the firm is classified as a related diversifier (RD). Otherwise, it is

TABLE 11.1 Distribution of the sample firms by industry and management ownership concentration (MOC)

Industry	Low MOC	Medium MOC	High MOC	All
Property	9	9	9	27
Manufacturing	2	6	4	12
Hospitality (hotels, restaurants, etc.)	4	0	3	7
Wholesaling and retailing	5	2	4	11
Transport	1	0	1	2
Communications	2	0	1	3
Total	23	17	22	62

TABLE 11.2   Distribution of the sample firms by industry and diversification strategy (two levels: dominant and diversified)

Industry	Dominant	Diversified
Property	13	14
Manufacturing	4	8
Hospitality (hotels, restaurants, etc.)	6	1
Wholesaling and retailing	5	6
Transport	2	0
Communications	3	0
Total	33	29

classified as an unrelated diversifier (UD). Among the 29 diversified firms, 11 were related diversifiers, while 18 were unrelated diversifiers. TABLE 11.3 reports the distribution of the sample firms by industry and the three-level diversification strategy.

Firm Performance (ROAP)

A firm's performance was measured by the average of its return on total assets (ROA) for the fiscal years 1990, 1991, and 1992. Using a lagged average to measure a firm's performance can reduce the influence of short-term temporal factors and capture the longer-term effect of a firm's strategy. The average ROA of a firm was further adjusted by subtracting the average performance of all firms within the same industry so as to control for the industry effect. The resulting variable is called performance premium (ROAP), and is used in the analyses below. Using the ROAP has the advantage of removing the possibility of a firm reportedly outperforming other firms of a different industry simply because the industry it belongs to is more profitable (Michel & Hambrick, 1992).

TABLE 11.3   Distribution of the sample firms by industry and diversification strategy (three levels: dominant, related, and unrelated diversified)

Industry	Dominant	RD	UD
Property	13	4	10
Manufacturing	4	5	3
Hospitality (hotels, restaurants, etc.)	6	1	0
Wholesaling and retailing	5	1	5
Transport	2	0	0
Communications	3	0	0
Total	33	11	18

Firm size

Since prior research suggests that firm size may have an effect on a firm's performance and ownership structure (Banz, 1981; Demsetz & Lehn, 1985), it has to be controlled for in this study. We measure firm size by the natural logarithm of sales. The use of natural logarithm transformation of sales is expected to rectify the rightward skewness of the distribution of the variable.

METHODS OF ANALYSIS

Since we hypothesized that the relationship between MOC and firm performance is non-monotonic, a quadratic regression model, in addition to a linear model, was employed. In this study, the firm performance premium (ROAP) is taken as the dependent variable, the firm size (SIZE) is the control variable, and the management ownership concentration (MOC) is the independent variable.

Moreover, as one further step, firms were grouped into different cells according to their degree of MOC and diversification categories. Both the two-level (dominant and diversified) and the three-level (dominant, RD, and UD) schemes of diversification strategy were used to investigate the effect of diversity on the relationship between management ownership concentration and firm performance. Specifically, we compared the performance of firms in different cells by means of *t*-tests, and chi-square tests were done to detect the distribution pattern of the described categorizations.

RESULTS

The descriptive statistics of the variables ROAP, SIZE, and MOC are shown in TABLE 11.4. The variable MOC has a significant negative correlation with SIZE, suggesting that the larger the firm, the more dispersed the firm's ownership. One explanation for this is that when a firm grows in size, it becomes more difficult to maintain the same percentage of stockholding since more capital will be needed. Our result is basically consistent with that of Demsetz & Lehn (1985).

TABLE 11.5 shows the regression results of the relationship between MOC and firm performance. For the linear model, none of the explanatory variables is significant. For the quadratic model, the variable SIZE remains insignificant. Although the *F*-value is marginally significant at the 10% level, the variables MOC and MOC^2 become significant at the 5% level. The results suggest that the quadratic model is better than the linear model in

TABLE 11.4   Descriptive statistics of variables (correlation coefficients)

	Mean (SD)	ROAP	SIZE
ROAP	0.59 (7.10)		
SIZE	14.26 (1.10)	0.1030	
MOC	31.11 (27.34)	0.0297	−0.2716**

Full sample: $N = 62$.
* $p \le 0.10$; ** $p \le 0.05$; *** $p \le 0.01$.

explaining the impact of MOC on firm performance. More specifically, in Hong Kong firms with either relatively higher or lower MOC outperform those with medium MOC. This supports the hypothesis that the relationship between MOC and firm performance is non-monotonic.

Grouping firms into different cells based on the classifications of MOC and diversification strategy helps analyze the relationships among MOC, diversification strategy, and firm performance. TABLE 11.6 shows the results of a chi-square test and the *t*-tests based on the two-level diversification categorization scheme. The significant chi-square statistic indicates that the diversification choice is affected by the MOC of a firm. The distribution reveals that, relatively speaking, more low-MOC firms adopt the dominant strategy, while firms with relatively high MOC tend to be more diversified.

TABLE 11.5   Regression results

	Linear model	Quadratic model
Dependent variable	ROAP	ROAP
Independent variable		
SIZE	0.1199	0.1205
MOC	0.0622	−1.0750**
MOC^2		1.1744**
Total R^2	0.0142	0.0997
Adj. R^2	−0.0192	0.0531
F	0.4249	2.1412
p-value	0.6558	0.1048
N	62	62

* $p \le 0.10$; ** $p \le 0.05$; *** $p \le 0.01$.
Note: When comparing the linear with the quadratic model, $\Delta R^2 = 0.0855$ ($p < 0.05$), implying that the quadratic model is significantly better than the linear model in explaining the variance in the dependent variable.

TABLE 11.6   Performance comparisons of sample firms according to classifications of
MOC and diversification strategy (two levels: dominant and diversified)
(a) Performance = mean ROAP (s.d.)

| | MOC | | | |
	Low	Medium	High	Total
Dominant	2.80 (9.42) $n = 18$	−1.94 (0.49) $n = 5$	5.72 (6.89) $n = 10$	2.96 (8.16) $n = 33$
Diversified	−1.48 (3.68) $n = 5$	−2.81 (3.45) $n = 12$	−1.66 (5.64) $n = 12$	−2.11 (4.41) $n = 29$
Total	1.87 (8.61) $n = 23$	−2.56 (2.90) $n = 17$	1.69 (7.15) $n = 22$	0.59 (7.10) $n = 62$

n = number of observations.
According to the distribution: $\chi^2 = 10.1964$ ($p < 0.01$).

(b) t-test results

Groups	t-value
Dominant versus diversified	3.09***
Low MOC versus medium MOC	2.29**
Low MOC versus high MOC	0.07
Medium MOC versus high MOC	2.53**
Dominant/low MOC versus dominant/medium MOC	2.12**
Dominant/low MOC versus dominant/high MOC	0.86
Dominant/medium MOC versus dominant/high MOC	3.50***
Diversified/low MOC versus diversified/medium MOC	0.71
Diversified/low MOC versus diversified/high MOC	0.07
Diversified/medium MOC versus diversified/high MOC	0.60

* $p \le 0.10$; ** $p \le 0.05$; *** $p \le 0.01$.

This result is consistent with the agency hypothesis that owner managers adopt diversity in order to reduce the risk of their personal investments in their respective companies. As such, our finding is in contrast to that of Fox & Hamilton (1994), who, using New Zealand data, reported no significant relationship between management ownership concentration and diversification strategy.

The results of t-tests shown in TABLE 11.6 show that dominant firms significantly outperform diversified firms. This provides evidence that the negative relationship between diversity and performance also applies to an important emerging economy which has different cultural characteristics from Western economies.

The results also show that firms with either low MOC or high MOC significantly outperform firms with medium MOC. There is, however, no significant difference between low MOC firms and high MOC firms. This reinforces the non-monotonic relationship between MOC and firm performance. Our finding is, thus, basically consistent with that of Morck, Schleifer & Vishny (1988). Such results, in general, provide additional evidence for the agency hypothesis concerning the effects of management ownership concentration on firm performance as discussed above. Specifically, it supports the notion that the managerial labor market functions well in disciplining those managers who have little stockholding, but is less effective when managers have secured enough stockholdings. When managers' stockholdings are so high that their self-interest is in line with that of the external shareholders, the agency problems arising from the separation of ownership and control may become insignificant.

We further investigated whether such a non-monotonic relationship exists after controlling for the firms' diversification strategy. It is clear that the relationship is retained only for dominant firms but not for diversified ones. More interestingly, the superior performance for the low and high MOC concentration firms disappears when owner managers of these firms choose to diversify their business. As such, our findings provide strong support for the hypothesis that a firm's decision to diversify is driven by non-value-maximization motivation.

Previous research has reported that the impacts of related diversification and unrelated diversification on firm performance may differ (Hoskisson *et al.*, 1993; Palepu, 1985; Rumelt, 1974). Therefore, both chi-square tests and *t*-tests were repeated for the distribution using the three-level diversification categorization scheme. The results are shown in TABLE 11.7. As noted, an empty cell is found for low MOC and RD. Therefore, the chi-square test cannot be applied. The *t*-test results indicate that firms classified as dominant or RD significantly outperform those classed as UD, but there is no significant difference between dominant and RD firms. It is found that the relatively high performance of firms with both low and high MOC extends from dominant strategy to RD as RD/high MOC firms perform better than RD/medium MOC firms. Thus, separating related diversification from unrelated diversification strategy provides more valuable information for strategy analysis.

SUMMARY AND DISCUSSION

This study investigates the interrelationship among management ownership concentration, diversification strategy, and firm performance of an emerging economy with an oriental cultural background. Contrary to some recent findings from non-Western economies, which show no significant relationship between management ownership concentration and diversification

TABLE 11.7 Performance comparisons of sample firms according to classifications of MOC and diversification strategy (three levels: dominant, related and unrelated diversified)

(a) Performance = mean ROAP (s.d.)

	MOC			
	Low	Medium	High	Total
Dominant	2.80 (9.42) $n = 18$	−1.94 (0.49) $n = 5$	5.72 (6.89) $n = 10$	2.96 (8.16) $n = 33$
RD	$n = 0$	−2.60 (4.08) $n = 7$	3.84 (5.19) $n = 4$	−0.26 (5.35) $n = 11$
UD	−1.48 (3.68) $n = 5$	−3.11 (2.73) $n = 5$	−4.42 (3.52) $n = 8$	−3.24 (3.41) $n = 18$
Total	1.87 (8.61) $n = 23$	−2.56 (2.90) $n = 17$	1.69 (7.15) $n = 22$	0.59 (7.10) $n = 62$

n = number of observations.
According to the distribution: χ^2 cannot be computed because of an empty cell.

(b) *t*-test results

Groups	*t*-value
Dominant versus RD	1.22
Dominant versus UD	3.80***
RD versus UD	1.84*
Low MOC versus medium MOC	2.29**
Low MOC versus high MOC	0.07
Medium MOC versus high MOC	2.53**
Dominant/low MOC versus dominant/medium MOC	2.12**
Dominant/low MOC versus dominant/high MOC	0.86
Dominant/medium MOC versus dominant/high MOC	3.50***
RD/low MOC versus RD/medium MOC	
RD/low MOC versus RD/high MOC	
RD/medium MOC versus RD/high MOC	2.29**
UD/low MOC versus UD/medium MOC	0.79
UD/low MOC versus UD/high MOC	1.44
UD/medium MOC versus UD/high MOC	0.71

* $p \leq 0.10$; ** $p \leq 0.05$; *** $p \leq 0.01$.

strategy, we found that, from a sample of large listed firms in Hong Kong, those with higher management ownership concentration are more inclined to diversify than those with lower management ownership concentration. Furthermore, consistent with the literature, high performance is associated with low and high, but not medium, levels of management ownership concentration.

When firms are controlled for their diversification strategies, however, such a non-monotonic relationship is retained only for dominant firms and partially for related diversifiers but not for unrelated diversifiers. More specifically, the superior performance of the low and high management ownership concentration firms disappears as these firms choose unrelated diversification as a corporate strategy. As such, this lends support to the hypothesis that diversification decisions are driven by non-value-maximization motivation. Our results are consistent with the agency hypothesis—in order to reduce the risks of their relatively undiversified portfolios, the managers of a firm with high management ownership concentration will have a greater incentive to adopt a diversification strategy even if such a strategy will result in lower performance.

The results of this study are consistent with both the resource-based theory (Barney, 1991) and the core competence theory (Prahalad & Hamel, 1990). Dominant firms have developed their competence and benefited from focusing their resources in their core businesses. Similarly, related diversifiers may generate competitive advantage by transferring core resources across related businesses (Datta, Rajagopalan & Rasheed, 1991).

As a direction of future research, it will be interesting to investigate the causality between diversification and firm performance in emerging economies. Does diversification lead to poor performance, or vice versa, or perhaps they are reciprocally interrelated? A longitudinal analysis may help to answer the question.

The recent financial crisis in Asia has shown that the world's economies are actually interconnected. Financial crisis can be contagious. The problems of one country can spread to another. Moreover, the resulting impacts may take place at both the macro and the micro levels. As is noted in both Korea and Indonesia, The International Monetary Fund (IMF) has demanded that the respective governments commit themselves to fundamental changes in the economic environments of these countries before providing any substantial financial supports. Some important changes have already taken place; more changes are anticipated, not only in the economic and financial systems, but also in the ownership structure of corporations. The resulting impacts of the changes in ownership structure on corporate strategic behavior as well as on firm performance in emerging economies are worthy of investigation.

It is interesting to note that significant changes have been taking place in the ownership structure of Hong Kong business firms in recent years, both before and after the handover of Hong Kong to China on 1 July 1997. Firstly, the increasing number of large mainland Chinese state-owned enterprises listed in Hong Kong (the so-called ''red chips'') has already reshaped the landscape of the local financial market. Secondly, due to market concerns and for political reasons, some major local firms have offered a significant stockholding to firms or individuals that are closely associated with the mainland Chinese authorities. The impact of such changes on strategic behavior has yet to be investigated.

Based on the recent developments in the ownership structure of quite a large number of Hong Kong firms, if, as we argue, ownership background is an important constituent of the strategic resources of a firm, the relationship among ownership background, strategic behavior, and performance of firms in emerging economies is a research area that cannot be ignored.

The practical relevance of our study is that our results may help multinational firms which are actively seeking strategic partners in emerging economies to identify suitable firms. Leaving other considerations aside, it appears that dominant firms with low management ownership concentrations will make suitable partners.

ACKNOWLEDGEMENTS

We would like to thank Michael Hitt and Robert Nixon for their very helpful comments and constructive suggestions. We have also received helpful comments from Robert Hoskisson and other participants at the 17th Annual International Conference of the Strategic Management Society. Financial support received from the Hong Kong Research Grant Council (RGC grant CUHK331/95H for Dennis Fan, and RGC grant CUHK170/96H for Chun-Cheong Wan) is gratefully acknowledged.

REFERENCES

Banz, R.W. (1981). The relationship between return and market value of common stocks. *Journal of Financial Economics*, **9**(1), 3–18.

Barnea, A., Haugen, R. & Senbet, L. (1985). *Agency Problems and Financial Contracting*. Englewood Cliffs, NJ: Prentice Hall.

Barney, J.B. (1991). Firm resources and sustained competitive advantage. *Journal of Management*, **17**, 99–120.

Baysinger, B. & Hoskisson, R. (1990). The composition of boards of directors and strategic control: effects on corporate strategy, *Academy of Management Review*, **15**(1), 72–87.

Bettis, R. (1981). Performance differences in related and unrelated diversified firms. *Strategic Management Journal*, **2**, 379–393.

Bowman, E. & Singh, H. (1993). Corporate restructuring: reconfiguring the firm. *Strategic Management Journal*, **14**, 5–14.

Campbell, A. & Luchs, K. (1992). *Strategic Synergy*. London: Butterworth Heinemann.

Christensen, K. and Montgomery, C. (1981). Corporate economic performance: diversification strategy versus market structure. *Strategic Management Journal*, **2**, 327–343.

Datta, D.K., Rajagopalan, N. & Rasheed, A.M.A. (1991). Diversification and performance: critical review and future directions. *Journal of Management Studies*, **28**, 529–558.

Demsetz, H. and Lehn, K. (1985). The structure of corporate ownership: causes and consequences. *Journal of Political Economy*, **93**, 1155–1177.

Drucker, P. (1954). *The Practice of Management*. New York: Harper & Row.

Fama, E. & Jensen, M. (1983). Separation of ownership and control. *Journal of Law and Economics*, **26**, 301–325.

Finkelstein, S. (1992). Power in top management teams: dimensions, measurement, and validation. *Academy of Management Journal*, **35**(3), 505–538.

Finkelstein, S. & Hambrick, D. (1996). *Strategic Leadership: Top Executives and their Effect on Organizations*. St Paul, MN: West Publishing.

Fox, M. & Hamilton, R. (1994). Ownership and diversification: agency theory or stewardship theory. *Journal of Management Studies*, **31**, 69–81.

Goold, M. & Luchs, K. (1993). Why diversify? Four decades of management thinking. *Academy of Management Executive*, **7**(3), 7–24.

Hamilton, R. & Shergill, G. (1993). Extent of diversification and company performance: the New Zealand evidence. *Managerial and Decision Economics*, **14**, 47–52.

Hill, C.W.L. (1994). *International Business*. Burr Ridge, IL: Irwin.

Hitt, M. & Ireland, R. (1986). Relationships among corporate level distinctive competencies, diversification strategy, corporate structure and performance. *Journal of Management Studies*, **23**, 401–416.

Hoskisson, R. & Hitt, M. (1990). Antecedents and performance outcomes of diversification: a review and critique of theoretical perspectives. *Journal of Management*, **16**(2), 461–509.

Hoskisson, R. & Hitt, M. (1994). *Downscoping: How to Tame the Diversified Firm*. New York: Oxford University Press.

Hoskisson, R. & Turk, T. (1990). Corporate restructuring: governance and control limits of the internal capital market. *Academy of Management Review*, **15**, 459–477.

Hoskisson, R., Johnson, R. & Moesel, D. (1994). Corporate divestiture intensity in restructuring firms: effects of governance, strategy, and performance. *Academy of Management Journal*, **37**(5), 1207–1251.

Hoskisson, R., Hitt, M., Johnson, R. & Moesel, D. (1993). Construct validity of an objective (entropy) categorical measure of diversification strategy. *Strategic Management Journal*, **14**, 215–235.

Hoskisson, R., Hitt, M., Johnson, R. & Grossman, W. (1996). Conflicting voices: the effects of ownership heterogeneity and internal governance on corporate strategy, working paper, Texas A&M University.

Jarrell, G., Brickley, J. & Netter, J. (1988). The market for corporate control: the empirical evidence since 1980. *Journal of Economic Perspective*, **2** (1), 49–68.

Jensen, M. (1986). The takeover controversy: analysis and evidence. *Midland Corporate Finance Journal*, **3**, 6–32.

Jensen, M. & Meckling, W. (1976). Theory of the firm: managerial behavior, agency costs and ownership structure. *Journal of Financial Economics*, **3**, 305–360.

Johnson, R., Hoskisson, R. & Hitt, M. (1993). Board of director involvement in restructuring: the effects of board versus managerial controls and characteristics. *Strategic Management Journal*, **14**, 33–50.

Judelson, D. (1969). The conglomerate-corporate form of the future. *Michigan Business Review*, July, 8–12.

Kanter, R. (1989). *When Giants Learn to Dance*. London: Simon & Schuster.

Katz, R. (1955). Skills of an effective administrator. *Harvard Business Review*, **33**(1), 37.

Koontz, H. (1961). The management theory jungle. *Academy of Management Journal*, 4(3), 175.

Lang, L. & Stulz, R. (1994). Tobin's Q, corporate diversification and firm performance. *Journal of Political Economy*, **102**(6), 1248–80.

Lloyd, W. & Jahera, J. Jr (1994). Firm-diversification effects on performance as measured by Tobin's q. *Managerial and Decision Economics*, **15**, 259–266.

Michel, J.C. & Hambrick, D.C. (1992). Diversification posture and top management team characteristics. *Academy of Management Journal*, **35**, 9–37.

Morck, R., Schleifer, A. & Vishny, R. (1988). Management ownership and market valuation: an empirical analysis. *Journal of Financial Economics*, **20**, 293–315.

Palepu, K. (1985). Diversification strategy, profit performance, and the entropy measure of diversification. *Strategic Management Journal*, **6**, 239–255.

Porter, M. (1985). *Competitive Advantage*. New York: Free Press.

Porter, M. (1987). From competitive advantage to corporate strategy. *Harvard Business Review*, **65**(3), 43–59.

Prahalad, C.K. & Hamel, G. (1990). The core competence of the corporation. *Harvard Business Review*, **68**(3), 79–91.

Ramanujam, V. & Varadarajan, P. (1989). Research on corporate diversification: a synthesis. *Strategic Management Journal*, **10**, 523–551.

Rumelt, R. (1982). Diversification strategy and profitability. *Strategic Management Journal*, **3**, 359–369.

Rumelt, R. (1974). *Strategy, Structure, and Economic Performance*. Cambridge, MA: Harvard University Press.

Trautwein, F. (1990). Merger motives and merger prescriptions. *Strategic Management Journal*, **11**, 283–295.

12

Founding Effects on Complex Adaptive Organizations: Birth Constraints in the Spanish Newspaper Population

ISABEL GUTIÉRREZ, CLARA-EUGENIA GARCIA, MANUEL NÚÑEZ-NICKEL

INTRODUCTION

This chapter explores how initial conditions constrain organizational dynamics within a specific population, and how the set of organizational core features acquired at founding affects organizations' survival prospects. The effects of founding conditions and characteristics acquired by organizations are critical; it is the stage where the organization needs to mobilize a substantial amount of resources, the basic product portfolio is defined, and its social impact is settled.

Core features at founding determine the early strategic decisions of firms (Boeker, 1989). An initial erroneous strategy becomes an *original sin* which is difficult to rectify, especially when managers face higher uncertainty in a

New Managerial Mindsets: Organizational Transformation and Strategy Implementation.
Edited by M.A. Hitt, J.E. Ricart i Costa and R.D. Nixon.
© 1998 John Wiley & Sons Ltd.

more interconnected world. Consequently, choices concerning core characteristics and strategies at founding may be particularly significant for corporations that operate in several environments (e.g. in different countries) and decide to start up a new business; they must consider the founding features that lead to a higher life expectancy.

Several theoretical as well as practical concerns generate interest in the founding event. Organizational founding plays an essential role within evolutionary perspectives of organizational change aimed at specifying the mechanisms of variation and of selective retention in the organizational realm. Organizational ecology has stressed how competition for a common set of economic and social resources and the impact of early environmental conditions lead to differential founding attempts in a population (Carroll & Delacroix, 1982; Baum & Oliver, 1996). Current research has focused on the effects of organizational demographics and competitive concentration or density dependence (Tucker *et al.*, 1988; Carroll & Hannan, 1989; Hannan & Carroll, 1992; Lomi, 1995a).

In contrast, history-dependence theories explain the persistence of particular organizational features and patterns of behavior. Organizational evolution is driven by variety at an early point in time, and whenever there is stability in such differences there is opportunity for differential survival chances and selection. History-dependence theories include the imprinting hypothesis, path dependence, and lock-in processes.

Empirical studies investigating the effects of early strategy on organizational results bear some similarity to this chapter. Romanelli (1989) explores the strategies followed by an organization during its early years to exploit environmental conditions. Her main conclusions indicate that, for most environmental conditions, specialist and aggressive strategies increase early survival. Freeser & Willard (1990) claimed that the founding strategies of high and low growth firms differ systematically among the organizations studied. Eisenhardt & Schoonhoven (1990) found significant interaction effects for top management teams at founding and the market stage on a firm's growth. In contrast, this chapter places less emphasis on the impact of an isolated early strategy on a particular measure of firms' results. We focus on the simultaneous effects of the set of organizational founding core features, and seek to prove if these in turn may enhance organizational life chances.

Our investigation attempts to fill several research gaps concerning founding characteristics as a predictor of firm survival. First, little is known about the extent to which a firm's core elements show different long-run survival prospects in comparison to organizations that own a different set of core features. Second, there is no available evidence as to which founding features are more persistent and have stronger impact over time.

The specific argument of this chapter is that imprinting and path-dependence processes compromise the survival chances of organizational forms. We depart from Stinchcombe's previous hypothesis (1965, p. 159):

> structural characteristics of a type of organization tend to persist, and consequently there is a strong correlation between the age at which industries were developed and their structure at the present time.

Hence, there are two sets of founding characteristics that influence organizational dynamics: (i) the environmental conditions at that time, and (ii) the organizational characteristics adopted that persist after the founding of firms. Stinchcombe's strong argument (1965) on imprinting of environmental conditions at the time of an organization's founding has been extended to the imprinting of the set of features acquired at founding.

We assume that survival chances of existing organizational forms are highly sensitive to initial conditions that may lead to inefficient/efficient but unpredictable results. Initial conditions and the characteristics of organizational features acquired at founding constrain change. High levels of interdependence between core features will increase path-dependence processes. Our interest is in testing both the imprinting and the path-dependence hypotheses. Imprinting provides an extreme case of the mismatch of time scales; that is, when the environment changes much more rapidly than organizations' response to time, core features occur that may have been adaptive in the past but are no longer so. Note that this argument does not imply that core features acquired at founding cannot change but that the probability of change and adaptation is constrained by early characteristics and by the previously adopted set of strategies (Eisenhardt & Schoonhoven, 1990).

In this chapter we evaluate the effects on an organization's survival of the core attributes acquired at founding according to Hannan & Freeman's definition (1984, p. 156):

> (1) its stated goals—the basis of which legitimacy and other resources are mobilized; (2) forms of authority within the organization and the basis of exchange between members and the organization; (3) core technology, especially as encoded in capital investment, infrastructure, and the skills of members; and (4) marketing strategy in a broad sense—the kind of clients (or customers) to which the organization orients its production and the ways in which it attracts resources from the environment.

The basic building blocks of this chapter are: (i) the selective long-run impact of history and context embodied in a set of core features acquired at founding; such features are not merely historical accidents but rather the reflection of evolution and previous events, and (ii) survival chances are constrained by imprinting as initial organizational features and decisions generate advantages.

The implications of imprinting and path-dependence processes in organizational survival will be discussed next, leading to a set of propositions to be tested empirically on the entire population of Spanish newspapers during the period 1966–1993. Dramatic institutional, organizational, and technological changes experienced in Spain in the past two decades provide an excellent social laboratory within which to examine organizational survival in a dynamic and turbulent environment.

The chapter is organized in five sections discussing the theoretical framework of the study; the set of propositions, data and analysis; the empirical results obtained; and their consequences in the context of current theoretical discussions within evolutionary theories of organizational change.

EVOLUTION, SOURCES OF DIVERSITY AND FOUNDING CHARACTERISTICS

Organizational life as well as economic phenomena represents a wide domain of nonbiological questions which have been subject recently to the search for evolutionary explanations. Evolutionary thinking has given way to much research on organizational demographics (Hannan & Freeman, 1989), the theory of the firm (Nelson & Winter, 1982), and business strategy (Barnett & Burgelman, 1996). Despite the use of a common set of biological metaphors, organizational evolution is compatible with different causal explanations that contain conflicting views, from Lamarckian theories supporting individual adaptation (Nelson & Winter, 1982) to a Darwinian explanation that goes by the workings of natural selection (Hannan & Freeman, 1977). The existence of differing perspectives within the evolutionary literature has been recognized for some time (Romanelli, 1991).

Major differences are drawn on behavioral assumptions, the hypotheses concerning the sources of organizational variety, and the unit of evolution (Barnett & Carroll, 1995). Notwithstanding the differences, evolutionary perspectives converge around the assumption that evolution needs both systematic and stochastic elements (Nelson, 1994).

This chapter provides the basic theoretical tenets of organizational founding effects based on the imprinting and the path-dependence hypotheses within an evolutionary view. Seen in an evolutionary perspective, imprinting and path dependence are not deterministic but highly uncertain. We depart from the assumption that the observed distribution of organizational forms reflects heterogeneity as a result of differences in the distribution of social and institutional characteristics.

To avoid any confusion, we shall refer to imprinting in order to indicate the high persistence of a set of specific core features acquired at founding and, thus, to reflect the idea that intertemporal relationships exist. We shall refer to the process that explains how a historically given organizational setting may lock in a suboptimal path as path dependence. We claim that both imprinting and path dependence represent the two necessary theoretical elements to understand differential survival chances exhibited by organizations within a population subject to the same environmental conditions. Imprinting, as emphasized by population ecology, has to be complemented by path dependence, as recent developments within evolutionary economics point out. It is our basic assumption in this chapter that if interdependence between core features prevails, as stated by Hannan & Freeman (1984), the probability of path dependence increases accordingly, and consequently suboptimal lock-in arises as reflected in differential survival chances.

Organizations select at founding alternative features, the contribution of which to survival chances is unknown. We adopt the imprinting hypothesis by assuming an intertemporal relationship between core features acquired at founding and long-run survival chances. Imprinting theories help to explain why two organizational settings will respond in very different ways when exposed to the same selection pressures. We also assume that path-dependence phenomena are the cornerstone of such differences.

The core of the organizational form represents an idiosyncratic combination of traits that may protect the organization from selection pressures. Altogether, core features are highly interdependent and, consequently, any change within the core will increase the probability of failure (Hannan & Freeman, 1984). The initial conditions at founding are measured by the influence of the set of core features acquired, which according to Hannan and Freeman (1984) includes organizational goals, forms of authority, core technology, and marketing strategy. The differential contribution to survival of core features at the initial moment is unknown, and inefficiencies are not remediable. Furthermore, survival prospects are not equally conditioned by these four core features; they represent a hierarchical list (Barnett & Carroll, 1995) and, consequently, we should expect strong imprinting and path dependence related to the organization's mission, its authority structure, its technological core, and lastly its marketing strategy in a broad sense.

Core features embody ecological factors, including the availability of resources, customers, suppliers, and support from the environment. Evolutionary economics has pointed out that customers, suppliers, tangible assets, and financial assets represent state variables. Such variables cannot be altered over a wide range of choices but may or may not change in the long-run, any change being critical to the success or failure of an organization (Winter, 1987).

Population ecology has built a coherent set of models and theories based on selection criteria as a major building block. The basic insight is that organizational forms fail because of systematic environmental pressures acting on structural features that determine the fitness of each organizational form. Survival chances are influenced by the environmental conditions and features of new organizational forms, the particular niches they might find, and the probability of failure shown by existing forms.

Conversely, the view of business organizations developed within evolutionary economics is based on a loose coupling between biological analogies and the behavioral theory of the firm (Cyert & March, 1963). It focuses on lower-level evolutionary processes concerning individual adaptation in order to increase the organization's subjective survival probability. The role of adaptive learning behavior is explained by path-dependence processes at the level of routines and capabilities. Despite standard views of organizational adaptation in order to fit environmental conditions (e.g. contingency theory) the major concern here is not to divorce adaptation from evolutionary processes. Bounded rationality and mistake-ridden actions provide the basis for imperfect environmental fitting and, thus, adaptation remains evolutionary. Organizations are not rational entities able to adopt the required forms or characteristics (Dosi, 1991).

Notwithstanding this debate, we contend that differences at the founding stage—either minor or negligible—related to the organization's mission, forms of authority, technology, and marketing strategy may have important and irreversible influences on the survival chances of organizational forms. This chapter focus on how and to what extent founding core features influence differential survival not as result of deterministic forces and intrinsic characteristics but of imprinting and path dependence. In the following sections we explore the impact of this statement, departing from a set of propositions concerning the expected potential effects of organizational core features. Following this argument, our overall premise is that differences in any of the core features at founding are translated into differences in survival prospects.

BACKGROUND AND PROPOSITIONS

ORGANIZATIONAL MISSION

The social acceptance of the organization at founding is linked to a set of external or ecological factors, including the availability of resources, customers, suppliers, financial support, and the ability to capitalize on specific opportunities. The organizational mission serves as a major source of legitimacy to suppliers, customers, and employees as well as to political and social actors. The bases on which legitimacy and other resources are mobilized closely refer to the mission of the organization. The organizational mission represents the most difficult to change acquired feature. Hence, abrupt breaks concerning the mission of the organization lead to unnecessary losses increasing the threat of ambiguity and failure (Amburgey, Kelly & Barnett, 1993).

The mission embodies the organization's identity with reference to its constituencies, both internal and external; it is difficult to change because any change would require a substantial variation in the institutional status of the organization. Altogether, the mission underlies the basic organizing and economic principles through which the organization gains legitimacy and stability. Moreover, the definition of an organization's mission should consider: (i) the basic methods or ways of acting with which it should be identified, and (ii) its place within the competitive space conformed by the organizations that carry on similar activities (Selznick, 1957).

The capacity of organizations to respond to changing levels of resources and to react to competitors defines a population's tolerance. Ecological research has investigated in depth the effects of differential levels of tolerance, defined as niche width, by focusing on the degree to which an organization follows a specialist or generalist product-market strategy (Freeman & Hannan, 1983). Firms address broad or narrow market segments depending on the range of resources available that they attempt to exploit. Generalist organizations operate in almost any conditions (Carroll, 1985). In contrast, specialist organizations focus on a relatively narrow band of available resources and they concentrate in a particular market segment. Implicitly, population ecology takes as a crucial assumption that these two broad forms respond differently to environmental changes and market conditions, and consequently they have different fitness functions. Hence, the mission of the organization, either generalist or specialist, will constrain the options, activities, and strategies it has available, thus influencing survival chances.

In essence, specialization requires lower levels of investment and expenditure of fewer resources than generalist strategies. Specialization helps organizations to compete in a market segment that is free of competition from larger firms either if the market is mature (competitive concentration), new or declining (Romanelli, 1989). We therefore formulate the following proposition:

> **Proposition 1:** Specialist organizations will have a higher likelihood of survival than generalist organizations.

FORMS OF AUTHORITY

Forms of authority within population ecology are a core feature grounded on the perspective of the mobilization of resources. Whereas conceptually it has not been clearly established, Hannan & Freeman (1984) explicitly excluded authority linked to structure, in the narrow sense, as well as to different hierarchical levels. Hence, forms of authority are taken as regarding "the basis of exchange between members and the organization" (Hannan & Freeman, 1984, p.156).

Whether different forms of authority can be established in meaningful ways and instrumentally approached is an interesting question. Regardless of the characteristics of authority within organizations linked to either position or leadership, authority can be understood in a fundamental sense as the exercise of legitimate power and control (Stinchcombe, 1968). From an economic perspective control rests upon ownership. Thus, we shall take ownership structure as a plausible proxy of forms of authority, and the source of legitimate power based on the set of residual control rights granted to owners.

The ownership structure becomes a critical feature acquired at founding, influencing both the allocation of assets and the capacity of particular types of organizations to claim for reliable performance and to account rationally for their actions. In creating their business, entrepreneurs in different countries relied on different types of institutional arrangements. Hence, we differentiate between organizations emerging at the time of founding as legal entities taking the form of individual businesses and those that took the legal status of corporations or stock companies (Allen & Sherer, 1995). Individual businesses are organizations in which the owner devotes to the business the human and financial resources available, and, being limited, they cannot easily be removed without dissolving the firm. Conversely, corporations are characterized by the high mobility of their resources. Corporations do not depend upon a particular owner.

Some investigations have focused on a team approach to founding. They found that top management teams exhibit higher growth and survival probabilities (Cooper, 1986; Eisenhardt & Schoonhoven, 1990). They concluded that risk sharing in corporations may enhance the prospects for subsequent high performance (Freeser & Willard, 1990). Within the field of organization theory, the contribution made by population ecologists stresses that turbulent and dynamic socio-economic systems favor the organizations that can demonstrate reliable performance and can account rationally for their actions (Hannan & Freeman, 1989). Hence, we assume that corporations are characterized by higher levels of reliability and accountability and, consequently, they are favored by environmental selection conditions.

From a different perspective, most of the research within managerial economics has dealt with the effects of corporations on social and economic structures and on the degree of efficiency with which corporations allocate resources and adjust to changing conditions. Among the different issues discussed in this literature are the impact of size on profitability, patterns of growth, and innovation. Contributions in this field postulated that the growth of the modern corporation has been an efficient response to the coordination of more complex problems (Chandler, 1962).

We take into consideration that higher levels of capitalization and financial slack should protect corporations from the negative influence of major changes. Selection pressures are prevented by the availability of free cash-flows that might increase the survival probability of the firm (Cyert & March, 1963). Thus, we deal with the implications of two simple but widely spread forms of ownership structure to test whether differences in survival chances are significant or not, and a second proposition may be established as follows:

Proposition 2: The ownership structure at founding of corporations bears a higher likelihood of survival than alternative forms of ownership such as individual businesses.

Furthermore, a second aspect has to be included to clarify the notion of ownership aimed at explaining why corporations began to internalize specific market transactions. The elimination of market exchanges is inherent in the concept of vertical financial ownership, and several implications have been pointed out from different theoretical stands (e.g. property rights approaches, transaction cost economics, agency theories, and strategic management) that examine the factors leading to vertical integration strategies, and to predict under which circumstances vertical integration will be more likely than market transactions. Traditionally the motives for vertical integration strategies have been classified into four major categories: (i) transaction costs, (ii) strategic choices, (iii) output and input price advantages, and (iv) structural uncertainty in cost and/or prices.

Most of the theoretical literature provides explanations for vertical integration strategies while understanding that the choice of governance structures is often misleading. In fact, in the absence of transaction cost and bureaucratic costs, alternative governance structures do not matter, and vertical financial ownership is an efficient alternative to vertical contracting. However, a world of zero transaction costs is a fiction.

We shall focus on differential survival chances exhibited by vertical financial ownership versus alternative governance structures. The former includes organizations that at founding decided to integrate, and to own nonhuman assets and physical equipment, which implied at that time an important investment decision. In contrast, alternative governance structures correspond to organizations that outsource a set of operational tasks relying on either market transactions, short-term contracts or long-term contractual arrangements (Williamson, 1991).

Supported by a large body of economic literature, we may conclude that vertical integration offers ownership, incentive, and governance structure advantages (Joskow, 1988; Masten, 1984; Riordan & Williamson, 1985). On the other hand, vertical financial ownership is negatively influenced by a set of factors, including bureaucratic costs, strategic costs (Rumelt, 1974), and production costs (Williamson, 1975). However, vertical financial integration results in economies of integration that may arise from reduced transaction-related costs, shared common cost, enhanced productivity, and increasing returns to scale that may slightly dominate bureaucratic costs (D'Aveni & Ravenscraft, 1994). Moreover, under plausible conditions, such as assets' complementarities and uncertainty, vertical financial ownership leads to efficiency (Mahoney, 1992). Empirical evidence suggests that where products or technologies are highly idiosyncratic, successful firms often control their assets through financial integration or quasi-integration arrangements (Harrigan, 1986; Monteverde & Teece, 1982). Hence, the degree of vertical financial integration will influence a firm's evolution, growth, and survival. Thus, a new proposition can be formulated:

Proposition 3: Organizations that exhibit vertical financial integration at founding will have a higher likelihood of survival than organizations adopting alternative governance structures.

TECHNOLOGICAL CORE

The technological core of an organization implies a particular combination of different sorts of knowledge attached to a particular technology embodied in capital goods, standard production operations, particular products, and specific investments. It is widely recognized that technology plays a critical role influencing the survival prospects of individual organizations. Technological change is often translated into a process of competence destruction if it makes existing skills, knowledge, and practices obsolete (Tushman & Anderson, 1986). Thus, a technological shock devalues the set of capabilities of incumbent firms (Dosi & Salvatore, 1992), negatively influencing their survival chances while favoring new entrants.

A particular technology is adopted at founding because it satisfies a need better than existing alternatives. Organizations face a choice dilemma if at founding there are several technologies that can potentially fulfill the same purpose. Technological choice, and consequently the set of needs to be met, is critical in terms of further success and survival. Technological choice is constrained by the levels of capital investment required, availability of well-trained employees, and levels of technological uncertainty, as well as by the minimization of subsequent changes (Freeser & Willard, 1990).

Several issues from an evolutionary perspective follow. First, prior experiences and applications of a particular technology shape future technological change and the adoption thereof. Second, technologies are characterized by a set of complementary assets built within the organization that limit adoption of a particular evolving technology. Accordingly, major limitations apply due to a variety of cost and investment requirements not only related to new capital goods but also to the development of new routines, competencies, and structures. Finally, population ecology scholars have predicted that organizations facing major technological changes and opportunities attempt to reorganize and adapt new developments but in such a process they alter their survival chances (Hannan & Freeman, 1984).

Despite the fact that where returns to one technology depend on users externalities, an early-start technology has greater advantages, the adoption at founding of well-established technologies may imply renewal in the short run. Moreover, because existing firms face real and perceived switching costs, new entrants using the new technology can circumvent the traditional entry barriers that once protected the established firms using prior technologies. On this basis, the following proposition argues that the adoption of new technologies will improve firms' survival likelihood:

Proposition 4: Organizations that adopt at founding an emerging technology will have a higher likelihood of survival than those organizations that adopt established technologies at founding.

MARKETING STRATEGY

Business organizations are continuously forming hypotheses about their external competitive environments, and their interpretations of them represent a variable for organizational behavior and strategies. One fundamental interpretation that firms have of their environment is related to their particular understanding of the characteristics of the markets in which they are going to compete. An organization's marketing represents a set of market-oriented and interrelated actions aimed at either protecting an established position in the marketplace or growing and strengthening a market position. However, as markets change over time as a result of external environment changes, marketing may also change; marketing is not a one-time proposition, and its effects on survival cannot be clearly anticipated ex-ante.

In essence, we have considered market positioning at founding as the first step of market-oriented actions that firms may follow. We assume that even if organizations change their marketing actions in response to perceived problems, market positioning at founding exhibits persisting properties.

Market positioning has a direct impact on the allocation of human, physical, and financial resources. Differences in market positioning are also associated with the later success or failure of business organizations. Research in marketing suggests that business organizations aware of their market position relative to competitors significantly outperformed their less aware cohorts, although little empirical work has investigated the effects on survival of differences in market positioning at founding. Our general understanding of market positioning at founding relates to the set of actions and decisions implemented by the organization to respond to customer needs and demands. Basically, in this chapter we take as one of the dimensions of market positioning at founding the aggressiveness argument stressed by Romanelli (1989). Market aggressiveness expresses the depth and rapidity of resource-acquiring activities in market domains, leading to the distinction between efficient and aggressive firms. Efficient firms seek to protect an established market position while aggressive firms spend corporate resources to grow and enhance a market position.

Market positioning must also be related to demand and competitive conditions at founding; the strength of competition in already saturated markets should lead to an efficient strategy in market positioning, while lower levels of concentration when demand is growing should lead to aggressive organizations according to the set of incentives offered to the organization.

In our analysis, organizations are characterized by a market positioning that involves a specific marketing mode adopted at founding to control a set of resources. From this perspective, and drawing on Romanelli's argument (1989), it is possible to formulate the following proposition:

Proposition 5: Aggressive organizations will exhibit a higher likelihood of survival than efficient organizations.

However, marketing problem solving at founding is also related to an organization's ability to accurately capture customers' patterns of consumption and routinized habits of behavior. Consequently, at founding organizations choose a set of commercial policies aimed at ensuring that the product/service reaches the market according to the perceived patterns of consumption/purchase. Commercial policies are measured in terms of such factors as distribution channels, and the timing at which the product is available. Differential levels of correspondence influence organizational survival. We have termed this strategy "market tuning." Usually, organizations at founding differ in their levels of market tuning or their ability to accurately capture the right timing between product availability and habits of purchase. Consequently, as path-dependence processes take place, they may lock-in a suboptimal identification of consumers' purchasing habits. We have differentiated between organizations that at founding implement high market tuning strategies and firms that lag behind consumer purchasing patterns. Hence, a new proposition is stated:

Proposition 6: Organizations that exhibit market tuning at founding will increase their likelihood of survival.

Data and Analysis

Sources of Data

The entire Spanish newspaper industry was used as the population of organizations, comprising all newspapers published in Spain during the period 1966–1993. Newspapers are defined as periodicals published at least four times a week and printed either in Spanish, Catalonian, Basque, or Gallego. Both generalist and specialist (e.g. sports, medicine) dailies covering either national or regional markets fall within the domain of this study.

The database was created by gathering information from two separate sources. The sources were set up as a consequence of the promulgation of the Press and Printing Act of 1966. The Act suppressed the existing censorship, instilling some elements of liberalization into the industry. Within this context, such sources of data were set up as venues for providing external parties with reliable information on press organizations.

The first source of data is the Press Registry (*Registro General de la Administración Pública*), which contains a census of all the daily newspapers published in Spain since 1966. Firms were obliged to deliver the following founding information to the Press Registry: newspaper's title, founders of the daily, legal status, ownership of the printing house, number of pages and price of the first issue at the founding stage, plus contents (e.g. general, commercial, etc.), and address.

The second source is the Media Guide of Spain (*Guía General de Medios de Comunicación Social*), a quarterly publication which reports detailed demographic data on each firm, including when it was founded, when it ceased operations (if applicable), the printing technology, the names of the directors of the newspaper, CEO of the company and advertising manager, the features of the design of the newspaper, the advertisement rates, and membership of the Spanish single party, *Prensa del Movimiento* (until 1977). The Media Guide provides a directory of all existing newspapers. Nevertheless, specific items of the comprehensive demographic list contained in the Guide are voluntarily supplied by press organizations. Moreover, any lack of data or any possible error in the information provided by the Press Registry was corrected by the information contained in the Media Guide.

The newspaper industry has been studied in different countries and major theoretical developments within population analysis have been empirically explored using data on newspaper publishing companies (e.g. Delacroix & Carroll 1983; Carroll 1987). A main difference between this chapter and existing evidence is that we use data concerning newspaper features at founding. Although businesses in this industry were asked to file information in 1966 about founding characteristics, some data may not be accurate. It seems plausible to consider that not all the data provided refer to the founding moment if changes prior to 1966 were introduced, which was the case for specific variables such as the legal status and the geographical coverage of the newspaper.

VARIABLES

Organizational Age at the Time of Failure

The age of each newspaper was calculated as the difference between its founding date and the date it ceased to exist. If the firm continued to exist as of 1993, it was treated as censured data (see Lawless, 1982, for a discussion on this issue). This variable is considered as dependent; that is, organizational age will be the variable to be explained in the model.

Organizational Mission

This closely refers to the newspaper's content (Amburgey, Kelly & Barnett, 1993). Newspapers differ in their general or specialized content, and the mission refers to the paper's overall breadth of subject matter. General content covers a wide variety of topics and, by definition, is not dominated by a single subject matter (Miner, Amburgey & Stearns, 1990). The specialized press includes medical, commercial, sport, and other papers. A dichotomous variable measures the mission of the newspaper, coded 1 if it is of general content and as 0 otherwise.

Forms of Authority

We approach forms of authority by both ownership structure and vertical financial integration of the printing house. Firms within the newspaper industry can be divided into individual businesses and corporations. An individual business is owned and controlled by one person. A stock company is owned by heterogeneous and not always constant holders. Differences in dispersion of ownership result in differences in control and authority (Haveman, 1993). The dummy variable *ownership structure* was coded 1 if the newspaper's legal status is a corporation, and 0 if the owner of the business is an individual. We also included the *ownership of the printing house* as a measure of vertical financial integration. The variable was coded 1 if the newspaper owned it, and hence it was integrated under common ownership, and 0 otherwise.

Core Technology

The printing technology used by the newspaper at founding was operationalized as the crucial component of the technological core. During the period under examination the set of technologies available to the newspaper industry included offset technology and other printing press systems (letterpress systems or letterpress in association with photogravure). The offset system represented the emerging technology in the newspaper population for the period under study while letterpress printing systems can be considered as a well-established technology in this industry. We included a dummy variable for the printing technology at founding coded 1 if the newspaper used *offset technology* and 0 otherwise.

Marketing Strategy

Newspapers rarely use pricing policies as a crucial marketing variable to compete. Moreover, retail price maintenance has been a common practice within the newspaper industry in Spain. Newspapers compete by addressing particular audiences (e.g. editorial policies in the case of generalist newspapers), and by a set of marketing actions related to market aggressiveness such as geographical coverage (e.g. national versus local diffusion) and the frequency of publication (Amburgey, Kelly & Barnett, 1993), and market tuning. We approached marketing aggressiveness by using three dummy variables related to a newspaper's geographical focus. Papers distributed to at least 15 Spanish provinces were considered to have *national coverage*. The dummy variable was coded 1 if the daily had national coverage and 0 otherwise. Newspapers distributed to fewer than 14 provinces and more than 1 were classified as having *regional coverage*, and coded 1 if they conformed to this criterion, and 0 otherwise. Concerning the frequency of publication, we included the *number of daily editions*. The variable was coded as 1 if the newspaper had more than a daily edition and 0 if it had only a daily edition. Finally, we included the moment at which the newspaper reached the market as a proxy of market tuning at founding aimed at catching consumers' habits of purchase. Our general understanding of this industry and conversations with industry analysts provided the information needed to determine that the dominant pattern of purchase is coincident with morning editions. Hence, the variable *morning edition* was taken as an appropriate measure of market tuning. This dummy variable (*morning edition*) was coded 1 if a paper reached the market early in the morning and 0 otherwise.

Control Variables

Previous research has indicated that failure rates (and survival) may be affected by organizational characteristics and population density or levels of competition and concentration within the industry. We have included six control variables that may influence newspapers' survival prospects. First, we have controlled the interorganizational linkages that could protect the newspaper from failure (Miner, Amburgey & Stearns, 1990). Newspapers belonging to the Spanish single party (*Prensa del Movimiento*) during the dictatorial Franco regime represent in this study the group of organizations with interorganizational linkages. This dummy variable was coded 1 if the newspaper was of the *Prensa del Movimiento* during the dictatorship, and 0 otherwise. In order to control for the bias introduced by this subsample of survivors, we introduced as a control variable *newspapers started before 1966* and coded 1 if the newspaper was founded before 1966, and 0 otherwise. Competitive conditions were controlled by *density* (number of operating newspapers at the time of failure) and by *square of density/100* variables (Lomi, 1995b). This analysis included as control variables the general conditions that may influence market prospects and failure rates of the newspaper industry in Spain. We introduced *potential market* as the population (in thousands) of literate people older than 16 years. Data were gathered from the Survey of Working Population, a quarterly report published by the National Bureau of Statistics (*Instituto Nacional de Estadística*). To measure the situation of the newspaper industry we entered a control variable on *consumption of newsprint* (in 100 000 tons), quoted by OECD. Finally, as an indicator of the general economic conditions (Carroll & Delacroix, 1982), we introduced the *Gross National Product* (GNP, in billion peseta). Information about the GNP was collected from OECD annual reports. They are shown in constant currency in comparison to the 1986 GNP value.

Model

We used lifetime data models (Lawless, 1982), due both to the dynamic characteristics of the phenomenon of organizational mortality and to the existence of censored values. First, a parametric analysis was conducted to test the distribution fit by applying the criteria established by Akaike and Schwarz. Application of both criteria to newspaper organizations can be found in Levinthal (1991). TABLE 12.1 shows the log-likelihood of the four statistical distributions currently used in survival analysis. The optimal distribution is the lognormal since it maximizes both criteria. Consequently, we shall account for a linear distribution between the log of the dependent variable organizational age and the set of independent variables. Hence, models contained in this study can be expressed in the following form:

$$\log (t) = \alpha + \beta X + \sigma \varepsilon$$

where t is the organizational age, β is a vector of coefficients for the independent variables, X (exogenous and control variables), σ is a scale parameter, and ε is a random error. If β is positive, it means that founding features increase life expectations within the population of newspapers or increase survival probabilities, while negative values of β imply the opposite. The influence of independent variables on failure rates may be analyzed as follows:

$$r(t) = f(t)/S(t)$$

where $f(t)$ is the density function of the t lognormal variable and $S(t)$ the survival function of t.

Proposition 1 is supported if the β coefficient is negative and statistically significant, while propositions 2, 3, 4, and 6 are supported if the β coefficients are positive and statistically significant. On the other hand, proposition 5 is supported if the coefficients of β for geographical coverage are statistically significant but the β of *national coverage* is higher than the coefficient of *regional coverage*. Moreover, proposition 5 is supported if the β of *national coverage* only is positive and statistically significant.

The survival probabilities stated in the different propositions were estimated through two regressions. First, we estimated a regression model including all the control variables to show their influence in the population under study (Model 1). Second, Model 2 shows the full model for main effects of environmental conditions represented by control variables and core features acquired at founding that represent the set of independent variables as previously defined, including the newspapers' content (Proposition 1), ownership structure related to forms of authority (Proposition 2), vertical financial ownership (Proposition 3), technological core (Proposition 4), market aggressiveness (Proposition 5), and market tuning (Proposition 6).

We estimated the lifetime data models which test the various propositions through entering into the location parameter the values of the exogenous and control variables. The coefficients were estimated using the LIFEREG method (SAS Institute, 1990, pp.997–1025).

TABLE 12.1   Statistical distribution for organizational age

	Loglikelihood	Location	Scale
Lognornal	−632.2735	3.5911	2.6780
Loglogistic	−636.8669	0.0950	0.6499
Weibull	−637.5385	0.0125	0.5415
Gompertz	−664.2276	−3.4843	0.0236

RESULTS

TABLE 12.2 presents descriptive population statistics, and TABLE 13.3 shows means, standard deviations, and correlations for variables at founding. From TABLE 12.3 we must conclude that there is no collineality among the independent variables. Although a medium-size correlation (0.52) appears between newspaper content and national coverage, it is insignificant when we isolate the influences on the dependent variable.

For this reason, TABLE 12.4 only shows the results of the two regressions (Models 1 and 2). In this table, the logarithm of organizational life is the dependent variable, the different founding characteristics are the independent variables, and environmental conditions are represented by control variables. Model 2 shows that the coefficient of the newspaper's content variable lacks significance. This result does not provide support for Proposition 1, hence specialist newspapers at founding do not increase their survival chances as predicted.

We found statistical evidence on the effects on survival of forms of authority evaluated both by ownership structure at the founding stage and by the common ownership of the printing house or vertical financial integration. Newspapers legally founded as corporations show higher chances of survival than those founded as individual businesses. Ownership structure is significant at the 0.05 level, and the estimated coefficient has a positive sign, as expected. Hence, we may conclude that Proposition 2 receives statistical support. We found support for Proposition 3 at the 0.01 level, showing that vertical financial integration at founding increases the survival likelihood of organizations in comparison with the organizations that selected alternative governance forms at founding.

As for the technological core, the significant finding is that the type of technology chosen at founding does not influence survival chances in this population as represented by the lack of significance of the coefficients. This

TABLE 12.2 Population characteristics

Features at founding time	Number of newspapers
Ownership structure	133
Offset technology	111
Letterpress technology	111
Own printing house	110
General content newspapers	238
State party press	42
Total number of newspapers (1966–1993)	276

TABLE 12.3 Means, standard deviations, and correlations

Variables	Means	s.d.	1	2	3	4	5	6	7	8	9	10	11	12	13	14
Prensa del Movimiento	0.15	0.35														
Firms started before 1966	0.42	0.49	0.49													
Density	132.11	12.60	-0.16	-0.15												
Density²/100	177.56	33.42	-0.16	-0.04	0.99											
Potential market	28184	2286	-0.24	-0.13	0.71	0.73										
Newsprint	3600	1062	-0.24	-0.10	0.86	0.87	0.94									
GNP	46174	7163	-0.22	-0.14	0.77	0.78	0.97	0.93								
Newspaper content	0.91	0.28	0.09	0.11	0.00	-0.00	-0.47	-0.02	-0.05							
Ownership structure	0.89	0.30	0.20	0.27	-0.00	-0.00	0.04	-0.00	0.05	0.17						
Own printing house	0.76	0.42	0.31	0.65	0.19	0.19	0.22	0.23	0.23	0.37	0.23					
Offset technology	0.46	0.49	-0.40	-0.76	0.10	0.10	0.23	0.20	0.23	-0.07	-0.15	-0.19				
National coverage	0.10	0.31	-0.08	-0.01	0.03	0.03	0.06	0.05	0.06	-0.52	0.06	-0.21	0.00			
Regional coverage	0.20	0.40	-0.03	0.09	0.10	0.11	0.11	0.10	0.11	0.08	0.19	0.01	-0.05	-0.17		
Morning edition	0.78	0.41	0.03	-0.10	0.39	0.39	0.31	0.36	0.33	0.07	-0.10	0.18	0.14	-0.18	0.16	
Edition number	1.00	0.07	-0.04	-0.09	-0.10	-0.10	-0.07	-0.09	-0.08	-0.27	0.02	-0.18	0.11	0.20	-0.04	-0.14

TABLE 12.4   Effects of founding characteristics on survival

Variables	Model 1	Model 2
Prensa del Movimiento	0.0242	–0.5916**
	(0.320)	(0.217)
Firms started before 1966	3.5176****	2.1621****
	(0.244)	(0.265)
Density	–1.1561***	–0.9891***
	(0.319)	(0.266)
Density^2/100	0.4969***	0.3966***
	(0.127)	(0.107)
Potential market	0.0005*	–0.0000
	(0.000)	(0.000)
Newsprint	–0.0010**	0.0001
	(0.000)	(0.000)
GNP	–0.0000	0.0000
	(0.000)	(0.000)
Newspaper content		0.3545
		(0.483)
Ownership structure		0.8592*
		(0.333)
Own printing house		0.7333**
		(0.242)
Offset technology		–0.2932
		(0.256)
National coverage		–0.0020
		(0.327)
Regional coverage		–0.2255
		(0.241)
Edition number		0.4062
		(0.764)
Morning edition		0.3484*
		(0.176)
Constant	58.8468**	61.1420***
	(21.390)	(17.171)
Chi-square	9.4249****	207.591****
f.d.	7	15

**** $p \leq 0.0001$; *** $p \leq 0.001$; ** $p \leq 0.01$; * $p \leq 0.05$.
Standard errors are in parentheses.

finding is surprising since prior literature, as well as logic, suggests that new firms adopting new core technologies should possess strong technological skills with a positive effect on their survival chances. Hence, we do not find support for Proposition 4.

Marketing strategy as represented by market aggressiveness and measured by geographical coverage and frequency of publication has no positive influence on survival, although we found that the likelihood of organizational survival is increased for the set of newspapers that serve customers' needs in the morning at the 0.5 level of statistical significance. These results show that in the newspaper industry market positioning at founding is not determinant in terms of survival, while customer-oriented firms able to accurately capture consumption patterns and customers' habits increase their survival chances.

DISCUSSION AND CONCLUSIONS

The analysis of the effects of organizational features acquired at founding provides a promising way to approach and summarize institutional conditions and individual differences. The prediction that founding characteristics have persistent effects over time is at least implicitly suggested by several research traditions (e.g. neo-institutional theories, population ecology, and history-dependence theories). In our opinion, there are strong theoretical arguments for assuming imprinting and path-dependence processes for historically given organizational settings. As an organization's traits and strategies contribute to stability and are highly interdependent, the impact of environmental selection forces acting upon them may be further enhanced. However, the empirical testing of this proposition has been overlooked by organizational scholars remarking that core features acquired at founding result in differential survival chances for organizations. The empirical findings presented in this chapter, however, suggest some support for the notion of imprinting and path-dependence but show weak support for the notion that founding characteristics are determinants for the life expectations of organizations.

The empirical evidence provided in this chapter is supported by an investigation of the entire Spanish newspaper industry during the period 1966–1993. In this setting we have evaluated the effects on survival of the four core characteristics at founding stated by Hannan & Freeman (1984): organizational goals, forms of authority, core technology, and marketing strategy. Our findings and conclusions rely on the quality of the databases used for the purposes of this research. We gathered information on characteristics at founding for the entire population and measured the independent variables at a point in time before the dependent variable was measured (see Miner, Amburgey & Stearns, 1990, p.708). This allowed us to explore the possible causal relationship between founding features and organizational survival.

Concerning the basic arguments in this chapter, we found that the organizational mission at founding cannot be considered as a critical feature in terms of organizational survival. This conclusion contrasts with the results of previous research in population ecology, which supported the positive effect of specialist strategies on early survival chances (e.g. Romanelli, 1989). Therefore, this implies that the mission is not an end in itself but instead a prerequisite for additional actions and improvements necessary to create economic value, to adapt, and to ensure survival. Hence, firms may adapt the mission as defined at founding to environmental changes. In this line, Amburgey, Kelly & Barnett (1993) showed the negative effects on survival of any change concerning an organization's goals. Thus, we may conclude that any change in the organization's mission may be critical and increase the probability of failure while in the absence of changes differences in the organizational mission at founding may be neutral in terms of survival chances.

The positive effects on the likelihood of survival linked to corporations and related control structures indicated that organizations started as corporations show higher survival chances due to higher levels of mobility and easy reallocation of valuable assets.

The greater survival chances exhibited by corporations highlight the impact of ownership structure on securing the external resources needed when facing major changes and turbulence; in complex environments in which organizations face strong competitive pressures, individual businesses no longer remain an efficient type of organizational form. The lower levels of survival recorded for individual businesses must be related to differences in initial endowments, as equity and assets, which constrain the probability of success along the organization's history in collecting resources from the environment.

We have found that common ownership and vertical integration have a beneficial effect on survival prospects, increasing the competitive superiority of integrated organizations. In a world in which contracts are incomplete, control over nonhuman assets, and hence vertical financial integration, can be interpreted as a way of enhancing one's ability to benefit from the returns of specific investments.

The neutral effects on survival of differences at founding concerning the technological core lead us to consider that early technological choices, in this specific industry, may not be directly translated into differential survival. Technological adaptation is the logical explanation. During the time period covered by our analysis the offset technology, defined as emerging technology, was adopted by organizations that had introduced at founding alternative technologies (e.g. letterpress). Such organizations recorded adaptive capabilities enhancing their survival probabilities. Thus, the general claim held by population ecologists concerning inertia inherent to the organizational form, and structured around the set of capabilities geared to the old technology, must be tempered. Hence, when a particular technology is valuable within an established firm, and becomes dominant within the industry, it is likely to be adopted regardless of the risk the choice may involve.

In addition, the offset technology has to be interpreted as a technological discontinuity, in the sense that it defined a fundamentally new way of making a product. Offset printing changed the internal division of labor within the newspaper organization, bringing about decisive cost, performance, and quality advantages over prior technologies. Hence, it should be pointed out that the new opportunities presented by the offset technology were met by old organizations that adapted themselves to technological changes as well as by emerging firms that selected at founding the offset technology.

This chapter does not support the notion that marketing strategy is a core feature acquiring at founding with direct implications in terms of survival. In contrast, marketing strategy has to be understood as a set of strategic decisions aimed at providing the basis for continuous adaptation to environmental changes. Marketing strategy at founding has to be considered as the starting point on which the organization may base future strategies. However, what we define in this chapter as market tuning has an influence on long-term survival expectations; initial mistakes concerning the lack of correspondence with defined and routinized patterns of purchasing habits imply poorer survival prospects for organizations.

Taken together, our results and testing for the six propositions do not support the general idea that birth features are critical for survival, i.e. managers have an important role and opportunity for action. Thus, strategic management plays an important role in survival and represents a crucial component to overcome founding constraints. However, organizational features acquired at founding shape future options; they limit the set of strategic choices available but are not lethal characteristics.

The results of this study also provide some insight into the most critical features with regard to survival prospects, and consequently into the founding characteristics that represent harder constraints for future success and strategic management. We find that decisions at founding on ownership structure, vertical integration, and market tuning have more impact on the future life prospects than other early decisions.

However, the strengths of the aforementioned research setting also bear considerable limitations. In the light of our results, we have assumed that the core features identified by previous research (Hannan & Freeman, 1984) may not accurately measure the critical dimensions that introduce differential survival within a population of organizations. Thus, the factors that make for organizational survival are not necessarily the core features emphasized by population ecologists. In our opinion, an extension of this research could be to introduce new, different organizational features acquired at founding that directly influence survival. We suggest that further research in this field should pay more attention to economic-oriented features and propositions rather than to pure organizational-based characteristics.

We must conclude that for core features to have a definitive impact on organizational survival based on imprinting and path dependence, they must be characterized by high levels of interdependence. Interdependence among core features has a twofold dimension. Firstly, any change in one core attribute may shift the overall fitness function of the organization and, secondly, even in the absence of change, organizations facing similar environmental pressures would show differential survival functions due to their specific mix of core features.

Finally, we should point out that the Spanish society faced a turbulent environment, which resulted in strong institutional and market pressures on organizations. Therefore, only further research on the relationship between birth features and organizational survival in a more stable environment would shed light on the generalization of our conclusions.

Summarizing, this study shows that biological evolutionary models and ideas cannot be adapted uncritically, it being necessary to consider the social and economic structure in which organizations develop and are embedded, as well as the effects of strategic management and decision making. The set of core features embodied in organizational forms that influence survival are far from strictly random; some of them may be derived from a general institutional framework. Core features are selected within a limited set of options in order to capitalize on specific opportunities and they are history- and time-constrained. Hence, the limitations shown in this chapter do not justify abandoning research on the effects of the characteristics and strategies defined at founding.

ACKNOWLEDGMENTS

Financial assistance from the Spanish Commission for Science and Technology (CICYT project 96–0637) made this research possible. The authors wish to thank this volume's editors for their helpful comments, encouragement and support.

REFERENCES

Allen, F. & Sherer, P.D. (1995). The design and redesign of organizational form. In E. Bowman & B. Kogut (eds) *Redesigning the Firm*. New York: Oxford University Press, pp.183–196.

Amburgey, T.L., Kelly, D. & Barnett, W.P. (1993). Resetting the clock: the dynamics of organizational change and failure. *Administrative Science Quarterly*, **38**, 51–73.

Barnett, W.P. & Burgelman, R.A. (1996). Evolutionary perspectives on strategy. *Strategic Management Journal*, **17**, 5–19.

Barnett, W.P. & Carroll, G.R. (1995). Modeling internal organizational change. *Annual Review of Sociology*, **21**, 217–236.

Baum, J.A. & Oliver, C. (1996). Toward an institutional ecology of organizational founding. *Academy of Management Journal*, **39**, 1378–1427.

Boeker, W. (1989). Strategic change: the effects of founding and history. *Academy of Management Journal*, **23**, 489–515.

Carroll, G. R. (1985). Concentration and specialization dynamics of niche width in populations of organizations. *American Journal of Sociology*, **90**, 1262–1283.

Carroll, G.R. (1987). *Publish and Perish: The Organizational Ecology of Newspaper Industries*. Greenwich, CT: JAI Press.

Carroll, G.R. & Delacroix, J. (1982). Organizational mortality in the newspaper industries of Argentina and Ireland: an ecological approach. *Administrative Science Quarterly*, **27**, 169–198.

Carroll, G. R. & Hannan, M.T. (1989). Density delay in the evolution of organizational populations: a model and five empirical tests. *Administrative Science Quarterly*, **34**, 411–430.

Chandler, A. D. Jr. (1962). *Strategy and Structure: Chapters in the History of the American Industrial Enterprise*. Cambridge, MA: MIT Press.

Cooper, A.C. (1986). Entrepreneurship and high technology. In D.L. Sexton & R.W. Smilor (eds) *The Art and Science of Entrepreneurship*. Cambridge, MA: Ballinger, pp.158–186.

Cyert, R. M. & March, J.G. (1963). *A Behavioural Theory of the Firm*. Englewood Cliffs, NJ: Prentice Hall.

D'Aveni, R.A. & Ravenscraft, D.J. (1994). Economies of integration versus bureaucracy costs: does vertical integration improve performance? *Academy of Management Journal*, **37**, 1167–1206.

Delacroix, J. & Carroll, G.R. (1983). Organizational foundings: an ecological study of the newspaper industries of Argentina and Ireland. *Administrative Science Quarterly*, **28**, 274–291.

Dosi, G. (1991). Perspectives on evolutionary theory. *Science and Public Policy*, **18**, 353–361.

Dosi, G. & Salvatore, R. (1992). The structure of industrial production and the boundaries between firms and markets. In M. Storper & J.A. Scott (eds) *Pathways to Industrialization and Regional Development*. London: Routledge, pp.171–192.

Eisenhardt, K. M. & Schoonhoven, C.B. (1990). Organizational growth: linking founding team, strategy, environment and growth among US semiconductor ventures, 1978–1988. *Administrative Science Quarterly*, **35**, 504–529.

Freeman, J. & Hannan, M.T. (1983). Niche width and the dynamics of organizational populations. *American Journal of Sociology*, **88**, 1116–1145.

Freeser, H.R. & Willard, G.E. (1990). Founding strategy and performance: a comparison of high and low growth high tech firms. *Strategic Management Journal*, **11**, 87–98.

Hannan, M.T. & Carroll, G.R. (1992). *Dynamics of Organizational Populations: Density, Legitimation, and Competition*. New York: Oxford University Press.

Hannan, M.T. & Freeman, J. (1977). The population ecology of organizations. *American Journal of Sociology*, **82**, 929–964.

Hannan, M.T. & Freeman, J. (1984). Structural inertia and organizational change. *American Sociological Review*, **49**, 149–164.

Hannan, M.T. & Freeman, J. (1989). *Organizational Ecology*, Cambridge, MA: Harvard University Press.

Harrigan, K.R. (1986). Matching vertical integration strategies to competitive conditions. *Strategic Management Journal*, **7**, 535–555.

Haveman, H.A. (1993). Organizational size and change: diversification in the savings and loan industry after deregulation. *Administrative Science Quarterly*, **38**, 20–50.

Joskow, P.L. (1988). Asset specificity and the structure of vertical relationships: empirical evidence. *Journal of Law, Economics, and Organization*, **4**, 95–117.

Lawless, J.F. (1982). *Statistical Models and Methods for Lifetime Data*. New York: John Wiley and Sons.

Levinthal, D.A. (1991). Random walks and organizational mortality. *Administrative Science Quarterly*, **36**, 397–420.

Lomi, A. (1995a). The population and community ecology of organizational founding: Italian co-operative banks, 1936–1989. *European Sociological Review*, **11**, 75–98.

Lomi, A. (1995b). The population ecology of organizational founding: location dependence and unobserved hetereogeneity. *Administrative Science Quarterly*, **40**, 111–144.

Mahoney, J.T. (1992). The choice of organizational form: vertical financial ownership versus other methods of vertical integration. *Strategic Management Journal*, **13**, 559–584.

Masten, S. (1984). The organization of production: evidence from the aerospace industry. *Journal of Law and Economics*, **27**, 403–417.

Miner, A.S., Amburgey, T.L. & Stearns, T.M. (1990). Inter-organizational linkages and population dynamics: buffering and transformational shields. *Administrative Science Quarterly*, **35**, 689–713.

Monteverde, K. & Teece, D.J. (1982). Supplier switching costs and vertical integration in the automobile industry. *Bell Journal of Economics*, **13**, 206–213.

Nelson, R.R. (1994). Evolutionary theorizing about economic change. In N. Smelser & R. Swedberg (eds) *The Handbook of Economic Sociology*. Princeton, NJ: Princeton University Press, pp.108–136.

Nelson, R.R. & Winter, S.G. (1982). *An Evolutionary Theory of Economic Change*. Cambridge, MA: Belknap Press.

Riordan, M. & Williamson, O.E. (1985). Asset specificity and economic organization. *International Journal of Industrial Organization*, **3**, 365–378.

Romanelli, E. (1989). Environments and strategies of organization start-up: effects on early survival. *Administrative Science Quarterly*, **34**, 369–387.

Romanelli, E. (1991). The evolution of new organizational forms. *Annual Review of Sociology*, **17**, 79–103.

Rumelt, R.P. (1974). *Strategy, Structure and Economic Performance*. Boston, MA: Harvard University Press.

SAS Institute (1990). *SAS/STAT User's Guide*, Version 6, 4th Edn, vol. 2. SAS Institute Inc.

Selznick, P. (1957). *Leadership in Administration. A Sociological Interpretation*. Berkeley, CA: University of California Press.

Stinchcombe, A.L. (1965). Social structure and organizations. In J.G. March (ed.) *Handbook of Organizations*. Chicago, IL: Rand McNally and Co, pp.142–193.

Stinchcombe, A.L. (1968). *Constructing Social Theories*. Chicago, IL: University of Chicago Press.

Tucker, D., Singh, J.V., Meinhard, A.G. & House, R.J. (1988). Ecological and institutional sources of change in organizational populations. In G.R. Carrol (ed.) *Ecological Models of Organizations*. Cambridge, MA: Ballinger, pp.127–152.

Tushman, M.L. & Anderson, P. (1986). Technological discontinuities and organizational environments. *Administrative Science Quarterly*, **31**, 439–465.

Williamson, O.E. (1975). *Markets and Hierarchies: Analysis and Antitrust Implications*. New York: Free Press.

Williamson, O.E. (1985). *The Economic Institutions of Capitalism: Firms, Markets, Relational Contracting*. New York: Free Press.

Williamson, O.E. (1991). Comparative economic organization: the analysis of discrete structural alternatives. *Administrative Science Quarterly*, **36**, 269–296.

Winter, S.G. (1987). Knowledge and competence as strategic assets. In D.J. Teece (ed.) *The Competitive Challenge*. New York: Harper & Row, pp.159–164.

13

Opportunities and Constraints: The Impact of Production and Organizing Intangible Resources on Multidimensional Firm Performance

KAREN BANTEL, DANIEL BYRD, WILL MITCHELL

A fundamental question in strategy research is why some firms outperform others. Several recent research streams highlight intangible resources as key causes of differential firm performance. Intangible resources receive many names, including inimitable resources (Barney, 1991), idiosyncratic exchange relationships (Teece, 1986), core competencies (Prahalad & Hamel, 1990), and isolating mechanisms (Rumelt, 1984). These terms share the common idea that intangibles are firm-specific, knowledge-based assets that intertwine with a business's tacit organizational routines. Many key questions remain open concerning how intangibles affect firm performance. Conceptual arguments sometimes view intangibles as having a monotonically

New Managerial Mindsets: Organizational Transformation and Strategy Implementation.
Edited by M.A. Hitt, J.E. Ricart i Costa and R.D. Nixon.
© 1998 John Wiley & Sons Ltd.

positive influence on performance. Empirical studies tend to show that intangibles associate with positive performance, but often center on single industries, specific intangibles, and single measures of performance (e.g. Henderson & Cockburn, 1994; Levinthal & Myatt, 1994; Maijoor & Van Witteloostuijn, 1996). In practice, though, intangible resources and performance are multidimensional concepts (Eccles, 1991; Mitchell, 1991; Amit & Schoemaker, 1993). If intangibles and performance decompose into multiple dimensions, what general relationships between the elements should one expect? Several conceptual features of intangibles suggest that intangibles present constraints for firms as well as competitive opportunities (Hannan & Freeman, 1977; Nelson & Winter, 1982; Wernerfelt, 1984; Leonard-Barton, 1992). If so, then possession of intangible resources will often produce tensions that result in tradeoffs along different performance dimensions.

This chapter attempts to determine how different types of intangibles account for differential firm performance along several performance dimensions. We emphasize the distinction between three types of resources: production resources, organizing intangibles based on internal routines, and organizing intangibles based on interorganizational relationships. In turn, we consider potential tradeoffs for profitability, growth, productivity, and survival performance. The research offers three contributions to our understanding of business strategy and performance. First, the chapter suggests that intangibles create opportunities and constraints on strategy, which in turn lead to performance tradeoffs. These tradeoffs may involve different performance dimensions at a particular time and performance tradeoffs over time along a particular dimension. Second, the chapter shows that the performance tradeoffs differ for varying types of intangibles. Third, the empirical operationalization of intangibles offers insights to aid development of generalizable theory.

BACKGROUND: INTANGIBLE RESOURCES

RELEVANT LITERATURES

Several literature streams contribute to our understanding of intangible resources. Five key literatures are: the resource-based view of the firm, transaction cost theory, behavioral theories, interorganizational network theories, and evolutionary theories.

The resource-based view of the firm gives the most extensive treatment on the subject of intangibles. Resource-based theorists describe intangibles as knowledge-based assets (Penrose, 1959). There are many typologies of intangible resources, with common distinctions between technical, manufacturing, marketing, managerial, and financial resources (Barney, 1986, 1991;

Chatterjee & Wernerfelt, 1991; Amit & Schoemaker, 1993; Capron, Dussauge & Mitchell, 1998). More generally, Kogut & Zander (1992) refer to first-order and second-order intangible resources. First-order intangibles are resources that yield direct design, manufacturing, marketing, and other commercialization advantages, while second-order intangibles consist of knowledge on how to put assets to use. Similarly, Henderson & Cockburn (1994) distinguish between component competencies, which are abilities that apply to day-to-day problem solving, and architectural competence, which is the ability to use and integrate component competencies. The key distinction in these discussions is that some resources directly create commercial advantage, while others create commercial advantage because they help a firm organize and apply its first-order resources. As Penrose (1959, p.54) put it, "A firm may achieve rents not because it has better resources, but rather the firm's distinctive competence involves making better use of its resources." We will refer to first-order component resources as production resources. We will refer to second-order architectural intangibles as organizing resources. The distinction between production resources and organizing resources provides a useful overarching resource typology. Later in the chapter, we will also develop the distinction between organizing resources that a firm holds within its boundaries and organizing resources that span organizational boundaries.

The basic argument of the resource-based view is that financial performance tends to increase with the degree to which a firm possesses valuable, scarce, and inimitable intangible resources. At the same time as an intangible resource may create value, however, the inimitability of a once-valuable resource may also constrain a firm in its attempts to change the resource when competitive conditions change. We will return to the issue of resource-based constraints later in the chapter.

The second literature, transaction cost theory, brings additional insight to the concepts of production and organizing resources, emphasizing economizing issues (Williamson, 1991a). Transaction cost economics argues that firms form governance relationships that minimize the combined costs of producing goods and protecting their value. In this view, the critical issue is to protect the value of idiosyncratic, transaction-specific assets. In some cases, such assets are tangible physical assets with dedicated uses. Often, though, transaction-specific assets involve substantial degrees of knowledge-based intangibility. Moreover, in the transaction cost view, the tacit nature of intangible resources typically creates a substantial degree of asset specificity (Williamson, 1985). Thus, the transaction cost and resource-based views examine intangible resources from converse sides. Where resource-based arguments emphasize that intangibles may create value, transaction cost arguments emphasize that firms must create governance mechanisms that protect the value of intangible resources. The mechanisms must deal with the governance of internal activities and with the governance of external exchanges involving transaction-specific assets that enjoy specialization economies and therefore suit external production (Williamson, 1975). The governance regime concept in the transaction cost view is the converse side of the organizing resource concept that arises in the resource-based view.

The performance implication of the transaction cost view is that firms must construct governance regimes that allow the optimal combination of production economies and governance economies. The governance regime must provide short-term incentives to undertake specialized investments, protect the value of the investments, and encourage valuable knowledge exchange among firms (Arrow, 1971; Grossman & Hart, 1986). An appropriate governance regime can also help managers to minimize the cost of achieving flexibility in the exchange arrangement over time. Several empirical studies in the transaction cost literature and in the related international business field of internalization theory offer support for this view (e.g. Armour & Teece, 1982; Morck & Yeung, 1992).

Despite the value of governance regimes, the short-term goal of exploiting the current value of a relationship and achieving long-term flexibility may sometimes conflict. The greater the investment in governance regimes that protect transaction-specific assets, the less attractive will be alternative options apart from current internal and external relationships. This is the basis of the fundamental transformation phenomenon that Williamson (1985) describes, whereby a large numbers bargaining situation evolves into a small numbers bargaining relationship once a firm makes a particular governance choice. In turn, this transformation may create path dependency and inadaptability of reorganizing intangibles over time.

In the third literature, behavioral theories of the firm take an introspective view of firms. Under these views, business actions derive from managers with finite analytical capacity and potentially self-serving motivations. As a result, firms are successful to the degree that they provide their employees with the right decision rules (March & Simon, 1958; Cyert & March, 1963) and incentive systems (Barnard, 1938; Cyert & March, 1963; Jensen & Meckling, 1976). Such decision rules and incentive systems constitute the firm's bureaucratic systems, and commonly involve substantial tacit, routine-based elements. In parallel with the resource-based and transaction cost views, these bureaucratic systems constitute a firm's set of organizing intangibles. Despite their necessity, the bureaucratic systems often detract from firm performance over time, because their routine-based nature makes them difficult to change. Organizational rules, heuristics, and other bureaucratic mechanisms can take on a life of their own (Zhou, 1993). Because of the institutional nature of rules and systems, bureaucratic systems may continue to govern firm actions long after the rules have served their initial usefulness in prompting profit-seeking behavior (Meyer & Rowan, 1977). In other words, once-valuable organizing resources can detract from performance when competitive environments change.

Interorganizational network theories, which constitute the fourth literature, lend a more macro perspective to the discussion of intangibles. A network position is the nexus of a set of a firm's interorganizational relationships. A firm's network position tends to result from its possession of resources, such as technical capability, that attract other firms as exchange partners. Although such resources may be scarce tangible assets, the most attractive resources will tend to be intangibles, due to their inimitability. From a network theoretical perspective, more central positions in networks of relationships confer second-order opportunities for firms to exploit resources throughout the network, in addition to their own resources (Baker, 1990). In this sense, network positions create organizing resources that allow firms to use production resources throughout a network of firms. Thus, network positions closely correspond to the concept of intangible resources. Network positions are valuable in that they determine access to information and resources (Powell, 1990; Burt, 1992) and may protect a firm from environmental threats (Baum and Oliver, 1991). Moreover, the organizing resources that arise from central network positions must be both scarce and imperfectly imitatable or else all organizations would be equally capable of assuming the most favorable position. Once established, network positions and their underlying internal intangibles may mutually reinforce themselves through reputational effects, the ability to influence market standards, path dependence in investment, and other forces (Podolny, 1993; Methe *et al.*, 1997). At the same time, though, central network positions may be the most at risk if environmental pressures come to bear upon key elements of the entire network (Singh & Mitchell, 1996). Positions at the margin that allow for more boundary spanning may allow firms to observe and prepare for environmental change (Cohen & Levinthal, 1990; Granovetter, 1985).

Finally, in the fifth literature, evolutionary theories such as evolutionary economics and organizational ecology contribute to our understanding of intangibles in at least two ways. First, organizational routines provide the locus for intangible assets (Nelson & Winter, 1982). Second, evolutionary theories emphasize dynamic perspectives in which intangibles contribute to some aspects of adaptation while hindering others. Organizational ecology stresses that routines are valuable because they contribute to reliability, which in turn is necessary for survival (Hannan & Freeman, 1984). Evolutionary economics provides a fuller characterization of routines, addressing three sets of issues. First, routines are tacit in nature, which makes them hard to imitate but also makes it difficult for the focal organization to replicate or change its own routines (Nelson & Winter, 1982; Henderson & Clark, 1990). Second, routines affect firm behavior on three levels of activities. At the lowest-level, operational routines provide the basis for reliability (Nelson & Winter, 1982). At the next level, organizational routines provide coordination and investment rules that bridge operational routines. In turn, firms use a third level of routines, which Amburgey, Kelly & Barnett (1993) refer to as modification routines, to restructure existing routines. Modification routines, the underpinnings of dynamic capabilities (Teece, Pisano & Shuen, 1997), trigger path-dependent adaptation and innovation by recombining operational and organizational routines (Henderson & Clark, 1990; Amburgey, Kelly & Barnett, 1993; Lei, Hitt & Bettis, 1996). In an evolutionary view, then, intangible resources contribute to current firm performance and influence the way in which firms respond to competitive changes.

AN INTEGRATED VIEW OF INTANGIBLES

These five sets of literature share two themes. First, the literatures have similar underlying definitions of the concept of intangible resources. Second, the literatures either explicitly or implicitly suggest that intangible resources create both opportunities and constraints on superior performance (Leonard-Barton, 1992). These themes lead to four propositions concerning how different types of intangibles will influence different types of performance.

The Concept of Intangible Resources

One common element of the literatures is that they view intangibles as firm-specific, knowledge-based assets that intertwine with a business's tacit organizational routines. The tacitness of organizational routines yields two additional properties of intangibles (Nelson & Winter, 1982). First, intangibles are unique to the firm for some time. Second, people both inside and outside the firms only partially understand the intangibles.

Intangibles emerge from a firm's choice of what activities to pursue and its choice of structures with which to govern those activities (Mosakowski, 1993). These two aspects of intangibles correspond to production and organizing intangibles. Organizing intangibles further divide into two subcategories: those that govern intra-firm relationships and those that govern inter-firm relationships. The strength of an intangible resource will increase as the intensity of the production activity or governing relationship increases. The strength of an intangible will also increase as the duration of a firm's experience with the intangible increases. At the same time, though, greater experience may create greater inertia and difficulty in adapting to environmental changes. Although the concept of third-level modification routines tempers the inertia concern, even modification routines tend to induce path-dependent responses to environmental changes, responses that may still be maladaptive.

Contributions to Current and Future Performance

Because they are only imperfectly imitatable, intangible resources provide a source of sustained advantages in production and organization. The advantages, in turn, contribute to superior performance. Production intangibles contribute to future performance as well as current performance. The non-depleting nature of production intangibles affords growth opportunities (Penrose, 1959). Once a firm has secured a valuable intangible asset, its marginal cost of expansion is minimal and the firm has a growth advantage over firms that lack the intangible base.

Organizing intangibles contribute to future performance as well as current performance. Organizing intangibles, including those that stem from intra-firm routines and those that derive from inter-firm routines, affect a firm's ability to use current knowledge. Effective intra-firm organizing routines aid the efficiency of knowledge use (Teece, 1982; March, 1991; Kogut & Zander, 1992; Henderson & Cockburn, 1994; Conner & Prahalad, 1996). Meanwhile, organizing routines that facilitate inter-firm collaboration allow the firm to access a broad base of knowledge (Powell, 1990; Henderson & Cockburn, 1994; Powell, Koput & Smith-Doerr, 1996).

Intra-firm and inter-firm organizing routines also affect a firm's flexibility to put new knowledge to use. Utilization of new knowledge often calls for a reconfiguration of organizing routines (Henderson & Clark, 1990). Successful reconfiguration, in turn, requires two types of flexibility: negotiating flexibility, which is the ease with which parties can agree upon required changes, and structural flexibility, which is the capacity to implement agreed upon changes. In an uncertain environment with boundedly rational individuals and incomplete contracting, internal governance affords greater negotiating flexibility (Masten, 1988; Williamson, 1991b; Conner & Prahalad, 1996; Mitchell & Singh, 1996a). With internal control, authority dictates at will unless the employment contract specifically restricts the action. By contrast, external relationships typically involve greater bargaining (Williamson, 1991b). On the other hand, inter-firm collaboration offers greater structural flexibility than does hierarchy (Powell, 1990). Compared to internal routines, inter-firm routines are apt to couple more loosely with a firm's full set of routines. Thus, restructuring of inter-firm routines, through dissolution or reconstitution, should be easier, assuming that the parties agree on the necessary changes.

In assessing the respective advantages of different types of intangibles, no one type of intangible would seem to have a dominant impact on firm performance. Both production resources and organizing resources will contribute to performance, because firms require both intrinsic production capabilities and the ability to organize their production skills. Moreover, both organizing intangibles that derive from intra-firm routines and organizing intangibles that stem from inter-firm routines may contribute, although with somewhat different tradeoffs. The inertial forces involved in hierarchical relationships enhance survival by decreasing variance in performance, but this low variance may hurt the conditional expectation of financial performance given firm survival (March, 1991). Firms that pursue collaborative relationships may increase their opportunities for primacy and their conditional expected performance, but the gains may come at a higher risk of failure due to greater performance variability. Theoretically, then, each type of intangible creates its own set of opportunities for superior performance. These opportunities are perhaps best realized when firms use the different types of intangible resources in combination.

Constraints on Current and Future Performance

Intangibles create two forms of constraints on performance, including temporal traps and incompatible concurrent performance goals. Temporal traps are perhaps the most obvious constraint. Intangibles that were sources of advantage under past conditions become constraints as environmental change over time calls for adaptation. Three types of temporal traps may emerge. The first are structural traps stemming from path dependencies. A firm may see the need to change and desire to do so, but may be unable to recombine its routines to respond appropriately (Dierickx & Cool, 1989; Henderson & Clark, 1990; Amburgey, Kelly & Barnett, 1993). Although selection pressure may come to bear upon a specific routine (Miner & Haunschild, 1995), the intertwined, complementary nature of routine-based resources can make adaptation disruptive for the whole organization (Teece, 1986; Amburgey, Kelly & Barnett, 1993; Helfat, 1994). The second type of temporal trap stems from myopia. Management may fail to perceive the need for change due to its focus on its current knowledge trajectory (Levinthal & March, 1993). Intangibles enhance learning within a firm's existing knowledge domain but may retard awareness of developments outside the domain (Cohen & Levinthal, 1990). The third type of temporal trap is that the success that intangibles initially yield can breed complacency. The complacency trap occurs when management is lulled into a false sense of security that change is not necessary since it has discovered the right formula (Cyert & March, 1963; Levinthal & March, 1993).

In addition to temporal traps, the nature of intangibles may create conflicts among performance goals, because the same intangible may present an opportunity to improve one type of performance while constraining another performance dimension. For instance, growth and current profitability may conflict. Growth goals may require ongoing investment in intangibles in order to maintain them (Nelson & Winter, 1982; Mosakowski, 1993), while profitability goals may drive a cash-cow, exploitation approach towards firm resources.

The different types of intangibles may present differing degrees of constraints. Two differences arise among the constraints. The first difference concerns production versus organizing intangibles. The second difference arises with respect to internal versus inter-firm organizing intangibles.

First, temporal traps will tend to differ for production and organizing intangibles. Organizing intangibles create more frequent and greater temporal constraints than production intangibles. The difference arises because competitive environments are more likely to require changes in organizing intangibles than production intangibles and because changing organizing intangibles is potentially more damaging than changing production intangibles. To reach this conclusion, we must first recall that temporal traps arise from environmental changes. Henderson & Clark (1990) categorize types of environmental change as incremental, architectural, modular, and radical. At the extremes, incremental changes require few new production and organizing intangibles, while radical changes require changes in both production technology and organizing intangibles. Modular and architectural environmental shifts represent intermediate levels of change. Modular changes require new production intangibles and architectural changes require new organizing intangibles.

Different sets of changes present different constraints. Under incremental or radical environmental change, production and organizing intangibles present the same level of constraint. Under incremental change they both pose little constraint, while under radical change they pose a severe dual constraint. Note, though, that the two intermediate cases of architectural and modular environmental change have different implications for production and organizing intangibles. Architectural change, which requires new organizing intangibles, tends to be more common than modular change, which requires new production intangibles (Tushman & Anderson, 1986). Thus, the need to modify organizing routines will exceed the need to modify production routines. Moreover, technology theorists tend to view architectural adaptation as more difficult than modular adaptation because architectural adaptation requires a reassembling of the firm's communication pathways and problem-solving strategies (Henderson & Clark, 1990). By contrast, when faced with the need to revamp production technology during modular changes, firms can still rely upon their current organizational structure to develop solutions. These arguments suggest that organizing intangibles will present greater and more frequent inter-temporal constraints than production intangibles.

The second difference in the constraints is that a firm's mix of internal and inter-firm organizing intangibles will tend to affect the type of constraints that the firm encounters. Until this point in the discussion, we have presented organizing intangibles based on internal and inter-firm relationships as independent constructs. However, a choice to govern an activity using internal relationships often represents a decision not to use inter-firm relationships and vice versa. In addition, the overall balance of internal versus inter-firm routines that a firm uses to manage its knowledge may be critical in determining the effective utilization of that knowledge. Using a diffusion model based on individual agents, March (1991) posits that organizations maximize learning by having an appropriate mix of what he calls efficient learners and diverse learners. Taking this abstraction of efficiency and diversity to the level of routines suggests that some mix of exploitation-oriented routines and exploration-oriented routines will maximize an organization's knowledge utilization. As we noted earlier, internal routines often aid exploitation of current knowledge, while inter-firm routines are likely to aid exploration. Thus, a firm's mix of internal and inter-firm routines may create tradeoffs for current and future performance.

We can illustrate the interdependent nature of organizing intangibles based on internal and inter-firm routines by examining the consequences of having extreme levels of either. Firms that primarily rely on inter-firm routines, with little capability based on internal routines, may be able to tap a large knowledge pool but may be unable to absorb and apply the knowledge (Cohen & Levinthal, 1990). A firm might also become extremely dependent on other firms due to its lack of bargaining power and lack of unique capabilities (Pfeffer & Salancik, 1978; Singh & Mitchell, 1996). At the other extreme, firms that primarily rely on intra-firm routines, with little capability based on inter-firm relationships, may miss opportunities to exploit new markets due to lack of information and lack of attention to developments outside their immediate domain. This type of myopia will cause a firm to miss growth opportunities (Slater & Narver, 1995; Mitchell & Singh, 1996b).

Thus, firms will tend to require some mix of internal and inter-firm intangibles. Maintaining a correct mixture is particularly difficult since strengthening of one often comes at the expense of the other. As a result, nonlinear and nonmonotonic relationships between levels of each organizing intangible and performance may well arise. The arguments concerning opportunities and constraints lead us to the following summary logic and resulting propositions.

Propositions

Production intangibles present an inter-temporal constraint with respect to obsolescence of technical or marketing knowledge. Although product obsolescence may occur, obsolescence of the underlying production knowledge will be less common under mere incremental or architectural environmental change. Under these conditions, production intangibles afford great opportunities with little short-term constraint. Even under modular change, many firms can use their production experience as the basis for adapting their production technologies. Hence, production intangibles that are valuable for today's financial performance should also enhance survival prospects until the next technical shock, which is a rare event in most industries.

Proposition 1: In the absence of radical environmental change, greater levels of production intangibles will contribute to superior financial performance and greater likelihood of survival.

Internal governance increases inertial forces which, in turn, enhance reliability. Information flows are also more reliable under internal governance (Helfat & Teece, 1987). Reliable, low variance performance, in turn, enhances survival prospects (Hannan & Freeman, 1984). This effect, which centers on a reduction in performance variance, may be independent of the impact on expected financial performance (Helfat, 1988). We also expect that integration towards the edges of a firm's environment will help focus managerial attention on critical factors for survival, such as technical changes and customer needs.

Proposition 2: Greater levels of internal organizing intangibles will contribute to greater likelihood of survival.

Clearly, some degree of expertise in managing internal or external relationships contributes to financial performance. Firms need to be able to manage knowledge within the firm for exploitative purposes and knowledge outside the firm for exploratory purposes. However, too little or too much experience with either form of governance will lead to underutilization of knowledge and cause performance problems. Thus, when observed in isolation, we expect moderate levels of organizing intangibles, either internal or inter-firm based, to exhibit the most favorable impact on financial performance.

Proposition 3: Greater levels of organizing intangibles will exhibit a curvilinear relationship with financial performance, in which performance first rises and then falls.

Firms often face tradeoffs in satisfying various dimensions of financial performance. For example, investments to support growth may have a detrimental short-term impact on profitability. Similarly, collaborations that aid productivity by leveraging internal resources may compromise the development of unique firm capabilities and thereby undermine prospects for sustained growth.

> **Proposition 4:** A given intangible resource will have non-uniform influences on different dimensions of financial performance.

The propositions focus on relationships that no one traditional research perspective predicts. The resource-based view presents a primarily static view of the relationship between intangibles and performance, thus under-emphasizing the inter-temporal constraints that intangibles present. Transaction cost economics also takes an equilibrium view of intangibles. The theory acknowledges the need to evaluate the most advantageous governance form over time, but avoids explicit discussion of structural flexibility, which is the capacity to make desired structural changes. Behavioral arguments focus on internal, organizing intangibles such as decision rules and incentive systems, rather than production intangibles, inter-firm relationships, and environmental influences. By contrast with behavioral views, interorganizational network views focus on external relationships while tending to under-emphasize internal processes. Lastly, evolutionary views explore the link between firm intangibles and survival prospects over time, but lack explanatory power in assessing differences in current financial performance between firms. Thus, an integrated view of intangibles that cuts across literature streams offers a unique contribution to understanding the sources of differential firm performance. By taking an integrated view we can compensate for the limitations of each individual perspective. Empirical support for the propositions will help develop this integrated approach.

DATA AND METHODS

The data set we used for the empirical analysis included 141 Midwestern US adolescent firms in technology industries such as telecommunications, medical devices, instrumentation, computers, and semiconductors. By adolescent, we mean firms from 5 to 20 years of age. The firms responded to a 1993 mail survey. We used the responses to the 1993 survey to operationalize the measures of intangibles and current performance. We then obtained follow-up information on the firms' status via telephone interviews in 1997, which we used for the survival measure. Adolescent firms in technology-intensive industries suit this study for several reasons. Adolescent firms are past the high risks of early failure due to the liability of newness (Stinchcombe, 1965) but have not yet reached the extremes of age-induced inertia (Barron, West

& Hannan, 1994). Adolescent firms commonly remain in their growth stage, typically within one main industry. Using technology-intensive industries helps ensure that the firms face changing competitive environments that create adaptation requirements. TABLE 13.1 reports the descriptive statistics and correlation matrix for the data set.

INTANGIBLE VARIABLES

This chapter deals with three categories of intangible resources: production intangibles, organizing intangibles based on internal routines, and organizing intangibles based on inter-firm relationships. TABLE 13.2 lists the survey items we used to operationalize these constructs. By measuring the activities and relationships that produce intangibles, these constructs seek to test our propositions.

We constructed two measures of production intangibles: technical capability and market scope. The evolutionary economics literature stresses the importance of firm-specific technical capability in shaping a firm's prospects for survival and financial performance (Nelson & Winter, 1982; Dosi, 1988; Henderson & Cockburn, 1994). We operationalized technical capability as R&D leadership and R&D productivity using four items. Market scope seeks to capture the underlying level of marketing expertise available to the firm. Marketing expertise allows the firm to participate successfully in multiple product markets. This broad participation, in turn, reinforces the underlying marketing expertise (Mahoney & Pandian, 1992; Slater & Narver, 1995). We operationalized marketing expertise with four items that measured breadth of experience across product and geographic markets.

We used marketing integration to operationalize our concept of organizing intangibles based on internal routines. Marketing integration is the degree to which firms integrate towards the customer by internalizing distribution, sales, and service functions. Marketing integration reflects the extent to which firms use intra-firm routines to manage their marketing know-how. Internally-oriented routines may be valuable in helping firms to focus managerial attention on the customer or become more efficient in transferring knowledge about how to satisfy market needs (Teece, 1982; Helfat & Teece, 1987; Kogut & Zander, 1992). We determined marketing integration with three items that measured internal control over distribution, sales and service to end customers. Of course, some of the expertise that a firm develops as a result of its market activities may reside in inter-firm relationships as well as in internal routines. We include this element of marketing expertise in our measures of organizing intangibles based on inter-firm relationships.

We constructed two measures of organizing intangibles based on inter-firm relationships: vertical relationships with suppliers and customers, and

TABLE 13.1 Summary statistics and product moment correlations

Correlations

Variable	1	2	3	4	5	6	7	8	9	10	11	12	13
1 Productivity	1												
2 Sales growth	0.24	1											
3 Profitability	-0.04	0.33	1										
4 Business survival	0.02	0.15	0.19	1									
5 Technical capability	0.19	0.22	-0.03	-0.07	1								
6 Market scope	0.14	0.08	0.05	0.05	0.15	1							
7 Marketing integration	-0.07	-0.17	-0.12	-0.13	0.14	-0.08	1						
8 Horizontal relationships	-0.12	-0.02	-0.08	-0.03	0.09	0.00	0.02	1					
9 Vertical relationships	0.14	0.18	-0.06	-0.04	0.21	0.16	0.02	0.17	1				
10 Firm age	-0.24	-0.23	-0.13	0.07	-0.17	-0.02	0.05	-0.01	-0.05	1			
11 Firm size	0.24	0.02	-0.14	-0.06	0.03	0.20	-0.07	-0.05	0.08	0.15	1		
12 Environmental turbulence	0.07	0.04	-0.26	-0.03	0.32	0.20	0.14	0.09	0.15	0.00	0.12	1	
13 Environmental munificence	-0.09	0.26	0.38	-0.14	-0.11	0.02	-0.08	0.01	0.04	0.08	-0.07	-0.44	1
Summary statistics													
Mean	111 151	3.48	4.13	0.84	4.4	3.86	5.23	0.13	0.83	8.89	24.44	3.97	3.85
Standard deviation	67 563	1.26	1.54	0.36	1.36	1.38	1.39	0.23	1.05	3.39	68.79	1.19	1.34
Minimum	20 000	1	1	0	1	1	1	0	0	5	1	1.4	1
Maximum	350 000	6	6	1	7	6.75	7	1.2	4.15	20	740	7	7
Cases	99	141	141	141	141	141	141	141	141	141	141	141	141

TABLE 13.2 Items used to measure constructs

Construct		Wording	Load
A	Production intangibles		
1a	Technical capability	Continuous new product development	0.595
1b	Technical capability	Products are customized to customer requirements	0.654
1c	Technical capability	Product leader	0.667
1d	Technical capability	R&D expenditures are relatively high	0.736
2a	Market scope	Provide a broad range of products	0.594
2b	Market scope	Serve broad geographic markets	0.604
2c	Market scope	Sell to numerous market segments with large potential	0.584
2d	Market scope	Many channels of distribution	0.626
B	Organizing intangibles based on internal routines		
3a	Marketing integration	All marketing done in-house	0.499
3b	Marketing integration	Direct product sales to customers	0.627
3c	Marketing integration	Do our own after-sales service	0.626
C	Organizing intangibles based on inter-firm routines		
4a	Horizontal relationships	Joint purchasing agreements with competitors	0.471
4b	Horizontal relationships	Joint sales agreements with competitors	0.471
4c	Horizontal relationships	Engaged in a joint venture with competitors	0.725
4d	Horizontal relationships	Engaged in joint research with competitors	0.633
4e	Horizontal relationships	Engaged in joint advertising with competitors	0.408
4f	Horizontal relationships	Engaged in licensing agreements with competitors	0.391
5a	Vertical relationships	Joint venture with suppliers or customers	0.636
5b	Vertical relationships	Joint research with suppliers or customers	0.677
5c	Vertical relationships	Joint advertising with suppliers or customers	0.427
D	Other influences		
6a	Environmental turbulence	Our firm must change its marketing practices extremely frequently	0.445
6b	Environmental turbulence	The rate of obsolescence is very high	0.720
6c	Environmental turbulence	Actions of competitors are unpredictable	0.449
6d	Environmental turbulence	Consumer demand and tastes are unpredictable	0.590
6e	Environmental turbulence	The mode of production/service changes often and in a major way	0.661
7a	Environmental munificence	Very safe, little threat to the survival and well-being of the firm	0.694
7b	Environmental munificence	Rich in investment and marketing opportunities	0.859
7c	Environmental munificence	An environment which the firm can control and manipulate to its own advantage	0.683

horizontal relationships with competitors. Both constructs consider the degree to which firms use inter-firm relationships to manage upstream or downstream activities such as research or advertising. A firm's position among a network of firms and its skill in managing a web of relationships is the essence of this particular intangible (Kogut, 1988; Powell, 1990; Burt, 1992). The key difference between vertical and horizontal relationships is the type of firm with which the firm collaborates. Horizontal relationships are with competitors, while vertical relationships are with customers and suppliers. We measured horizontal relationships with six items and vertical relationships with three items.

We measured technical capability, market scope, and marketing integration using seven-point Likert scales. Following recommended practice, we used an unweighted average of the responses for each set of items to develop the scores. For horizontal and vertical relationships, we transformed checklist responses into binary code. These scores, like the others, were unweighted averages for each set of responses.

We checked the fit of the measurement model using Lisrel 8.14, which yielded fit parameters within acceptable range (Cudeck & Browne, 1983), especially given the macro nature of our constructs. We confirmed internal consistency by calculating Cronbach's alphas for technical capability (0.76), market scope (0.70), marketing integration (0.61), horizontal relations (0.68), and vertical relations (0.60). We confirmed discriminant validity with Lisrel's phi matrix, which captures the correlation between constructs. The matrix yielded low values (0.33 or less) that were only on the margin of significance (alpha = 0.10). Thus, there is strong support for reliability and discriminant validity.

PERFORMANCE VARIABLES

We divided performance into two subcategories, financial performance and survival. Financial performance served as an indicator of performance in the recent past, while survival served as an indicator of long-term performance. We measured financial performance on three dimensions: productivity, sales growth, and profitability. We derived each measure from self-report data obtained in the 1993 survey and then validated the measures with information from published reports. We measured productivity as a continuous variable recording dollar sales per full-time equivalent (FTE) employee, which is an indicator of labor productivity. We measured sales growth as percentage sales growth from the prior year. We measured profitability as income before taxes as a percentage of sales. The growth and profitability measures were categorical variables derived from survey responses. Respondents chose one of six response categories indicating their most recent year's performance.

We determined survival status in 1997, four years after the initial survey, using phone interviews and follow-up investigation of firms that we could not contact via phone. Of the 141 firms, 118 cases (84%) were still operating as either independent firms (112 cases, 80%) or acquired businesses (6 cases, 4%). The remaining 23 firms (16%) had shut down.

We obtained growth, profitability, and survivor status information for all 141 firms, but only 99 firms had complete sales per FTE data. We corrected the productivity models for sample selection bias.

CONTROL VARIABLES

We used control variables for environmental and firm-level factors to help isolate the impact of intangibles on performance. Since our sample was a cross-industry data set, we used the environmental factors of industry munificence and turbulence as controls. We measured these variables with survey response data, using three items for munificence (alpha = 0.79) and five items for turbulence (alpha = 0.77), as TABLE 13.2 reports. We also used the firm-level factors of size, measured in FTE employees, and age, measured as years since founding.

METHODS

We used two sets of models, as FIGURE 13.1 summarizes. One set of models predicted financial performance. Another set of models predicted survival. We approached survival prediction in two ways. The first model sought to identify the impact of intangibles (I) on survival (S) without controlling for financial performance (I → S; model 2a in FIGURE 1). The second model, (I, P → S; model 2b in FIGURE 13.1), adds controls for financial performance (P). The distinction between the two models is important because there are two mechanisms by which intangibles could influence survival chances. First, intangibles might affect financial performance directly, which, in turn, would influence survival chances. In this first case, intangibles affect survival only indirectly, through their influence on financial performance. The alternative argument is that intangibles have a residual direct impact on survival, net of their impact on financial performance. That is, intangibles may influence a firm's survival chances independent of their contribution to current performance. The second survival model seeks to estimate any direct influence of intangibles on survival by controlling for financial performance.

We used two approaches to estimate influences on financial performance. The first approach examined the impact of intangibles on each dimension of

Model

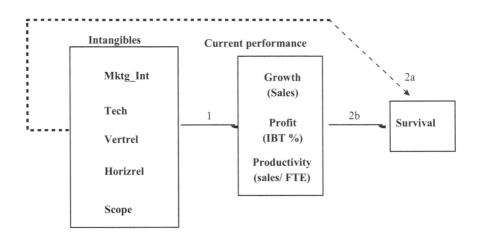

1. Financial performance: 2. Survival:

Linear models	Nonlinear models

1a. I, P => Productivity   1d. I, I^2, P => Productivity   2a. I=> S,

1b. I, P => Growth   1e. I, I^2, P => Growth   2b. I, P=>S,

1c. I, P => Profits   1f. I, I^2, P => Profits

FIGURE 13.1   The two sets of models

financial performance (i.e. productivity, growth, and profitability), while controlling for the remaining financial performance factors. When attempting to model growth, for example, it may be important to control for profitability and productivity because the individual dimensions of financial performance are likely to interact. The second set of models examined the possibility of curvilinear relationships between intangibles and financial performance by incorporating a squared term for each intangible. We used this approach to test proposition 3, which predicted curvilinear relationships between organizing intangibles and financial performance.

We used maximum-likelihood, binomial logit analysis for all survivor models because the dependent variable, survival status, was binary. We used two different methods to estimate models predicting the dimensions of financial performance. We used the Grouped Data Regression Model in the statistical package LIMDEP to analyze factors affecting sales growth and profitability. Growth and profitability are both categorical variables with known ranges. The case is similar to those in which one might use an ordered probit model, but the Grouped Data Regression Model is more efficient than ordered probit because it permits one to specify the categorical ranges when known (Greene, 1995). Productivity, a continuous variable that was only available for a subset of the sample, required a different modeling approach. We used two-stage, maximum-likelihood regression with correction for sample selection bias. In addition to the constant, we used four parameters for the selection equation: age, FTEs, growth, and profitability. These parameters reflect assumptions regarding the factors that would influence the probability of a firm responding to a request for financial information.

RESULTS

TABLES 13.3 and 13.4 present the results. Productivity failed to show any significant relationships as an independent variable with survival or as a

TABLE 13.3 Binomial logit estimates of influences on business survival from 1993 to 1997 (141 cases, 23 shut down)

	1 Intangibles → Survival	2 Intangibles, Performance → Survival
Intangibles		
Marketing integration	0.256	0.347*
Market scope	−0.244	−0.292
Horizontal relationships	0.053	0.309
Vertical relationships	0.015	0.010
Technical capability	0.082	0.046
Financial performance		
Sales growth		0.129
Profitability		0.377**
Other influences		
Firm age	−0.079	−0.065
Firm size	0.010	0.014
Environmental turbulence	0.226	0.260
Environmental munificence	0.460**	0.254
Constant	−1.080	−2.680
Loglikelihood	−55.7	−52.8
Loglikelihood ratio χ^2, full model versus constant and controls (d.f.)	4.4(5 d.f.)	10.2 (7 d.f.)
Loglikelihood ratio χ^2, model 2 versus model 1 (2 d.f.)		5.8*

* $p < 0.10$; ** $p < 0.05$ (two-tailed tests).

TABLE 13.4 Grouped data regression estimates of linear and nonlinear influences on financial performance in 1993 (141 cases)

	1 I, P → Sales growth	2a I, I2, P → Sales growth	2b joint test [a] p-value	3 I, P → Profitability	4a I, I2, P → Profitability	4b joint test [a] p-value
Intangibles						
Marketing integration	-1.820**	1.610		-0.218	-2.790	
Marketing integration squared		-0.360	0.07		0.270	0.57
Market scope	-1.040	-0.892		0.532	1.610	
Market scope squared		-0.028	0.46		-0.141	0.49
Horizontal relationships	-1.260	37.20**		-1.510	5.990	
Horizontal relationships squared		-54.70**	0.01		-9.520	0.54
Vertical relationships	1.680	3.630		-0.745	-0.610	
Vertical relationships squared		-0.618	0.19		-0.008	0.59
Technical capability	1.720*	0.326		0.121	-2.080	
Technical capability squared		0.153	0.22		0.260	0.63
Financial performance						
Sales growth						
Profitability	1.890**	1.570**		1.570**	1.390**	
Other influences						
Firm age	-0.872**	-0.910**		-0.162	-0.237	
Firm size	0.004	0.001		-0.014	-0.001	
Environmental turbulence	2.520**	2.700**		—	1.010*	-1.040*
Environmental munificence	2.190**	2.150**		1.300**	1.380**	
Constant	0.10	-5.010		3.940	12.30	
Sigma	12.60**	12.20**		6.560**	6.580**	
Loglikelihood	-251.4	-245.8		-229.6	-229.0	
Loglikelihood ratio *-2, full model versus constant and controls (d.f.)	15.6(5)**	26.8(10)**		12.6(5)**	13.8(10)	
Loglikelihood ratio *-2, main effects versus squared terms model (d.f.)		11.2(5)**		1.2(5)		

* $p < 0.10$, ** $p < 0.05$ (two-tailed tests).
[a] The joint test p-value compares the model to estimates that omit each individual intangible and its squared effect.

dependent variable with intangibles. Even the selection equation for productivity information failed to produce any significant results. Thus, we removed productivity from further consideration in order to work with the full data set. As we noted earlier, the subset of cases with productivity data included 99 of the 141 cases. Removing productivity from further consideration allowed us to use all 141 cases in the remaining analysis. Thus, the productivity analysis does not appear in the reported results.

Survival Models

TABLE 13.3 reports the main effects of intangibles on survival. We first consider the results without performance controls (I → S; model 1). When we fail to control for financial performance, it appears that none of the intangibles has a significant impact on survival. This result proves to be misleading because the direct impact of intangibles and indirect impact of intangibles via financial performance intertwine, thereby masking significant relationships. Only industry munificence appears to impact performance in the first column of TABLE 13.3.

Once we control for financial performance in TABLE 13.3 (I, P → S; model 2), we see that marketing integration has a positive, direct impact on survival. None of the other intangibles has a significant direct impact on survival. The marketing integration result is consistent with proposition 2 and highlights the positive effect of organizing intangibles based on internal routines on survival.

Notice also that profitability strongly affects survival in column 2 of TABLE 13.3, while the effect of munificence disappears in model 2. In the financial performance models that follow, munificence proves to relate positively with profitability. These two results suggest that munificence influences survival only to the degree that firms translate environmental benevolence into profits.

Linear and Curvilinear Financial Performance Models (I, P → P; I, I², P → P)

Column 1 of TABLE 13.4 reports the linear influences of intangibles on growth. Technical capability and profitability positively influence growth, while marketing integration negatively influences growth. The causal direction between profitability and growth is likely to be mutual. Profitability may generate the funds to fuel investments that support growth. Reciprocally, growth indicates an increase in sales volume and eventually sales margins as concentration rises, thereby leading to increased profits.

Column 3 of TABLE 13.4 reports linear influences of intangibles on profitability. Beyond the control variables, only growth influences profitability. However, recall that technical capability and marketing integration influence growth; therefore, an indirect relationship likely exists between these intangibles and profitability via growth. Since profitability contributes to survival, intangibles share an indirect influence on survival via growth and profitability.

Column 2a of TABLE 13.4 reports the curvilinear influences of intangibles on growth. From the change in the chi-squared statistic relative to model 1 ($\Delta \chi^2 = 11.2$, $\Delta d.f. = 5$), we see that the curvilinear model is a significant improvement over the linear model ($p < 0.05$). Marketing integration and horizontal relationships provide the increased explanatory power of model 2. The curvilinear effect of marketing integration reaches moderate statistical significance. As FIGURE 13.2 depicts, marketing integration has an inverted-U relationship with growth. At moderate levels, marketing integration has a positive influence on growth. However, high levels of marketing integration influence growth negatively. The mean level of marketing integration is high, which leads to the results in the linear model in column 1 where the relationship with growth was negative and significant. The curvilinear influence of horizontal relationships on growth in model 2 of TABLE 13.4 is highly significant. Like marketing integration, horizontal relationships also have an inverted-U relationship with growth, as FIGURE 13.2 depicts. At moderate levels, horizontal relationships have a positive influence on growth, while high levels of horizontal relationships reduce growth.

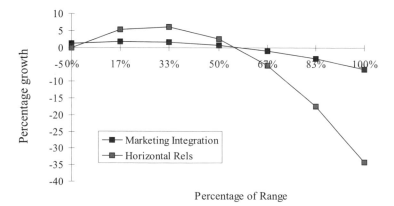

FIGURE 13.2   Impact of organizing intangibles on percentage growth

The positive relationship that technical capability shows in the linear model appears to lose its statistical significance in the curvilinear model of column 2 in TABLE 13.4. However, the loss of significance occurs only because the result spreads across the technical capability and the technical capability squared coefficients, which both have positive relationships with growth. In fact, the overall influence of technical capability on growth remains positive.

Model 4a of TABLE 13.4 investigates the possible presence of curvilinear influences of intangibles on profitability. No such influences emerge. The profitability results in model 4 are similar to the results of the linear model in column 2. As before, only growth, turbulence, and munificence hold significant relationships. Compared to the linear model, the curvilinear model is not a significant improvement ($\Delta \chi^2 = 1.2$, Δd.f. = 5). Thus, there are no observable nonmonotonic relationships between intangibles and profitability.

DISCUSSION AND FUTURE RESEARCH

TESTS OF PROPOSITIONS

Several results stand out. The results offer moderate support for proposition 1, which predicted that production intangibles would contribute to financial performance and survival, barring radical environmental changes. Consistent with the proposition, technical capability, which is a production intangible, has a positive impact on financial performance, specifically on growth. This relationship is linear rather than nonlinear, which would imply the presence of some constraint. Technical capability also has an indirect, positive impact on survival, via growth and profitability. On the other hand, market scope, which is the other production intangible that we measured, holds no significant relationship with either financial performance or survival.

The results support propositions 2 and 3. Consistent with proposition 2, internal organizing intangibles, in the form of marketing integration, contribute to survival. Consistent with proposition 3, internal organizing intangibles, again in the form of marketing integration, and inter-firm organizing intangibles, in the form of horizontal relationships, exhibit a curvilinear relationship with growth, first rising and then falling.

The results provide weak support for proposition 4, which predicted that a given intangible resource will have non-uniform influences on different dimensions of financial performance. There are no cases in which an intangible has a positive impact on one financial performance dimension and a negative impact on another dimension. However, we observe cases in which an intangible significantly influences one dimension of financial performance while having no impact on other dimensions. This outcome is true for technical capability, marketing integration and horizontal relationships.

CONCEPTUAL IMPLICATIONS

The results suggest three conceptual implications, concerning balancing issues for organizing intangibles, unambiguous effects of production intangibles, and lack of impact by market scope and vertical relationship intangibles. First, our results suggest that firms face delicate balancing issues and some dilemmas regarding the organizing intangibles that result from governance choices. A balanced mix of internal and inter-firm governing relationships seems to yield the greatest contribution to firm growth. This is consistent with March's concept (1991) of balanced exploration and exploitation. However, survival chances appear to improve with greater reliance upon internal routines, which aid exploitation of existing knowledge and contribute to reliable performance through inertial forces.

Marketing integration, in its turn, involves an apparent paradox. High levels of marketing integration have a direct positive benefit for survival prospects. Firms that have pursued forward integration are more likely to be keenly aware of the needs of existing customers. Internal structures may also aid efficient transfer and exploitation of this customer knowledge (Teece, 1982; Helfat & Teece, 1987; Kogut & Zander, 1992; Conner & Prahalad, 1996). These same structures strengthen inertial forces, making reliable performance and survival more probable. At the same time, however, growth goals call for a low to moderate degree of marketing integration. It is likely that a moderate amount of marketing integration helps supply the minimum amount of customer awareness necessary for growth and helps increase the firm's absorptive capacity for understanding and applying knowledge regarding new markets. A high degree of marketing integration, while enhancing survival directly, may induce a myopia that limits awareness of new markets for growth (Slater & Narver, 1995). When high levels of marketing integration hinder growth, the lack of growth creates an indirect, negative impact on survival via lower profitability, thus partially offsetting the direct positive benefit of marketing integration on survival. Therefore, firms concerned about survival face a tension. As marketing integration increases beyond moderate levels, the direct impact on survival chances is positive. But the increase of marketing integration may also create countervailing, negative pressure on survival via the constraint on growth and profitability.

As is the case with marketing integration, a moderate array of horizontal relationships aids growth. However, over-dependence on horizontal relationships may preclude the development of unique firm knowledge. The over-dependence may also block the development of the minimum amount of internal routines necessary to absorb and apply outside knowledge (Cohen & Levinthal, 1990), thus negating much of the benefit of horizontal relationships. Alternatively, though, it is possible that reverse causality is at work at high levels of horizontal relationships. That is, poor performance may force a firm into the arms of its competitors, as a rescue strategy. In turn, though, such relationships born of necessity will have a direct, negative influence on performance, because they may further jeopardize the weaker firm's growth prospects.

In the end, firms will need to create a mix of internal and inter-firm routines. Extreme forms of organization, such as the "virtual corporation", invite peril. In assessing the appropriate mix, managers must weigh survival concerns against the search for primacy. If survival concerns outweigh the latter, then our research suggests that firms should conduct more of their marketing, distribution, sales, and service activities themselves. If the search for primacy predominates then the firm should engage in a greater degree of collaboration in order to tap the rich pool of knowledge outside the firm.

The second implication is that, in contrast to the give-and-take results for organizing intangibles, production intangibles have strictly monotonic influences on performance. Modular environmental change is infrequent and radical environmental change is even less frequent (Tushman & Anderson, 1986). Therefore, most or all of the firms in our sample likely faced only incremental or architectural change during the four-year period of the study. Thus, the constraint issue associated with core production intangibles did not arise as a performance factor in most cases. In the short run, firm investments in technical capability provide substantial opportunities, yielding an unambiguous, positive impact on growth and, indirectly, on survival.

The third implication concerns the two intangibles, market scope and vertical relationships, that demonstrated no significant relationships with performance. This outsome might have occurred for several reasons. First, it could be true that the opportunities and constraints presented by these resources offset each other at all levels of the intangible. A second possibility might exist for vertical relationships. From a transaction cost perspective, the null result for the vertical relationship is the expected result. This is because transaction-level characteristics determine the decision to integrate, features of which are likely to have a random distribution across countless transactions for a variety of firms in a variety of industries. In this view, an observed link between vertical relationships and performance would require the presence of systemic, transaction-level traits across the firms in our sample, which is an improbable scenario.

One final explanation for the insignificant results could be measurement error on any of three dimensions, including marketing know-how, vertical relationships, and relative magnitude. First, we used marketing scope to attempt to determine the level of marketing know-how. The question arises, however, whether marketing know-how is a function of marketing breadth or depth. We chose to measure the breadth of marketing knowledge. Different results might be obtained if one instead measured a firm's depth of marketing knowledge, perhaps using cumulative advertising spending as a measure. Second, our measure of vertical relationships combines two types of relationships—links with suppliers and links with customers—but these two sets of relationship may have different effects, despite the close empirical relationship in our data. Relationships with suppliers tend to focus on the management of technical knowledge, while relationships with customers tend to build around the management of marketing knowledge. Separating these two effects in a larger sample might yield significant relationships. Third, for all intangibles we measured absolute amounts rather than levels relative to an industry. As Barney (1991) pointed out, intangibles may enhance survival but only lead to competitive parity in financial performance if they are not scarce. As a result, measurement of absolute rather than relative intangible amounts may have also been responsible for the non-results. Nonetheless, we believe that the overarching contribution of the results is significant.

Our effort at understanding the complexities involved in the relationship between production and organizing intangibles and multiple dimensions of performance has produced useful results. Future research should help validate these initial results and address open issues. A first step would be refinement of measures, particularly for marketing know-how and vertical relationships. Second, we plan to obtain another wave of data for intangibles and performance in this sample. This should help to tease out some of the causal relationships and allow examination of whether the stock of intangibles or changes in the level of intangibles has greater influence on performance.

REFERENCES

Amburgey, T., Kelly, D. & and Barnett, W. (1993). Resetting the clock: The dynamics of organizational change and failure. *Administrative Science Quarterly*, **38**, 51–73.

Amit, R. & Schoemaker, P. (1993). Strategic assets and organizational rent. *Strategic Management Journal*, **14**, 33–46.

Armour, H. & Teece, D. (1982). Vertical integration and technological innovation. *Review of Economics and Statistics*, **62**, 470–474.

Arrow, K. (1971). *Essays in the Theory of Risk Bearing*. Chicago, IL: Markham.

Baker, W. (1990). Markets, networks and corporate behavior. *American Journal of Sociology*, **96**, 589–625.

Barnard, C. (1938). *The Functions of the Executive*. Cambridge, MA: Harvard University Press.

Barney, J. (1986). Strategic factor markets: expectations, luck and business strategy. *Management Science*, **32**, 1231–1241.

Barney, J. (1991). Firm resources and sustained competitive advantage. *Journal of Management*, **17**, 99–120.

Barron, D. West, E. & Hannan, M. (1994). A time to grow and a time to die: growth and mortality of credit unions in New York City, 1914–1990. *American Journal of Sociology*, **100**, 381–421.

Baum, J. & Oliver, C. (1991). Institutional linkages and organizational mortality. *Administrative Science Quarterly*, **36**, 187–218.

Burt, R. (1992). *Structural Holes*. Cambridge, MA: Harvard University Press.

Capron, L., Dussauge, P. & Mitchell, W. (1998). Resource redeployment following horizontal mergers and acquisitions in Europe and the United States, 1988–1992. *Strategic Management Journal*, forthcoming.

Chatterjee, S. & Wernerfelt, B. (1991). The link between resources and type of diversification: theory and evidence. *Strategic Management Journal*, **12**, 33–48.

Cohen, W. & Levinthal, D. (1990). Absorptive capacity: a new perspective on learning and innovation. *Administrative Science Quarterly*, **35**, 128–152.

Conner, K. & Prahalad, C.K. (1996). A resource-based theory of the firm: knowledge versus opportunism. *Organization Science*, **7**, 477–501.

Cudeck, R. & Browne, M. (1983). Cross-validation of covariance structures. *Multivariate Behavioral Research*, **18**, 147–167.

Cyert, R. & March, J. (1963). *A Behavioral Theory of the Firm*. Englewood Cliffs, NJ: Prentice Hall.

Dierickx, I. & Cool, K. (1989). Asset stock accumulation and sustainability of competitive advantage. *Management Science*, **35**, 1504–11.

Dosi, G. (1988). Sources, procedures, and microeconomic effects of innovation. *Journal of Economic Literature*, **26**, 1120–1230.

Eccles, R. (1991). The performance manifesto. *Harvard Business Review*, **69**, 131–137.

Granovetter, M. (1985). Economic action and the social structure: the problem of embeddedness. *American Journal of Sociology*, **91**, 481–510.

Greene, W. (1995). *LIMDEP Version 7.0 User's Manual*. Plainview, NY: Econometric Software.

Grossman, S. & Hart, O. (1986). The costs and benefits of ownership: a theory of vertical and lateral integration. *Journal of Political Economy*, **94**, 691–719.

Hannan, M. & Freeman, J. (1977). The population ecology of organizations. *American Sociological Review*, **82**, 929–964.

Hannan, M. & Freeman, J. (1984). Structural inertia and organizational change. *American Sociological Review*, **49**, 149–164.

Helfat, C. (1988). *Investment Choices in Industry*. Cambridge, MA: MIT Press.

Helfat, C. (1994). Firm-specificity in corporate applied R&D. *Organization Science*, **5**, 173–184.

Helfat, C. & Teece, D. (1987). Vertical integration and risk reduction. *Journal of Law, Economics and Organization*, **3**, 47–67.

Henderson, R. & Clark, K. (1990). Architectural innovation: the reconfiguration of existing product technologies and the failure of the established firms. *Administrative Science Quarterly*, **33**, 9–30.

Henderson, R. & Cockburn, I. (1994). Measuring competence? Exploring firm effects in pharmaceutical research. *Strategic Management Journal*, **15**, 63–84.

Jensen, M. & Meckling, W. (1976). The theory of the firm: managerial behavior, agency costs and ownership structure. *Journal of Financial Economics*, **3**, 305–360.

Kogut, B. (1988). Joint ventures: theoretical and empirical perspectives. *Strategic Management Journal*, **9**, 319–332.

Kogut, B. & Zander, U. (1992). Knowledge of the firm, combinative capabilities and the replication of technology. *Organizational Science*, **3**, 383–397.

Lei, D., Hitt, M. & Bettis, R. (1996). Dynamic core competences through meta-learning and strategic context. *Journal of Management*, **22**, 549–569.

Leonard-Barton, D. (1992). Core capabilities and core rigidities: a paradox in managing new product development. *Strategic Management Journal*, **13**, 111–125.

Levinthal, D. & March, J. (1993). The myopia of learning. *Strategic Management Journal*, **14**, 95–112.

Levinthal, D. & Myatt, J. (1994). Co-evolution of capabilities and industry: the evolution of mutual funds processing. *Strategic Management Journal*, **15**, 45–62.

Mahoney, J. & Rajendran Pandian, J. (1992). The resource-based view within the conversation of strategic management. *Strategic Management Journal*, **13**, 363–380.

Maijoor, S. & Van Witteloostuijn, A. (1996). An empirical test of the resource-based theory: strategic regulation in the Dutch audit industry. *Strategic Management Journal*, **17**, 549–569.

March, J. (1991). Exploration and exploitation in organizational learning. *Organizational Science*, **2**, 71–87.

March, J. & Simon, H. (1958). *Organizations*. New York: Wiley.

Masten, S. (1988). A legal basis for the firm. *Journal of Law, Economics, and Organization*, **4**, 181–198.

Methe, D., Mitchell, W., Miyabe, J. & Toyama, R. (1997). Overcoming a standard bearer: challenges to NEC's personal computer in Japan, working paper, Kobe University.

Meyer, J. & Rowan, B. (1977). Institutionalized organizations: formal structure as myth and ceremony. *American Journal of Sociology*, **83**, 340–363.

Miner, A. & Haunschild, P. (1995). Population level learning. In B. Staw (ed.) *Research in Organizational Behavior*, **17**. Greenwich, CT: JAI Press, pp.115–166.

Mitchell, W. (1991). Dual clocks: entry order influences on industry incumbent and newcomer market share and survival when specialized assets retain their value. *Strategic Management Journal*, **12**, 85–100.

Mitchell, W. & Singh, K. (1996a). Survival of businesses using collaborative relationships to commercialize complex goods. *Strategic Management Journal*, **17**, 169–195.

Mitchell, W. & Singh, W. (1996b). Entrenched success: the reciprocal relationship between interfirm collaboration and business sales growth. *Proceedings of the Academy of Management*, 31–35.

Morck, R. & Yeung, B. (1992). Internalization: an event study test. *Journal of International Economics*, **33**, 41–56.

Mosakowski, E. (1993). A resource-based perspective on the dynamic strategy–performance relationship: an empirical examination of the focus and differentiation strategies in entrepreneurial firms. *Journal of Management*, **4**, 819–839.

Nelson, R. & Winter, S. (1982). *An Evolutionary Theory of Economic Change*. Cambridge, MA: Harvard University Press.

Penrose, E. (1959). *The Theory of the Growth of the Firm*. New York: Wiley.

Pfeffer, J. & Salancik, G. (1978). *The External Control of Organizations*. New York: Harper & Row.

Podolny, J. (1993). A status-based model of market competition. *American Journal of Sociology*, **98**, 829–872.

Powell, W. (1990). Neither market nor hierarchy: network forms of organization. In B. Staw and L.L. Cummings (eds) *Research in Organizational Behavior*, vol. 12. Greenwich, CT: JAI Press, pp. 295–336.

Powell, W., Koput, K. & Smith-Doerr, L. (1996). Interorganizational collaboration and the locus of innovation: networks of learning in biotechnology. *Administrative Science Quarterly*, **41**, 116–145.

Prahalad, C.K. & Hamel, G. (1990). The core competence of the corporation. *Harvard Business Review*, **68**, 79–91.

Rumelt, R. (1984). Toward a strategic theory of the firm. In R. Lamb (ed.) *Competitive Strategic Management*. Englewood Cliffs, NJ: Prentice Hall, pp. 556–570.

Singh, K. & Mitchell, W. (1996). Precarious collaboration: business collaboration after partners shut down or form new partnerships. *Strategic Management Journal*, **17**, 99–115.

Slater, S. & Narver, J. (1995). Market orientation and the learning organization. *Journal of Marketing*, **59**, 63–74.

Stinchcombe, A. (1965). Social structure and organizations. In J.G. March (ed.) *Handbook of Organizations*. Chicago, IL: Rand McNally, pp. 153–193.

Teece, D. (1982). Towards an economic theory of the multiproduct firm. *Journal of Economic Behavior and Organization*, **3**, 39–63.

Teece, D. (1986). Profiting from technological innovation. *Research Policy*, **15**, 285–305.

Teece, D., Pisano, G. & Shuen, A. (1997). Dynamic capabilities and strategic management. *Strategic Management Journal*, **18**, 507–533.

Tushman, M. & Anderson, P. (1986). Technological discontinuities and organizational environments. *Administrative Science Quarterly*, **31**, 439 465.

Wernerfelt, B. (1984). A resource-based view of the firm. *Strategic Management Journal*, **5**, 171–180.

Williamson, O. (1975). *Markets and Hierarchies*. New York: Free Press.

Williamson, O. (1985). *The Economic Institutions of Capitalism*. New York: Free Press.

Williamson, O. (1991a). Strategizing, economizing an economic organization. *Strategic Management Journal* **12**, 75–94.

Williamson, O. (1991b). Comparative economic organization: the analysis of discreet structural alternatives. *Administrative Science Quarterly*, **36**, 269–296.

Zhou, X. (1993). The dynamics of organizational rules. *American Journal of Sociology*, **98**, 1134–1166.

14

The Quality of Inter-Unit Relationships in MNEs as a Source of Competitive Advantage

TATIANA KOSTOVA

INTRODUCTION

Strategic management research has identified various sources of firms' competitive advantage including countries' competitive advantages (Porter, 1990), industry characteristics (Cool & Schendel, 1988; Porter, 1979), firm's strategy, resources and core competencies (Barney, 1991; Lippman & Rumelt, 1982; Nelson, 1991), and firms' institutional capital (Oliver, 1996), among many others. Most of the work in this area has examined factors of competitive advantage that are predominantly economic in nature and that operate at the level of the organization or higher, i.e. industry and nation state. Relatively less has been done at the levels of organizational units and individual employees and in regard to factors of an organizational and managerial nature. Among the notable exceptions are the work by Hansen & Wernerfelt (1989), Oliver (1996), and Barney & Zajac (1994), which have addressed in various ways the effects of organizational and managerial factors.

This chapter contributes to the existing research on firm's competitive advantage by focusing on a potentially critical but seldom examined factor,

New Managerial Mindsets: Organizational Transformation and Strategy Implementation.
Edited by M.A. Hitt, J.E. Ricart i Costa and R.D. Nixon.

that of the relationships between the organizational units of the firm. The central proposition is that the relationships that exist between the units of a firm are a potential source of competitive advantage because they affect the firm's ability to learn and, as part of this, to transfer knowledge between its units in an effective and efficient way. This proposition is consistent with a recently advanced idea that the social capital of the firm creates value by facilitating the development of its intellectual capital (Nahapiet & Ghoshal, 1998). Among the distinct contributions of this chapter is that it examines attitudinal inter-unit relationships in addition to structural relationships, an aspect which has been addressed only to a limited extent and not necessarily at this level of analysis. This chapter employs a multidisciplinary approach as it draws from organization theory and organizational behavior to conceptualize and operationalize inter-unit relationships and to examine their effects on firms' learning and competitive advantage.

Furthermore, it examines the theoretical model in the context of the multinational enterprise (MNE), which is interesting in a number of ways. First, organizational ability to learn, although recognized as an important feature of successful organizations in general, has been singled out perhaps as the most critical factor of success for MNEs. It is widely believed in the theory of foreign direct investment that the primary advantage a firm brings to foreign markets is its possession of superior knowledge (Kogut & Zander, 1993) and its ability to transfer this knowledge using intra-organizational instead of open market mechanisms. Capitalizing on the diverse competencies of the multiple national locations of the MNE and utilizing these dispersed competencies by transferring them between geographical locations and between people is a key characteristic of the successful "transnational" organization (Bartlett & Ghoshal, 1989) and the so-called "heterarchy" (Hedlund, 1986).

The MNE context is also interesting because it brings out the critical importance of inter-unit relationships in organizations. Due to the geographical distance and the economic, political, and cultural differences between the organizational units of the MNE, establishing and maintaining good relationships between them is relatively difficult, as evidenced by many cases in the practice of international management. At the same time, establishing good relationships between the units of the MNE is perhaps more critical compared to domestic organizations. As discussed above, cross-unit knowledge transfer is an important activity in MNEs as it is a major source of competitive advantage. However, MNEs have limited possibilities for using more formal means of control and coordination to support the processes of knowledge transfer across units. Therefore, MNEs have to rely to a greater extent on less formal mechanisms for coordination and control such as constructive and cooperative relationships between their organizational units.

It should be noted, however, that the theoretical model developed in this chapter is not MNE-specific, i.e. it is conceptually generalizable to any organization and not just MNEs. The case of the MNE is chosen here not because it is in any way unique for this theory but because it accentuates some of the most important aspects of the phenomenon under study. For example, the MNE context illustrates well the importance of organizational learning through transfer of knowledge between units, the challenges associated with the developing of good relationships between organizational units, and the importance of such relationships for the success of knowledge transfer.

The chapter first presents the development of a theoretical model of the effects of the quality of inter-unit relationships on the competitive advantage of MNEs. The model draws on a number of concepts and perspectives from organization theory, organizational behavior, and strategic management. Then, the particular study conducted to test the theoretical model is described, which presents only one of the many possible alternatives for testing the model. More specifically, this study examines 104 dyadic relationships between parent companies and foreign organizational units. It explores the effects of these relationships on the success of cross-border transfers of organizational practices from parent companies to foreign units. The particular practice examined here is that of quality management. The results of the study as well as the significance of this research and its implications for theory and practice are discussed.

THEORETICAL MODEL

In this section, I present a theoretical model (see FIGURE 14.1) of the relationship between three broad constructs: intra-organizational inter-unit relationships, organizational learning, and firms' competitive advantage. The central proposition is that the quality of intra-organizational relationships, i.e. the relationships between the different units in an organization, is an important factor of the organization's competitive advantage. Furthermore, the effect of inter-unit relationships on competitive advantage is realized through the organization's ability to learn—the better the relationships between the organizational units, the higher the organization's potential to learn, and the stronger its competitive advantage.

As noted above, the three constructs in the model are very broad and can be conceptualized and operationalized in various ways. For example, intra-organizational relationships have been studied in the context of interdependencies (Martinez & Jarillo, 1989; Roth & Nigh, 1992; Van de Ven, Delbecq & Koenig, 1976), power dependence (Pfeffer & Salancik, 1978), social networks (Burt, 1992; Granovetter, 1985), and social capital (Nahapiet & Ghoshal,

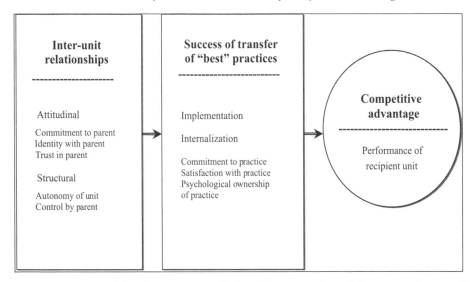

FIGURE 14.1   Model of inter-unit relationships, transfer of best practices and competitive advantage

1998). Organizational learning has also been conceptualized and operationalized in different ways, as has firms' competitive advantage.

The particular approach to studying inter-unit relationships, organizational learning, and competitive advantage adopted in this study is as follows: (i) the model is developed in the context of the MNE; (ii) the focus is on the dyadic relationships between parent companies and foreign subsidiaries; (iii) organizational learning is examined in the context of the transfer of best organizational practices from parent companies to foreign subsidiaries; (iv) competitive advantage is defined in terms of performance of foreign subsidiaries; and (v) the particular practice of Total Quality Management (TQM) is examined.

While recognizing that there are many alternatives for studying the general phenomena of inter-unit relationships, organizational learning, and competitive advantage, I suggest that the particular context selected in this chapter is both representative for all types of organizations and generalizable as a whole. Thus, I expect that the findings about transfers of TQM practices from a parent company to its foreign subsidiary will hold for transfers in all organizations (not only MNEs), for other organizational practices (for example, HRM or environmental protection), and for other directions of transfer (for example, between foreign subsidiaries or between a foreign subsidiary and a parent company when the transfer originates at the subsidiary). In the following sections I briefly introduce the main concepts and then develop a model of their relationships.

TRANSFER OF "BEST" PRACTICES AND ORGANIZATIONAL LEARNING

Organizational learning can occur in various ways, such as learning by individual employees, generation of knowledge somewhere in the organization, and acquisition of knowledge from outside sources. An important component of the processes of organizational learning is the transfer of knowledge between different organizational units in which organizations engage to achieve synergy and efficiency. Organizations typically transfer manufacturing and organizational practices that have been successful in one of their units to other units within the organization as they usually reflect the core competencies and superior knowledge of particular divisions, plants, and sites. Practices are transferred across organizational units to improve the efficiency and overall performance and to create a more isomorphic and uniform intra-organizational environment, a more distinct and cohesive organizational climate and culture, an organization-wide perception of "this is how we do things here." Booklets of "best practices" may even be put together and sent out to all units and employees, and various mechanisms are frequently used to ensure implementation of these practices organization-wide.

While the internal transfer of practices is important for all business organizations, it is extremely salient in the context of the MNE. Foreign direct investment theory suggests that the primary advantage a firm brings to foreign markets is its possession of superior knowledge. As Kogut & Zander (1993) state, "Foreign direct investment is the transfer of an intermediate good, called knowledge, which embodies a firm's advantage, whether it be the knowledge underlying technology, production, marketing or other activities." The notions of a successful multinational, more specifically, the so-called "transnational organization" (Bartlett & Ghoshal, 1989) and "heterarchy" (Hedlund, 1986), clearly suggest the idea of capitalizing on differences and diversity among national locations and of utilizing strengths and competencies dispersed worldwide by transferring them across units.

Despite the well-recognized strategic importance of these types of exchanges, the transfer process is not always smooth and successful, especially when it spans national borders. Managers in foreign affiliates of MNEs often report frustration with headquarters' requests for implementation of "yet another" new program. This may lead to local decisions not to implement the practice while reporting otherwise to headquarters. Affiliate managers may implement the practices only partially by adopting those components that they feel "people here will buy in" and ignoring the rest (quotations are from interviews with European subsidiaries managers of US-based MNEs). In some extreme cases, local managers feel alienated from the parent company to the extent that they do not believe in the parent's motives and do not even consider complying with the requests for transfer. For example, a general manager of a national subsidiary in Europe said regarding the US-based headquarters of the company, "They don't have the foggiest idea about what is going on really. They get the numbers. They get $100 million a year in profits and that is probably about as much as they want to know" (Ghoshal & Nohria, 1987).

Obviously, the formal process of transfer of a "best" organizational practice does not always result in organizational learning at the recipient unit, and, therefore, does not always lead to higher competitiveness of the recipient unit and the whole organization. In order for learning to occur in real organizations, in the context of transfers of best practices, it is necessary that the practice is transferred successfully to the recipient unit. Drawing on institutional theory and more specifically on "old" institutional theory, I define success of transfer as the degree of institutionalization of the practice at the recipient unit, i.e. the degree to which the practice is considered by the employees at the recipient unit as the "taken-for-granted way" of conducting a particular activity and the degree to which it is "infused with value," i.e. it has a symbolic meaning for employees that goes beyond the formal set of rules and procedures associated with it (Selznick, 1957). As Selznick (1957) suggested, such institutionalization shapes organizational identity and attaches a meaning to the practice as a source of organizational competitiveness.

In summary, I propose that organizational learning may result from inter-unit transfer of "best" organizational practices and that a necessary condition for organizational learning to occur is the institutionalization of the practice that is being transferred at the recipient unit.

INTER-UNIT RELATIONSHIPS AND TRANSFER OF "BEST" PRACTICES

The processes of transfer of organizational practices across units is embedded in the relationships between the units involved in the transfer. A transfer of a given practice is only one of a series of interactions between the parent company and the recipient unit. Therefore, the transfer process should be examined in the context of the relationships that have developed between the units over time. As suggested in social psychology, many of our impressions and judgments are primarily a result of inference from earlier judgments (Ebbesen & Allen, 1979; Tesser, 1978; both cited in Markus & Zajonc, 1985, p.159). Moreover, since the transfer and implementation of an organizational practice is a process that may take significant resources and time, it requires strong motivation and commitment on behalf of the local management. Motivation of the managers of the recipient unit to implement a practice may result either from the perceived value of the practice for the unit or from the perceived value of the mere act of compliance with the parent company's requests for transfer, as suggested by expectancy theories of motivation (Kanfer, 1990). In both cases, the perceived value is affected by the overall quality of past relationships with the parent company—the better the relationships, the stronger the motives to engage in implementation of the practice being transferred.

In his work on transfer of knowledge inside the firm, Szulanski (1996) recognizes the organizational embeddedness of the process of transfer. Drawing on communication theory (Arrow, 1971), he proposed that transfers are impeded by the phenomenon of "stickiness," i.e. difficulty of transferring knowledge. He suggested two origins of "stickiness." The first is intrinsic to the knowledge transferred and includes characteristics such as ambiguity in the use of knowledge and proof of the usefulness of the knowledge. The second is extrinsic and pertains to the situation in which the transfer takes place. Characteristics of the situation include motivation of the source of transfer, perceived reliability of the source, motivation of the recipient of the transfer, absorptive and retentive capacity of the recipient, a barren organizational context, and arduousness of the relationship between the source and the recipient.

In this study the organizational embeddedness of the transfer and learning process is conceptualized by the construct of interorganizational, inter-unit relationships. This is a complex multidimensional and multilevel construct as the relationships between organizational units may include various aspects such as financial, technological, administrative, and legal. Relationships may be exhibited at different levels and in different ways. For the purposes of this study, I am using such aspects of interorganizational relationships that are most likely to affect the motivation of employees at recipient units to engage in transfer processes and that are most likely to affect the degree to which the practice that is being transferred will be institutionalized at the recipient unit and therefore learning will occur. I examine two types of relationships between organizational units and parent companies, which I call *attitudinal* and *structural*.

Attitudinal relationships between a parent company and a recipient organizational unit reflect the prevailing attitudes of the employees at the recipient unit towards the parent company. While there are many possible attitudes that employees may hold, in this chapter I focus on three particular attitudes that are thought to affect the processes of practice transfer—commitment of the employees at the recipient unit to the parent company, identity of the employees at the recipient unit with the parent company, and trust of the employees at the recipient unit in the parent company.

Adapting the concept of organizational commitment by Mowday, Steers & Porter (1979), I define *commitment* of an organizational unit's employees to the parent company as the relative strength of that unit's employees' identification with and involvement in the parent company, which can be characterized by at least three related factors: (i) a strong belief in and acceptance of the parent company's goals and values, (ii) a willingness to exert considerable effort on behalf of the parent company, and (iii) a strong desire to maintain membership in the parent company. The degree of commitment of the recipient unit's employees to the parent company will be directly related to the willingness and the motivation of that unit's employees to exert effort on behalf of the parent's requests for implementation of a practice.

Identity of the recipient unit's employees with the parent company reflects the degree to which people at the recipient unit experience the state of identity with the parent company. Identity has been originally defined at the individual level as one of the three psychological states of an individual's attachment to the organization (O'Reilly & Chatman, 1986). This definition was based on Kagan's (1958) work, which suggested that individuals can accept influence in three conceptually distinct ways: compliance or exchange, identification or affiliation, and internalization or value congruence. Attachment to an individual, object, group, or organization results from identification with the attitudes, values or goals of the model, i.e. some of the attributes, motives, or characteristics of the model are accepted by the individual and become incorporated into the cognitive response set of that individual. In the context of this study, higher degrees of identification among the recipient unit's employees with the parent company will be associated with higher motivation to adopt or replicate what has been done at the parent company, i.e. to implement the practice that is being transferred.

Adapting Bromiley & Cummings's (1995) definition of interorganizational trust, I define *trust* of the recipient unit in the parent company as a common belief among employees of the unit that the parent company: (i) makes good faith efforts to behave in accordance with any commitments, whether explicit or implicit; (ii) is honest in whatever discussions preceded such commitments; and (iii) does not take excessive advantage of the unit even when the opportunity is available. Higher levels of trust in the parent will reassure the management at the recipient unit about the goodwill motives of the parent company in transferring the practice, and will, therefore, lower the resistance of the unit to change, thus increasing the likelihood of a successful implementation of a practice.

The attitudinal relationships between recipient unit and parent company might be an especially salient factor for transfer success when the practice is complex and ambiguous and its value for the subsidiary is difficult to assess. In this case, the recipient unit's decision on whether to engage in implementation of a particular practice and how much effort to put into this could be affected to a greater extent by less direct factors, such as commitment to, trust in, and identity with the parent company. Furthermore, poor attitudes of the recipient unit's employees to the parent company may create "stickiness" and thus have a negative effect on the implementation of the practice even when the recipient unit is aware of the value of the practice itself.

My interviews with foreign subsidiary managers gave support for this line of reasoning. A Japanese interviewee, for example, explained that they had a lot of problems implementing practices imported from the US headquarters, but "everything changed once we were able to build trust between us and the headquarters." A Canadian interviewee, on the other hand, was very sensitive about the unique self-identity of the plant where he was a general manager. He insisted that they are completely autonomous, that they have their own identity which is different from the identity of the parent company and that they, therefore, "do not import practices from the parent at all." This leads to the following proposition:

P1: The quality of the attitudinal relationships between an organizational unit and a parent company including commitment of that unit's employees to the parent, identity with parent, and trust in parent, is positively associated with the success of transfer of organizational practices from the parent company to the organizational unit.

Structural relationships are based on the formal power and authority structure of the organization. Drawing on organization theory and, more specifically, on the resource dependence perspective (Pfeffer & Salancik, 1978), I focus on one aspect of the formal relationships between parent companies and organizational units, i.e. the power/dependence between them which reflects the non-symmetric, hierarchical nature of the relationships between the parent company and the recipient unit. While the idea of power/dependence in the context of MNEs has been widely explored in international management research (Gladwin & Walter, 1980), it has been applied mainly to the conceptualization of relationships between a parent company and a local host country political environment. In this study the concept of dependence refers to the intra-organizational, inter-unit relationships, e.g. the relationships between a parent company and another organizational unit of the multinational company. In this perspective, the transfer of a practice is examined as a power-based interaction between parties differently positioned in the power structure of the organization. Accordingly, units that perceive to be dependent on the parent company will comply to a greater extent with any requests coming from the parent company, including those of implementation of practices that are being transferred, as compared to units not dependent on the parent.

P2: The perceived dependence of an organizational unit on the parent company is positively associated with the success of transfer of organizational practices from the parent company to that unit.

Transfer of "Best" Practices and Competitive Advantage

There is sufficient theoretical reason to suggest that a successful transfer of a "best" organizational practice is likely to increase the competitive advantage of the recipient unit. Arguments can be drawn from a number of literatures. First of all, "best" organizational practices, i.e. practices that are thought to constitute the most efficient ways of conducting certain organizational tasks, reflect the collectively shared organizational knowledge and the core competencies of the firm. Organizational knowledge has been consistently recognized as a valuable organizational resource by both economists and organization theorists. Marshall (1965, p.115), for example, argued that "knowledge is our most powerful engine of production." In a similar vein, Quinn (1992, p.6) suggested that with rare exceptions, the economic and producing power of the firm lies more in its intellectual capabilities than its hard assets and that most successful corporations "are becoming dominantly repositories and coordinators of intellect." Furthermore, firm-specific organizational resources and competencies are a source of competitive advantage, as proposed by research on core competencies of the firm and the resource-based view of the firm (Barney, 1991; Nelson, 1991). Therefore, the successful transfer of a best practice resulting in the creation of organizational knowledge and in the building of core competencies at the recipient unit will likely increase the competitive advantage of that unit.

Additional arguments for this proposition can be drawn from institutional theory and more specifically from "old" institutionalism. Selznick (1957, p.17) argued that organizational practices become institutionalized in organizations over time, i.e. they become "infused with value" as they adopt a symbolic meaning for employees that goes beyond "the technical requirements of the task at hand." Once institutionalized, practices become valued for themselves, "not as a tool but as an institutional fulfillment of group integrity and aspiration" (Selznick, 1957, p.16). He has further suggested that institutionalization is important for the accomplishment of organizational goals and mission because it helps to create and preserve the institutional integrity of the organization, which, in turn, reflects the organization's distinctive competencies. Therefore, a successful transfer of a best organizational practice resulting in the institutionalization of the practice at the recipient unit is likely to increase the competitive advantage of the recipient unit.

The above arguments are valid for all "best" organizational practices that have been successfully transferred to an organizational unit, i.e. institutionalized at that unit. In addition, there might be practice-specific effects on competitive advantage that result from the value of the particular practice. For example, the organizational practice examined in this study, the quality management practice, is likely to have an effect by itself on the competitive advantage of the recipient unit. As demonstrated by organizational researchers, quality management practices are of strategic importance for firms because they help create and sustain firms' competitive advantage (e.g. Hunt, 1993; Spencer, 1994). Success in deployment of quality practices results in improvement of customer satisfaction, and the internal sharing of these practices maximizes quality resources and accelerates organizational learning worldwide (Powel, 1995).

In summary, I propose that the success of transfer of a particular practice, i.e. the degree to which the practice has been successfully institutionalized at the recipient unit, will have an effect on that unit's competitive advantage reflected in its performance:

> P3: The success of transfer of an organizational "best" practice from a parent company to a given organizational unit of the company, i.e. the degree of institutionalization of the practice at the recipient unit, is positively associated with that unit's performance.

STUDY DESIGN

This study is the first step in testing the theoretical model described above. While the model is sufficiently general to accommodate various practical cases of MNEs and intra-organizational transfers of practices, here it is tested for a particular type of MNE, for a particular practice, and for a particular type of transfer—USA MNEs and the practices of quality management that are being transferred from US-based parent companies to their foreign subsidiaries. Quality management practices were chosen for this study because they are of strategic importance for US multinational companies (Hunt, 1993; Sitkin, Sutcliffe & Schroeder, 1994; Spencer, 1994) and many large MNEs are transferring these practices across borders. Further, the theoretical model fully applies to quality management practices. Finally, the problems experienced during transfer of quality practices seem to be representative and typical of the problems associated with the transfer of other practices in US MNEs. While there is sufficient evidence that transfers of practices within MNEs may take various directions (Kogut & Zander, 1993; Zander & Kogut, 1995), I chose to study transfers from parent to foreign organizational units because this remains a common and important direction for knowledge-based transfers.

SAMPLE DESCRIPTION

The study employs cross-sectional field methodology and falls into the category of ecological studies (Leung & Bond, 1989) which work with aggregate measures of variables collected from *N* individuals belonging to *n* different cultures. The data was collected at two different levels: individual employee and location, which, in this study, is defined as the relatively autonomous organizational unit which belongs simultaneously to the corresponding product division on a worldwide basis and to the national subsidiary in a particular country. Two large MNEs were used for the study. The first served as a site in the model development stage of the study. A total of eighteen interviews were conducted with managers of foreign subsidiaries of this company who were visiting the corporate headquarters on different assignments. The second (called hereafter "Globe" for confidentiality) served as a site for testing the model. Globe is a large agricultural company with more than 73 000 employees and presence in about 60 countries in North America, South America, Asia, Australia, Europe, Africa, and the Pacific Rim. The company has a product divisional structure with several major divisions and multiple lines of business within each division.

The sample for this study consisted of all Globe's plants, offices, and sites located in nine foreign countries, all of which had been involved in importing quality management practices from the US parent company. Countries included Canada, Argentina, the United Kingdom, the Netherlands, France, Spain, Australia, Portugal, and Malaysia. In addition to the foreign locations, three US-based plants of the company were also included in the sample. With few exceptions, all company locations from the selected countries and all senior managers of these locations were included in the study. In summary, the total number of countries included in the study was 10, the total number of locations invited to participate was 111, and the total number of surveys sent out to individual senior managers of locations was 1070.

OPERATIONALIZATION AND MEASUREMENT

The model uses two dependent variables, "first-order" dependent variable success of transfer, and a "second-order" dependent variable location's performance. *Success of transfer* of an organizational practice is defined as the degree of institutionalization of the practice at the recipient unit. It is conceptualized at two different levels and is operationalized with two sets of variables, respectively implementation and internalization. *Implementation* reflects the degree to which the various components of the quality management program have actually been implemented in a location. It is measured with a 30-item scale based on the application guidelines for the Globe Chairman's Quality Award (corporate publication, 1996). The scale measures the actual implementation of the seven components of the quality management practice such as customer satisfaction, process improvement, and employee involvement. *Internalization* is defined as the degree to which the practice has been "infused with value" (Selznick, 1957) at the recipient location. It is operationalized with a set of traditional organizational behavior constructs that, as suggested here, reflect the concept of internalization, including employee *commitment* to the practice, employee *satisfaction* with the practice, and employee *psychological ownership* of the practice.

Employee *commitment* to the practice of quality management was measured with an eight-item adapted version of the Organizational Commitment Questionnaire (OCQ; Mowday, Steers & Porter, 1979), which has face validity in the context in which commitment is used here, i.e. commitment to an organizational practice. Employee *satisfaction* with the practice was defined as the degree to which employees feel they are satisfied with the quality management practice and, more specifically, with its different components. It was measured with a seven-point scale consisting of one item for each of the seven components of the quality process, for example, "I really like the customer satisfaction component of the quality process." Employee *psychological ownership* of the practice was measured with an adaptation of Pierce, Van Dyne and Cummings' (1992) five-item measurement instrument which includes statements like "this is OUR quality process."

The second-order dependent variable, *location's performance*, was operationalized with four performance measures that are widely used in the company and that apply across divisions, countries, and locations, namely earnings per employee, output per production employee, return on assets, and gross profit per unit produced. Explaining performance based on the adoption of an organizational practice, the quality management practice in this case, is definitely a challenge. The economic performance of an organizational unit at any particular moment in time is the result of a variety of factors, and the adoption of a quality management practice is only one of them. In this study the "control" for the other possible factors of performance was done in several ways. First, the model was tested on organizational units from a single company, most of which operate in the same industry. Second, relative rather than absolute measures of performance were used, which allows greater comparability across locations. Two relative measures of performance were used in this study, average annual growth rates of the four performance measures for the period 1991–1995 and five-year growth rates of the four performance measures over the same period. This five-year period was chosen for testing the relationships between performance and success of quality practices transfer because the quality deployment effort in the company began in 1989–1990 and had been effective during these five years; hence, if there were any relationships between quality implementation and performance, they would have become apparent in this period.

Attitudinal relationships between the parent company and the foreign location was operationalized with three constructs: commitment of the location to the parent company; identity of the location with the parent company; and trust of the location in the parent company. *Commitment* of the location to the parent company was measured with an adapted nine-item version of Mowday, Steers & Porter's (1979) OCQ. *Identity* of location with parent was measured with a six-item scale based on some recent work in organizational identity (Dukerich, Golden & Shortell, 1995; Gioia & Schultz, 1995; Gioia & Thomas, 1995; Saranson, 1995). *Trust* of location in the parent company was measured with an adapted version of the nine-item short form of the Organization Trust Inventory (OTI) instrument developed by Cummings & Bromiley (1995).

The *structural relationship* between a location and the parent company was operationalized as perceptions of the senior management people at the location about that location's relative *autonomy* from the parent company and the parent's *control* over the location. Operationalization was based on previous research in the field of interorganizational relationships (Van de Ven, Delbecq & Koenig, 1976) and research in international management studying relationships between parent companies and their foreign locations (Ghoshal & Bartlett, 1988). The instrument consisted of two sections—one for autonomy and one for control. The autonomy scale measured the perceived autonomy of the location relative to the parent company in making several important decisions such as the location's goals and plans, modification of a production process or technology, and recruitment and career development plans for the location's managers. The control scale measured the perceived degree of control of the location by the parent in several important tasks and functions, including new product development, financial resources, location's performance, manufacturing technologies and processes, and human resource management.

DATA COLLECTION

Aimed at using the most appropriate source of information for each construct as well as at avoiding the potential common source biases problems, I used two different surveys in this study. Survey 1, completed by divisions' central offices at the corporate headquarters, collected the performance data. Survey 2, completed by the senior managers at each location, collected data on attitudinal and structural relationships between locations and the parent company as well as implementation and internalization of the quality program at the recipient location.

All survey instruments were developed with the active participation of the Corporate Quality Department in Globe. Survey 2 used in the participating countries was double-reverse translated—to and from French, UK English, Dutch, Spanish, Portuguese, and Bahasa Malay. Survey 2 was distributed to all locations in the 10 countries included in the study. The distribution scheme was complex and was carried out by the researcher and a team of company employees. Seven countries administered the survey on-site. Two countries—France and the Netherlands—mailed the survey to employees' home addresses. Canada used a mixed scheme. All surveys were returned directly to the researcher in an attempt to ensure confidentiality and anonymity, as promised in the covering letter in the survey. The actual results of the survey administration efforts with a breakdown by country are presented in TABLE 14.1.

As can be seen from the table, 534 copies of survey 2 (from Globe's locations' managers) were collected from 104 locations of the company in 10 countries. In addition, 104 surveys (Survey 1) were sent out to Globe division managers closely associated with the 104 locations in the sample. Currently, 27 of those surveys have been completed and analyzed. The response rate of 50% for survey 2 was acceptable given the nature and the scope of the study. The response rate for survey 1 was disappointing but can be explained by the nature of the information requested, i.e. detailed 5-year performance data for all 104 locations of a privately held company located in 10 different countries. Follow-up efforts are currently being made to collect additional survey 1 information for the missing locations. Of the respondents, 30% were female and 70% were male. The average age of respondents was 42 years and the average tenure in Globe was over 13 years. Respondents were citizens of 14 countries and spoke 12 native languages.

RESULTS AND DISCUSSION

This study employed a variety of analytical procedures to test the psychometric properties of the measurement instruments and the propositions.

TABLE 14.1 Results of survey administration

No	Country	Locations	Survey 2		
			Distributed	Responded	Response rate (%)
1	Canada	33	250	130	52
2	USA	3	25	19	76
3	Argentina	12	200	63	32
4	UK	10	125	62	50
5	Holland	12	50	26	52
6	France	8	200	83	42
7	Spain	17	93	82	88
8	Australia	7	100	52	52
9	Portugal	1	7	7	100
10	Malaysia	1	20	10	50
	Total	104	1070	534	50

Similar to other studies in international management, this study faced the challenging issue of *levels of analysis*. The propositions were formulated for the level of location while most of the definitions drew on theory developed at the individual level. Furthermore, the data was collected at different levels of analysis: the performance data at the level of the location (separate organizational unit); the data for attitudinal and structural relationships at the level of the location (although from individuals who served as informants for a given location); the implementation and the internalization data at the level of the individual (individuals were treated as respondents for this matter).

In an attempt to pick the theoretically appropriate level of analysis and at the same time to utilize the richness of the collected data, the statistical analyses were performed at multiple levels. The analysis of the psychometric properties of the measurement instruments was done at the level at which the data was collected. The correlation analysis and the testing of propositions 1 and 2 were done at both individual and location level. Proposition 3 was tested at the level of location. Thus, the data was transformed into two different sets. For the individual-level data set, each individual respondent participated with his/her individual responses for the implementation and the internalization data as well as for the attitudinal and structural relationships variables. For the location-level data set, individual responses were aggregated to the level of the location. As a result, the number of data points was reduced to 80 (locations that had at least one management and five non-management respondents). Aggregation was done only after ANOVA testing of the within and between variance in the data showed that the between-location variance was significantly larger than the within-location variance. Since the two sets of tests (individual-level and location-level) produced similar overall results, I here report the results of the individual-level tests for the correlations and for proposition 1 and 2 and the location-level tests for proposition 3.

PSYCHOMETRIC PROPERTIES OF THE MEASUREMENT INSTRUMENTS

The psychometric analysis of the measurement instruments employed in the study included tests of reliability, exploratory factor analysis, and confirmatory factor analysis. *Reliability* tests were performed on all multiple-item scales measuring the independent and dependent variables and on all sub-scales measuring dimensions of the multidimensional scales. The reliability analysis was conducted across countries, i.e. with the all-country data set. Item–total correlation statistics were used to improve the reliability of the scales where possible. Slight improvement of the reliability statistics was achieved by dropping an item from each of the following scales: employee commitment to practice (initially eight items), commitment of location to parent (initially nine items), and trust of location in parent (initially nine items). Overall, the reliability statistics (Cronbach's alpha) by scales and subscales showed satisfactory levels of internal consistency, with Cronbach's alphas ranging from 0.79 for autonomy of subsidiary from parent to 0.95 for implementation. Reliability coefficients are reported on the diagonal of TABLE 14.2.

Exploratory and *confirmatory* factor analyses were used to examine whether the hypothesized factor structures of the scales hold in this data set as well as to examine the factor structure of the complex, multidimensional scales that were used in the study (detailed description of the results are available from the author upon request). The results of the exploratory and confirmatory factor analyses suggested to retain for the propositions testing the following structure of the independent and dependent variables: all three dimensions of attitudinal relationships (commitment to parent, identity with parent, and trust in parent); two dimensions of the structural relationships (autonomy of location and control by parent); and four dimensions of the internalization scale instead of the proposed three (commitment to practice, satisfaction with practice, psychological ownership-I and psychological ownership-WE. Based on the factor loadings, the psychological ownership dimension was broken into two dimensions. Psychological ownership-I represents the sense of ownership that an organizational member has developed individually and is reflected in statements like "This is MY quality process." Psychological ownership-WE represents the sense of ownership that an individual has developed together with the other members of the organization and is reflected in statements like "This is OUR quality process". (The construct psychological ownership is relatively new in the organizational behavior field and its use in this study is exploratory. Further examination of the theoretical rationale for the two dimensions of psychological ownership and the cross-country equivalence of the measure of psychological ownership is needed.)

In summary, the reliability analysis and the exploratory and confirmatory factor analyses demonstrated that the measurement instruments used in the study provided valid measures of the constructs. The scales were reliable. The overall fit of the measurement models was satisfactory. The factor structure of the scales was generally consistent with the theorized structure of the constructs.

DESCRIPTIVE STATISTICS

TABLE 14.2 presents the descriptive statistics and the correlation coefficients for the main variables measured in the study. All correlation coefficients

TABLE 14.2 Descriptive statistics

	Mean	SD	Commitment to parent	Identity with parent	Trust in parent	Autonomy of location	Control by parent	Implementation	Commitment to practice	Satisfaction with practice	Psychological ownership-I	Psychological ownership-WE
Commitment to parent	5.04	0.88	**0.87**									
Identity with parent	4.73	1.04	0.71**	**0.83**								
Trust in parent	5.00	1.02	0.60**	0.57**	**0.93**							
Autonomy of location	4.26	1.10	0.09*	0.015	0.16**	**0.79**						
Control by parent	4.66	1.19	0.061	0.10*	0.03	−0.25**	**0.83**					
Implementation	4.93	0.85	0.45**	0.48**	0.43**	0.13**	0.020	**0.95**				
Commitment to practice	5.40	0.95	0.33**	0.30**	0.26**	0.03	0.05	0.37**	**0.92**			
Satisfaction with practice	5.72	0.69	0.31**	0.30**	0.33**	0.03	0.12*	0.44**	0.65**	**0.90**		
Psychological ownership-I	4.34	1.36	0.24**	0.21**	0.12**	0.05	−0.06	0.35**	0.46**	0.27**	**0.82**	
Psychological Ownership-WE	5.32	1.23	0.31**	0.28**	0.31**	0.06	−0.02	0.49**	0.53**	0.44**	0.32**	**0.86**

** Correlation is significant at the 0.01 level (2-tailed).
* Correlation is significant at the 0.05 level (2-tailed).
 Cronbach alphas reported on the diagonal.

were consistent with the expectations in terms of both significance and direction of the relationship. In addition, analysis of variance (ANOVA) tests were performed on all variables by country. The results showed significant country differences for all variables except the three attitudinal relationship variables—commitment to parent, identity with parent, and trust in parent—which were not significantly different between countries, a finding worth examining further.

PROPOSITIONS TESTING

The central proposition in this study, that inter-unit intra-organizational relationships in MNEs are a source of competitive advantage because they affect organizational learning through cross-unit transfers of "best" organizational practices, was empirically supported in this data set. Propositions 1 and 2 were tested with a series of regression analyses where each of the dependent variables (implementation, commitment to practice, satisfaction with practice, psychological ownership of practice-I, and psychological ownership of practice-WE) were regressed on the entire set of independent variables, including commitment to parent, identity with parent, trust in parent, autonomy of location, and control of location by parent. In addition, nine dummy variables were included to control for country. The results of the regression analyses are presented in TABLE 14.3.

Proposition 1

Proposition 1, which suggested that the success of transfer of an organizational practice from a parent company to a recipient location will be positively associated with the attitudinal relationships between the parent company and that location, was fully supported. The results demonstrate that organizational practices tend to be more successfully transferred to organizational units whose employees are more committed to the parent company, have a stronger sense of identity with the parent company, and have a higher level of trust in the parent company. More specifically, commitment, identity, and trust were all significant predictors of implementation (regression equation 1); commitment, identity, and trust predicted commitment to practice (regression equation 2); commitment and trust predicted satisfaction with practice (regression equation 3); commitment and identity predicted psychological ownership-I (regression equation 4); and commitment and trust predicted psychological ownership-WE (regression equation 5). These results are generally consistent with previous research in organizational behavior, intra-organizational relationships, and knowledge transfer. The contribution of this study lies in applying traditional

TABLE 14.3   Results of regression analysis for testing propositions 1 and 2

Independent variables	Dependent variables				
	Imple-mentation	Commitment to practice	Satisfaction with practice	Psycho-logical ownership–I	Psycho-logical ownership–WE
Equation number	(1)	(2)	(3)	(4)	(5)
Constant	2.294**	3.685**	4.079**	3.355**	3.111**
Commitment to parent	0.154**	0.301**	0.167**	0.153**	0.221**
Identity with parent	0.261**	0.246**	0.110	0.053**	0.038
Trust in parent	0.182**	0.099**	0.138**	–0.035	0.137**
Autonomy of location	0.104**	0.049	0.034	0.136	0.039
Control by parent	0.028	–0.013	0.060	–0.054	–0.061
Country 1	–0.135	–0.222	–0.112	–0.179	–0.122
Country 2	–0.040	–0.012	0.038	–0.111	0.012
Country 3	–0.147	–0.049	0.036	–0.111	–0.064
Country 4	–0.130	–0.324**	–0.122	–0.237**	–0.199*
Country 5	–0.155**	–0.248**	0.033	–0.183 **	–0.206**
Country 6	–0.211*	–0.257**	–0.203	–0.383**	–0.160
Country 7	–0.135	0.018	0.053	–0.160	–0.018
Country 8	–0.133	–0.137	–0.075	–0.139	–0.026
Country 9	–0.052	–0.053	0.026	–0.138**	–0.019
R square	0.30	0.26	0.21	0.13	0.18
Adjusted R square	0.28	0.23	0.18	0.10	0.16
F regression	13.08**	10.89**	7.07**	4.59**	7.16**

** $p < 0.01$.
* $p < 0.05$.

organizational behavior constructs to a new level of analysis (organization unit) and in the context of a non-traditional issue (knowledge transfer). This study provides evidence that any single interaction between organizational units is likely to be affected by the overall quality of past relationships between these units reflected in the mutual commitment, identity, and trust.

Proposition 2

This proposition tested the effects of structural relationships on transfer success and performance. More specifically, it tested the power/dependence argument, suggesting that organizational units that perceive themselves to be dependent on the parent, i.e. are less autonomous from and are controlled more by the parent, would put more effort into the transfer initiative because of the danger of unfavorable consequences in case of non-compliance. If the power/dependence motive were true, higher dependence would be associated with higher levels of transfer success. The results for this proposition were weak (see TABLE 14.3). Control of location by parent was not found to be a significant predictor of any of the dependent variables. Autonomy of location was significant for only one dependent variable—implementation—but was insignificant for the rest of the independent variables. Therefore, the degree of implementation was not affected by the perceptions of the location of being controlled by, i.e. dependent on, the parent company. The internalization of the quality practice at the recipient location was not affected in this sample either by the perceived autonomy of the location, or by the control of the location by the parent company.

It is interesting to note that autonomy of location in decision making yielded results opposite to what was proposed by the power/dependence argument. It was found that autonomy, which is a measure of relative power rather than dependence, affected positively implementation of practice. Locations that considered themselves to be relatively autonomous and independent from the parent company had achieved higher success in implementation of the practice transferred from the parent company. Although inconsistent with the proposition based on power/dependence logic, this finding is interpretable theoretically if examined in the context of the organizational behavior literature on participation in decision making and empowerment.

Proposition 3

The results provided partial support for proposition 3, as only some of the performance measures were significantly and positively correlated with some of the variables measuring implementation and internalization of the quality process at the recipient unit. As presented in TABLE 14.4, the average annual growth rate of output per production employee was significantly and positively correlated with implementation, employee commitment to the quality practice, and psychological ownership-WE. The average annual growth rates of earnings per employee and return on assets were positively correlated with psychological ownership-WE. The five-year growth rates of performance measures had only one significant relationship with measures of transfer success—output per production employee was positively correlated with psychological ownership-WE.

Although the empirical support for proposition 3 appears to be relatively weak, I am not surprised with the results and consider them to be generally supportive. A possible reason for the "weak" results is that performance is determined by various factors, and institutionalization of the quality process is only one of them. This is especially true for the types of industries in this sample, i.e. agriculture and commodity trading. Further, for reasons beyond my control, such as reluctance of some corporate offices to provide confidential performance data or incomplete and missing data for some indicators, the sample size for testing this proposition was relatively small. The

TABLE 14.4   Summary of testing results for proposition 3

Performance transfer success	Average annual growth rates of performance	Five-year growth rates of performance
Implementation	Significant correlation with: output per production employee ($r=0.52; p < 0.05$)	Non-significant correlations
Employee commitment to quality practice	Significant correlation with: output per production employee ($r=0.52; p < 0.05$)	Non-significant correlations
Employee satisfaction with quality practice	Non-significant correlations	Non-significant correlations
Psychological ownership–I	Non-significant correlations	Non-significant correlations
Psychological ownership–WE	Significant correlations with: output per production employee ($r=0.59; p < 0.01$) earnings per employee ($r=0.48; p < 0.05$) Return on assets ($r=0.57; p< 0.05$)	Significant correlations with: output per production employee ($r=0.56; p < 0.05$)

total number of locations for which performance data was available was 36 and for some correlation pairs N equaled 27.

SIGNIFICANCE AND CONTRIBUTION

This study is significant for several reasons. First of all, it addresses a question of practical relevance and strategic importance for multinational companies which has not been examined previously, i.e. the effects of inter-unit relationships in MNEs on their competitive advantage. The study also contributes to the literature on organizational learning and knowledge transfer in MNEs as it relates the success of these processes to the inter-unit relationships in the organization as well as to the performance of organizational units involved in knowledge transfer. Furthermore, the practice of quality management in the context of which the theoretical model advanced here was tested is of strategic significance for US companies as it provides advantages in the global competition.

Among the theoretical contributions of the study is its interdisciplinary nature. It draws from and integrates several disciplinary areas—

international management, organization theory, and organizational behavior—to develop a cross-level model of success of knowledge transfer and competitive advantage. It uses past research from these areas to better conceptualize and operationalize the key constructs. In doing so it links traditional concepts coming from relatively independent established fields. The study crosses levels of analysis, applying for example, organizational behavior constructs to operationalize concepts from institutional theory. A key construct that was conceptualized and operationalized in this way was the concept of success of practice transfer. In addition to the more traditional measures of implementation of the practice at the recipient unit, this study looked at the internalization of the transferred practice by the employees at the recipient unit and provided an original operationalization for internalization ("infusion with value"). It was shown here that these two measures of success may both be significantly related to and may also differ in their association with the independent variables (i.e. inter-unit relationships) and with the second-order dependent variable (i.e. recipient unit's performance).

The results of this study support the central idea that inter-unit relationships in organizations may be a source of competitive advantage as they affect the organization's ability to transfer best practices across units. Strong empirical support is provided for the importance of inter-unit relationships in organizations. All attitudinal variables examined here, including commitment to, identity with, and trust in the parent company, were shown to be significant predictors of both implementation and internalization of the practice at the recipient unit. This finding adds to both the research on intra-organizational relationships and the research on transfer of practices across organizational units. It has very strong practical implications as well, suggesting that building healthy inter-unit relationships is an investment strategy that pays off.

An interesting finding regarding the attitudinal relationships was that they were not significantly different across countries, i.e. organizational units from around the world seemed to have similar attitudes towards the parent company. This could be the result of a strong organizational culture of mutual trust, identity, and commitment, which was apparent in the interviews that I conducted with company employees from various countries and locations. Interesting theoretical questions, then, would be "What is the impact of national culture, if any, on the attitudinal relationships between parent companies and foreign affiliates?", "How do multinationals develop good relationships with their foreign affiliates?", and "What are the determinants of commitment to parent, identity with parent, and trust in parent?"

Furthermore, empirical evidence is provided here that the successful transfer of best practices is significantly associated with organizational units' performance. In addition to confirming some previous findings that the implementation of quality management practices improves competitive advantage (Powel, 1995), this study also showed that internalization re-flected in the employees' attitudes towards the quality practice is signifi-cantly related to performance as well. A particularly interesting finding (given the exploratory stage of the work on psychological ownership) is that the sense of ownership that employees at the recipient unit develop of the practice as a collectivity (psychological ownership-WE) is a significant pre-dictor of that unit's performance.

This study has some conceptual and methodological limitations. Concep-tually, the model could be expanded to include other determinants of organ-izational learning (transfer success) and competitive advantage. For example, the current conceptualization of structural relationships as power/dependence relationships is somewhat limited. It could be suggested, based on the literature on network theory and organizational interdependencies (e.g. Burt, 1992; Granovetter, 1985), that horizontal relationships between units be added to the model. This would be especially appropriate when structural relationships between units positioned at the same hierarchical level in the organization are examined, for example, between two or more subsidiaries of an MNE instead of the relationships between parent com-panies and subsidiaries. Methodologically, the cross-sectional variance methodology employed here could be complemented by a longitudinal methodology, which would allow a more detailed examination of the "why" and "how" questions of processes of transfer. Another limitation of the study is the testing of the model in a single company.

Overall, the results of this study are encouraging. In a broader sense, they provide evidence for the socio-organizational embeddedness of the pro-cesses of organizational learning that occurs through cross-unit transfer of "best" organizational practices as well as for the significance of both organ-izational learning and quality of inter-unit relationships for organizational performance and competitive advantage.

REFERENCES

Arrow, K. (1971). *Classificatory Notes on the Production and Transmission of Technical Knowledge.* Amsterdam: North Holland.

Barney, J.B. (1991). Firm resources and sustained competitive advantage. *Journal of Management,* **17**, 99–120.

Barney, J. & Zajac, E. (1994). Competitive organizational behavior: toward an organizationally-based theory of competitive advantage. *Strategic Management Journal,* **15**, 5–9.

Bartlett, C. & Ghoshal, S. (1989). *Managing across Borders: The Transnational Solution.* Boston, MA: Harvard Business School Press.

Bromiley, P. & Cummings, L. (1995). Transactions costs in organizations with trust. In R. Bies, R. Lewicki & B. Sheppard, (eds) *Research in Negotiation in Organizations,* vol. 5. Greenwich, CT: JAI Press, pp. 219–247.

Burt, R. (1992). The social structure of competition. In N. Nohria & R.G.Eccles (eds) *Networks and Organizations: Structure, Form and Action*. Boston, MA: Harvard Business School Press.

Cool, K. & Schendel, D. (1988). Performance differences among strategic group members. *Strategic Management Journal*, **9**, 207–223.

Cummings, L. L. & Bromiley, P. (1995). The Organizational Trust Inventory (OTI): development and validation. In R. Kramer & T. Tyler (eds) *Trust in Organizations: Frontiers of Theory and Research*. Thousand Oaks, CA: Sage, pp. 302–330.

Dukerich, J., Golden, B. & Shortell, S. (1995). Testing a model of physician identification with a vertically integrated healthcare system, paper presented at the *Identity II Conference*, Park City, UT.

Ghoshal, S. & Bartlett, C. (1988). Creation, adoption, and diffusion of innovations by subsidiaries of multinational corporations. *Journal of International Business Studies*, Fall, 365–388.

Ghoshal, S. & Nohria, N. (1987). Multinational corporations as differentiated networks, INSEAD working paper no. 87/13, INSEAD, Fontainebleau.

Gioia, D. & Schultz, M. (1995). The interrelationship of identity and image, paper presented at the *Identity II Conference*, Park City, UT.

Gioia, D. & Thomas, J. (1995). Institutional identity, image and issue interpretation: sensemaking during strategic change in academia, working paper, Smeal College of Business, Pennsylvania State University.

Gladwin, T. & Walter, I. (1980). How multinationals can manage social and political forces. *Journal of Business Strategy*, **3**, 54–68.

Granovetter, M. (1985). Economic action and social structure: the problem of embeddedness. *American Journal of Sociology*, **91**. 481–510.

Hansen, G.S. & Wernerfelt, B. (1989). Determinants of firm performance: the relative importance of economic and organizational factors. *Strategic Management Journal*, **10**, 399–411.

Hedlund, G. (1986). The hypermodern MNC: a heterarchy? *Human Resource Management*, **25**(1), 9–13.

Hunt, V. D. (1993). *Managing Quality: Integrating Quality and Business Strategy*. Homewood, IL: Irwin.

Kagan, J. (1958). The concept of identification. *Psychological Review*, **65**, 296–305.

Kanfer, R. (1990). Motivation theory and industrial and organizational psychology. In M. Dunnette & L. Hough (eds) *Handbook of Industrial and Organizational Psychology*, vol. 1, 2nd edn. Palo Alto, CA: Consulting Psychologist Press, 1: pp. 75–170.

Kogut, B. & Zander, U. (1993). Knowledge of the firm and the evolutionary theory of the multinational corporation. *Journal of International Business Studies*, **4**, 625–645.

Leung, K. & Bond, M. (1989). On the empirical identification of dimensions for cross-cultural comparisons. *Journal of Cross-Cultural Psychology*, **20**, 133–151.

Lippman, S. & Rumelt, R. (1982). Uncertain imitability: an analysis of interfirm differences in efficiency under competition. *Bell Journal of Economics*, **13**, 418–438.

Markus, H. & Zajonc, R. B. (1985). The cognitive perspective in social psychology. In C. Lindzey & E. Aronson (eds) *Handbook of Social Psychology*, vol. 1, 3rd edn. New York: Random House, pp. 137–230.

Marshall, A. (1965). *Principles of Economics*. London: Macmillian.

Martinez, J. & Jarillo, J. (1989). The evolution of research on coordination mechanisms in multinational corporations. *Journal of International Business Studies*, **20**, 489–514.

Mowday, R., Steers, R. & Porter, L. (1979). The measurement of organizational commitment. *Journal of Vocational Behavior*, **14**, 224–247.

Nahapiet, J. & Ghoshal, S. (1998). Social capital, intellectual capital and the organizational advantage. *Academy of Management Review*, **23**(2), 242–266.

Nelson, R. (1991). Why are firms different and why does it matter? *Strategic Management Journal*, **12**, 61–74.

Oliver, C. (1996). Sustainable competitive advantage: combining institutional and resource based views. *Strategic Management Journal*, **18**(9), 697–713.

O'Reilly III, C. & Chatman, J. (1986). Organizational commitment and psychological attachment: the effects of compliance, identification, and internalization on prosocial behavior. *Journal of Applied Psychology*, **71**, 492–499.

Pfeffer, J. & Salancik, J. (1978). *The External Control of Organizations: A Resource Dependence View*. New York: Harper & Row.

Pierce, J., Van Dyne, L. & Cummings, L. (1992). Psychological ownership: a conceptual and empirical analysis, unpublished manuscript.

Porter, M. (1979). The structure within industries and companies' performance. *Review of Economics and Statistics*, **61**, 214–227.

Porter, M. (1990). *The Competitive Advantage of Nations*. New York: Free Press.

Powel, A. (1995). Global quality: competitive successes and challenges, the Conference Board, report number 1125–95-RR.

Quinn, J. (1992). *Intelligent Enterprise*. New York: Free Press.

Roth, K. & Nigh, D. (1992). The effectiveness of headquarters–subsidiary relationships: the role of coordination, control, and conflict. *Journal of Business Research*, **25**, 277–301.

Saranson, Y. (1995). Operationalizing organizational identity: the case of the Baby Bells, paper presented at the *Identity II Conference*, Park City, UT.

Selznick, P. (1957). *Leadership in Administration: A Sociological Interpretation*. New York: Harper & Row.

Sitkin, S., Sutcliffe, K. & Schroeder, R. (1994). Distinguishing control from learning in Total Quality Management: a contingency perspective. *Academy of Management Review*, **19**, 537–564.

Spencer, B. (1994). Models of organization and Total Quality Management: a comparison and critical evaluation. *Academy of Management Review*, **19**, 446–471.

Szulanski, G. (1996). Exploring internal stickiness: impediments to the transfer of best practice within the firm. *Strategic Management Journal*, **17**, 27–44.

Van de Ven, A., Delbecq, A. & Koenig, R. (1976). Determinants of coordination modes within organizations. *American Sociological Review*, **41**, 322–338.

Zander, U. & Kogut, B. (1995). Knowledge and the speed of the transfer and imitation of organizational capabilities: an empirical test. *Organization Science*, **6**, 76–92.

15

Planning the Migration: Rewriting the Script for the Corporate Centre

YASMIN MERALI, JOHN MCGEE

INTRODUCTION

Over the past decade there has been a growth of interest in the changing structure, styles and role of corporate headquarters (Goold & Campbell, 1991; Goold, Campbell & Alexander, 1994; Uscem & Gottlicb, 1990). The headquarters can add value by playing a variety of roles, ranging from simple uniform controlling and checking to complex coordination and knowledge management. Success in the multinational corporation (MNC) context is about managing strategically in an interconnected world where inter- and intra-organizational relationships and the local/global dynamic are complex. For MNCs the task of managing the tradeoffs between the global integration of business activities (for benefits of scale and scope economies) and the need for local responsiveness (for reaping advantages of fit with the local market characteristics) is an intricate one (Bartlett & Ghoshal, 1987; Prahalad & Doz, 1987). The way that the headquarters relates to each business and its role in coordinating collaboration across businesses is an important determinant of corporate success (e.g. Ghoshal & Nohria, 1989, 1993).

For multi-business MNCs operating in highly dynamic contexts, the role of the headquarters in knowledge management and the leveraging of competences across divisional and business boundaries is critical (Ghoshal &

New Managerial Mindsets: Organizational Transformation and Strategy Implementation.
Edited by M.A. Hitt, J.E. Ricart i Costa and R.D. Nixon.

Nohria, 1989, 1993). This chapter is concerned with the role that the head-quarters plays in facilitating these activities by developing and realizing a congruent corporate self concept through the enactment of headquarters–business relationships. Self concept is a perception of that which we call our identity (see Weick, 1995 for a treatment of identity). The realization of the corporate self concept embraces features of dominant logic enactment (Prahalad & Bettis, 1986, 1995), and has a marked resonance with recent literature on dynamic capabilities and strategic management (Lei, Hitt & Bettis, 1996; Teece, Pisano & Shuen, 1997). The corporate self concept oper-ates at a primordial level, and provides a useful lens for reviewing ideas about learning and transformation in MNCs, while reconciling the enact-ment of what Prahalad & Bettis (1995) refer to as "contradictory dominant logics".

In an earlier paper (Merali & McGee, 1998) we proposed a framework for understanding distinctive headquarters behaviours in terms of their infor-mation and learning characteristics. In this chapter we extend that earlier work by addressing the question of transformation. We focus on issues of migration faced by headquarters in attempting to move from one established style of behaviour to a significantly different one. We suggest that in extreme cases, such a move requires a fundamental change in the foundational perceptions that support and sustain the headquarters' self concept. This will result in consequent changes in the headquarters' primary focus, values, aspirations, structures, attitudes and relationship manage-ment mechanisms.

Recent academic literature on headquarters styles highlights a contempo-rary shift away from formal, hierarchic mechanisms of communication and control to more flexible and less formal ways of managing headquarters–business relationships (Ferlie & Pettigrew, 1996). Our work on archetypes (Merali & McGee, 1998) suggests that a variety of mechanisms coexist within the context of the multibusiness, multinational corporation. The central management imperative here is about obtaining the optimal "value creating arrangement" where

- there is effective utilization of resources and competences (local and cen-tral) for sustained viability and competitive success, and
- resources and competences (business and corporate) are developed and utilized effectively to achieve a desired and feasible balance between the individual interests of the constituent divisions/businesses and the corp-orate interest in total value creation.

Each headquarters–division–business relationship is a distinctive one, geared towards obtaining a good fit between the coordination mechanism employed and the needs of the business in its particular competitive and national environment. In this situation it becomes essential that the business, divisional and headquarters staff are capable of sustaining high rates of learning in order to act appropriately in the changing external context. The planning of migrations in headquarters style within such contexts is a complex task.

The first part of this chapter defines a framework for characterizing migrations in the pattern of headquarters–business relationship. We then employ the framework to examine the case of an international corporation ("Groupe Tulip") that is currently engaged in a migration from a predominantly formalized, hierarchically structured headquarters style to a more networked and communicative one.

In tracking the migration of the headquarters behaviour style we found that the change in style is effected not by radical transformation but by the enactment of a thematic script through accumulated change and adaptation. We propose that in the world of high growth and internationalization, the corporate headquarters can play a significant role in value creation by sponsoring growth within a framework of dynamic coordinated integrative mechanisms.

THE MIGRATION FRAMEWORK

HEADQUARTERS ARCHETYPES

Previously, we proposed a framework of headquarters archetypes that is useful in attempting to understand the relationship between headquarters and its associated businesses (Merali & McGee, 1998). The model interpreted the enactment of this relationship as mediated through, and evidenced by, its *transactions* (c.f. Berne, 1961). We commented on how transactions are influenced by the perceptions of the participants and used the concept of *scripts* to describe the perceptions and their influence on the transactions.

The headquarters–business relationship is a key component of the headquarters knowledge acquisition structure: it acts as a significant filter for what enters the headquarters knowledge base. Whether formalized or not, the knowledge base of the headquarters is an inherent structural component of the script. Implied in the context of the headquarters script is a perception of the channel of communication: within the script, each headquarters–business relationship has a "bandwidth" and "integrity rating" associated with its value as an information conduit for the headquarters' knowledge acquisition activity.

The framework (FIGURE 15.1) proposed a two-by-two matrix to distinguish four archetypal headquarters scripts. The two defining dimensions used were *management focus* and *Weltanschauung. Management focus* is a dimension whose extremes are defined respectively as *capability focus* and *product focus. A capability* focus exists when management engagement and concern is focused predominantly on the capabilities and competences of the business. A *product focus* exists when management engagement and concern is focused predominantly on the product/output of the business. The *Weltanschauung* (i.e. "world outlook") for the enactment of the script is a dimension whose extremes are defined respectively as *programmatic* and *emergent*. A *programmatic Weltanschauung* exists when the relationship is acted out in a fashion predicated on a mindset where the world is largely "planned for", and actions and behaviours are designed to deliver explicit outcomes. An *emergent Weltanschauung* exists when the relationship is acted out in a dynamic, interactive mode predicated on a mindset where the world is viewed as uncertain, "shapeable" and "shaping".

We called the four quadrants defined by these two dimensions *archetypes* and named them *Lion Tamer, Trainer, Leader* and *Mentor*. These archetypes are "pure" and fictional, each operating exclusively within a single paradigm. Nonetheless, they represent useful analogues to help our understanding of the enactment of headquarters scripts.

Characteristics associated with each archetype are shown in FIGURE 15.2. We demonstrated that our framework is consistent with Burrell & Morgan's (1979) scheme. We further discussed the implications of information and learning styles of the archetypes and suggested that these too are characteristic.

Learning styles are characterized using Ashby's (1940) concepts of single-loop and double-loop learning in the context of Argyris & Schon's (1978) model of organizational learning. The *Lion Tamer* is not actively engaged in promoting learning in the businesses. The *Trainer* (with its commitment to the promotion of centrally determined, programmatic incremental learning) is predominantly engaged in single-loop learning of the adaptive type. The *Leader* is focused on process issues and though a strength in adaptive

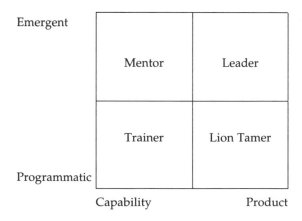

FIGURE 15.1   The archetype matrix

The four archetypes: competence characteristics

	Capability	Product
Emergent	**Mentor** – knowledge diffusion and organizational competence – cross boundary learning – innovation networks – double loop learning	**Leader** – effectiveness oriented – resource management – directional operational/tactical networks – self concept enhancement – disciplined creativity – coordination competence
Programmatic	**Trainer** – discrete individual competences – task-related training – centralized innovation – single-loop learning	**Lion Tamer** – efficiency oriented – resource management – linear communication – conformance orientation – regulation competence

Weltanschauung (vertical axis: Emergent / Programmatic) — *Management focus* (horizontal axis: Capability / Product)

The four archetypes: outlook and management focus

	Product	Capability
Emergent	**Mentor** Focus: external Horizon: long term Locus of control: embedded in relationships	**Leader** Focus: external Horizon: medium/long term Locus of control: discrete, delegated
Programmatic	**Trainer** Focus: internal Horizon: long term Locus of control: centrally distributed	**Lion Tamer** Focus: internal Horizon: short term Locus of control: discrete, control

Weltanschauung (vertical axis: Emergent / Programmatic) — *Management focus* (horizontal axis: Product / Capability)

FIGURE 15.2 Archetype characteristics

learning is one of its characteristics, it has a strong external focus and encourages "bounded innovation" at the business level (to accommodate changes in the local external environment). In this sense the *Leader* shows a certain predisposition towards the generative learning style. The *Mentor* is concerned with championing double-loop learning. It typically does this by providing contexts within which cross-boundary discourse and the process of organizational inquiry can be situated, and the requisite variety of models (Ashby, 1956) can be generated to spawn innovative ways of leveraging organizational core competences.

The corporate *Weltanschauung* acts as a filter for viewing the world, and determines the type of information that is considered to be relevant for making sense of the environment. The information matrix in FIGURE 15.3 provides a schematic representation of the types of information that underpin and characterize the enactment of each archetype. The *shared model* for a given archetype characterizes the dominant headquarters perception about what constitutes the ultimate set of values that all meaningful endeavour is designed to satisfy (i.e. the ultimate "pay off" towards which the script is directed). *Feedback information* is the type of information that is used by the headquarters to monitor what is happening within the business context. This is the information that is used to assess the congruence between the business's endeavours and the headquarters' perception of the shared model. *Dominant control instrument* characterizes the means (or instruments)

Archetype	Shared model	Feedback information	Dominant control instrument	Communications system
Lion Tamer	Operational efficiency	Efficiency data	Preset internal targets	Formal, linear
Leader	Economic performance	Performance figures	External performance targets	Formal hierarchically integrated
Trainer	Complex matrix	Discrete task-related competence measures	Formal standards and protocols	Formal functional/ process integration
Mentor	Trans-formation capability	Progress and positioning indicators	Empowerment	Formal and informal information networking

FIGURE 15.3   Information characteristics of the four archetypes

employed by the headquarters to shape the business' endeavours. *Communication system* characteristics reflect the communications infrastructures that are necessary for the enactment of the archetype.

The *Lion Tamer*, with its focus on operational efficiency, will employ systems that provide financial data about the business, and evaluate individual output against preset internal targets, using financial reward mechanisms to reinforce "appropriate" business behaviour. The communication infrastructure is characterized by formal protocols for linear communication through functional hierarchies.

The *Leader* with its focus on economic performance through process efficacy, will employ systems that provide performance figures about the business and evaluate individual business performance against external benchmarks, using "best practice" transfer mechanisms to implant "appropriate" business behaviour. The communication structure is predominantly formal in style, characterized by vertical control channels with transverse integration linkages (or networks) between businesses for purposes of tactical and operational coordination.

The *Trainer*, with its focus on internal effectiveness based on business competence, will employ discrete, function/task-related competence measures to monitor business performance, using formal standards and protocols to orchestrate the development of specific competences in individual businesses so that these map on to the headquarters' blueprint of the corporate competence matrix in a complementary fashion alongside the other businesses in the portfolio. The communications structure will tend to reflect the matrix structure, with formal function/process integration.

The *Mentor*, with its focus on developing capabilities that can both generate and survive discontinuities in the competitive and strategic contexts, will employ progress and positioning indicators to assess the nature and value of the capabilities being developed by the individual businesses and to learn about the mode in which these capabilities are leveraged by the businesses. The *Mentor* is concerned with aspects of effective organizational learning, and perceives the headquarters–business relationship as one within which a learning partnership exists. Accordingly, it reinforces "appropriate" business behaviour through continued empowerment of the business within the relationship context. The communications structure is an organic one, characterized by a fusion of formal and informal communications (and relationship) networks linking the individual businesses with each other and the headquarters.

THE MIGRATION MAPS

In our earlier work (Merali & McGee, 1998) we articulated the positioning challenge that arises when the headquarters finds itself situated squarely within a given quadrant of our archetype framework and decides to migrate across the framework to reposition itself in a different quadrant. We suggested that such a migration requires a change in fundamental perceptions underpinning the headquarters' self-script, resulting in changes in its primary focus, values, aspirations, behaviours, structures, attitudes and relationship scripts.

This chaper is concerned with describing how such a change can be effected. We use our framework to construct a migration map for an international corporation (Groupe Tulip) that is currently migrating from the *Lion Tamer* quadrant to the *Leader* quadrant. The "map" for the journey associated with the planned migration is defined in terms of changes in the headquarters' self concept and relationship scripts, the evolution of learning and knowledge networks and the development of new capabilities.

CASE STUDY: CONTEXT

The organization in this case study (Groupe Tulip) is an international group of natural resource companies with two joint European parents. Historically the company was vertically integrated, with extensive, formal planning procedures. The procedures had evolved from being directive to being more indicative in style. Its businesses range from exploration and extraction of resources ("upstream") to consumer product marketing ("downstream"). The gains from integrating activities along the supply chain were historically important. In recent years a degree of vertical disintegration has resulted in upstream and downstream companies acquiring more distinct identities and benefiting from economies directly attainable within the scope of the business (as opposed to corporate) operations. The corporate headquarters staff is divided between the two parent countries. The parent companies directly or indirectly own the shares in the Groupe Tulip holding companies, but are not themselves part of the Groupe Tulip. They appoint directors to the boards of the Groupe Tulip holding companies, from which they receive dividends. The company shares are listed and traded on the stock exchanges in nine countries.

Groupe Tulip has recently completed a major restructuring exercise, accompanied by a fundamental change in the headquarters self concept, and resulting in significant changes in the headquarters–business relationships. The headquarters has now launched a "Transformation" initiative aimed at enabling Groupe Tulip companies to develop more independently and more effectively in the uncertainty that is held to be the future scenario in the industry. This section traces the changing scenario leading up to the recent restructuring and the "rewriting" of the script for the corporate headquarters. The period preceding the restructuring will be referred to as the "pretransformational era".

GROUPE TULIP STRUCTURE IN THE PRE-TRANSFORMATION ERA

The period that led up to the restructuring exercise of the mid-1990s is important because it provides the basis necessary for understanding the migration of the 1990s. The following narrative outlines the Groupe Tulip structure and organizational context that preceded the restructuring of the 1990s.

The last major restructuring in Groupe Tulip was in the 1950s, when the organization created a matrix of geographical *regions*, business *sectors* and service *functions* (e.g. manufacturing, research and development, marketing), as illustrated in FIGURE 15.4. The US outfit operated as an independent subsidiary outside of the European matrix organization.

Local operating units belonged to specific business sectors and were managed along regional lines. Regions acted as the shareholder representatives and were responsible for appointing operating unit heads, and service companies were responsible for providing functional specialisms across the board: these functions provided expertise to the operating companies around the world, and directed corporate-wide research programmes.

HEADQUARTERS–BUSINESS RELATIONSHIPS AND THE HEADQUARTERS SELF CONCEPT IN THE PRE-TRANSFORMATIONAL ERA

The headquarters was "hands-off" in its management style and the local operating companies enjoyed a very high degree of autonomy under the regional umbrella. From the 1960s to the mid-1980s the matrix structure was perceived to be an enabling one, providing requisite flexibility and integration across the business sectors (e.g. where the output from one sector was the feedstock for another). Resources were plentiful and local businesses developed in a manner largely unconstrained by the headquarters. Accountability to shareholders was managed at the regional level. The local operating companies had a very strong "local company" identity, while the corporate logo and name afforded them the hallmark of quality and respectability. The role of the service companies was central in providing technological expertise. The business sectors were active in coordination.

Retrospectively, when asked about the pre-transformation era, headquarters managers characterize the headquarters as having been like an unenthusiastic Lion Tamer: the headquarters perceived its role as one of overseeing the efficient operation of the businesses and of having accountability for the financial performance of the group (the reward and incentive structure was based on the financial performance of the business units). The

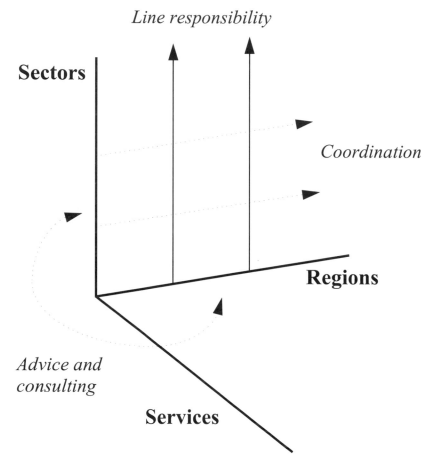

FIGURE 15.4   The matrix structure

headquarters focused on output measures for the businesses. Communications channels had a loosely command-and-control formalised structure.
While the corporate structure was centralized in terms of control over the
financial outcomes, there was minimal intervention by the headquarters in the
process of development within the regional and business domains. It was this
laissez-faire attitude that betrayed its lack of enthusiasm for being an effective
Lion Tamer. The booming economy of the early 1980s and the favourable
industry context allowed the headquarters to maintain this state comfortably.

The headquarters did not actively engage in knowledge management or
in leveraging competences across business boundaries. The pre-
transformation information and competence profile for the headquarters–
business relationship fitted the Lion Tamer profile (with some strengths in

other quadrants). The headquarters' self-script appeared to be predominantly rooted in the maintenance of "typical" Lion Tamer characteristics:

Shared model:	Profitability
Control mechanism:	Performance targets
Feedback:	Financial performance figures
Communications:	Formal, command and control style between headquarters & businesses

Some features in the enactment of the script exhibited characteristics more typical of other archetypes. For example, the policy of transferring managers frequently across different regions and businesses (to broaden their experience base) had engendered the development of very extensive informal networks (a characteristic more typically associated with the Mentor archetype). The dedication to technical expertise resulted in very efficient mechanisms for technology skills transfer (a characteristic more typically associated with the Trainer archetype). Networking and technology skills transfer went on between individuals at the regional and business levels, but the headquarters was too far removed from this level to play a direct role in leveraging these capabilities.

RESTRUCTURING

THE IMPETUS FOR RESTRUCTURING

The Lion Tamer profile from the 1950s era was adequate for overseeing the business performance in the very prosperous industry and economic context of the 1960s through to the 1980s. However the appropriateness of the matrix structure was seriously challenged by the emerging events of the mid-1980s to early 1990s.

Politically, the 1990s were relatively dynamic, with marked instability in some of the local business environments. Because the company had a high international visibility, the strong local presence and influence that went with the "local company" identity needed to be managed in a way that was consistent with the corporate image and policy.

Economically, the global recession of the 1980s had left its mark. Overall corporate performance was still healthy, but the businesses had not been left unscathed by the economic downturn. Many of the businesses were affected adversely by the turbulence of international markets and currency exchange rates. The late 1980s and early 1990s saw major changes in the industry (due to low demand, worldwide surpluses and over-production in the upstream business domains, and changes in the product market for the downstream businesses). The immediate impact of this within the businesses themselves was significant, resulting in rationalization and restructuring to produce lean, efficiency oriented units. At the strategic level, these changes prompted a move away from dependence on bulk commodity products and towards a focus on the development of a future portfolio of more specialized, high value products.

Socially, environmental and "green" issues were becoming increasingly important. They seriously affected the corporate image at an international level. It was becoming imperative that the way in which green/political issues and related incidents were handled at the local level was consistent with the corporate face at the global level.

Technologically the environment was challenging: the rapid rate of technological advances and the need to invest in technologies for future strategic developments meant that Groupe Tulip needed to make far-reaching, high level decisions about technology futures and investments. The scope and impact of these decisions were wider than the domain of any single business, and an effective mechanism was required to make these decisions more swiftly and effectively.

With its "unenthusiastic Lion Tamer" corporate *Weltanschauung*, Groupe Tulip had neither the will nor the sophisticated coordination competence required to get the best out of the matrix organization. In the dynamic context of the 1990s, with its attendant global recession, the pre-transformational matrix structure became cumbersome. As might be expected (Wilson & Rosenfeld, 1990, p.255) under the (relatively) impoverished resource conditions the consensus-style decision making process was increasingly problematic. Moreover, the matrix structure had become distorted over the years: the high local autonomy of the pre-transformational era nurtured the development of powerful "local barons". In the 1990s regional power games resulted in the gridlocking of critical corporate and business decisions (for example, decisions about business acquisitions and technology infrastructure investments). This occurred when globalization was becoming an increasingly important item on the corporate agenda, markets were shifting, and the need to show the world a strong, responsible, caring, outward-looking corporate face was paramount.

This was the situation that heralded a major restructuring exercise in the 1990s: political, economic, social and technological issues demanded more coordination in the decision making processes and in the way that the group presented itself on the international stage. The genesis of the transformation lay in that restructuring.

THE RESTRUCTURED GROUPE TULIP

The restructuring of the mid-1990s resulted in an organization comprised of four International Business Sectors (IBSs), as shown in FIGURE 15.5. Each IBS was headed by a Sector Committee made up of the operating company managing directors. The Sector Committees fed into the central Committee of Managing Directors (CMD), which in turn reported to the parent Board. The non-executive Chair of each Sector Committee represented the interests of the IBS on the CMD.

This new structure did not incorporate a discrete "regional coordination" layer: the CMD became responsible for the high-level coordination across geographical regions. The new structure expedited the corporate-level decision making process by creating direct headquarters–business links and building the business–regional coordination nodes into the structure of the CMD: besides representing an IBS, each member of the CMD was also responsible for one of the six geographical regions covered by Groupe Tulip. In this way the provision was made to scrutinize strategic decisions (e.g. business acquisition decisions) from the "regional perspective" at the CMD level. Local cooperative operational arrangements between business units were worked out on a personal basis. For the transition period, a central group was established to deal with remnants from the matrix era relating to cross-business issues, principally at the operational unit level.

FIGURE 15.5   The "new" structure

The corporate functions of the old matrix structure were absorbed/ evolved into individual IBSs. Corporate-wide issues such as environmental and health issues were managed by a central group. A new, centralized Professional Services organization was established to provide global support in general corporate-wide services (such as Human Resource and Information Services). The arrangement was flexible: services covered by Professional Services could also be outsourced, both centrally and by individual businesses. A group was established at the headquarters to manage the external interface and coordinate the international presentation of a consistent "Groupe Tulip Face".

THE MIGRATION

RE-EVALUATION OF THE HEADQUARTERS' SELF CONCEPT AND THE GENESIS OF THE MIGRATION

The restructuring exercise had been conceived as just that—the establishment of a structure that would (i) enable the streamlining of the corporate-wide decision making process, and (ii) provide a mechanism for presenting a consistent "Groupe Tulip Face" internationally (in particular, Groupe Tulip was concerned that local responses to environmentally sensitive issues were consistent with corporate policy guidelines on corporate citizenship, and that media reporting on Groupe Tulip's activities was based on congruent information from headquarters and business level sources).

On the face of it, the decision to restructure could be interpreted as a "phenomenon of the times". The global recession of the late 1980s and early 1990s induced many organizations in Western Europe and the US to carry out restructuring exercises aimed at enhancing their ability to compete more effectively in the global markets through improved efficiency. The change *process* initiated at the Groupe Tulip headquarters by the restructuring exercise resulted in achievements that went beyond efficiency honing: as shown in the following sections, it resulted in a fundamental re-evaluation of the headquarters' self concept and transformed the nature of the script for the enactment of the business–headquarters relationship.

There was a major movement of centre staff as a consequence of the restructuring. New people came into the corporate centre while centrally managed service functions moved out to the business divisions. The centre was thus closely connected with the reality of change.

A number of things contributed to the re-evaluation of the headquarters' self concept, including the vision of the new CEO, the recent public reaction to Groupe Tulip's decisions on environmentally sensitive issues, and a general realization that the future was going to be very different from the past.

The launch of the "Transformation" programme was a symbolic act by the headquarters for the manifestation of its new identity.

Two significant individually initiated events enabled the headquarters to change.

1. The Head of Corporate Strategy ran focused discussion groups. Through these, senior management became committed to leading a corporate change programme.
2. The new CEO (who arrived prior to the restructuring) was the corporate "Champion" of the Transformation concept. He had recently experienced a transformational exercise in a different context in the US (where a declining subsidiary had been turned around by a strong leadership and a people-centric consultancy input) and he brought the benefit of his experience and some of the US consultants to create workshops for senior managers. In these workshops senior managers re-evaluated their behaviours, attitudes and fundamental beliefs relating to the centre and its role in Groupe Tulip.

This was the foundation that enabled senior management to develop a coherent script for the future of the centre and its relationships with the businesses. Out of this came the renewed centre self concept, and the idea of launching a corporate-wide Transformation programme as a vehicle for the enactment of the script.

HEADQUARTERS–BUSINESS RELATIONSHIPS AND THE HEADQUARTERS' SELF CONCEPT

Headquarters' Self Concept

Collectively, the centre decided to assume leadership in a deeper sense than would have been required for merely orchestrating the restructuring exercise.

The desired change in headquarters' style was articulated as changing from being "directive" to being "influencing" and "interactive", from "telling" to "listening". The desired change in headquarters' role was articulated as changing from "overseeing" to "strategic leadership". The articulation of the "strategic leadership" role was heavily associated with the realization that the internally focused, programmatic Lion Tamer *Weltanschauung* was inadequate (for enabling Groupe Tulip to position itself favourably in the uncertain industry context that it faced). They saw that the leadership needed to facilitate the development of appropriate capabilities to deliver sustainable performance in the dynamic environment. The desired change in strategy was articulated as changing from being (loosely) planned to more "emergent". The desired processes required to enact the new role were variously articulated as "coaching and learning", "advisory" and "engagement". TABLE 15.1 summarizes the "7S" (Pascale & Athos, 1981) profile (for the "pre-transformational" entity) and shows the characteristics that the "new centre" aspired to cultivate.

The Migration Plan

The focus for the new business organization emphasized the achievement of high performance and the establishment of a socially responsible image that was consistent with the global corporate image. The focus of the headquarters–business relationship was intended to establish a coordinated, outward-looking performance culture. The Transformation programme was the vehicle for achieving this change.

TABLE 15.1   The "7S" characteristics for the old and the desired organizational profiles

	Old organizational profile	Desired profile
Strategy	(Loosely) planned	(More) emergent
Structure	Matrix dominated/distorted by powerful 'local barons'	Well-defined formal relationships and procedures, organic informal networking
Style	Closed, directive, command-and-control, reactive	Open, engaging, interactive, credible, proactive, collaborative
Staff	Professional, technically focused	Open, professional, organizationally focused
Systems	Implicit, organizational networks, with localized information gatekeepers, somewhat prone to political obfuscation	Visible, shared systems, exploiting internal and external intelligence and sustained by formal and informal networks
Skills	Technical excellence, political alacrity	Technical excellence, positioning skills (i.e. pursuing personal development in the context of a holistic organizational perspective)
Super-ordinate goals	Return to shareholders	Sustainable value to shareholders and industry leadership with integrity

Headquarters managers retrospectively likened this to a migration from the Lion Tamer quadrant to the Leader quadrant (as shown in FIGURE 15.6), with the Transformation programme being predominantly concerned with promoting an information and competence profile of the type characteristic of the Leader archetype. Consolidation in the Leader quadrant was evidenced by the establishment of an external focus, an effectiveness-oriented performance culture and the coordinated leveraging of business capabilities.

Signaling the "Performance Culture"

The headquarters signaled its commitment to a performance culture by providing a corporate-wide framework for target setting and performance evaluation. The pre-transformational focus was on financial performance of the business units in relation to centrally set internal targets. The new culture differed from this in three important aspects:

1. The new evaluation criteria included financial *and* non-financial aspects of business performance (e.g. pollution levels, ecological impact).
2. The new evaluation process was concerned with evaluating business performance against *external* benchmarks (c.f. the pre-transformational internal focus).
3. The new process for setting stretch targets incorporated self-evaluation against peer performance and external benchmarks (c.f. the pre-transformational centrally imposed targets).

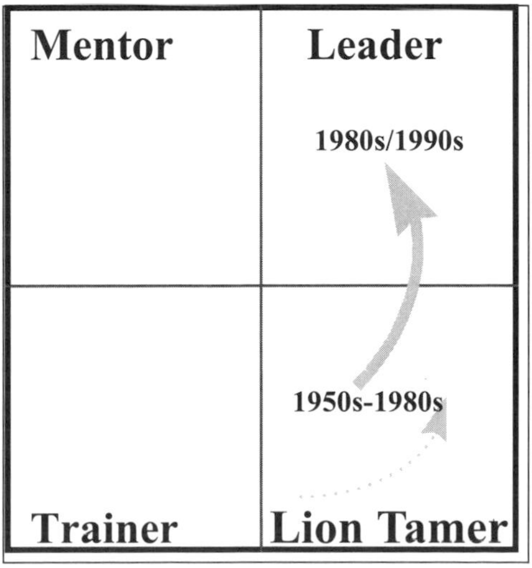

Mentor	Leader
	1980s/1990s
Trainer	Lion Tamer
	1950s-1980s

FIGURE 15.6   The migration plan

The balanced scorecard approach (Kaplan & Norton, 1992) was introduced as the corporate instrument for performance management. The centre developed a corporate scorecard template setting out fundamental criteria to be used for setting performance targets and for performance evaluation. The corporate template was adopted by all of the businesses with appropriate adaptations to reflect their specific contexts. Internal and external benchmarking was introduced as the basis for developing stretch performance targets. Businesses were encouraged to make their performance data visible across the corporation.

Establishing an External Focus

The focus on the management of external interfaces resulted in the establishment of procedures and centralized roles for dealing with external players. As discussed earlier, the new organization was particularly concerned to maintain an external image consistent with espoused corporate values and good corporate citizenship criteria. The new structure (with direct business–headquarters links) was designed to equip both headquarters and businesses with intelligence about the dynamic external environment (to enable both to be proactive in deploying resources to deal effectively with changes in the national and global contexts).

At a more fundamental level, the headquarters–business relationship was instrumental in revising the business self concept. For example, the enactment of externally-focused roles and procedures, and the inclusion of environmental criteria in individual business scorecards resulted in the development of an environmentally-conscious identity in the individual businesses.

Leveraging Business Capabilities

Although a number of important capabilities existed at the divisional and local levels, the "pre-transformational" headquarters did not play an active role in leveraging these across the corporate businesses. For example, the operating companies with their "local company" identities possessed significant local knowledge and had established powerful local networks. The "pre-transformational" headquarters was not active in leveraging these capabilities within the corporate template. In contrast, the new headquarters *Weltanschauung* incorporated this aspect: it was concerned with activating local networks within the corporate framework. If a division moved into a national context where another division already had an established presence, the headquarters would concern itself with ensuring that existing local networks and knowledge base were protected and utilized to enhance the corporate presence. Intervention by the headquarters was concerned with providing the information infrastructure to support cross-divisional knowledge transfer (the term "infrastructure" is used here to refer to both the technological infrastructure for cross-boundary data sharing and communication, and the relationship network for leveraging country-specific expertise).

Similarly, with regard to technological and operational expertise, the "pre-transformational" headquarters focused on skills transfer, but did not focus on issues of knowledge and core competence management. The restructured headquarters explicitly concerned itself with issues of knowledge management (e.g. through developing knowledge maps and creating international, inter-business projects aimed at developing a corporate knowledge network) and the leveraging of core competences. Best practice diffusion was actively managed and portfolio development was influenced by competence-based thinking (e.g. taking technological innovations and existing capabilities and developing them into new core businesses, which then became nuclei for the generation of new divisions). General portfolio management competences (e.g. risk management) are being aggressively evaluated and developed.

Exploiting Information Technology

Information technology (IT) was a key element of the forward thinking inspired by the new self concept. Intranet technology was introduced to provide the coordination infrastructure across the global business. IT was perceived to be important in developing a culture where the transfer of expertise and best practice was facilitated. Electronic media and the intranet were to be used for recording and disseminating best practice. Publication of performance data on the intranet by businesses was seen as a way of facilitating a culture of openness and as a means of motivating businesses to aspire to levels of excellence.

In the longer term, IT-enabled networks will provide a significant part of the organizational infrastructure for knowledge creation and for the corporate-level leveraging of existing knowledge. Corporate-wide communication on the global intranet is seen as an important step in providing an infrastructure that enables businesses to engage in "conversations" about change and development.

The then future significance of IT in organizational learning and knowledge management was signaled by the establishment of the new position of Corporate Knowledge Officer, who was charged with facilitating the establishment of electronically mediated organizational conversations across the global businesses.

In a symbolic act, the CEO engaged in an electronic dialogue with individuals on the subject of one of the headquarters-driven performance initiatives very early on in the change programme.

OBSERVATIONS ON THE TRANSFORMATION PROCESS

The case of Groupe Tulip suggests that the congruence of the headquarters' self concept with the desired archetype was key to the success of the migration, and that the *process* of migration can be used to develop complex competence bundles to enable future migratory endeavours.

Redefinition of the corporate self-concept resulted in a radically different enactment of the headquarters–business relationship. Communications channels are being developed to incorporate business knowledge into the corporate mental map (allowing the businesses to share and shape the corporate mental map). Societal processes play an important role in Groupe Tulip's schema for developing a corporate knowledge network. International, inter-business projects, and regular corporate-sponsored leaders forums are examples of mechanisms for enabling such processes. Congruence between the headquarters and business mental maps is reinforced by programmes such as the leadership development programme: younger managers (potential future leaders) from the businesses are seconded to the headquarters to work closely with senior corporate staff. The tradition of international transfers and strong informal networks continue to play an important "cross-pollinating" role in knowledge diffusion across businesses. Formal processes (such as peer-benchmarking, and the participative evaluation processes, described later) are designed to promote transfer of best practice. As discussed earlier, IT is intended to play an important role in knowledge dissemination and in facilitating global "conversations" to generate ideas about change and development.

BEHAVIOUR APPROXIMATING "PURE" ARCHETYPE

The articulated foci for the "new business organization" were on achieving high performance and a responsible corporate image. On the information matrix (FIGURE 15.3), the information characteristics of the "new" headquarters–business relationship conformed neatly to the profile for the Leader: they are externally focused and output directed. The performance culture, the coordination capability (as demonstrated in the establishment of performance management systems) and the early investment in corporate IT infrastructures (for use in the documentation and dissemination of best practice) also typify the Leader archetype. Of key importance within the Leader self concept is the maintenance of congruent dynamic leadership over time (to sustain a profile of high shareholder value in future years notwithstanding a changing industry context). The headquarters focused on the development of future leaders.

It would appear that the corporate management focus of Groupe Tulip was on developing the competence profile necessary for consolidating its presence in the Leader quadrant of the archetype matrix. The perception of headquarters managers at the time concurred with this view.

INDICATIONS OF MIXED TYPES OF BEHAVIOURS

An interesting picture emerges when we consider the *process* characteristics of the enactment of the script for the establishment of a "performance culture". While on the information matrix (FIGURE 15.3), the information characteristics of the headquarters–business relationship match the profile for the Leader (being externally focused and output directed), the processual characteristics actually developed capabilities that will facilitate a move to the Mentor quadrant (see FIGURE 15.7).

While performance was evaluated against the set scorecard targets, the stretch targets were set by the businesses themselves going through a process of facilitated *self-evaluation* (against internal and external benchmarks). For example, in one of the businesses the benchmarking and target-setting mechanism employed for "low-performing" businesses was a facilitated workshop. Participants in the workshop included managers of the organization undergoing evaluation, corporate experts and delegates from peer organizations. The process of self-evaluation, target-setting and resource allocation was done in a "problem solving" setting (where peer organizations could learn from each other and where peer networking could be reinforced). Target setting was therefore empowering, and the resulting self-evaluation capability is one that is more typically associated with the Mentor quadrant.

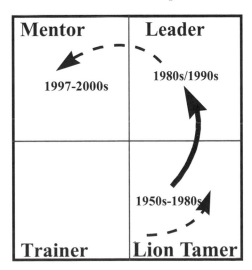

FIGURE 15.7   The actual migration map for Groupe Tulip

Training capabilities (previously used exclusively for developing technological excellence) were harnessed in a programme for developing leadership. For example, projects were set up whereby potential leaders from the global business were seconded to work with corporate executives on high profile projects. International leaders workshops were sponsored by the headquarters in order to promote the congruent development of leadership concepts. This intersubjective developmental exercise is more typically associated with the Mentor quadrant (directed development would be more characteristic of the Leader archetype). In the context of organizational learning, it is similar to the process of "organizational inquiry" postulated by Argyris & Schon (1978) as central to developing double-loop learning. At a more profound level, this type of engagement is instrumental in developing a congruent identity and self-concept.

The headquarters was strongly committed to continual investment in societal processes for transferring expertise. It actively invested in enhancing the high level of networking among individuals (that the original expatriate culture had generated) and in leveraging them for the transfer of expertise. To this end, cross-business conversations were engineered and international projects were set up to establish global networking capabilities across businesses. Future knowledge management will be facilitated by the use of IT, but the development of the societal knowledge network is a prerequisite for the success of organizational learning, and the processual intervention by the headquarters in this respect is Mentor-like.

The migration plan for Groupe Tulip was to move away from the Lion Tamer quadrant and consolidate in the Leader quadrant by establishing a performance culture and developing capabilities for the effective transfer of best practice. The Transformation programme was the vehicle for the planned migration, and the headquarters shaped the processes for corporate-wide target-setting and performance evaluation. Because the headquarters self concept was Mentor-like, the *process* of enactment of the headquarters–business relationship has shaped and cultivated cognitive, process and business capabilities that can support a future migration into the Mentor quadrant.

PATH DEPENDENCY IN THE DEVELOPMENT OF COMPETENCE BUNDLES

As we suggested in our earlier work (Merali & McGee, 1998):

> there is a "progression" in terms of the complexity of coordination mechanisms and competence repertoires of the different archetypes. The Lion Tamer

is the most "primitive" form in this context, with the Trainer and Leader assuming an intermediate position and the Mentor being the most "advanced". Taking a resource-based view (Wernerfelt, 1984; Peteraf, 1993) of the four archetypes, it is likely that the value creating potential of the headquarters is a function of its *co-specialized* resource and competence "bundles" (rather than being simply a function of individual competences). The relative complexity of the competence bundle associated with each archetype is directly related to the complexity of behaviour of the archetype.

There is an element of path dependency in the migration map for Groupe Tulip (see FIGURE 15.7). Increasingly complex resource bundles are being developed as the organization progresses with its journey round the matrix. The case illustrates two of the general points made in our earlier work.

The first of these points concerns competence management. While establishing its identity in a given quadrant, the headquarters will focus on developing and establishing headquarters–business relationships to generate quadrant-specific behaviours and competences within the businesses. Once the script is established, and business commitment is realized, the new behaviours and competences are integral. When (as in the case study) a migration to a different quadrant is undertaken, previously acquired competences do not cease to be relevant or important—they become part of the current competence pool. The focus of the headquarters' efforts moves on to develop different competences.

The second point concerns the transition phase of the journey. In the case of Groupe Tulip, while management focus is primarily on consolidation in the Leader quadrant, the *process* (of arriving at the desired outcomes) resulted in the development of more complex competences and Mentor-like cognitive characteristics. These are self-evaluation and empowerment, congruent corporate identity, deep networking capabilities, vertical and horizontal collaboration, and the intersubjective development of organizational identity. The pattern of migration suggests that the realization of a changing headquarters self concept is effected not by radical transformation but by the enactment of a thematic script through accumulated change and adaptation.

DISCUSSION

The organizational process has three roles in dynamic core competence management (Teece, Pisano & Shuen, 1997): coordination (a static concept), learning (a dynamic concept) and reconfiguration (a transformational concept). Our work with Groupe Tulip in using the self concept and archetype models (which focus on the issues of transformation and migration) is entirely consistent with this view. Coordination/integration was evidenced by the establishment of the performance evaluation systems; learning was evidenced by the development of new capabilities, and reconfiguration was evidenced by the consolidation in the Leader quadrant. A "good" migration process could be said to encapsulate all three roles.

THE IMPORTANCE OF THE SELF CONCEPT

This case study shows that the headquarters self concept is powerful in shaping the development and leveraging of dynamic corporate competences. We propose that in the world of high growth and internationalization, the development and enactment of appropriate headquarters–business relationship scripts plays a significant role in value creation by providing a framework of intelligent dynamic coordinated integrative mechanisms. Weick (1995, p.160) highlights the importance of identity as a focus for sensemaking and as a basis for congruent action:

> Each . . . organization chooses who it will be by first choosing what actions, if any it needs to explain, and second by choosing which explanations for these actions it will defend. An inability or unwillingness to choose, act and justify these leaves people with too many alternatives and too few certainties. Binding decisions affect the tasks we are attracted to, the reasons that move us, the values we try to realize, the plans we admire, and the people we seek out. Avoidance of such decisions slows down the development of attractions, reasons, values, plans and associates.

Thus, for an organization that is operating in a dynamic environment, and for which knowledge acquisition and evaluation are significant activities, the establishment and understanding of its own identity is particularly important. In the sense of our chapter, self concept arises from being and gives rise to doing.

The dominant logic (Prahalad & Bettis, 1986, 1995) is active in filtering and assessing features of the environment in order to design viable actions and procedures for dealing with that environment. The multiplicity of (sometimes contradictory) dominant logics observed in multibusiness MNCs is to be expected in diverse national and industrial contexts. Here, success is often determined by the goodness of fit of the logic with distinctive individual national market characteristics. The dominant logics of a given organization arise out of (and are therefore grounded in) the same self concept (irrespective of their individual natures). This necessarily reconciles different dominant logics insofar as providing an overall framework (within which each dominant logic is congruent with the self concept).

PATH DEPENDENCY AND THE DEVELOPMENT OF NEW CAPABILITIES

There is clear evidence in our case study (compare the pre- and post-migration characteristics described above) of a path dependency in migration maps, resulting in the development of increasingly complex competence bundles with the transition states in migration displaying mixed archetype behaviours.

We do not subscribe to the concept of "unlearning" as a mechanism for developing new capabilities and behaviours. In our view, competence bundles develop over time, and the difference in the relative importance of the various competences in the enactment of new scripts accounts for externally observable "transformations" over time. Competences that are not used and are not nurtured and renewed will atrophy and disappear, appearing to be "displaced" by other, newly acquired or newly selected, capabilities. Capabilities that are not embedded in the organizational self concept will be destroyed by excision of the people who once realized those capabilities.

We believe that the concept of "unlearning" is appealing when describing the artefacts of this type of change—e.g. when new "skills" are observed to replace "old" ones or when new behaviour patterns are established (as in the implementation of Argyris & Schon's (1978) notion of single-loop learning. However, if we consider the development of deep knowledge or the accumulation of wisdom (knowing what is appropriate when) learning happens through recognizing the inappropriateness of a behaviour and developing a new suitable response for the newly perceived situation. The meta-level knowledge gained and retained through this experience becomes available for sensemaking in a future "different situation".

THE IMPORTANCE OF THE PROCESS OF MIGRATION

It is not sufficient in examining the process of migration to consider merely the start and end points of the process.

What emerged from our case study showed that the process (i.e. the specific mechanisms put in place in order to achieve the migration) was highly significant. In particular, because Groupe Tulip approached the process through a mixture of formal and informal participative and societal processes, they generated (cognitive and process) capabilities and resources that went beyond those required for consolidation in the Leader quadrant. These additional capabilities and resources (self-evaluation and empowerment, congruent corporate self concept, deep networking capabilities, vertical and horizontal collaboration, and the intersubjective development of organizational identity) are *en route* for a likely future continuance of their migration process that will ultimately take them into the Mentor quadrant.

It was also importantly apparent that the process fitted well with the idea of a "good" migration process as described earlier.

CONCLUSION

Recent literature (Lei, Hitt & Bettis, 1996; Teece, Pisano & Shuen, 1997) highlights the importance of the role of headquarters, path dependency, and collective organization-specific learning for the development of dynamic capabilities in complex dynamic environments. Our work with Groupe Tulip concurs with these assertions. As evidenced by our migrational maps, there appears to be a path dependency in the development of increasingly complex competence bundles. The *process* of migration was observed to be of key importance in the emergence of cognitive structures and development of knowledge networks.

As illustrated in the Groupe Tulip case, the headquarters self concept is powerful in shaping the development and leveraging of corporate competences. In an interconnected world of high growth and internationalization, success in the MNC context is about managing strategically the tradeoffs between the global integration of business activities and the need for local responsiveness. The development and enactment of appropriate headquarters–business relationship scripts can play a significant role in value creation by providing a framework of intelligent dynamic coordinated integrative mechanisms.

The self concept and archetype framework for the enactment of the headquarters–business relationships is useful in this context because it:

- provides a (new) descriptor language for macroscopic corporate change processes;
- provides a rational context for the simultaneous operation of multiple dominant logics;
- suggests possible ways in which dominant logics change and develop over time;
- identifies path dependencies in the development of dynamic capabilities.

REFERENCES

Ashby, W. R. (1940). Adaptiveness and equilibrium. *Journal of Mental Science*, **8**, 478–483.

Ashby, W. R. (1956). *An Introduction to Cybernetics*. London: Chapman & Hall.

Argyris, C. & Schon, D. A. (1978). *Organisational Learning*. Reading, MA: Addison-Wesley.

Bartlett, C. A. & Ghoshal, S. (1987). Managing across borders: new organizational responses. *Sloan Management Review*, **29**(1), 43–53.

Berne, E. (1961). *Transactional Analysis in Psychotherapy*. New York: Grove Press.

Burrell, G. & Morgan, G. (1979). *Sociological Paradigms and Organisational Analysis*. London: Heinemann.

Ferlie, E. & Pettigrew, A. (1996). The nature and transformation of corporate headquarters: a review of recent literature and a research agenda. *Journal of Management Studies*, **33**(4), 495–523.

Ghoshal, S. & Nohria, N. (1989). Internal differentiation within multinational corporations. *Strategic Management Journal*, **10**(4), 323–338.

Ghoshal, S. & Nohria, N. (1993). Horses for courses: organisational forms for multinational corporations. *Strategic Management Journal*, **14**.

Goold, M. & Campbell, A. (1991). *Corporate Strategy and Parenting Skills*. London: Ashridge Strategic Management Centre.

Goold, M., Campbell, A. & Alexander, M. (1994). *Corporate-Level Strategy*. New York: Wiley.

Kaplan, R.S. & Norton, D.P. (1992). The balanced scorecard: measures that drive performance. *Harvard Business Review*, January/February, 71–79.

Lei, D., Hitt, M.J. & Bettis, R. (1996) Dynamic core competences through meta-learning and strategic context. *Journal of Management*, **22**, 549–569.

Merali, Y. & McGee, J. (1998). Information competences and knowledge creation at the corporate centre. In G. Hamel, C. K. Prahalad, H. Thomas & D. O'Neal (eds) *Strategic Flexibility: Managing in a Turbulent Economy*. Chichester: Wiley.

Pascale, R.T. & Athos, A.G. (1981). *The Art of Japanese Management*. Hammondsworth: Penguin.

Peteraf, M.A. (1993). The cornerstones of competitive advantage: a resource-based view. *Strategic Management Journal*, **14**, 179–191.

Prahalad, C.K. & Bettis, R.A. (1986). The dominant logic: a new link between diversity and performance. *Strategic Management Journal*, **7**, 485–501.

Prahalad, C.K. & Bettis, R.A. (1995). The dominant logic: retrospective and extension. *Strategic Management Journal*, **16**, 5–14.

Prahalad, C. K. & Doz, Y. L. (1987). *The Multinational Mission: Balancing Local Demands and Global Vision*. New York: Free Press.

Teece, D.J., Pisano, G. & Shuen, A. (1997). Dynamic capabilities and strategic management. *Strategic Management Journal*, **18**, 509–533.

Useem, M. & Gottlieb, M. M. (1990). Corporate restructuring:, ownership, disciplined alignment and the reorganisation of management. *Human Resource Management*, **29**(3), 285–306.

Wernerfelt, B. (1984). A resource-based view of the firm. *Strategic Management Journal*, **5**, 171–180.

Weick, K. E. (1995). *Sensemaking in Organizations*. Thousand Oaks, CA: Sage.

Wilson, D. C. & Rosenfeld, R. H. (1990). *Managing Organisations*. London: McGraw-Hill.

Index

Index compiled by Geoffrey C. Jones